Lecture Notes in Computer Science 15840

Founding Editors

Gerhard Goos
Juris Hartmanis

AF167407

The series Lecture Notes in Computer Science (LNCS), including its subseries Lecture Notes in Artificial Intelligence (LNAI) and Lecture Notes in Bioinformatics (LNBI), has established itself as a medium for the publication of new developments in computer science and information technology research, teaching, and education.

LNCS enjoys close cooperation with the computer science R & D community, the series counts many renowned academics among its volume editors and paper authors, and collaborates with prestigious societies. Its mission is to serve this international community by providing an invaluable service, mainly focused on the publication of conference and workshop proceedings and postproceedings. LNCS commenced publication in 1973.

M. Dolores Jiménez López · György Vaszil
Editors

Languages of Cooperation and Communication

Essays Dedicated to Erzsébet Csuhaj-Varjú to Celebrate Her Scientific Career

 Springer

Editors
M. Dolores Jiménez López (iD)
Universitat Rovira i Virgili
Tarragona, Spain

György Vaszil (iD)
University of Debrecen
Debrecen, Hungary

ISSN 0302-9743   ISSN 1611-3349 (electronic)
Lecture Notes in Computer Science
ISBN 978-3-031-97273-7   ISBN 978-3-031-97274-4 (eBook)
https://doi.org/10.1007/978-3-031-97274-4

Preface

This volume brings together 16 double-blind peer-reviewed contributions by 36 authors who, through their work, wish to pay tribute to the academic legacy and the human quality of Erzsébet Csuhaj-Varjú. The chapters presented here reflect the depth and breadth of her scientific influence and are also a gesture of admiration and gratitude from colleagues, students, and friends whose paths have crossed hers throughout a long and fruitful career.

Erzsébet Csuhaj-Varjú is Professor Emerita at the Faculty of Informatics of the Eötvös Loránd University (ELTE) in Budapest, and has also served as Research Professor at the Institute for Computer Science and Control (SZTAKI) of the Hungarian Academy of Sciences. With decades of experience in academia and research, she has earned international recognition as a leading figure in theoretical computer science. Her distinguished career spans key institutions in Hungary and abroad, and numerous collaborations with international research groups and universities. She has played pivotal roles as a researcher, professor, mentor, and leader in multiple scientific and academic communities. From her early training in mathematics and computer science, she has continually expanded the frontiers of knowledge through her pioneering work, tireless energy, and generous spirit.

In the course of her career, Erzsébet Csuhaj-Varjú initiated and carried out important work in several scientific directions and research areas in the theory of formal languages, automata, and bio-inspired computation. These results contributed to the conceptual development of the fields. Each of these areas has been shaped by her original insights and her collaborations with some of the most respected researchers in the field. Her work has not only led to the creation of new theoretical models, but has also inspired new research directions and generations of young scientists.

The articles collected in this Festschrift are situated in the three main areas where Professor Csuhaj-Varjú has made particularly significant contributions: (1) grammars, grammar systems, and automata, (2) networks of language processors, (3) bio-inspired models and membrane systems.

In the early 1990s, she introduced—together with Jürgen Dassow—the concept of cooperating/distributed grammar systems (CD grammar systems), laying the groundwork for a formal language-theoretic treatment of distributed and cooperative processes. This foundational contribution culminated in the influential monograph Grammar Systems: A Grammatical Approach to Distribution and Cooperation, co-authored with Jürgen Dassow, Jozef Kelemen, and Gheorghe Păun in 1994.

She developed the concept of networks of language processors, which is a framework for networks of grammars (rewriting systems) in a general sense. The first variant of the model was published with Arto Salomaa on networks consisting of Lindenmayer systems. Her work in this area opened several novel research directions, including the development of the theory of networks of evolutionary processors.

A particularly impactful contribution was her joint paper with Lila Kari and Gheorghe Păun on test tube systems based on splicing, which demonstrated for the first time the existence of a Turing machine equivalent, programmable computational model based on operations that mimic the recombinant behavior of DNA strands.

In the area of membrane computing, she introduced, in collaboration with György Vaszil, the concept of the P automaton—a formal model combining the characteristics of classical finite automata and a membrane system variant using communication rules only. This model has since evolved into an independent and active subfield within membrane computing. She has also made notable contributions to the development of generalized communicating P systems (with Sergey Verlan) and P colonies (with Lucie Ciencialová).

Over her prolific academic career, Erzsébet Csuhaj-Varjú has authored around 250 publications—including 131 journal articles—which have received approximately 1600 citations. She has given more than 100 talks at international conferences and workshops as a contributing or invited speaker, and she has given lectures, tutorials, or advanced courses at several research centers and universities of Europe. She serves on the editorial boards of several major journals, and she has held key roles in the organization of more than 120 international conferences and workshops. Her body of work has not only advanced the state of the art in theoretical computer science but also helped shape the evolution of the field through visionary thinking, deep collaborations, and a remarkable sense of scientific community.

Erzsébet Csuhaj-Varjú's outstanding contributions have been recognized with numerous prestigious awards. These include the "Best Supervisor" award in 2000, the "Medal of the Faculty of Informatics" from the University of Debrecen in 2019, the "Pro Universitate Medal" from the Eötvös Loránd University in 2021, and the "Pro Facultate Informatica Medal" from the Faculty of Informatics in 2022. In 2021, she was also honored with a shared Academy Award from the Hungarian Academy of Sciences, alongside György Vaszil, for their outstanding work in the theory of formal languages, automata, and unconventional computation.

It is impossible to overlook the broader impact of Erzsébet Csuhaj-Varjú's career as a woman who has excelled and led in a domain historically dominated by men. Her success brings essential visibility to women in science and highlights the value of diverse perspectives in research and academic leadership. She has served—both explicitly and through her example—as a role model, reminding us that excellence and empathy are not only compatible but mutually reinforcing.

Beyond her scientific achievements, those who know Erzsébet also recognize her exceptional human qualities. Her career is marked by a spirit of collaboration, reflected in a wide network of co-authors and in the many institutions and projects she has been part of. She has guided and mentored numerous students and young researchers, always with care, generosity, and encouragement. What stands out in every professional interaction with Erzsébet is the respect she extends to all, regardless of their academic rank, and the warmth and kindness she brings to every exchange—often accompanied by her characteristic smile.

While no single volume can fully capture the depth of our gratitude and recognition for Erzsébet Csuhaj-Varjú's outstanding contributions and support, it is the only means available to us as academics to honor her legacy. We therefore extend our sincere thanks to all those who contributed to the realization of this Festschrift: the authors and reviewers for their valuable input and timely cooperation, and the team at Springer for their friendly collaboration and support throughout the preparation of this volume.

We close this preface with our deepest gratitude to Erzsébet Csuhaj-Varjú—for everything she has accomplished, but above all, for the way in which she has done it: with brilliance, with integrity, and with humanity. Her scientific work continues to inspire, and her presence continues to uplift all those around her. We hope that this volume serves as something special for her, a true reflection of the affection, respect, and admiration we all feel for her and her remarkable contributions.

May 2025

M. Dolores Jiménez López
György Vaszil

Contents

Bio-inspired Models and Membrane Systems

Grammars, Grammar Systems, and Automata

Controlled Hybrid CD Grammar Systems

Maurice H. ter Beek$^{(\boxtimes)}$ [ID]

CNR–ISTI, Pisa, Italy
`maurice.terbeek@isti.cnr.it`

Abstract. We study the generative power of hybrid CD grammar systems whose derivations are controlled by a graph, a hypothesis language or a generalized sequential machine. We relate them to the families of languages generated by matrix grammars with appearance checking. We thus characterise language families that lie in between that of the families of context-free and context-sensitive languages, which are of particular interest to linguists. In particular, we show that controlled hybrid CD grammar systems can generate the non-context-free features multiple agreements, crossed agreements and (re)duplication that occur in many natural languages.

Keywords: Grammar systems · controlled derivation · non-context-free

1 Introduction

Erzsébet Csuhaj-Varjú's impressive legacy includes the introduction and development of (cooperating/distributed) grammar systems to formalize the relations between the blackboard model of (cooperative) problem solving (by multi-agent systems) known from Artificial Intelligence and formal languages [19,21]. The cooperating agents are modelled as grammars that edit the blackboard by distributed rewriting of a sentential form taking turns. Their problem-solving strategy is regulated by derivation modes and the solutions are represented by terminal words. Since their introduction, grammar systems have been studied intensively, including well-motivated extensions like *controlled* and *hybrid* CD grammar systems, *teams* in CD grammar systems and combinations thereof [4,5,23,24,34,37,41,42,44,45].

In this paper, we report on the generative power of several kinds of controlled hybrid CD grammar systems, in particular their relations with the family of languages generated by matrix grammars with appearance checking. The reason is that the generative power of this family is known to lie in between that of the family of languages generated by context-free grammars and that of the one generated by context-sensitive grammars, which has been a sweet spot of particular interest to linguists for many decades. Since 1959, Chomsky has inspired

© The Author(s), under exclusive license to Springer Nature Switzerland AG 2025
M. D. Jiménez López and G. Vaszil (Eds.): Erzsébet Csuhaj-Varjú Festschrift,
LNCS 15840, pp. 3–25, 2025.
https://doi.org/10.1007/978-3-031-97274-4_1

many linguists and theoretical computer scientists to wonder about the position of natural languages in what is now known as the Chomsky hierarchy [18]:

> *"the main problem of immediate relevance to the theory of language is that of determining where in the hierarchy of devices the grammars of natural languages lie."*

While the exact position remains to be settled, linguists have narrowed it down since they apparently agree that many natural languages contain non-context-free constructions [51] while at the same time the generative power of context-sensitive grammars is too computationally expensive to parse [33]. The three basic features that occur in natural languages like English [35], Dutch [36], Swiss German [17], Mali's lingua franca Bambara [22] and Chinese [46] are so-called *multiple agreements, crossed agreements* and *(re)duplication* [2,27]. Languages with these three features can be generated by (controlled) (hybrid) CD grammar systems, as we will show in Examples 1, 2 (and 4) and 3, respectively.

Outline. In Sect. 2, we define some basic notions from formal language theory, such as Chomsky grammars and matrix grammars, followed by the definition of CD grammar systems in Sect. 3. We then extend the latter to hybrid CD grammar systems in Sect. 4, to controlled CD grammar systems in Sect. 5 and to various types of controlled hybrid CD grammar systems in Sect. 6. Section 7 presents the results obtained for the newly defined families of languages and positions them in the literature, followed by concluding remarks in Sect. 8.

2   Preliminaries

In this section, some prerequisites necessary for understanding the sequel are defined. For details and unexplained notions, the reader is referred to [48–50] for formal languages in general and in particular for L systems [38,47], regulated rewriting [25,27] and grammar systems [20,26].

The set of all non-empty strings over an *alphabet* V is denoted by V^+; V^* if the *empty string* λ is included. The *length* of a string x is denoted by $|x|$; $|\lambda| = 0$. Set *inclusion* is denoted by $\subseteq$, *proper inclusion* by $\subset$ and set *difference* by $\setminus$.

A *Chomsky grammar* of *type* i ($i \in \{0, 1, 2, 3\}$) is a construct $G = (N, T, P, S)$, where N is the set of *nonterminals*, T is the set of *terminals*, $N \cap T = \varnothing$, $S \in N$ is the *axiom* and P is a finite set of *productions* of the form i, defined as follows:

(0) $\alpha \to \beta$, for $\alpha, \beta \in (N \cup T)^*$ and $|\alpha|_N \geq 1$,
(1) $w_1 A w_2 \to w_1 x w_2$, for $w_1, w_2 \in (N \cup T)^*$, $x \in (N \cup T)^+$ and $A \in N$, and $S \to \lambda$ is allowed iff S does not occur in the right-hand side of any production,
(2) $A \to x$, for $A \in N$ and $x \in (N \cup T)^*$, and
(3) $A \to xB$ or $A \to x$, for $A, B \in N$ and $x \in T^*$.

Moreover, two other well-known types of grammars G are used in the sequel, defined with a finite set of productions P of the form j, with $j \in \{4, 5\}$, as follows:

(4) $A \rightarrow x_1 B x_2$ or $A \rightarrow x$, for $A, B \in N$ and $x, x_1, x_2 \in T^*$, and

(5) $A \rightarrow x_1 B x_2$ or $A \rightarrow x$, for $A, B \in N$ and $x, x_1, x_2 \in T^*$, and productions of the form $S \rightarrow x_1 A_1 x_2 A_2 \ldots x_n A_n x_{n+1}$ are allowed for $A_i \in N$, $x_i \in T^*$ and $1 \leq i \leq n$ iff S does not appear in the right-hand side of any production.

A string x *directly derives* a string y in G, denoted by $x \Longrightarrow_G y$, iff $x = w_1 \alpha w_2$, $y = w_1 \beta w_2$ and $\alpha \rightarrow \beta \in P$, for $w_1, w_2 \in (N \cup T)^*$. This is also called a one-step derivation in G; consequently a k-step derivation (for $k \geq 0$) in G, denoted by $\Longrightarrow_G^k$, is defined for $x, y \in (N \cup T)^*$ as $x \Longrightarrow_G^k y$ iff there are words $x_0, x_1, \ldots, x_k$ such that $x = x_0$, $y = x_k$ and $x_i \Longrightarrow_G x_{i+1}$, with $0 \leq i \leq k-1$. If G is clear from the context, it is omitted, writing only $\Longrightarrow$ and $\Longrightarrow^k$, respectively. This applies to all definitions of derivation steps in the sequel. The transitive (and reflexive) closure of the one-step derivation is denoted by $\Longrightarrow^+$ ($\Longrightarrow^*$).

The language generated by G is denoted by $L(G)$ and it is defined by:

$$L(G) = \{ w \in T^* \mid S \Longrightarrow_G^* w \}.$$

A word $w \in (N \cup T)^*$ is called a *sentential form* (*terminal word* if $w \in T^*$) of G iff $S \Longrightarrow_G^* w$, so the language generated by G consists of all terminal words of G.

A language is said to be of type i iff it is generated by a Chomsky grammar of type i, with $i \in \{0, 1, 2, 3\}$. Type 0 grammars are also called *phrase structure grammars* and the family of type 0 languages is called *recursively enumerable*, denoted by RE.

Type 1 grammars and language are also called *context-sensitive* and their family of languages is denoted by CS. A *non-contracting* (or length-increasing, monotonous) grammar is a Chomsky grammar (N, T, P, S) such that the productions in P are of the form $\alpha \rightarrow \beta$, for $\alpha, \beta \in (N \cup T)^+$ and $|\alpha| \leq |\beta|$, and $S \rightarrow \lambda$ is allowed iff S does not occur in the right-hand side of any production. Context-sensitive grammars and non-contracting grammars generate the same family of languages CS.

Type 2 grammars and languages are also called *context-free* and their family of languages is denoted by CF.

In the literature, type 3 grammars and languages are called *right-linear*. When in condition (3) above the requirement $x \in T^*$ is replaced by $x \in T$, the definition of a *simply regular* grammar is obtained. Right-linear and simply regular grammars generate the same family of languages. In the sequel, grammars in the sense of condition (3) will be considered and are called *regular*; their family of languages is denoted by REG.

Furthermore, grammars and languages of type 4 (5) are called *linear* (*metalinear*) and their family of languages is denoted by LIN ($MLIN$).

Finally, a grammar is called λ-*free* if it does not contain any production $\alpha \rightarrow \lambda$, or if the only λ-production it contains is $S \rightarrow \lambda$, with S the axiom not appearing in the right-hand side of any production of the grammar.

A *generalized sequential machine* (gsm) is a construct $g = (K, I, O, s_0, \delta, H)$, where K is a finite non-empty set of *states*, I is the non-empty *input* alphabet,

O is the non-empty *output* alphabet, $s_0 \in K$ is the *initial state*, $H \subseteq K$ is the set of *final states* and δ is a finite set of productions of the form:

$$s_i v \to w s_j, \text{ for } s_i, s_j \in K, \ v \in I \text{ and } w \in O^*.$$

Let $\Rightarrow^*$ denote the transitive and reflexive closure of $\to$. For a word $v \in I^+$, let

$$g(v) = \{w \mid s_0 v \Rightarrow^* w s_z \text{ for some } s_z \in H\}.$$

Then we define a *gsm mapping*, for a gsm g and a language L over I, as follows:

$$g(L) = \{z \mid z \in g(v) \text{ for some } v \in L\}.$$

Without providing its definition, in the sequel we will also refer to the family of languages generated by ET0L systems (*ET0L*) without using it in any construction in the proofs. Definitions of this language family can be found in, e.g., [47, 48]. The family of languages that is used in the proofs is defined next.

A *matrix grammar (with appearance checking, ac for short)* [1] is a construct $G = (N, T, S, M, F)$, where N is the set of nonterminals, T is the set of terminals, $S \in N$ is the axiom, M is a finite set of *matrices* of the form $m : (r_1, r_2, \ldots, r_n)$, where $r_i : \alpha_i \to \beta_i$ are productions over $N \cup T$ and $|\alpha_i|_N \geq 1$, with $1 \leq i \leq n$, and F is a set of occurrences of productions in M. For $w, w' \in (N \cup T)^*$ and $m : (\alpha_1 \to \beta_1, \alpha_2 \to \beta_2, \ldots, \alpha_n \to \beta_n) \in M$ it is said that w directly derives w', written as:

$$
\begin{aligned}
w \Longrightarrow w' \quad \text{iff} \quad & \text{there exist } w_0, w_1, \ldots, w_n \in (N \cup T)^* \text{ such that} \\
& w_0 = w \text{ and } w_n = w' \text{ and, for all } 0 \leq i \leq n - 1, \\
\text{either} \quad & w_{i-1} = w'_{i-1} \alpha_i w''_{i-1} \text{ and } w_i = w'_{i-1} \beta_i w''_{i-1}, \\
& \text{for some } w'_{i-1}, w''_{i-1} \in (N \cup T)^*, \\
\text{or} \quad & \text{the production } \alpha_i \to \beta_i \text{ cannot be applied to } w_{i-1}, \\
& \alpha_i \to \beta_i \in F \text{ and } w_i = w_{i-1}.
\end{aligned}
$$

If $F = \varnothing$, the matrix grammar is called *without appearance checking* and F is omitted from the construct. The language generated by G is $L(G) = \{w \in T^* \mid S \Longrightarrow^* w\}$, where $\Longrightarrow^*$ denotes the reflexive and transitive closure of $\Longrightarrow$.

The family of languages generated by matrix grammars with appearance checking with λ-free context-free productions of type 2 is denoted by MAT_{ac} (MAT_{ac}^λ when not restricted to λ-free productions); MAT for matrix grammars without appearance checking. The following hierarchy, which includes the so-called Chomsky hierarchy for Chomsky grammars, is well known:

$$REG \subset LIN \subset MLIN \subset CF \subset MAT \subset MAT_{ac} \subset CS \subset MAT_{ac}^\lambda = RE.$$

3 CD Grammar Systems

Cooperating grammar systems were introduced in [40], the motivation coming from the theory of two-level grammars. Ten years later, they received renewed attention when a link with the notion of the blackboard model of problem solving from the theory of AI was established in [21], as described in the Introduction. A more general form was introduced in [19] and is presented next.

Definition 1. *A cooperating distributed grammar system, CD grammar system for short, is a construct* $\Gamma = (N, T, S, P_1, P_2, \ldots, P_n)$, *where* N *is the set of nonterminals,* T *is the set of terminals,* $S \in N$ *is the axiom and each* P_i, *with* $1 \leq i \leq n$, *is a finite set of productions over* $N \cup T$, *called a* component *of* Γ.

CD grammar systems rewrite differently than the grammars presented so far.

Definition 2. *Let* $\Gamma = (N, T, S, P_1, P_2, \ldots, P_n)$ *be a CD grammar system. Then* Γ *can rewrite according to one of the following five modes of derivation. For all modes, let* $x, y, z \in (N \cup T)^*$, $k \geq 1$, $1 \leq i \leq n$ *and* $\Longrightarrow_{P_i}^{\ell}$ *is used for the ℓ-step derivation* $\Longrightarrow^{\ell}$ *as defined for a Chomsky grammar* (N, T, S, P_i).

$\leq k$ *This mode corresponds to* at most k *direct derivation steps in succession by some component* P_i *in the CD grammar system:*

$$x \Longrightarrow_{\Gamma}^{\leq k} y \text{ iff there exists } P_i \text{ such that } x \Longrightarrow_{P_i}^{0} y \text{ or } x \Longrightarrow_{P_i}^{k'} y \text{ for some } k' \leq k.$$

$= k$ *This mode corresponds to* exactly k *direct derivation steps in succession by some component* P_i *in the CD grammar system:*

$$x \Longrightarrow_{\Gamma}^{=k} y \text{ iff there exists } P_i \text{ such that } x \Longrightarrow_{P_i}^{k} y.$$

$\geq k$ *This mode corresponds to* at least k *direct derivation steps in succession by some component* P_i *in the CD grammar system:*

$$x \Longrightarrow_{\Gamma}^{\geq k} y \text{ iff there exists } P_i \text{ such that } x \Longrightarrow_{P_i}^{k'} y \text{ for some } k' \geq k.$$

$*$ *This mode corresponds to* an arbitrary number *of direct derivation steps in succession by some component* P_i *in the CD grammar system:*

$$x \Longrightarrow_{\Gamma}^{*} y \text{ iff there exists } P_i \text{ such that } x \Longrightarrow_{P_i}^{0} y \text{ or } x \Longrightarrow_{P_i}^{k} y \text{ for some } k.$$

t *This mode corresponds to* maximal *derivations by some component* P_i *in the CD grammar system (i.e., the component must rewrite the sentential form as long as it is able to):*

$$x \Longrightarrow_{\Gamma}^{t} y \text{ iff there exists } P_i \text{ such that } x \Longrightarrow_{P_i}^{*} y \text{ and no } z \text{ such that } y \Longrightarrow_{P_i} z.$$

The language generated by a CD grammar system depends on the mode of derivation according to which it rewrites.

Definition 3. *Let* $\Gamma = (N, T, S, P_1, P_2, \ldots, P_n)$ *be a CD grammar system. The language generated by* Γ *in derivation mode* f, *for* $f \in \{\leq k, = k, \geq k \mid k \geq 1\} \cup \{*, t\}$, *is denoted by:*

$$L_f(\Gamma) = \{z \in T^* \mid S \Longrightarrow_{\Gamma}^{f} w_1 \Longrightarrow_{\Gamma}^{f} \cdots \Longrightarrow_{\Gamma}^{f} w_m = z, \ m \geq 1\}.$$

The family of languages that is generated by CD grammar systems $(N, T, S, P_1, P_2, \ldots, P_m)$ with only λ-free context-free productions of type 2 in each P_j, working in derivation mode f, and $1 \le j \le m \le n$, is denoted by $CD_n(f)$. Denote $CD(f) = \bigcup_{n \ge 1} CD_n(f)$.

This definition is illustrated by the following example.

Example 1. Consider the CD grammar system

$$\Gamma_1 = (\{S, A, B, A', B'\}, \{a, b, c\}, S, P_1, P_2, P_3),$$

where

$$P_1 = \{S \to AB, A' \to A, B' \to B\},$$
$$P_2 = \{A \to a^4 A' b^4, B \to c^4 B'\} \text{ and}$$
$$P_3 = \{A \to ab, B \to c\}.$$

Suppose that this CD grammar system works in the maximal derivation mode t. Clearly, the first component to be applied is P_1, resulting in AB. Then either component P_3 is used, resulting in the terminal word abc, or P_2 is used. After using P_2, the sentential form is $a^4 A' b^4 c^4 B'$ and only P_1 can be used, resulting in $a^4 A b^4 c^4 B$. Using P_2 and P_1 iteratively, strings of the form $a^i A b^i c^i B$ are generated, where $i \bmod 4 \equiv 0$. This string can be rewritten into a terminal one by using P_3 and hence the language generated by Γ_1 operating in mode t is:

$$L_t(\Gamma_1) = \{ a^n b^n c^n \mid n \bmod 4 \equiv 1, \ n \ge 1 \}.$$

This language is not a context-free language, thus demonstrating that CD grammar systems with context-free components are able to produce languages not in the context-free language class.

In fact, concerning the generative power of CD grammar systems, we know from [19,20] that for $f \in \{ =k, \ge k \mid k \ge 2 \}$, $k \ge 1$ and $k', k'' \ge 2$, holds that:

$$CF = CD(=1) = CD(\ge 1) = CD(*) = CD(\le k) \subset (CD(=k') \cap CD(\ge k'')),$$
$$CF = CD_1(f) \subset CD_2(f) \subseteq CD_3(f) \subseteq \ldots \subseteq CD(f) \subseteq MAT \text{ and}$$
$$CF = CD_1(t) = CD_2(t) \subset CD_3(t) = CD(t) = ET0L.$$

4 Hybrid CD Grammar Systems

The idea of considering the agents of a multi-agent system to have different capabilities, formally modelled by allowing different modes of derivation to be associated with different components, was introduced into the model of CD grammar systems in [42]. This has resulted in hybrid CD grammar systems [42,43], a.k.a. *externally* hybrid CD grammar systems to distinguish them from *internally* hybrid CD grammar systems [29–31]. In the latter, not only different components may work according to different (classical) modes of derivation (e.g., in the $\le k$-mode a component has to perform at most k steps) but components may moreover work according to arbitrary Boolean combinations of classical modes of derivation (e.g., in the $(t \wedge \le k)$-mode a component has to perform as many derivation steps as possible, but at most k steps).

Definition 4. *A hybrid cooperating distributed (CD) grammar system is a construct* $\Gamma = (N, T, S, (P_1, f_1), (P_2, f_2), \ldots, (P_n, f_n))$, *where* N *is the set of nonterminals,* T *is the set of terminals,* $S \in N$ *is the axiom,* $P_1, P_2, \ldots, P_n$ *are the components as for usual CD grammar systems and* $f_i \in \{\leq k, = k, \geq k \mid k \geq 1\} \cup \{*, t\}$ *is the mode of derivation associated with the component* P_i, *with* $1 \leq i \leq n$. *The language generated by* Γ *is:*

$$L(\Gamma) = \{ z \in T^* \mid S \Longrightarrow_{P_{i_1}}^{f_{i_1}} w_{i_1} \Longrightarrow_{P_{i_2}}^{f_{i_2}} \cdots \Longrightarrow_{P_{i_m}}^{f_{i_m}} w_{i_m} = z,$$
$$1 \leq i_j \leq n, \ 1 \leq j \leq m \}.$$

The family of languages that is generated by hybrid CD grammar systems $(N, T, S, (P_1, f_1), (P_2, f_2), \ldots, (P_m, f_m))$ with only λ-free context-free productions of type 2 in each P_j and $1 \leq j \leq m \leq n$, is denoted by HCD_n. Denote $HCD = \bigcup_{n \geq 1} HCD_n$.

Also this definition is illustrated by an example.

Example 2. Consider the hybrid CD grammar system

$$\Gamma_2 = (\{S, A, B, C, D, A', B', C', D'\}, \{a, b, c, d\}, S,$$
$$(P_1, = 1), (P_2, = 2), (P_3, = 2), (P_4, t), (P_5, = 4)),$$

where

$$P_1 = \{S \rightarrow ABCD\},$$
$$P_2 = \{A \rightarrow aA', C \rightarrow cC'\},$$
$$P_3 = \{B \rightarrow bB', D \rightarrow dD'\},$$
$$P_4 = \{A' \rightarrow A, B' \rightarrow B, C' \rightarrow C, D' \rightarrow D\} \text{ and}$$
$$P_5 = \{A \rightarrow a, B \rightarrow b, C \rightarrow c, D \rightarrow d\}.$$

Obviously, every successful derivation starts with the application of P_1, thus generating $ABCD$. There are three possibilities to continue. When P_5 is applied, the terminal word $abcd$ is generated since P_5 operates in mode $= 4$. Otherwise, either P_2 or P_3 has to be used in mode $= 2$, resulting in $aA'BcC'D$ or $AbB'CdD'$, respectively. Then, in case P_2 (P_3) was used in the last step, the derivation can proceed with P_3 (P_2) or P_4. Using P_2 as well as P_3, the only possibility to continue is by using P_4. Hence, in all cases (basically only two different ones) there comes a time when P_4 is used. This P_4 works in mode t, which makes it possible to remove the primes from only A and C or from only B and D or from all four of them, in all cases leaving no primed nonterminals and thus fulfil the stop condition of mode t. Consequently, this process can be iterated until eventually P_5 is used to replace A, B, C and D and thus fulfilling the stop condition for mode $= 4$. This explanation shows that the generated language is:

$$L(\Gamma_2) = \{a^n b^m c^n d^m \mid m, n \geq 1\}.$$

Like the language generated in Example 1, this language is non-context-free.

Concerning the generative power of hybrid CD grammar systems, we know from the definitions and [42,43] that for $f \in \{\leq k, = k, \geq k \mid k \geq 1\} \cup \{*, t\}$, $n' \geq 1$ and $n \geq 4$, holds that:

$$CF = CD_1(f) = HCD_1 \subset HCD_2 \subseteq HCD_3 \subseteq HCD_4 = HCD_n = HCD \subseteq MAT_{ac},$$
$$ET0L = CD_3(t) \subseteq HCD_3,$$
$$CD(f) \subseteq HCD_3,$$
$$ET0L \subset HCD_4 \text{ and}$$
$$CD_{n'}(f) \subseteq HCD_{n'}.$$

Furthermore, in [42] it was shown that for each hybrid CD grammar system, an equivalent hybrid CD grammar system can be constructed that contains three components working in the t-mode and one in the $= k$-mode, for some $k \geq 1$.

For the generative devices mentioned so far, only the notation for λ-free context-free productions of type 2 was given. Here and in the sequel, however, when productions are of type X, for $X \in \{REG, LIN, MLIN, CF, CS, RE\}$, a subscript X may be added to the notation; moreover, a superscript λ is added when not restricted to λ-free productions.

Concerning the generative power of hybrid CD grammar systems with sub-context-free productions, we know from [3,5,20,42] that for $f \in \{\leq k, = k, \geq k \mid k \geq 1\} \cup \{*, t\}$ holds that:

$$REG = CD_{REG}(f) = HCD_{REG},$$
$$LIN = CD_{LIN}(f) = HCD_{LIN} \text{ and}$$
$$MLIN = CD_{MLIN}(f) = HCD_{MLIN}.$$

5 Controlled CD Grammar Systems

Apart from hybrid CD grammar systems, numerous other types of CD grammar systems have been defined and investigated in the literature, among which grammar systems controlled by a directed graph, in which derivations are guided by paths in the graph (cf., e.g., [19,24,28,34,40]), or by a Petri net (cf. [15]), which allow (vector controlled) concurrent rewriting, grammar systems whose sentential forms are put into a gsm before another derivation step can take place (cf., e.g., [41,44]), and grammar systems whose sentential forms are compared to a (regular) hypothesis language, accepting only those sentential forms satisfying the format of the hypothesis language (cf., e.g., [23,44]).

We denote the above mentioned families of languages that are generated by CD grammar systems with graph control (GC), with a hypothesis language (HL) and with a gsm (GSM), with only λ-free productions of type X, for $X \in \{REG, LIN, MLIN, CF, CS, RE\}$, and working in derivation mode f, for $f \in \{\leq k, = k, \geq k \mid k \geq 1\} \cup \{*, t\}$, by $YCD_X(f)$, where $Y \in \{GC, HL, GSM\}$. Typically, subscript X is omitted if $x = CF$.

To put the results in this section in a proper perspective, we restate some results from [19, 23, 41] in the following lemma.

Lemma 1. *For $k, k' \geq 1$ and $f \in \{\leq k, =k, \geq k \mid k \geq 1\} \cup \{*, t\}$ holds that:*

1. $GCCD_{REG}(=k) = GCCD(\leq k) = GCCD(=k) = MAT$,
   $GCCD(\geq k) = GCCD(\geq k') \subseteq MAT$ and
   $CF = GCCD(*) \subset GCCD_{REG}(t) = GCCD(t) = ET0L$,
2. $HLCD(f) = CS$ and
3. $GSMCD(f) = CS$.

It is not difficult to see that every (hybrid) CD grammar system is also a controlled (hybrid) CD grammar system.

Lemma 2. *For $X \in \{REG, LIN, MLIN, CF, CS, RE\}$, $Y \in \{GC, HL, GSM\}$ and $f \in \{\leq k, =k, \geq k \mid k \geq 1\} \cup \{*, t\}$ holds that:*

1. $CD_X(f) \subseteq YCD_X(f)$ and
2. $HCD_X \subseteq YHCD_X$.

Proof. The inclusions follow when the controlling devices impose no restriction. Thus for $Y = GC$, consider the complete graph C_n with n nodes. For $Y = HL$, consider the regular language $R = (N \cup T)^* \setminus T^*$. For $Y = GSM$, finally, consider the gsm that does not translate but only copies the string it receives as input, i.e., $g = (\{s_0\}, N \cup T, N \cup T, s_0, \{(s_0 x, x s_0) \mid x \in (N \cup T)\}, \{s_0\})$. $\qquad\square$

6   Controlled Hybrid CD Grammar Systems

In this section, we combine the ideas from the previous sections and investigate the generative power of controlled hybrid CD grammar systems. These results, most of them originally reported in the MSc thesis [3], have not been published before. Lemma 4 is new.

6.1   Hybrid CD Grammar Systems with Static Control

First the case of a graph as *static* control mechanism is considered. The control is called static, since the current state of the problem is not taken into consideration. The notion of derivations controlled by a directed graph has already been presented in [19, 28, 40, 52] for Chomsky grammars, cooperating grammar systems, CD grammar systems and CD grammar systems with singleton components (or, equivalently, graph-controlled grammars with derivation modes) working in classical modes or internally hybrid modes (i.e., arbitrary Boolean combinations of classical modes, cf. Sect. 4). Results on graph controlled CD grammar systems with appearance checking and characterizations of graphs associated to specific language classes can be found in [24, 34].

Definition 5. *A hybrid CD grammar system with graph control is a construct*

$$\Gamma = (N, T, S, (P_1, f_1), (P_2, f_2), \ldots, (P_n, P_n), U),$$

where $(N, T, S, (P_1, f_1), (P_2, f_2), \ldots, (P_n, P_n))$ *is a hybrid CD grammar system and* $U = (V, E)$ *is a directed graph with set of nodes* V *and set of edges* E, *the* n *nodes of which are labelled by* P_i, *with* $1 \leq i \leq n$.

For $f_i \in \{\leq k, = k, \geq k \mid k \geq 1\} \cup \{*, t\}$ *and* $1 \leq i \leq n$, *the language generated by* Γ *and controlled by* U *is:*

$$L^U(\Gamma) = \{ z \in T^* \mid S \Longrightarrow_{P_{i_1}}^{f_{i_1}} w_{i_1} \Longrightarrow_{P_{i_2}}^{f_{i_2}} \cdots \Longrightarrow_{P_{i_m}}^{f_{i_m}} w_{i_m} = z,$$

$$(P_{i_k}, P_{i_{k+1}}) \in E, \ 1 \leq i_j \leq n, \ 1 \leq j \leq m, \ 1 \leq k \leq m-1 \}.$$

Note that the graph has exactly one node for each component labelled by the component.

The family of languages that is generated by hybrid CD grammar systems with graph control $(N, T, S, (P_1, f_1), (P_2, f_2), \ldots, (P_m, f_m), U)$ with only λ-free context-free productions of type 2 in each P_j and $1 \leq j \leq m \leq n$, is denoted by $GCHCD_n$. Denote $GCHCD = \bigcup_{n \geq 1} GCHCD_n$.

The next example illustrates hybrid CD grammar systems with graph control.

Example 3. Consider the hybrid CD grammar system with graph control

$$\Gamma_3 = (\{S, A, B\}, \{a, b\}, S, (P_1, t), (P_2, =1), (P_3, t), (P_4, t), (P_5, t), U),$$

where

$$P_1 = \{S \to ABS, S \to AB\},$$
$$P_2 = \{A \to a\},$$
$$P_3 = \{B \to bB'\},$$
$$P_4 = \{B \to b\},$$
$$P_5 = \{B' \to B\} \text{ and}$$

U is the following graph:
$$\begin{array}{c} P_1 \to P_2 \to P_4 \\ \nearrow \ \downarrow \\ P_5 \leftarrow P_3 \end{array}$$

Using P_1 for i times results in the sentential form $(AB)^i$, with $i \geq 1$. Then every time P_2 changes one A into an a, the components P_3 and P_5 change all B's into bB. This is repeated until there is only one A remaining in the sentential form, after which another path in the graph is taken to replace also this last A by a and consequently replacing all B's by b, thus obtaining a terminal string. No terminal string can be obtained if the last A's replacement by a is followed by replacing all B's by bB' since this would eventually require another application of P_2 before yielding a terminal string, which is not possible due to the absence of A's. It is thus clear that

$$L^U(\Gamma_3) = \{(ab^n)^n \mid n \geq 1\}.$$

Hence already only one non-metalinear production and a simple graph suffice to generate a non-ET0L language.

The proof of the next lemma makes use of the *domain* of a component P of a grammar system with set N of nonterminals, which is defined as $dom(P) = \{ A \in N \mid A \to x \in P \}$.

Lemma 3. *It holds that* $GCHCD \subseteq MAT_{ac}$ *and* $GCHCD^{\lambda} \subseteq MAT_{ac}^{\lambda}$.

Proof. Consider a graph controlled hybrid CD grammar system

$$\Gamma = (N, T, S, (P_1, f_1), (P_2, f_2), \ldots, (P_n, f_n), U).$$

To simulate this hybrid CD grammar system with graph control, construct the following matrix grammar with appearance checking

$$G' = (N', T', S', M', F'),$$

where

$$
\begin{aligned}
N' \;=\;& N \cup \{S'\} \cup \{ [P_i, f_i], [P_i, \geq k]' \mid (P_i, f_i), (P_i, \geq k) \in \Gamma,\; 1 \leq i \leq n \},\\
T' \;=\;& T \cup \{z\},\\
M' \;=\;& \{ (S' \to S[P_i, f_i]) \mid f_i \in \{ \leq k, = k, \geq k \mid k \geq 1 \} \cup \{*, t\},\; 1 \leq i \leq n \} \cup\\
& \{ ([P_i, \leq k] \to [P_j, f_j],\; A_1 \to x_1, A_2 \to x_2, \ldots, A_h \to x_h) \mid\\
& \quad A_g \to x_g \in P_i,\; f_j \in \{ \leq k, = k, \geq k \mid k \geq 1 \} \cup \{*, t\},\; 1 \leq g \leq h \leq k,\\
& \quad (P_i, P_j) \in E,\; 1 \leq i, j \leq n \} \cup\\
& \{ ([P_i, \leq k] \to [P_j, f_j]) \mid f_j \in \{ \leq k, = k, \geq k \mid k \geq 1 \} \cup \{*, t\},\\
& \quad 1 \leq i, j \leq n \} \cup\\
& \{ ([P_i, = k] \to [P_j, f_j],\; A_1 \to x_1, A_2 \to x_2, \ldots, A_k \to x_k) \mid\\
& \quad A_g \to x_g \in P_i,\; f_j \in \{ \leq k, = k, \geq k \mid k \geq 1 \} \cup \{*, t\},\; 1 \leq g \leq k,\\
& \quad (P_i, P_j) \in E,\; 1 \leq i, j \leq n \} \cup\\
& \{ ([P_i, \geq k] \to [P, \geq k]',\; A_1 \to x_1, A_2 \to x_2, \ldots, A_k \to x_k) \mid\\
& \quad A_g \to x_g \in P_i,\; 1 \leq g \leq k,\; 1 \leq i \leq n \} \cup\\
& \{ ([P_i, \geq k]' \to [P_i, \geq k]',\; A \to x) \mid A \to x \in P_i,\; 1 \leq i \leq n \} \cup\\
& \{ ([P_i, \geq k]' \to [P_j, f_j]) \mid f_j \in \{ \leq k, = k, \geq k \mid k \geq 1 \} \cup \{*, t\},\\
& \quad (P_i, P_j) \in E,\; 1 \leq i, j \leq n \} \cup\\
& \{ ([P_i, *] \to [P_i, *],\; A \to x) \mid A \to x \in P_i,\; 1 \leq i \leq n \} \cup\\
& \{ ([P_i, *] \to [P_j, f_j]) \mid f_j \in \{ \leq k, = k, \geq k \mid k \geq 1 \} \cup \{*, t\},\\
& \quad (P_i, P_j) \in E,\; 1 \leq i, j \leq n \} \cup\\
& \{ ([P_i, t] \to [P_i, t],\; A \to x) \mid A \to x \in P_i,\; 1 \leq i \leq n \} \cup\\
& \{ ([P_i, t] \to [P_j, f_j],\; A_{i_1} \to F, A_{i_2} \to F, \ldots, A_{i_{s_i}} \to F) \mid\\
& \quad dom(P_i) = \{ A_{i_1}, A_{i_2}, \ldots, A_{i_{s_i}} \},\; f_j \in \{ \leq k, = k, \geq k \mid k \geq 1 \} \cup \{*, t\},\\
& \quad (P_i, P_j) \in E,\; 1 \leq i, j \leq n \} \cup\\
& \{ ([P_i, f_i] \to z) \mid f_i \in \{ \leq k, = k, \geq k \mid k \geq 1 \} \cup \{*, t\},\; 1 \leq i \leq n \} \text{ and}
\end{aligned}
$$

in F' are all the productions $A \to F$ appearing in M'.

The simulation starts with applying a production $S' \rightarrow S[P_i, f_i]$, where S is the original axiom and $[P_i, f_i]$ a marker, indicating which component is being simulated and what its mode of derivation is. From S, the language of the graph controlled hybrid CD grammar system will be generated and the marker will control this generation.

When the mode is $\leq k$, indeed less than k times a production from the corresponding component is used before handing over control to another component. Furthermore, this other component has to be connected to the current component by an edge in the controlling graph. This test is done throughout the whole construction, before handing over control to another component. In the case of mode $= k$, exactly k productions are used. For mode $\geq k$, first exactly k productions are used, after which the primed version of $[P_i, \geq k]$ is used to hand over control to another component only after another zero or more rewriting steps.

If the mode is $*$, an arbitrary number of productions is used before handing over control. Finally, in mode t the same construction is used to rewrite an arbitrary number of times. Moreover, the productions in the set F' guarantee that in this mode control can only be handed over to another component when no more production of the particular component can be used. In the case of mode $\leq k$ and $*$ the control can also directly be given to another component, corresponding to the case when the less than k or arbitrary number of rewriting steps is in fact zero.

Eventually, the marker is replaced by z thus yielding $L(G') = L(\Gamma)\{z\}$. This z can be removed by a morphism and thus, since it is known (cf., e.g. [25]) that the family MAT_{ac} is closed under restricted morphisms, $L(\Gamma) \in MAT_{ac}$ and the first statement of the lemma is proved.

The second statement of the lemma can be proved by a similar construction, even simplified since the marker can be replaced by λ instead of z, making the use of a morphism unnecessary.   □

Lemma 4. *It holds that* $MAT_{ac} \subseteq GCHCD$ *and* $MAT_{ac}^{\lambda} \subseteq GCHCD^{\lambda}$.

Proof. Consider a matrix grammar with appearance checking

$$G = (N, T, S, M, F).$$

Denote $M = \{m_1, m_2, \ldots, m_m\}$. Moreover, assume that any matrix m_i, with $1 \leq i \leq m$, contains at most one production in F; it is known (cf., e.g., [25]) that this is a normal form for matrix grammars.

To simulate this matrix grammar with appearance checking, construct the following graph controlled hybrid CD grammar system

$$\Gamma' = (N, T, S, (P_1, f_1), (P_2, f_2), \ldots, (P_n, f_n), U),$$

such that $(P_1, f_1), (P_2, f_2), \ldots, (P_n, f_n)$ contains the below components, for every matrix $m_i : (\alpha_{i_1} \rightarrow \beta_{i_1}, \alpha_{i_2} \rightarrow \beta_{i_2}, \ldots, \alpha_{i_{\ell_i}} \rightarrow \beta_{i_{\ell_i}}) \in M$, with $1 \leq i \leq m$, and U is as below.

If m_i contains no production which is in F, then for all $1 \le j \le \ell_i$, we add a component

$$(P_{i_j}, = 1), \text{ where } P_{i_j} = \{\alpha_{i_j} \to \beta_{i_j}\}.$$

Else, let $\alpha_{i_t} \to \beta_{i_t}$, for some $1 \le t \le \ell_i$, be the production of m_i which is in F. Then we add a component

$$(P'_{i_t}, t), \text{ where } P'_{i_t} = \{\alpha_{i_t} \to \alpha_{i_t}\}.$$

Moreover, $U = (V, E)$, where U and V are as follows, for every matrix m_i : $(\alpha_{i_1} \to \beta_{i_1}, \alpha_{i_2} \to \beta_{i_2}, \ldots, \alpha_{i_{\ell_i}} \to \beta_{i_{\ell_i}}) \in M$, with $1 \le i \le m$:

$$V = \{ P_{i_j} \mid 1 \le j \le \ell_i, \ 1 \le i \le m \} \cup \{ P'_{i_t} \mid 1 \le t \le \ell_i, \ 1 \le i \le m \} \text{ and}$$
$$E = \{ (P_{i_j}, P_{i_{j+1}}) \mid 1 \le j \le \ell_i, \ 1 \le i \le m \} \cup \{ (P_{i_{\ell_i}}, P_{k_1}) \mid 1 \le i, k \le m \} \cup$$
$$\{ (P_{i_{t-1}}, P'_{i_t}), \ (P'_{i_t}, P_{i_{t+1}}) \mid 1 \le t \le \ell_i, \ 1 \le i \le m \}.$$

For every production in matrices of M, a component P_{i_j} is constructed operating in mode $= 1$. Additionally, for every production in F, an 'appearance checking' component P'_{i_t} is constructed operating in mode t. The strict ordering of productions in matrices of M is preserved by the graph. After all productions of a matrix have been used, a new matrix can be started by beginning with its first production. This is all imposed by the graph. Since the productions are put in different components following each other, it is clear that a production can rewrite nonterminals introduced by a production from the same matrix which precedes it in the ordering.

The appearance checking works as follows. First assume that α_{i_t} occurs in the sentential form. Then the production $\alpha_{i_t} \to \beta_{i_t}$ of component P_{i_t} can be applied and matrix simulation can continue with component $P_{i_{t+1}}$. However, P'_{i_t} works in the t-mode and since α_{i_t} is present, this component will continue working without ever obtaining a terminal string.

Next assume that α_{i_t} does not occur in the sentential form. Then the derivation cannot continue by applying component P_{i_t}, since it works in mode $= 1$, which is impossible. However, component P'_{i_t} works in the t-mode, meaning that it can be applied zero times if the left-hand side of its production does not occur in the sentential form, and matrix simulation can continue with component $P_{i_{t+1}}$. This shows that the appearance checking case is simulated correctly.

It is thus clear that $L(\Gamma') = L(G)$ and that both statements of the lemma are now proved. $\square$

To put these results in perspective, the following results now hold, for $f \in \{\le k, = k, \ge k \mid k \ge 1\} \cup \{*, t\}$ and $k \ge 1$:

$$\begin{array}{ccc}
CS = & HLCD(f) & = & GSMCD(f) \\
\cup & & & \\
MAT_{ac} = & GCHCD & \supseteq & HCD \\
\cup & & & \\
MAT = & GCCD_{[REG]}(=k) & & ET0L = GCCD_{[REG]}(t) = CD(t) \\
\cup & & & \\
CF = & GCCD(*) & = & CD(*)
\end{array}$$

Families which are not connected are not necessarily incomparable. The reported statements can be found in Sects. 2–5 and in Lemma 3 and 4, or are obvious.

Note that hybridity strictly increases the generative power of graph controlled CD grammar systems, whereas it remains an open problem whether control by a graph strictly increases the generative power of hybrid CD grammar systems. A solution to this problem could shed light on the relation between hybrid CD grammar systems and matrix grammars, or perhaps even solve this open problem first stated in [43].

6.2   Hybrid CD Grammar Systems with Dynamic Control

Next the case of a hypothesis (or target) language or a gsm as *dynamic* control mechanism is considered. This kind of control is called dynamic, since the current state of the problem is taken into consideration by assuming a hypothesis (target) language with which the sentential forms are compared during derivation, or a gsm that translates sentential forms during derivation.

We first define hybrid CD grammar systems with a (regular) hypothesis language. The notion of a hypothesis language (or the slightly different concept of regular restriction) to compare sentential forms with during derivation has already been introduced in [23, 32, 44] for context-free grammars, CD grammar systems and colonies, which is a subclass of CD grammar systems with components generating finite languages (cf. [39] for a result on context-free grammars with a weak regular restriction).

Definition 6. *A hybrid CD grammar system with a (regular) hypothesis language is a construct*

$$\Gamma = (N, T, S, (P_1, f_1), (P_2, f_2), \ldots, (P_n, f_n), R),$$

where $(N, T, S, (P_1, f_1), (P_2, f_2), \ldots, (P_n, f_n))$ *is a hybrid CD grammar system and R is a regular language in $(N \cup T)^* \setminus T^*$.*

A derivation consists of accepted derivation steps, where a derivation step $x \Longrightarrow_{P_i}^{f_i} y$, *for* $f_i \in \{\leq k, = k, \geq k \mid k \geq 1\} \cup \{*, t\}$ *and* $1 \leq i \leq n$, *is accepted iff* $y \in R$ *or* $y \in T^*$. *The language generated by Γ with hypothesis language R is:*

$$L^R(\Gamma) = \{ z \in T^* \mid S \Longrightarrow_{P_{i_1}}^{f_{i_1}} w_{i_1} \Longrightarrow_{P_{i_2}}^{f_{i_2}} \cdots \Longrightarrow_{P_{i_m}}^{f_{i_m}} w_{i_m} = z,$$

$$w_{i_k} \in R, \ 1 \leq i_j \leq n, \ 1 \leq j \leq m, \ 1 \leq k \leq m - 1 \}.$$

Note that no hypothesis is made about the final terminal string. The regularity of the hypothesis language is motivated by the fact that the test for the condition $y \in R$ can be done in linear time.

The family of languages that is generated by hybrid CD grammar systems with a hypothesis language $(N, T, S, (P_1, f_1), (P_2, f_2), \ldots, (P_m, f_m), R)$ with only λ-free context-free productions of type 2 in each P_j and $1 \leq j \leq m \leq n$, is denoted by $HLHCD_n$. Denote $HLHCD = \bigcup_{n \geq 1} HLHCD_n$.

We now define hybrid CD grammar systems with a gsm. The notion of a gsm that translates sentential forms during derivation has already been introduced in [41, 44] for CD grammar systems and colonies.

Definition 7. *A hybrid CD grammar system with a gsm is a construct*

$$\Gamma = (N, T, S, (P_1, f_1), (P_2, f_2), \dots, (P_n, f_n), g),$$

where $(N, T, S, (P_1, f_1), (P_2, f_2), \dots, (P_n, f_n))$ *is a hybrid CD grammar system and*

$$g = (K, N \cup T, N \cup T, s_0, \delta, H)$$

is a gsm.

For $f_i \in \{\leq k, = k, \geq k \mid k \geq 1\} \cup \{*, t\}$ *and* $1 \leq i \leq n$, *the language generated by* Γ *with gsm* g *is:*

$$L^g(\Gamma) = \{ z \in T^* \mid S \Longrightarrow_{P_{i_1}}^{f_{i_1}} w_{i_1} \Longrightarrow g(w_{i_1}) \Longrightarrow_{P_{i_2}}^{f_{i_2}} w_{i_2} \Longrightarrow g(w_{i_2}) \Longrightarrow_{P_{i_3}}^{f_{i_3}} \cdots$$
$$\cdots \Longrightarrow_{P_{i_m}}^{f_{i_m}} w_{i_m} = z, \ 1 \leq i_j \leq n, \ 1 \leq j \leq m \}$$

The family of languages that is generated by hybrid CD grammar systems with a gsm $(N, T, S, (P_1, f_1), (P_2, f_2), \dots, (P_m, f_m), g)$ with only λ-free context-free productions of type 2 in each P_j and $1 \leq j \leq m \leq n$, is denoted by $GSMHCD_n$. Denote $GSMHCD = \bigcup_{n \geq 1} GSMHCD_n$.

The next example illustrates hybrid CD grammar systems with a gsm.

Example 4. Consider the hybrid CD grammar system with a gsm

$$\Gamma_4 = (\{S, A, B, C, D\}, \{a, b, c, d\}, S, (P_1, =1), (P_2, =2), (P_3, =2), (P_4, =4), g),$$

where

$$P_1 = \{S \rightarrow abcd\},$$
$$P_2 = \{A \rightarrow aa, C \rightarrow cc\},$$
$$P_3 = \{B \rightarrow bb, D \rightarrow dd\},$$
$$P_4 = \{A \rightarrow a, B \rightarrow b, C \rightarrow c, D \rightarrow d\} \text{ and}$$
$$g = (\{s_a, s_b, s_c, s_d, s_z\}, I, O, s_a, \delta, \{s_z\}),$$
with $I = O = \{S, A, B, C, D, a, b, c, d\}$ and
$$\delta = \{s_a a \rightarrow A s_b, s_a A \rightarrow A s_b, s_b a \rightarrow a s_b, s_b b \rightarrow B s_c, s_b B \rightarrow B s_c,$$
$$s_c b \rightarrow b s_c, s_c c \rightarrow C s_d, s_c C \rightarrow C s_d, s_d c \rightarrow c s_d, s_d d \rightarrow D s_z,$$
$$s_d D \rightarrow D s_z, s_z d \rightarrow d s_z\}.$$

Initially, only P_1 can be used, resulting in the sentential form *abcd*. This component can now never be used again. The gsm translates this string into *ABCD*. The gsm always translates the first a, b, c and d that it meets into A, B, C and D, respectively, if this particular nonterminal is not yet present in the sentential form, meanwhile skipping specific intermediate terminals and nonterminals. From *ABCD*, the derivation can be continued by using either P_2, P_3 or P_4.

Component P_4 results in the terminal string $abcd$. Using P_2 (P_3) leads to $aaBccD$ ($AbbCdd$), which the gsm thus translates into $AaBCcD$ ($ABbCDd$). Repeating this process, strings of the form $Aa^i b^j Cc^i d^j$ or $a^i Bb^j c^i Dd^j$ are translated into strings of the form $Aa^i Bb^j Cc^i Dd^j$, with $i \geq 1$ and $j \geq 0$ ($i \geq 0$ and $j \geq 1$). Finally, component P_4 can then be used (only after translation since it requires the presence of A, B, C and D in the sentential form) to obtain terminal strings of the form $a^i b^j c^i d^j$, with $i \geq 1$ and $j \geq 1$. It is thus clear that

$$L^g(\Gamma_4) = \{\, a^n b^m c^n d^m \mid m, n \geq 1 \,\}.$$

Note that the gsm in the example is in fact a Mealy machine since it is deterministic and every production in the set δ has only one output letter. Hence already regular productions and a restricted gsm suffice to generate a non-context-free language.

The following lemma leads to a result (cf. Theorem 1) that is not limited to hybrid CD grammar systems with control by a gsm, but that also holds for control by a hypothesis language.

Lemma 5. *It holds that GSMHCD $\subseteq$ CS.*

Proof. Consider a hybrid CD grammar system with a gsm

$$\Gamma = (N, T, S, (P_1, f_1), (P_2, f_2), \ldots, (P_n, f_n), g).$$

Furthermore, let

$$g = (S, I, O, s_0, \delta, F), \text{ where } I = O = (N \cup T).$$

To simulate this hybrid CD grammar system with a gsm, construct the following Chomsky grammar of type 1.

$$G' = (N', T', S', P'),$$

where

$$N' = N \cup \{S', T, T', s_0\} \cup \{\, [C_i, f_i, j], \ [C'_i, f_i, j], \ [C''_i, f_i, j] \mid (P_i, f_i) \in \Gamma,$$
$$f_i \in \{\leq k, = k, \geq k \mid k \geq 1\}, \ 1 \leq i \leq n, \ 0 \leq j \leq k\} \cup$$
$$\{\, [C_i, g_i], \ [C'_i, g_i], \ [C''_i, g_i] \mid (P_i, g_i) \in \Gamma, \ g_i \in \{*, t\}, \ 1 \leq i \leq n\} \cup$$
$$\{\, C_{t_i}, C'_{t_i} \mid (P_i, t) \in \Gamma, \ 1 \leq i \leq n\},$$
$$T' = T \cup \{L, R\} \text{ and}$$

$P' = \{S' \to LTSR\} \cup$

$\quad \{LT \to L[C_i, f_i, 0], \ LT \to L[C_i, g_i] \mid f_i \in \{\leq k, = k, \geq k \mid k \geq 1\},$

$\quad g_i \in \{*, t\}, \ 1 \leq i \leq n\} \cup$

$\quad \{[C_i, f_i, j]y \to y[C_i, f_i, j], \ [C_i', f_i, j]y \to y[C_i', f_i, j],$

$\quad y[C_i'', f_i, j] \to [C_i'', f_i, j]y \mid y \in (N \cup T), \ f_i \in \{\leq k, = k, \geq k \mid k \geq 1\},$

$\quad 0 \leq j \leq k, \ 1 \leq i \leq n\} \cup$

$\quad \{[C_i, g_i]y \to y[C_i, g_i], \ [C_i', g_i]y \to y[C_i', g_i], \ y[C_i'', g_i] \to [C_i'', g_i]y \mid$

$\quad y \in (N \cup T), \ g_i \in \{*, t\}, \ 1 \leq i \leq n\} \cup$

$\quad \{[C_i, f_i, j]A \to x[C_i', f_i, j] \mid A \to x \in P_i, \ f_i \in \{\leq k, = k, \geq k \mid k \geq 1\},$

$\quad 0 \leq j \leq k, \ 1 \leq i \leq n\} \cup$

$\quad \{[C_i, g_i]A \to x[C_i', g_i] \mid A \to x \in P_i, \ g_i \in \{*, t\}, \ 1 \leq i \leq n\} \cup$

$\quad \{[C_i, f_i, j]R \to [C_i'', f_i, j]R \mid f_i \in \{\leq k, = k, \geq k \mid k \geq 1\}, \ 0 \leq j \leq k,$

$\quad 1 \leq i \leq n\} \cup$

$\quad \{[C_i, g_i]R \to [C_i'', g_i]R \mid g_i \in \{*, t\}, \ 1 \leq i \leq n\} \cup$

$\quad \{L[C_i'', f_i, j] \to L[C_i, f_i, j + 1] \mid f_i \in \{\leq k, = k, \geq k \mid k \geq 1\},$

$\quad 0 \leq j \leq k - 1, \ 1 \leq i \leq n\} \cup$

$\quad \{L[C_i'', \leq k, j] \to Ls_0 \mid 0 \leq j \leq k, \ 1 \leq i \leq n\} \cup$

$\quad \{L[C_i'', = k, k] \to Ls_0 \mid 1 \leq i \leq n\} \cup$

$\quad \{L[C_i'', \geq k, k] \to L[C_i, \geq k, k], \ L[C_i'', \geq k, k] \to Ls_0 \mid 1 \leq i \leq n\} \cup$

$\quad \{L[C_i'', *] \to L[C_i, *], \ L[C_i'', *] \to Ls_0 \mid 1 \leq i \leq n\} \cup$

$\quad \{L[C_i, *] \to Ls_0 \mid 1 \leq i \leq n\} \cup$

$\quad \{L[C_i, t] \to LC_{t_i}, \ L[C_i'', t] \to LC_{t_i} \mid 1 \leq i \leq n\} \cup$

$\quad \{C_{t_i}y \to yC_{t_i} \mid y \to x \notin P_i, \ y \in (N \cup T)^+, \ x \subset (N \cup T)^*, \ 1 \leq i \leq n\} \cup$

$\quad \{C_{t_i}R \to C_i'R, \ yC_{t_i}' \to C_{t_i}'y, \ LC_{t_i}' \to Ls_0 \mid y \in (N \cup T), \ 1 \leq i \leq n\} \cup$

$\quad \{s_1x \to ys_2 \mid (s_1x, ys_2) \in \delta\} \cup \{sR \to TR \mid s \in F\} \cup$

$\quad \{yT \to Ty \mid y \in O\} \cup \{LT \to LT'\} \cup$

$\quad \{T'y \to yT' \mid y \in T\} \cup \{T'R \to R\}.$

Note that G contains non-contracting productions; it is known (cf., e.g., [48, 50]) that these can be transformed into context-sensitive productions.

The simulation starts by introducing the sentential form $LTSR$, where S is the original axiom, T is a marker and L and R are terminal symbols indicating the left and right end, respectively, of the sentential form. From S, the language of the hybrid CD grammar system with a gsm will be generated and the marker is non-deterministically replaced by a control symbol $[C_i, f_i, j]$ or $[C_i, g_i]$ indicating the use of a component P_i working in mode $f_i \in \{\leq k, = k, \geq k \mid k \geq 1\}$ or $g_i \in \{*, t\}$, respectively. In the case of a mode $f_i \in \{\leq k, = k, \geq k \mid k \geq 1\}$, a counter j, with $0 \leq j \leq k$, is used; in the case of mode $*$ or t this is not necessary.

The simulation continues by moving the control symbol to the right (skipping terminals and nonterminals) until a nonterminal is replaced by a production from the component P_i, consequently priming the control symbol. Then this primed version of the control symbol is moved completely to the right of the sentential from, where it becomes double primed and is moved completely to the left again. When it is completely on the left of the sentential form, some different cases need to be considered.

In the case of mode $\leq k$, $= k$ or $\geq k$ (for a $k \geq 1$) the counter is increased by one and the process is repeated. When exactly k productions of the component P_i are used (when j reaches the value k) and the mode is $= k$, the control symbol is replaced by s_0. In the case of mode $\leq k$, this can happen for every value of j between zero and k. For mode $\geq k$ this production can be used when j is equal to k, but also another process guided by the initial control symbol with counter k can be started. This allows the use of a production more than k times, indeed corresponding to mode $\geq k$, before replacing the control symbol by s_0.

In the case of mode $*$, the control symbol can be replaced by s_0 after using P_i an arbitrary number of times indeed. The same holds for mode t, except that before introducing s_0 a test is done to check if there is indeed no production left from P_i that can be used on the current sentential form. For this test, a test symbol C_{t_i} is introduced, indicating for which component (P_i) this test is done. This test symbol is moved from left to right over the sentential form, allowed to skip any terminals but only those nonterminals for which there is no production in component P_i being tested. When it reaches the right end, it is replaced by its primed version which is then moved completely to the left to be replaced by s_0.

In any mode, the result is the introduction of s_0 to indicate the end of the work of the component. This s_0 is the start symbol of the gsm. Next, the usage of the gsm is simulated on the sentential form remaining after using a component. It does its work as usual and when it reaches the right side of the sentential form in a final state, this final state symbol is replaced by the marker T again. This T is moved to the left, skipping only symbols from the output alphabet of the gsm, where it is replaced by T'. Finally, this T' is moved completely to the right skipping only terminals before it disappears.

From this detailed explanation it is clear that $L(G') = \{L\}L(\Gamma)\{R\}$ and, since it is known (cf., e.g., [50]) that the family CS is closed under cancellation of first and last letter, $L(G') \in CS$, and the lemma is thus proved.   □

This lemma leads to the final result of this paper, presented in below theorem.

Theorem 1. *For $f \in \{\leq k, = k, \geq k \mid k \geq 1\} \cup \{*, t\}$ holds that:*

$$CS = HLCD(f) = HLHCD = GSMHCD.$$

Proof. The first equality can be found in Lemma 1(2). Furthermore, the inclusion $HLCD(f) \subseteq HLHCD$ is obvious. It is also clear that a gsm can check whether a given input string is in a regular language; it can thus play the role of a hypothesis language and hence $HLHCD \subseteq GSMHCD$ holds. Finally, Lemma 5 finishes the proof of this theorem.   □

7   Results

To put the results of this paper in a proper perspective, the following diagram now holds, for $f \in \{\,\leq k, = k, \geq k \mid k \geq 1\,\} \cup \{*, t\}$ and $k \geq 1$, where families which are not connected are not necessarily incomparable and $[REG]$ means that the result holds with or without the restriction to regular productions of type 3:

$$
\begin{array}{rlllll}
RE = & MAT_{ac}^{\lambda} \\
\cup \\
CS = & HLCD(f) & = GSMCD(f) = HLHCD = GSMHCD \\
\cup \\
MAT_{ac} = & GCHCD & \supseteq & HCD \\
\cup & & & \curvearrowright \\
MAT = & GCCD_{[REG]}(=k) & & & ET0L & = & CD(t) & = GCCD_{[REG]}(t) \\
\cup & & & & & & \cup \\
CF = & CD(=1) & = & CD(\geq 1) & = CD(\leq k) = & CD(*) & = GCCD(*) \\
\cup \\
MLIN = & CD_{MLIN}(f) & = & HCD_{MLIN} \\
\cup \\
LIN = & CD_{LIN}(f) & = & HCD_{LIN} \\
\cup \\
REG = & CD_{REG}(f) & = & HCD_{REG}
\end{array}
$$

8   Conclusion

We have characterised the generative power of several types of hybrid CD grammar systems with controlled derivations, by relating them to the families of languages generated by matrix grammars with appearance checking and by context-sensitive grammars. In particular, due to the new Lemma 4, we now know that hybridity strictly increases the generative power of graph controlled CD grammar systems. However, it remains an open problem whether control by a graph strictly increases the generative power of hybrid CD grammar systems.

Moreover, we have shown that such formal languages can generate the non-context-free constructs known as multiple agreements, crossed agreements and (re)duplication, which linguists have identified as features of natural languages. In particular, graph controlled hybrid CD grammar systems can generate these non-context-free features. This is important, since their generative power is shown to be strictly less than that of context-sensitive grammars, which are known to be too computationally expensive to parse.

Acknowledgement. This paper is dedicated to Erzsébet Csuhaj-Varjú (Erzsi for friends like me) who has taught me everything I always wanted to know about CD grammar systems exactly 30 years ago when Grzegorz Rozenberg and Jetty Kleijn put me in contact with her. She was an excellent supervisor of my Master's thesis on teams in grammar systems [3], which has resulted in this paper and in three earlier papers

[4–6]. The concept of teamwork has been an important part of my research ever since. We continued to collaborate on CD grammar systems also while I was working on my PhD thesis on team automata [7], which have become a successful area of research [13,14]. This collaboration resulted in teams of pushdown automata [11,12] as well as in a series of papers in which we teamed up to study notions of competence in CD grammar systems [8–10]. For a special journal issue celebrating an earlier birthday of Erzsi, Jetty and I transferred the team automata concept of synchronised collaboration to teams of grammars [16]. For this Festschrift, I decided to return to the roots and report on specific types of CD grammar systems. Who knows what's next …

I would also like to thank the anonymous reviewers for their useful comments and suggestions. In particular, the proof that the statement of Lemma 4 holds for matrix grammars with appearance checking, and not just for matrix grammars without appearance checking as proved in [3], is due to one of the reviewers.

Disclosure of Interests. The author has no competing interests to declare that are relevant to the content of this article.

References

1. Abraham, S.: Some questions of phrase-structure grammars, I. Comput. Linguist. **4**, 61–70 (1965). https://doi.org/10.1515/ling.1967.5.31.5
2. Becerra-Bonache, L., Bel-Enguix, G., Jiménez-López, M.D., Martín-Vide, C.: Mathematical foundations: formal grammars and languages. In: Mitkov, R. (ed.) The Oxford Handbook of Computational Linguistics, Chap. 9, pp. 207–229. Oxford University Press (2003). https://doi.org/10.1093/oxfordhb/9780199573691.013.021
3. ter Beek, M.H.: Teams in grammar systems. Master's thesis, Leiden University, September 1996. https://theses.liacs.nl/716
4. ter Beek, M.H.: Teams in grammar systems: hybridity and weak rewriting. Acta Cybern. **12**(4), 425–444 (1996). https://cyber.bibl.u-szeged.hu/index.php/actcybern/article/view/3473
5. ter Beek, M.H.: Teams in grammar systems: sub-context-free cases. In: Păun, G., Salomaa, A. (eds.) New Trends in Formal Languages. LNCS, vol. 1218, pp. 197–216. Springer, Heidelberg (1997). https://doi.org/10.1007/3-540-62844-4_13
6. ter Beek, M.H.: Simple eco-grammar systems with prescribed teams. In: Păun, G., Salomaa, A. (eds.) Grammatical Models of Multi-Agent Systems. Topics in Computer Mathematics, vol. 8, pp. 113–135. Gordon and Breach, London (1999)
7. ter Beek, M.H.: Team automata: a formal approach to the modeling of collaboration between system components. Ph.D. thesis, Leiden University (2003). https://doi.org/https://hdl.handle.net/1887/29570
8. ter Beek, M.H., Csuhaj-Varjú, E., Holzer, M., Vaszil, G.: On competence in CD grammar systems. In: Calude, C.S., Calude, E., Dinneen, M.J. (eds.) DLT 2004. LNCS, vol. 3340, pp. 76–88. Springer, Heidelberg (2004). https://doi.org/10.1007/978-3-540-30550-7_7
9. ter Beek, M.H., Csuhaj-Varjú, E., Holzer, M., Vaszil, G.: On competence in CD grammar systems with parallel rewriting. Int. J. Found. Comput. Sci. **18**(6), 1425–1439 (2007). https://doi.org/10.1142/S0129054107005467
10. ter Beek, M.H., Csuhaj-Varjú, E., Holzer, M., Vaszil, G.: Cooperating distributed grammar systems: components with nonincreasing competence. In: Kelemen, J., Kelemenová, A. (eds.) Computation, Cooperation, and Life. LNCS, vol. 6610, pp. 70–89. Springer, Heidelberg (2011). https://doi.org/10.1007/978-3-642-20000-7_7

11. ter Beek, M.H., Csuhaj-Varjú, E., Mitrana, V.: Teams of pushdown automata. In: Broy, M., Zamulin, A.V. (eds.) PSI 2003. LNCS, vol. 2890, pp. 329–337. Springer, Heidelberg (2004). https://doi.org/10.1007/978-3-540-39866-0_32

12. ter Beek, M.H., Csuhaj-Varjú, E., Mitrana, V.: Teams of pushdown automata. Int. J. Comput. Math. **81**(2), 141–156 (2004). https://doi.org/10.1080/00207160310001650099

13. ter Beek, M.H., Hennicker, R., Proença, J.: Team automata: overview and roadmap. In: Castellani, I., Ticzzi, F. (eds.) COORDINATION 2024. LNCS, vol. 14676, pp. 161–198. Springer, Cham (2024). https://doi.org/10.1007/978-3-031-62697-5_10

14. ter Beek, M.H., Hennicker, R., Proença, J.: Overview and roadmap of team automata. Log. Methods Comput. Sci. (2025)

15. ter Beek, M., Kleijn, J.: Petri net control for grammar systems. In: Brauer, W., Ehrig, H., Karhumäki, J., Salomaa, A. (eds.) Formal and Natural Computing. LNCS, vol. 2300, pp. 220–243. Springer, Heidelberg (2002). https://doi.org/10.1007/3-540-45711-9_13

16. ter Beek, M.H., Kleijn, J.: On distributed cooperation and synchronised collaboration. J. Autom. Lang. Comb. **19**(1-4), 17–32 (2014). https://doi.org/10.25596/jalc-2014-017

17. Bresnan, J., Kaplan, R.M., Peters, S., Zaenen, A.: Cross-serial dependencies in Dutch. Linguist. Inq. **13**(4), 613–635 (1982). https://doi.org/10.1007/978-94-009-3401-6_11

18. Chomsky, N.: On certain formal properties of grammars. Inf. Control **2**(2), 137–167 (1959). https://doi.org/10.1016/S0019-9958(59)90362-6

19. Csuhaj-Varjú, E., Dassow, J.: On cooperating/distributed grammar systems. J. Inf. Process. Cybern. **26**(1–2), 49–63 (1990)

20. Csuhaj-Varjú, E., Dassow, J., Kelemen, J., Păun, G. (eds.): Grammar Systems: A Grammatical Approach to Distribution and Cooperation, Topics in Computer Mathematics, vol. 5. Gordon and Breach, London (1994)

21. Csuhaj-Varjú, E., Kelemen, J.: Cooperating grammar systems: a syntactical framework for the blackboard model of problem solving. In: Plander, I. (ed.) Proceedings of the 5th International Conference on Artificial Intelligence and Information-Control Systems of Robots (AIICSR 1989), North-Holland, pp. 121–127 (1989)

22. Culy, C.: The complexity of the vocabulary of Bambara. Linguist. Philos. **8**, 345–351 (1984). https://doi.org/10.1007/978-94-009-3401-6_14

23. Dassow, J.: Cooperating/distributed grammar systems with hypothesis languages. J. Exp. Theor. Artif. Intell. **3**(1), 11–16 (1991). https://doi.org/10.1080/09528139108915278

24. Dassow, J.: A remark on cooperating distributed grammar systems controlled by graphs. Wiss. Zeit. T.U. Magdeburg **35**, 4–6 (1991)

25. Dassow, J., Păun, G.: Regulated Rewriting in Formal Language Theory. EATCS Monographs on Theoretical Computer Science, vol. 18. Springer, Berlin (1989). https://www.springer.com/de/book/9783642749346

26. Dassow, J., Păun, G., Rozenberg, G.: Grammar systems. In: Rozenberg, G., Salomaa, A. (eds.) Handbook of Formal Languages, Volume 2: Linear Modeling: Background and Application, pp. 155–213. Springer, Heidelberg (1997). https://doi.org/10.1007/978-3-662-07675-0_4

27. Dassow, J., Păun, G., Salomaa, A.: Grammars with controlled derivations. In: Rozenberg, G., Salomaa, A. (eds.) Handbook of Formal Languages, Volume 2: Linear Modeling: Background and Application, pp. 101–154. Springer, Heidelberg (1997). https://doi.org/10.1007/978-3-662-07675-0_3

28. Fernau, H., Holzer, M.: Graph-controlled cooperating distributed grammar systems with singleton components. J. Autom. Lang. Comb. **7**(4), 487–503 (2002). https://doi.org/10.25596/JALC-2002-487
29. Fernau, H., Holzer, M., Freund, R.: Bounding resources in cooperating distributed grammar systems. In: Bozapalidis, S. (ed.) Proceedings of the 3rd International Conference on Developments in Language Theory (DLT 1997), pp. 261–272. Aristotle University of Thessaloniki (1997)
30. Fernau, H., Holzer, M., Freund, R.: Hybrid modes in cooperating distributed grammar systems: internal versus external hybridization. Theor. Comput. Sci. **259**(1–2), 405–426 (2001). https://doi.org/10.1016/S0304-3975(00)00022-0
31. Fernau, H., Holzer, M., Freund, R.: Hybrid modes in cooperating distributed grammar systems: combining the t-mode with the modes $\leq k$ and $= k$. Theor. Comput. Sci. **299**(1–3), 633–662 (2003). https://doi.org/10.1016/S0304-3975(02)00541-8
32. Friš, I.: Grammars with partial ordering of the rules. Inf. Control. **12**(5-6), 415–425 (1968). https://doi.org/10.1016/S0019-9958(68)90439-7. Errata in Inf. Control. **15**(5), 452–453 (1969). https://doi.org/10.1016/S0019-9958(69)90521-X
33. Gazdar, G., Pullum, G.K.: Computationally relevant properties of natural languages and their grammars. New Gener. Comput. **3**, 273–306 (1985). https://doi.org/10.1007/978-94-009-3401-6_17
34. Gheorghe, M., Păun, G.: Further remarks on cooperating/distributed grammar systems. Bull. Math. Soc. Sci. Math. Roumanie **34(82)**(3), 231–245 (1990). http://www.jstor.org/stable/43678342
35. Higginbotham, J.: English is not a context-free language. Linguist. Inq. **15**(2), 225–234 (1984). https://doi.org/10.1007/978-94-009-3401-6_13
36. Huijbregts, R.: The weak inadequacy of context-free phrase structure grammars. In: de Haan, G.J., Trommele, M., Zonneveld, W. (eds.) Van Periferie Naar Kern, pp. 81–99. Foris (1984)
37. Kari, L., Mateescu, A., Păun, G., Salomaa, A.: Teams in cooperating grammar systems. J. Exp. Theor. Artif. Intell. **7**(4), 347–359 (1995). https://doi.org/10.1080/09528139508953816
38. Kari, L., Rozenberg, G., Salomaa, A.: L systems. In: Rozenberg, G., Salomaa, A. (eds.) Handbook of Formal Languages, Volume 1: Word, Language, Grammar, pp. 253–328. Springer, Heidelberg (1997). https://doi.org/10.1007/978-3-642-59136-5_5
39. Král, J.: A note on grammars with regular restrictions. Kybernetika **9**(3), 159–161 (1973). http://www.kybernetika.cz/content/1973/3/159
40. Meersman, R., Rozenberg, G.: Cooperating grammar systems. In: Winkowski, J. (ed.) MFCS 1978. LNCS, vol. 64, pp. 364–373. Springer, Heidelberg (1978). https://doi.org/10.1007/3-540-08921-7_84
41. Mitrana, V.: Pairs grammar systems - transducers. Ann. Univ. Buc. Ser. Matem.-Inform. **39**, 73–81 (1990)
42. Mitrana, V.: Hybrid cooperating distributed grammar systems. Comput. Artif. Intell. **2**, 83–88 (1993)
43. Păun, G.: On the generative capacity of hybrid CD grammar systems. J. Inf. Process. Cybern. **30**(4), 231–244 (1994)
44. Păun, G.: On the generative capacity of colonies. Kybernetika **31**(1), 83–97 (1995). http://www.kybernetika.cz/content/1995/1/83
45. Păun, G., Rozenberg, G.: Prescribed teams of grammars. Acta Inform. **31**(6), 525–537 (1994). https://doi.org/10.1007/BF01213205
46. Radzinski, D.: Unbounded syntactic copying in Mandarin Chinese. Linguist. Philos. **13**, 113–127 (1990). https://doi.org/10.1007/BF00630518

47. Rozenberg, G., Salomaa, A.: The Mathematical Theory of L Systems. Academic Press, New York (1980)
48. Rozenberg, G., Salomaa, A. (eds.): Handbook of Formal Languages, Volume 1: Word, Language, Grammar. Springer, Heidelberg (1997). https://doi.org/10.1007/978-3-642-59136-5
49. Rozenberg, G., Salomaa, A. (eds.): Handbook of Formal Languages, Volume 2: Linear Modeling: Background and Application. Springer, Heidelberg (1997). https://doi.org/10.1007/978-3-662-07675-0
50. Salomaa, A.: Formal Languages. Academic Press, New York (1973)
51. Shieber, S.M.: Evidence against the context-freeness of natural language. Linguist. Philos. **8**(4), 333–343 (1985). https://doi.org/10.1007/978-94-009-3401-6_12
52. Wood, D.: Bicolored digraph grammar systems. RAIRO **R-1**, 45–52 (1973). http://www.numdam.org/item/M2AN_1973__7_1_45_0

Binary Right-Distinguishability Operation

Cezar Câmpeanu[✉]

University of Prince Edward Island, Charlottetown, PE C1A4P3, Canada
ccampeanu@upei.ca

Abstract. In this paper we investigate the state complexity of operations related to the binary distinguishability operation defined as a combination of a closure operator and a specific Boolean formula. The extensions provided by changing the closure operator in a paper published in 2016 for the unary distinguishability operation have inspired the new operations studied here.

Keywords: Regular languages · distinguishability · equivalence relation

1 Introduction

Testing the equivalence of regular languages and the devices recognizing them has been of great interest to researchers since the early days of automata theory. One example is the paper of E. F. Moore written in 1958, "Gedanken-Experiments On Sequential Machines", [7].

Moore's paper influenced the study of the language of words that can distinguish various non-equivalent states of machines, distinct words, or distinct languages. Thus, we can define unary and binary distinguishability operations on words, states, and languages.

The distinguishability operation can be defined as a combination of a closure operator and a few specific Boolean operations for languages. Moreover, using the Kuratowski theorem [6], one can observe that the distinguishability operation can be extended in various ways by replacing the closure operator. Please see [3,4] for complete details and definitions.

In [4], two extensions of the distinguishability operation are considered: right-distinguishability and two-sided distinguishability. In both cases, the operator is a unary one. These operations can be generalized to binary operations, and by replacing the closure operator with others like scattered superstring insertion, [8], or scattered substring insertion, [8], we can obtain other interesting operations. Of course, one can add to the mix other closure operators. Thus, the number of possible new operations can be very large. Therefore, it can extend the area of application of the distinguishability operation.

Although one may think this is a purely theoretical exercise, these extensions may be of interest when we study languages that are not equivalent for a closure

M. D. Jiménez López and G. Vaszil (Eds.): Erzsébet Csuhaj-Varjú Festschrift,
LNCS 15840, pp. 26–40, 2025.
https://doi.org/10.1007/978-3-031-97274-4_2

operator[1]. The last statement, where two objects represented by languages can be considered in the same class of objects if they are equivalent for some closure operator, may be of interest in machine learning, where we could distinguish several families of objects. This way, the distinguishability language could speed up the learning algorithms or classify objects, and we plan to address it in future studies.

This paper will only focus on the binary right-distinguishability operation, introducing the basic notations and definitions in Sect. 2. Fundamental properties of binary right-distinguishability operation are proved in Sect. 3, with a special Subsect. 3.1 dedicated to the state complexity. The minimal distinguishability words for the binary left and right distinguishability operations are studied in Sect. 4.1 and Sect. 4.2, while the conclusion, open problems, and future work are discussed in Sect. 5.

2   Notations

We begin the section with basic notation from automata theory, focusing only on the case of regular languages and deterministic finite automata. For subclasses or superclasses of regular languages and other representations of languages, we leave the study for subsequent papers.

An alphabet, usually denoted by Σ, is a finite non-empty set. A sequence of letters $a_1, a_2, \ldots, a_n \in \Sigma$, written as $w = a_1 a_2 \ldots a_n$, is a word over the alphabet Σ, and n is the length of the word w, denoted by $|w|$. In case $n = 0$, the word w has no letters and is denoted by ε.

The concatenation of two words $u = u_1 \ldots u_m$, $v = v_1 \ldots v_n$ is the word $uv = u_1 \ldots u_m v_1 \ldots v_n$. The set of all words over Σ is $\Sigma^\star$ and $(\Sigma^\star, \cdot, \varepsilon)$ is the free monoid generated by Σ with the operation of concatenation. The reverse of a word $w = w_1 \ldots w_n$ is $w^R = w_n \ldots w_1$, and $L^R = \{x \mid x = w^R, w \in L\}$.

A word u is a prefix/suffix/infix of another word v, if there exists $y \in \Sigma^\star / x \in \Sigma^\star / x, y \in \Sigma^\star$, such that $v = uy$ / $v = xu$ / $v = xuy$. We denote this by $u \preceq_p v / u \preceq_s v / u \preceq_i v$. All these relations are order relations.

The set of prefixes of a word is $\mathsf{pref}(v) = \{u \in \Sigma^\star \mid u \preceq_p v\}$, and prefixes of a language is $\mathsf{pref}(L) = \{u \mid u \in \mathsf{pref}(v), v \in L\}$. In a similar way, we define the set of suffixes $\mathsf{suff}(\cdot)$, and the set of infixes, $\mathsf{infix}(\cdot)$.

In case the alphabet $\Sigma = \{a_0, a_1, \ldots, a_{k-1}\}$ is ordered, i.e., $a_i < a_{i+1}$, for all i, $0 \leq i \leq k - 2$, we can also define the quasi-lexicographical order as follows:

$$x \preceq_l y \text{ iff } |x| < |y| \text{ or } x = u a_i v, y = u a_j w \text{ and } i < j.$$

We have the following relations:

$$\mathsf{suff}(L) = \mathsf{pref}(L^R)^R, \text{ and } \mathsf{pref}(L) = \mathsf{suff}(L^R)^R \tag{1}$$

$$\overline{L}^R = \overline{L^R} \tag{2}$$

For automata theory, we follow the notations and definitions in [5].

---

[1] Thus, two languages would be considered "equivalent" or similar, if they have the same closure.

Definition 1. *A deterministic finite automaton is a quintuple* $\mathcal{A} = (Q, \Sigma, \delta, q_0, F)$, *where* Q *and* Σ *are finite non-empty sets,* $\delta : Q \times \Sigma \longrightarrow Q$ *is the transition function,* $q_0 \in Q$ *is the initial state, and* $F \subseteq Q$ *is the set of final states.*

The transition function δ can be naturally extended from $Q \times \Sigma$ to $Q \times \Sigma^\star$ as follows: $\overline{\delta}(q, \varepsilon) = q$, $\overline{\delta}(q, wa) = \delta(\overline{\delta}(q, w), a)$. For simplicity, the extension $\overline{\delta}$ is also denoted by δ. The language accepted by a DFA $\mathcal{A} = (Q, \Sigma, \delta, q_0, F)$ is

$$L(\mathcal{A}) = \{ w \in \Sigma^\star \mid \delta(q_0, w) \in F \} .$$

Two automata $\mathcal{A}_i$, $i = 1, 2$ accepting the same language are called equivalent and we write it $\mathcal{A}_1 \sim \mathcal{A}_2$.

A DFA $\mathcal{A} = (Q, \Sigma, \delta, q_0, F)$ has all its states accessible if for all $q \in Q$ we can find $w \in \Sigma^\star$, such that $\delta(q_0, w) = q$. A state q is called useful if $\delta(q, w) \in F$ for some word $w \in \Sigma^\star$. A DFA is called trim if it has all its states accessible, and has at most one state that is not useful. That state, that is not useful, but accessible, is called the dead state or sink state. For any DFA there is an equivalent trim DFA. In what follows, we will use only trim automata.

The number of states of the minimal DFA recognizing a regular language L is denoted by $\mathsf{sc}(L)$.

The distinguishability operation was introduced in [4] as the language of words that can distinguish two non-equivalent words or states with respect to the Myhill-Nerode equivalence relation. It is a named left distinguishability as the words are appended to the right, and they distinguish the words on the left.

We can now introduce the binary distinguishability operation as it is done in [3].

Definition 2. *[3] The distinguishability operation of two languages* L_1 *and* L_2 *is* $\mathsf{D}(L_1, L_2) = (\mathsf{suff}(L_1) \cap \mathsf{suff}(\overline{L_2})) \cup (\mathsf{suff}(\overline{L_1}) \cap \mathsf{suff}(L_2))$.

We extend the definition by replacing the closure operator suff with another one $\mathsf{CL} \in \{\mathsf{pref}, \mathsf{infix}\}$, and study the complexity of the new operations.

Because $\mathsf{CL} \in \{\mathsf{pref}, \mathsf{infix}\}$ is a closure operator that commutes with intersection and union, we have the following.

Lemma 1. *Let* L_1, L_2 *be two languages. Then,*

1. $\mathsf{D_p}(L_1, L_2)$ *is a prefix closed set,*
2. $\mathsf{D_i}(L_1, L_2)$ *is an infix closed set.*

Since most of the properties of the left-distinguishability[2] have been studied in [3], in the next section we study the properties of binary right-distinguishability.

---

[2] In [3], binary left-distinguishability is simply called binary distinguishability.

3   Properties of Binary Right-Distinguishability

In case of prefix operator, we can observe that for the new operation we have:

$$\begin{aligned}
\mathsf{D_p}(L_1, L_2) &= (\mathsf{pref}(L_1) \cap \mathsf{pref}(\overline{L_2})) \cup (\mathsf{pref}(\overline{L_1}) \cap \mathsf{pref}(L_2)) \\
&= (\mathsf{suff}(L_1^R)^R \cap \mathsf{suff}(\overline{L_2^R})^R) \cup (\mathsf{suff}(\overline{L_1^R})^R \cap \mathsf{suff}(L_2^R))^R) \\
&= ((\mathsf{suff}(L_1^R) \cap \mathsf{suff}(\overline{L_2^R})) \cup (\mathsf{suff}(\overline{L_1^R}) \cap \mathsf{suff}(L_2^R)))^R \\
&= \mathsf{D}(L_1^R, L_2^R)^R.
\end{aligned}$$

This means that
$$\mathsf{D}(L_1, L_2)^R = \mathsf{D_p}(L_1^R, L_2^R). \tag{3}$$

The (left) quotient of the language L with respect to the word x is, [1,2],

$$x^{-1}L = \{w \in \Sigma^\star \mid xw \in L\}. \tag{4}$$

The right quotient of the language L with respect to the word x is

$$Lx^{-1} = \{w \in \Sigma^\star \mid wx \in L\}. \tag{5}$$

Using (5), we can rewrite $\mathsf{pref}(L) = \bigcup\limits_{x \in \Sigma^\star} Lx^{-1}$, therefore

$\mathsf{pref}(\overline{L}) = \bigcup\limits_{x \in \Sigma^\star} \overline{L}x^{-1} = \overline{\bigcap\limits_{x \in \Sigma^\star} Lx^{-1}}$. One can see that if x is not a suffix of
any word in L, $Lx^{-1} = \emptyset$. Hence, if one of the right quotients of L is $\emptyset$, then
$\mathsf{pref}(\overline{L}) = \Sigma^\star$.

If $x^{-1}L = \emptyset$, x is not a prefix of any word in L. If for any $x \in \Sigma^\star$, $x^{-1}L \neq \emptyset$,
there is $y \in \Sigma^\star$ such that $xy \in L$, then $\Sigma^\star \subseteq \mathsf{pref}(L)$, i.e., $\mathsf{pref}(L) = \Sigma^\star$.

We can also write that for $\mathsf{D_p}(L_1, L_2)$ we have:

$$\mathsf{D_p}(L_1, L_2) = \left(\bigcup_{x \in \Sigma^\star} L_1 x^{-1} \setminus \bigcap_{\mathsf{x} \in \Sigma^\star} L_2 x^{-1} \right) \cup \left(\bigcup_{x \in \Sigma^\star} L_2 x^{-1} \setminus \bigcap_{\mathsf{x} \in \Sigma^\star} L_1 x^{-1} \right).$$

Next, we verify the binary operation's properties corresponding to valid
results for the unary operation.

Lemma 2. *Let L_1, L_2 be two regular languages. The following statements are
true:*

1. *If L_1 and L_2 do not have $\emptyset$ as a quotient, then $\mathsf{D_p}(L_1, L_2) = \mathsf{pref}(\overline{L_1}) \cup \mathsf{pref}(\overline{L_2})$.*
2. *If L_1 and $\overline{L_1}$ do not have $\emptyset$ as a quotient, then $\mathsf{D_p}(L_1, L_2) = \Sigma^\star$.*
3. *If L_1 and L_2 have $\emptyset$ as a right quotient, then $\mathsf{D_p}(L_1, L_2) = \mathsf{pref}(L_1) \cup \mathsf{pref}(L_2)$.*
4. *If L_i, $i = 1, 2$, are prefix closed, and L_i, $i = 1, 2$, have $\emptyset$ as a right quotient,
   then $\mathsf{D_p}(L_1, L_2) = L_1 \cup L_2$.*

Proof. 1. Because $\emptyset$ is not a right quotient of L_i, $i = 1, 2$, we have $\mathsf{pref}(L_i) = \Sigma^*$,
$i = 1, 2$, therefore $\mathsf{D_p}(L_1, L_2) = (\mathsf{pref}(L_1) \cap \mathsf{pref}(\overline{L_2})) \cup (\mathsf{pref}(\overline{L_1}) \cap \mathsf{pref}(L_2)) = \mathsf{pref}(\overline{L_2}) \cup \mathsf{pref}(\overline{L_1})$.

2. Because $\emptyset$ is not a quotient of L_1, and $\overline{L_1}$, we have $\mathsf{pref}(L_1) = \Sigma^*$, and $\mathsf{pref}(\overline{L_1}) = \Sigma^*$, therefore $\mathsf{D_p}(L_1, L_2) = (\mathsf{pref}(L_1) \cap \mathsf{pref}(\overline{L_2})) \cup (\mathsf{pref}(\overline{L_1}) \cap \mathsf{pref}(L_2)) = \mathsf{pref}(\overline{L_2}) \cup \mathsf{pref}(L_2) = \Sigma^*$.

3. $\mathsf{D_p}(L_1, L_2) = \mathsf{D}(L_1^R, L_2^R)^R$. Since $\emptyset$ is a right quotient of L_i, $i = 1, 2$, $\mathsf{pref}(\overline{L_i}) = \Sigma^*$, so $\mathsf{D_p}(L_1, L_2) = \mathsf{pref}(L_1) \cup \mathsf{pref}(L_2)$.

4. $\mathsf{D_p}(L_1, L_2) = (\mathsf{pref}(L_1) \cap \mathsf{pref}(\overline{L_2})) \cup (\mathsf{pref}(\overline{L_1}) \cap \mathsf{pref}(L_2)) = (L_1 \cap \Sigma^*) \cup (\Sigma^* \cap L_2) = L_1 \cup L_2$.

$\square$

Corollary 1. *If L_1 and L_2 are finite languages, then $\mathsf{D_p}(L_1, L_2) = \mathsf{pref}(L_1) \cup \mathsf{pref}(L_2)$.*

3.1   State Complexity of Binary Right-Distinguishability

We start this section observing that for a minimal DFA $\mathcal{A} = (Q, \Sigma, \delta, q_0, F)$, the automaton $\mathcal{A}_{\mathsf{pref}} = (Q, \Sigma, \delta, q_0, F_{\mathsf{pref}})$ where $F_{\mathsf{pref}} = \{q \in Q \mid \delta(q, x) \in F$, for some $x \in \Sigma^*\}$ has the property that $L(\mathcal{A}_{\mathsf{pref}}) = \mathsf{pref}(L)$. Also, the automaton $\mathcal{A}_{\overline{\mathsf{pref}}} = (Q, \Sigma, \delta, q_0, F_{\overline{\mathsf{pref}}})$ where $F_{\overline{\mathsf{pref}}} = \{q \in Q \mid \delta(q, x) \notin F$ for some $x \in \Sigma^*\}$, has the property that $L(\mathcal{A}_{\overline{\mathsf{pref}}}) = \mathsf{pref}(\overline{L})$. Now, we are ready for the following result.

Theorem 1. *If L_1 is recognized by a minimal DFA with $n \geq 2$ states, and L_2 is recognized by a minimal DFA with $m \geq 2$ states, then $\mathsf{sc}(\mathsf{D_p}(L_1, L_2)) = mn$.*

Proof. For each $i = 1, 2$, if both L_i and $\overline{L_i}$ do not have $\emptyset$ as a quotient, then $\mathsf{D_p}(L_1, L_2) = \Sigma^*$ and only one state is needed for a DFA accepting $\mathsf{D_p}(L_1, L_2)$.

Otherwise, let $\mathcal{A}_i = (Q_i, \Sigma, \delta, q_{0,i}, F_i)$ be the minimal DFA recognizing L_i with $|Q_1| = n$, $|Q_2| = m$, $m, n \geq 2$.

We have that at least one of $\mathcal{A}_i$, or $\overline{\mathcal{A}_i}$, $i = 1, 2$, has a dead state, thus at least one of $F_{i\,\mathsf{pref}} \subset Q_i$ or $F_{i\,\overline{\mathsf{pref}}} \subset Q_i$ hold for both $i = 1, 2$.

To obtain a DFA for $\mathsf{D_p}(L_1, L_2)$, we build the DFA $\mathcal{A} = (Q, \Sigma, \delta, q_0, F)$ as follows: $Q = Q_1 \times Q_2$, $q_0 = (q_{0,1}, q_{0,2})$, $\delta : Q \times \Sigma \longrightarrow Q$ is defined as $\delta((p, q), a) = (\delta_1(p, a), \delta_2(q, a))$, for all $a \in \Sigma$, and $F = F_{1\,\mathsf{pref}} \times F_{2\,\overline{\mathsf{pref}}} \cup F_{1\,\overline{\mathsf{pref}}} \times F_{2\,\mathsf{pref}}$.

It is clear that $L(\mathcal{A}) = \mathsf{D_p}(L_1, L_2)$, and $\mathcal{A}$ has mn states. Therefore, the upperbound for the state complexity of $\mathsf{D_p}$ is mn. Because $L(\mathcal{A})$ is prefix closed, any minimal automaton for $L(\mathcal{A})$ will have at most one state that is not final and it will be the dead state.

For the lowerbound, we give two constructions. The first construction is for a ternary alphabet. Then we improve the result by constructing a witnesses for a binary alphabet.

If Σ has at least three letters, the following pair of automata will reach the upperbound mn:

$A_m = (Q_m, \{a, b, c\}, \delta_m^A, 0, F_m^A)$ and $B_n = (Q_n, \{a, b, c\}, \delta_n^B, 0, F_n^B)$, where $Q_r = \{0, 1, \ldots, r - 1\}$, $r \in \{m, n\}$,

$\delta_m^A(q,a) = (q+1) \bmod (m-1), 0 \le q \le m-2, \delta^A(m-1,a) = m-1,$
$\delta_m^A(q,b) = q, 0 \le q \le m-3, \delta(m-2,b) = m-1, \delta^A(m-1,b) = m-1,$
$\delta_m^A(q,c) = (q+1) \bmod (m-1), 0 \le q \le m-2, \delta^A(m-1,c) = m-1,$
$F_m^A = \{m-2\}$, and
$\delta_n^B(q,b) = (q+1) \bmod (n-1), 0 \le q \le n-2, \delta^B(n-1,a) = n-1,$
$\delta_n^B(q,a) = q, 0 \le q \le n-3, \delta(n-2,b) = n-1, \delta^B(n-1,b) = n-1,$
$\delta_n^B(q,c) = (q+1) \bmod (n-1), 0 \le q \le n-2, \delta^B(n-1,c) = n-1,$
$F_n^B = \{n-2\}$.

We must note that the only non-final state is $(m-1, n-1)$ and is reachable, as we will show bellow.

All pairs of states are reachable because we can advance independently with a on the first component of the cross product, b on the second component of the cross product, and c on both components. Thus, all states (p,q), $0 \le p \le m-2$ and $0 \le q \le n-2$, can be reached from $(0,0)$. By applying letter c once, we reach state $m-2$ on the first component, or $n-2$ on the second component, we can "return" to state 0 without getting the sink state of the two components, $m-1$ for the first one, and $n-1$ for the second one.

To get to the sink state, $m-2$, on the first component together with all other states on the second component, we apply letter b to $(m-2, q)$, then advance on the second component with b or c. Note that if we apply letter b to $(m-2, q)$, on the first component we will have only $m-1$. To get to the sink state, $n-2$, on the second component together with all other states on the first component, we apply letter a to $(p, n-2)$, then advance on the first component with a or c – thus, on the second component we will only have $n-1$. Hence, all states are reachable.

Now let us take a pair of states in the cross product automaton, (p,q) and (r,s), and assume $p < r < m-1$, and $q, s < n-1$.

We have $\delta((p,q), a^{m-2-r}b^{n-2-s}a) = (x,y)$, with $x \le m-2$ and $\delta((r,s), a^{m-2-r}b^{n-2-s}a) = (m-1, n-1)$. Since $x \le m-2$, the state $(x,y) \in F$, but $(m-1, n-1) \notin F$.

If $p < r < m-1$ and $q = n-1$, $\delta((p, n-1), a^{m-2-r}b^{n-2-s}a) = (x, n-1)$, with $x \le m-2$ and $\delta((r,s), a^{m-2-r}b^{n-2-s}a) = (m-1, n-1)$. The state $(x, n-1) \in F$, but $(m-1, n-1) \notin F$. If $p < r < m-1$ and $s = n-1$, $\delta((p,q), a^{m-2-r}b) = (x,y)$, with $x \le m-2$ and $\delta((r, n-1), a^{m-2-r}b) = (m-1, n-1)$. The state $(x, y) \in F$, but $(m-1, n-1) \notin F$. All the other cases are symmetric.

Therefore, all states are distinguishable, i.e., the automaton $\mathcal{A}$ constructed above is minimal. An example for the construction for $m = 3$ and $n = 3$ is depicted in Fig. 1.

We cannot use a similar construction for the binary alphabet, as it will not reach the upperbound. Two examples are depicted in Fig. 2 and Fig. 3.

For the binary case, the witnesses for the lowerbound are the automata C_m described below and B_n described above, but deleting the letter c from the alphabet.

$$C_m = (Q_m, \{a, b\}, \delta_m^C, 0, F_n^C)$$

Fig. 1. An example of two automata reaching the upperbound for the right-distinguishability operation with 4 states each, for a ternary alphabet. The cross-product minimal automaton for the language resulting from the binary right-distinguishability operation has 16 states.

Fig. 2. Two automata not reaching the upperbound for the right-distinguishability operation with 3 states each, in case of a binary alphabet. The binary right-distinguishability language has a cross-product minimal automaton with 8 states, where the state $(0, 1)$ is unreachable.

Fig. 3. Another example of two automata not reaching the upperbound for the right-distinguishability operation with 4 states each, in case of a binary alphabet. The binary right-distinguishability language has a cross-product minimal automaton with 15 states, where the state $(2, 2)$ is unreachable.

$\delta_m^C(q, a) = (q + 1) \bmod (m - 2)$, $0 \le q \le m - 3$, $\delta^C(m - 2, a) = m - 1$, $\delta^C(m - 1, a) = m - 1$,

$\delta_m^C(q, b) = (q + 1) \bmod (m - 1)$, $0 \le q \le m - 2$, $\delta(m - 1, b) = m - 1$,
$F_m^C = \{m - 2\}$.

To prove that all states are reachable, it is enough to see that we can advance only on the first component with letter a until we reach state $m - 3$. To move the first component with k positions from $m - 2$ and keep the second position in place, we can apply the word $b^k ab^{n-2-k}$. To avoid the transition $n - 2$ to $n - 1$ on the second component after applying b^k, we can replace some of the b's with a's in $b^k ab^{n-2-k}$, because after two b's, from $m - 3$ we can advance on the first component with either a's, or b's.

By applying a^{m-3} to a state where the first component is less than $m - 2$, we go back to a previous position, while on the second component, if we are not in position $n - 3$, we don't move. Thus, we can shift the first component independently of the second position to reach all states (p, q), such that $0 \leq p \leq m - 3$ and $0 \leq q \leq n - 2$. To reach states $(m - 2, y)$ we observe that $\delta((m - 3, q), b) = (m - 2, (q + 1) \bmod (n - 2))$. We also have $\delta((p, n - 2), a) = ((p + 1) \bmod (m - 2), n - 1)$, $\delta((m - 2, q), a) = (m - 1, q)$ for all $0 \leq q \leq n - 3$, $\delta((m - 2, n - 3), bba^{m-2-1}b) = (m - 2, n - 2)$, $\delta((m - 2, q), ab^i) = (m - 1, (q + i) \bmod (n - 2))$, if $q \neq n - 3$, $\delta((m - 2, n - 2), ab^i) = (m - 1, n - 1)$, and $\delta((p, n - 2), ba^i b^{n-3}) = ((p + n - 2 + i) \bmod (m - 2), n - 2)$ for all $p \neq m - 3$, and by subsequently applying b^{n-2}, $m - 3$ times, we get $((p + i) \bmod (m - 2), n - 2)$.

Therefore, all states are reachable.

Now, let (p, q) and (r, s) be two states, with $p, r \leq m - 2$, $q, s \leq n - 2$. We will construct a word w that will distinguish these two states, in steps.

We can assume that $q < s$. Thus, by applying to both pairs b^{n-2-s}, we obtain the new pairs (p_1, q_1), $(r_1, n - 2)$, $p_1, r_1 \leq m - 2$, $q_1 < n - 2$.

If $p_1 = r_1 = m - 2$ and by applying a, we get $(m - 1, q_1) \in F$, $(m - 1, n - 1) \notin F$.

If $r_1 = m - 2$, $p_1 < m - 2$ and by applying a, we get $(p_1 + 1, q_1) \in F$, $(m - 1, n - 1) \notin F$.

If $r_1 < m - 2$, $p_1 = m - 2$ and by applying b^{m-2-r_1}, we get these two pairs: $((2(m - 2) - r_1) \bmod (m - 1), (q_1 + m - 2 - r_1) \bmod (n - 1))$, $(m - 2, n - 1)$, or simplified, $(m - 3 - r_1, (q_1 + m - 2 - r_1) \bmod (n - 1))$ and $(m - 2, n - 1)$.

These states can be distinguishable with a, as the first pair goes to a final state, and the second pair in $(m - 1, n - 1) \notin F$.

We now consider pairs of the form $(p, q), (r, n - 1)$ and $(p, q), (m - 1, s)$, with $p, r \leq m - 2$, $q, s \leq n - 2$.

Case $(p, q), (r, n - 1)$, $p, r \leq m - 2$, $q \leq n - 2$.

If $q + m - 2 - r \neq n - 2$, we can use $w = b^{m-2-r}a$. If $q + m - 2 - r = n - 2$, we use $w = b^{m-2-r}ba^{m-3}ba$.

Case $(p, q), (m - 1, s)$, with $p \leq m - 2$, $q, s \leq n - 2$. We apply the word $w = b^{n-2-s}$. Thus, we get the pairs: $((p + n - 2 - s) \bmod (m - 1), (q + n - 2 - s) \bmod (n - 1))$ and $(m - 1, n - 2)$. If $(q + n - 2 - s) \bmod (n - 1) \neq n - 2$, these pairs are distinguishable with a. If $(q + n - 2 - s) \bmod (n - 1) = n - 2$, the pairs become $((p + n - 2 - s) \bmod (m - 1), n - 2)$ and $(m - 1, n - 2)$. If $(p + n - 2 - s) \bmod (m - 1) < m - 2$, they are distinguishable with a, otherwise we get the pairs $(m - 2, n - 1)$ and $(m - 1, n - 2)$. The word $ba^{m-3}ba$ will distinguish these two states.

For $(s, n - 1)$ and any other state (p, q) we first apply b^{m-2-s}, and we get $(m - 2, n - 1)$ and $((p + m - 2 - s) \bmod (m - 1), (q + m - 2 - s) \bmod (n - 2))$, case that was already analyzed above.

We now consider pairs of the form $(m - 1, q)$ and (r, s), $r \leq m - 2$, $q, s \leq n - 2$. We first apply b^{n-2-q} and we obtain a pair $(m - 1, n - 2)$ and $((r + n - 2 - q) \bmod (m - 1), (s + n - 2 - q) \bmod (n - 1))$. If $s \neq q$, the last pair of pairs of states are distinguishable with a. If $s = q$, we must check if $(r + n - 2 - q) \bmod (m - 1) = m - 2$. If not, we can use again a, otherwise we get the following pairs: $(m - 1, n - 2)$ and $(m - 2, n - 2)$. Applying to both pairs the word $ba^i b^{n-2}$, we get $(m-1, n-2)$ and $((i \bmod (m-2)+n-2) \bmod (m-1), n-2)$. These two states are distinguishable with a for an i chosen, such that $(i \bmod (m-2)+n-2) \bmod (m-1) < m-2$. This last case exhausts all possible cases. Therefore, all states are distinguishable, and the constructed automaton is minimal.   □

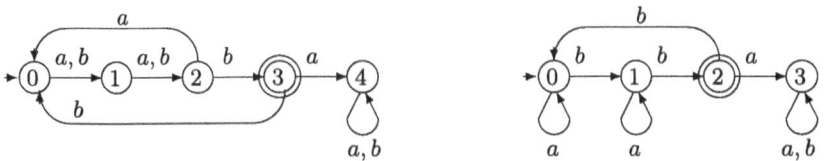

Fig. 4. An example of two automata reaching the upperbound for the right-distinguishability operation with 5 states and 4 states. The cross-product minimal automaton for the language resulting from the binary right-distinguishability operation has 20 states.

A witness for the lowerbound for the binary alphabet is in Fig. 4.

This is a new result and cannot be obtained from the limits of the binary distinguishability operation D, defined in [3]. Moreover, if we were to use the theoretical bounds for each of the operations using the limit for the reversal (see [9]), we would get an upperbound of $\mathsf{sc}(\mathsf{D_p}(L_1, L_2)) \leq 2^{2^{mn}-2^m-2^n+1}$. This upperbound is not even close to what we got from a direct analysis of the newly defined operation. However, by applying this new bound to get the state complexity for the (left)-binary distinguishability operation, and using (3) we get: $\mathsf{sc}(\mathsf{D}(L_1, L_2)) \leq 2^{mn}$, which is much closer to the exact bound $2^{mn}-2^m-2^n+1$, which was computed in [3].

4   Minimal Words for Binary Left and Right-Distinguishability Operation

This section defines the set of minimal distinguishability words for two languages. To this aim, we first need to check what words can distinguish two words for two languages, not just one language, as done in [4]. We will do it for each of the two types of distinguishability studied so far in [3,4] and this paper. We must emphasize that in [3], the minimal distinguishability words are defined only for DFAs, while here, we establish the same concept for languages.

4.1   Minimal Words for Binary Left-Distinguishability Operation

Let L_1 and L_2 be two languages, and x, y two words. We say that the words x and y are distinguishable with respect to the pair of languages L_1 and L_2 if the set

$$D_{L_1, L_2}(x, y) = \{w \mid (xw \in L_1 \land yw \notin L_2) \lor (xw \notin L_1 \land yw \in L_2)\}$$

is not empty.

Assume we have an order over the alphabet Σ. In case $D_{L_1,L_2}(x,y) \neq \emptyset$, we can define the minimal word distinguishing x and y with respect to L_1 and L_2 as

$$\underline{D}_{L_1,L_2}(x,y) = \min\{w \mid w \in D_{L_1,L_2}(x,y)\},$$

where minimum is considered with respect to the quasi-lexicographical order.

The set of all minimal distinguishability words with respect to the languages L_1 and L_2 is

$$\underline{D}(L_1, L_2) = \left\{\underline{D}_{L_1,L_2}(x,y) \mid x,y \in \Sigma^*, D_{L_1,L_2}(x,y) \neq \emptyset\right\}.$$

Example 1. Let $L_1 = \{aabb, abab\}$ and $L_2 = \{\varepsilon\}$. We have the following :

1. $\underline{D}_{L_1,L_2}(\varepsilon,\varepsilon) = \varepsilon$ ($\varepsilon \notin L_1$, $\varepsilon \in L_2$),
2. $\underline{D}_{L_1,L_2}(\varepsilon,a) = aabb$,
3. $\underline{D}_{L_1,L_2}(a,\varepsilon) = \varepsilon$ ($a \notin L_1$, $\varepsilon \in L_2$),
4. $\underline{D}_{L_1,L_2}(aa,\varepsilon) = \varepsilon$ ($aa \notin L_1$, $\varepsilon \in L_2$),
5. $\underline{D}_{L_1,L_2}(abb,\varepsilon) = \varepsilon$ ($abb \notin L_1$, $\varepsilon \in L_2$),
6. If $x \neq \varepsilon$:
   (a) $\underline{D}_{L_1,L_2}(a,x) = abb$, ($aabb \in L_1$, and $xabb \notin L_2$),
   (b) $\underline{D}_{L_1,L_2}(aa,x) = bb$, ($aabb \in L_1$, and $xbb \notin L_2$),
   (c) $\underline{D}_{L_1,L_2}(aab,x) = b$, ($aabb \in L_1$, and $xb \notin L_2$),
   (d) $\underline{D}_{L_1,L_2}(aabb,x) = \varepsilon$, ($aabb \in L_1$, and $x \notin L_2$),
   (e) $\underline{D}_{L_1,L_2}(ab,x) = ab$, ($abab \in L_1$, and $xab \notin L_2$),
   (f) $\underline{D}_{L_1,L_2}(aba,x) = b$, ($abab \in L_1$, and $xb \notin L_2$),
   (g) $\underline{D}_{L_1,L_2}(abab,x) = c$, ($abab \in L_1$, and $x \notin L_2$),
7. for all other words $u,v \notin \{\varepsilon, a, aa, ab, aab, aba, aabb, abab\}$, we have $\underline{D}_{L_1,L_2}(u,v)$ is undefined.

One can check using the definition that $\underline{D}_{L_1,L_2}(u,v)$ is undefined, for all $u \notin \mathsf{pref}(L_1)$, and $v \notin \mathsf{pref}(L_2)$, or $u \notin \mathsf{pref}(\overline{L_1})$ and $v \notin \mathsf{pref}(\overline{L_2})$. That is happening because in all these cases $D_{L_1,L_2}(u,v) = \emptyset$.

Hence, for Example 1, we get $\underline{D}(L_1, L_2) = \{\varepsilon, b, ab, bb, abb, aabb\}$.

Lemma 3. *The set of minimal distinguishability words with respect to two languages is suffix-closed.*

Proof. We follow the same reasoning as in Theorem 5.4 in [4], but using two languages instead of one. Let $w \in \underline{D}(L_1, L_2)$, and let $w = uv$, with $u,v \in \Sigma^*$. Because $w \in \underline{D}(L_1, L_2)$, we can find two other words, $x,y \in \Sigma^*$, such that $xw \in L_1$ and $yw \notin L_2$, or $xw \notin L_1$ and $yw \in L_2$. We consider only the case when $xw \in L_1$ and $yw \notin L_2$, the other case being similar. Thus, $xuv \in L_1$ and $yuv \notin L_2$. It follows that $v \in D_{L_1,L_2}(xu,yu)$. Since $v \in D_L(xu,yu)$, there exists $v' = \underline{D}_{L_1,L_2}(xu,yu)$ and $v' \preceq_l v$. Hence, $uv' \preceq_l uv$ and $uv' \in D_{L_1,L_2}(x,y)$, which implies $w = uv \preceq_l uv'$. Then we must have $uv' = uv$, which implies $v = v' = \underline{D}_{L_1,L_2}(xu,yu) \in \underline{D}(L_1, L_2)$. $\square$

So far, in this section we did not require the languages L_1 and L_2 to be regular. To keep the paper self-contained, we include here the definition of minimal words for the binary distinguishability operation on automata from [3].

Let $\mathcal{A}_i = (Q_i, \Sigma, \delta_i, q_{0,i}, F_i)$ two DFAs. The distinguishability language of two states $p \in Q_1$, $q \in Q_2$, with respect to their DFAs is

$$D_{\mathcal{A}_1,\mathcal{A}_2}(p,q) = \{w \in \Sigma^\star \mid \quad (6)$$
$$(\delta_1(p,w) \in F_1 \text{ and } \delta_2(q,w) \notin F_2)$$
$$\text{or } (\delta_1(p,w) \notin F_1 \text{ and } \delta_2(q,w) \in F_2)\}.$$

Definition 3. *[3] Let $\mathcal{A}_1$, $\mathcal{A}_2$ be two finite machines, and assume we have an order over the alphabet Σ.*

If $p \in Q_1$ and $q \in Q_2$, we define

$$\underline{D}_{\mathcal{A}_1,\mathcal{A}_2}(p,q) = \min\{w \mid w \in D_{\mathcal{A}_1,\mathcal{A}_2}(p,q)\},$$

where minimum is considered with respect to the quasi-lexicographical order. In case p is equivalent to q, $\underline{D}_{\mathcal{A}_1,\mathcal{A}_2}(p,q)$ is undefined. The set of minimal words distinguishing the states of the two finite machines $\mathcal{A}_1$, and $\mathcal{A}_2$ is

$$\underline{D}(\mathcal{A}_1,\mathcal{A}_2) = \{\underline{D}_{\mathcal{A}_1,\mathcal{A}_2}(p,q) \mid p \in Q_1, q \in Q_2\}.$$

The following result is an easy exercise left to the reader.

Lemma 4. *Let L_i, $i = 1,2$, be two regular languages such that $L_i = L(\mathcal{A}_i)$, $\mathcal{A}_i = (Q_i, \Sigma, \delta_i, q_{0,i}, F_i)$, where $\mathcal{A}_i, i = 1,2$, are trim DFAs. We have:*

1. *If $p \in Q_1$ and $q \in Q_2$ are such that $\delta_1(q_{0,1}, u) = p$, $\delta_2(q_{0,2}, v) = q$, then $\underline{D}_{L_1,L_2}(u,v) = \underline{D}_{\mathcal{A}_1,\mathcal{A}_2}(p,q)$.*
2. *$\underline{D}(L_1, L_2) = \underline{D}(\mathcal{A}_1, \mathcal{A}_2)$.*

The new terminology will help us infer the next results. Using Theorem 12 of [3], which establishes the number of minimal distinguishability words for states in two DFAs, and applying Lemma 4, Lemma 4 establishes the link between the distinguishability operation on states of a DFA and distinguishability operation on words, for the corresponding regular languages accepted by those DFAs, we get the following.

Theorem 2. *If L_1 and L_2 are regular languages such that $\mathsf{sc}(L_1) = m$ and $\mathsf{sc}(L_2) = n$, then $|\underline{D}(L_1, L_2)| \leq m + n - 1$.*

For the same reason as above, we must also have the following result.

Lemma 5. *If L_1 and L_2 are regular languages such that $\mathsf{sc}(L_1) = m$ and $\mathsf{sc}(L_2) = n$, then the length of minimal words that can distinguish between two other words is at most $2\min(n,m) - 1$ in case $m \neq n$, and $2\min(n,m) - 2$, otherwise. This upperbound is reached.*

These two results are nothing else than a reformulation of previous results obtained for DFAs to results on the regular languages accepted by the corresponding minimal DFAs.

4.2 Minimal Words for Binary Left and Right-Distinguishability Operation

For binary right-distinguishability, it is assumed that we have similar results as for the binary left-distinguishability operation. We want to verify each of the results of the previous section and check if the corresponding property holds for the new operation. As before, we assume we have an order over the alphabet Σ.

Definition 4. *Let L_1, and L_2 be two languages and x, y two words. We say that the words x and y are right-distinguishable with respect the languages L_1 and L_2 if the set*

$$\mathsf{D}^{(p)}_{L_1, L_2}(x, y) = \{w \mid (wx \in L_1 \ \wedge \ wy \notin L_2) \ \vee \ (wx \notin L_1 \ \wedge \ wy \in L_2)\}$$

is not empty.

In case $\mathsf{D}^{(p)}_{L_1, L_2}(x, y) \neq \emptyset$, we can define the minimal word distinguishing x and y with respect to L_1 and L_2 as

$$\underline{\mathsf{D}}^{(p)}_{L_1, L_2}(x, y) = \min \left\{ w \mid w \in \mathsf{D}^{(p)}_{L_1, L_2}(x, y) \right\},$$

where minimum is considered with respect to the quasi-lexicographical order.

The set of all minimal distinguishability words with respect to the languages L_1 and L_2 is

$$\underline{\mathsf{D}}^{(p)}(L_1, L_2) = \left\{ \underline{\mathsf{D}}^{(p)}_{L_1, L_2}(x, y) \mid x, y \in \Sigma^*, \mathsf{D}_{L_1, L_2}(x, y) \neq \emptyset \right\}.$$

Remark 1. Because of (1), we also have the following equalities:

$$\mathsf{D}^{(n)}_{L_1, L_2}(x, y) = \left(\mathsf{D}_{L_1^R, L_2^R}(x^R, y^R) \right)^R. \tag{7}$$

$$\mathsf{D}^{(p)}_{L_1^R, L_2^R}(x^R, y^R) = \left(\mathsf{D}_{L_1, L_2}(x, y) \right)^R. \tag{8}$$

Example 2. Let $L_1 = \{bbaa, baba\}$ and $L_2 = \{\varepsilon\}$. We have the following :

1. $\underline{\mathsf{D}}^{(p)}_{L_1, L_2}(\varepsilon, \varepsilon) = \{\varepsilon\}$ $(\varepsilon \notin L_1, \ \varepsilon \in L_2)$,
2. $\underline{\mathsf{D}}^{(p)}_{L_1, L_2}(\varepsilon, a) = \{bab\}$,
3. $\underline{\mathsf{D}}^{(p)}_{L_1, L_2}(a, \varepsilon) = \{\varepsilon\}$ $(a \notin L_1, \ \varepsilon \in L_2)$,
4. $\underline{\mathsf{D}}^{(p)}_{L_1, L_2}(aa, \varepsilon) = \{\varepsilon\}$ $(aa \notin L_1, \ \varepsilon \in L_2)$,
5. $\underline{\mathsf{D}}^{(p)}_{L_1, L_2}(baa, \varepsilon) = \{\varepsilon\}$ $(abb \notin L_1, \ \varepsilon \in L_2)$,
6. If $x \neq \varepsilon$:
   (a) $\underline{\mathsf{D}}^{(p)}_{L_1, L_2}(\varepsilon, x) = \{baba\}$, $(baba \in L_1, \text{ and } babax \notin L_2)$,
   (b) $\underline{\mathsf{D}}^{(p)}_{L_1, L_2}(a, x) = \{bab\}$, $(baba \in L_1, \text{ and } babx \notin L_2)$,
   (c) $\underline{\mathsf{D}}^{(p)}_{L_1, L_2}(aa, x) = \{bb\}$, $(bbaa \in L_1, \text{ and } bbx \notin L_2)$,
   (d) $\underline{\mathsf{D}}^{(p)}_{L_1, L_2}(baa, x) = \{b\}$, $(bbaa \in L_1, \text{ and } bx \notin L_2)$,

(e) $\underline{D}^{(p)}_{L_1,L_2}(bbaa, x) = \{\varepsilon\}$, $(bbaa \in L_1$, and $x \notin L_2)$,

(f) $\underline{D}^{(p)}_{L_1,L_2}(ba, x) = \{ba\}$, $(baba \in L_1$, and $bax \notin L_2)$,

(g) $\underline{D}^{(p)}_{L_1,L_2}(aba, x) = \{b\}$, $(baba \in L_1$, and $bx \notin L_2)$,

(h) $\underline{D}^{(p)}_{L_1,L_2}(baba, x) = \{\varepsilon\}$, $(baba \in L_1$, and $x \notin L_2)$,

7. for all other words $u, v \notin \{\varepsilon, a, aa, ba, bb, aba, baa, bbaa, baba\}$, we have $\underline{D}_{L_1,L_2}(u, v)$ is not defined.

Similar to the case of binary left-distinguishability operation, for binary right-distinguishability we have that $\underline{D}_{L_1,L_2}(u, v)$ is not defined for all $u \notin \mathsf{suff}(L_1)$ and $v \notin \mathsf{suff}(L_2)$, or $u \notin \mathsf{suff}(\overline{L_1})$ and $v \notin \mathsf{suff}(\overline{L_2})$.

Thus, for Example 2 we conclude that $\underline{D}^{(p)}(L_1, L_2) = \{\varepsilon, b, ba, bb, bab, baba\}$.

We would like to check if the relation between the binary left-distinguishability and binary right-distinguishability given by Eq. (3) or the Remark 1 can be adapted for minimal words, i.e., if

$$\underline{D}(L_1, L_2)^R = \underline{D}^{(p)}(L_1^R, L_2^R). \tag{9}$$

By comparing the Example 1 and Example 2, it follows that (9) is false.

This means that each of the properties proved in the previous section for $\underline{D}$ must be individually checked for $\underline{D}^{(p)}$, and we cannot use the symmetry of the two relations.

However, using (8), we also have that

$$D^{(p)}_{L_1,L_2}(x, y) \neq \emptyset \Longleftrightarrow D_{L_1^R,L_2^R}(x^R, y^R) \neq \emptyset. \tag{10}$$

With some rewording, the following result can be obtained from Lemma 3 and Remark 1. However, it is not a consequence of the previous result, and for this reason, we include a complete proof here, as the minimum is taken using the quasi-lexicographical order over a reverse of a set of words, which are also reversed.

Lemma 6. *The set of minimal right-distinguishability words with respect to two languages is prefix-closed.*

Proof. Let $w \in \underline{D}^{(p)}(L_1, L_2)$, and let $w = uv$, with $u, v \in \Sigma^*$. Because $w \in \underline{D}(L_1, L_2)$, we can find two other words, $x, y \in \Sigma^*$, such that $wx \in L_1$ and $wy \notin L_2$, or $wx \notin L_1$ and $wy \in L_2$. We consider only the case when $wx \in L_1$ and $wy \notin L_2$, the other case being similar. Thus, $uvx \in L_1$ and $uvy \notin L_2$. It follows that $u \in D^{(p)}_{L_1,L_2}(vx, vy)$. Since $u \in D^{(p)}_{L_1,L_2}(vx, vy)$, there exists $u' = \underline{D}^{(p)}_{L_1,L_2}((vx, vy)$ and $u' \preceq_l u$. Hence, $u'v \preceq_l uv$ and $u'v \in D^{(p)}_{L_1,L_2}(x, y)$, which implies $w = uv \preceq_l u'v$. Then, we must have $u'v = uv$, which implies $u = u' = \underline{D}^{(p)}_{L_1,L_2}(vx, vy) \in \underline{D}^{(p)}(L_1, L_2)$. $\square$

Using Lemma 3 and Remark 1, we get that the number of minimal left distinguishable words with respect to the languages L_1 and L_2 for the words u and v must be the same as the number of minimal right distinguishable words with respect to the languages L_1^R and L_2^R for words u^R and v^R, i.e., $|\underline{\mathsf{D}}^{(p)}(L_1, L_2)| = |\underline{\mathsf{D}}(L_1^R, L_2^R)|$.

Following Theorem 12 of [3] we have:

Theorem 3. *If L_1 and L_2 are regular languages such that $\mathsf{sc}(L_1) = m$ and $\mathsf{sc}(L_2) = n$, then $|\underline{\mathsf{D}}^{(p)}(L_1, L_2)| \leq 2^m + 2^n - 1$.*

5   Conclusion

We extended the definition of distinguishability to the right and two-side distinguishability for two languages. We proved that although the new operations have properties similar to the binary distinguishability operation, the state complexity bounds and the set of minimal words that can distinguish the two languages must be computed again. They cannot be derived from the minimal words obtained from the binary left-distinguishability operation. Furthermore, all state complexity upperbounds proved in the paper can be reached, i.e., they are also lowerbounds. The case of two-sided distinguishability is left for future papers. We must also note that there are multiple possibilities for extending this type of operation, either by changing the closure operator or by iterating some operations. For all possible extensions, the properties of these new operations can be of interest in building AI-backend engines, or for usage in other areas of computer science.

Acknowledgement. We want to thank the anonymous referees for their careful reviews, which helped improve the quality of the paper. This study was self-funded.

Disclosure of Interests. The author has no competing interests to declare that are relevant to the content of this article.

References

1. Brzozowski, J.A.: In search of most complex regular languages. Int. J. Found. Comput. Sci. **24**(6), 691–708 (2013)
2. Brzozowski, J., Tamm, H.: Theory of átomata. In: Mauri, G., Leporati, A. (eds.) DLT 2011. LNCS, vol. 6795, pp. 105–116. Springer, Heidelberg (2011). https://doi.org/10.1007/978-3-642-22321-1_10
3. Câmpeanu, C., Câmpeanu, C.A., Kozma, M.: Binary distinguishability operation. Theor. Comput. Sci. **1016**, 114782 (2024). https://doi.org/10.1016/J.TCS.2024.114782
4. Câmpeanu, C., Moreira, N., Reis, R.: Distinguishability operations and closures. Fundam. Informaticae **148**(3-4), 243–266 (2016). https://doi.org/10.3233/FI-2016-1434
5. Hopcroft, J.E., Ullman, J.D.: Introduction to Automata Theory, Languages and Computation. Addison Wesley (1979)
6. Kuratowski, C.: Sur l'operation $\overline{A}$ de l'analysis situs. Fundam. Math. **3**, 182–199 (1922)

7. Moore, E.F.: Gedanken-experiments on sequential machines. In: Automata Studies, Annals of Mathematics Studies, vol. 34, pp. 129–153 (1956)
8. Okhotin, A.: On the state complexity of scattered substrings and superstrings. Fundamenta Informaticae **99**(3), 325–338 (2010). https://doi.org/10.3233/FI-2010-252
9. Salomaa, A., Wood, D., Yu, S.: On the state complexity of reversals of regular languages. Theor. Comput. Sci. **320**(2), 315–329 (2004). https://doi.org/10.1016/j.tcs.2004.02.032. https://www.sciencedirect.com/science/article/pii/S0304397504001318

Further Remarks on Context-Free Grammars with Subregular Control Languages

Jürgen Dassow$^{(\boxtimes)}$ (iD)

Fakultät für Informatik, Otto-von-Guericke-Universität Magdeburg, PSF 4120,
39016 Magdeburg, Germany
`dassow@iws.cs.uni-magdeburg.de`

Abstract. A context-free grammar with appearance checking and control language is a triple (G, F, R), where $G = (N, T, P, S)$ is a context-free grammar, F is a subset of P, and the control language R is a subset of P^*. The language generated by (G, F, R) consists of all terminal words z with a derivation $S \overset{ac}{\underset{q}{\Longrightarrow}} z$ where q is a word of R and ac means that non-applicable rules can be skipped (without changing the sentential form), if they belong to F. It is known that, by the use of regular control languages, all recursively enumerable languages can be obtained. We prove that this statement also holds, if we use star-free, ordered, regular suffix-closed, union-free, and strictly locally (k)-testable language (where $k \geq 2$). On the other hand, if we restrict to combinational, definite, reverse definite, generalized definite, nilpotent, monoidal, or strictly locally 1-testable languages as control languages, then only context-free languages can be generated.

Keywords: grammars with controlled derivations · appearance checking · subregular languages

1 Introduction

It is a well-known fact that context-free grammars are not able to cover all phenomena of programming and natural languages. On the other hand, the more powerful context-dependent grammars have some bad properties (for instance, some decision problems are undecidable for them). Therefore, there is an interest in intermediate mechanisms which enlarge the generative power as well as have some good properties. Context-free grammars with control languages are one approach in this direction. Here it is required that the sequence of productions used in a derivation has to belong to a regular language called the control language. Such grammars were introduced in [16] by S. Ginsburg and E.H. Spanier. It turned out that this mechanism is equivalent to many other devices with a regulation of the derivation process as matrix grammars, programmed grammars, periodically time-variant grammars, and others. For details, we refer to monographs [11,23], Vol. 2, Chap. 3 [22].

M. D. Jiménez López and G. Vaszil (Eds.): Erzsébet Csuhaj-Varjú Festschrift,
LNCS 15840, pp. 41–53, 2025.
https://doi.org/10.1007/978-3-031-97274-4_3

It is known that some special languages are sufficient to obtain the same power as the set of all regular languages. An example are all languages of the form M^* where M is a finite set of words. This comes from the fact that each matrix in a matrix grammar corresponds to a finite sequence of applied rules and matrix grammars can therefore be described by a finite set of words which can iteratively be applied. Thus, it is a natural problem to study the generative power of context-free grammars with control languages where the control languages belong to subsets of the set of regular languages. The case of grammars with control languages (without appearance checking) was studied

- in [4,8] where it was shown that context-free grammars with monoidal, combinational, definite, nilpotent and regular commutative control languages generate only context-free languages whereas ordered, regular star-free, regular circular, strictly locally (k-)testable, union-free, and regular suffix-closed languages have the same power as all regular languages,
- in [5], where the subregular languages were defined by syntactic parameters as the number of nonterminals or productions, necessary to generate the control language (by a regular grammar),
- in [7], where it was proved that left and right ideals and arbitrary, prefix, suffix, bifix, infix, and solid regular codes have the same power as all regular sets whereas outfix, reflective, and uniform codes can generate only finite languages.

In [4,5,8], only the case without appearance checking was considered. In this paper, we continue these investigations by considering the case with appearance checking, that is, some rules can be skipped. This case is important because context-free grammars with erasing rules, regular control languages and appearance checking are as powerful as arbitrary grammars, that is, such grammars can generate all recursively enumerable languages.

We prove that most of the results for the case without appearance checking remain valid.

Finally, we mention that this research can be considered as a continuation of other investigations concerning the effect of subregular languages to the generative power (see, e.g., [6,9,10,12]), to the transformation of nondeterministic finite automata into deterministic finite automata (see [1]), or the operational complexity (see, e.g., [19] and Sect. 4.3 in [13]).

2   Definitions

We assume that the reader is familiar with the basic concepts of the theory of formal languages. In this section, we only recall some notations and some definitions such that a reader can understand the results and follow the argumentations. For more details, we refer to [22].

For an alphabet V, i.e., V is a finite non-empty set, the set of all words and all non-empty words over V are denoted by V^* and V^+, respectively. The empty word is denoted by λ. For a language L, let alph(L) be the minimal set V such that $L \subseteq V^*$.

The families of finite, regular, context-free, and recursively enumerable languages are denoted by *FIN*, *REG*, *CF*, and *RE*, respectively.

2.1   Subregular Families of Languages

The aim of this section is the definition of the subregular families of languages considered in this paper and the relations between them.

For a language L over V, we set

$$\text{Circ}(L) = \{vu \mid uv \in L, \ u, v \in V^*\},$$
$$\text{Suf}(L) = \{v \mid uv \in L, \ u, v \in V^*\}.$$

We consider the following restrictions for regular languages. Let L be a language with $V = \text{alph}(L)$ and k a natural number with $k \geq 1$. We say that L is

- a *combinational* language iff it can be represented in the form $L = V^*A$ for some subset $A \subseteq V$,
- a *definite* language iff it can be represented in the form $L = A \cup V^*B$ where A and B are finite subsets of V^*,
- a *reverse definite* language iff it can be represented in the form $L = A \cup BV^*$ where A and B are finite subsets of V^*,
- a *generalized* (or *symmetric*) *definite* language iff it can be represented in the form $L = A \cup BV^*C$ for some finite sets $A \subset V^*$, $B \subset V^*$, and $C \subset V^*$,
- a *nilpotent* language iff L is finite or $V^* \setminus L$ is finite,
- a *circular* language iff $L = \text{Circ}(L)$,
- a *suffix-closed* (or *fully initial* or *multiple-entry*) language iff $\text{Suf}(L) = L$,
- a *star-free* (or *non-counting*) language iff L can be described by a regular expression which is built by union, product, and complementation,
- a *union-free* language iff L can be described by a regular expression which is built by product and star,
- a *monoidal* language iff $L = V^*$,
- a *strictly locally k-testable* language iff there are three subsets A, B and C of V^k such that $a_1 a_2 \ldots a_n$ with $n \geq k$ and $a_i \in V$, $1 \leq i \leq n$, belongs to L if and only if $a_1 a_2 \ldots a_k \in A$, $a_{j+1} a_{j+2} \ldots a_{j+k} \in B$ for $1 \leq j \leq n - k - 1$, and $a_{n-k+1} a_{n-k+2} \ldots a_n \in C$,
- a *strictly locally testable* language iff it is strictly locally k-testable for some $k \geq 1$,
- an *ordered* language iff there are a deterministic finite automaton $\mathcal{A} = (Z, X, \delta, z_0, F)$ with the state set Z, the set X of input symbols, the transition function δ, the initial state z_0, and the set F of final states and a reflexive order $\preceq$ on the set Z such that $\mathcal{A}$ accepts L and, for all $a \in X$, $z \preceq z'$ implies $\delta(z, a) \preceq \delta(z', a)$.

A set $R \subset V^*$ is strictly locally 1-testable if and only if there are sets $A \subseteq V$, $B \subseteq V$, and $C \subseteq V$ such that $R = AB^*C \cup (A \cap C)$.

By $COMB$, DEF, $RDEF$, $GDEF$, NIL, $CIRC$, SUF, SF, UF, MON, SLT_k, $k \geq 1$, SLT, and ORD, we denote the families of all combinational, definite, reverse definite, generalized definite, nilpotent, regular circular, regular suffix-closed, star-free, union-free, monoidal, strictly locally k-testable, strictly locally testable, and ordered languages, respectively.

Definite languages occur already in the fundamental paper [20] on finite automata and seem to form the first class of subregular languages. Reverse and generalized definite languages were defined in [3, 17]. Star-free (or non-counting regular) and strictly locally testable, suffix-closed regular (or multiple-entry), union-free, and ordered languages were introduced in the papers [2, 15, 21, 25], respectively. Some properties of the above mentioned types of languages can be found in [14, 24, 26].

It is obvious that combinational, definite, reverse definite, generalized definite, nilpotent, union-free, star-free, ordered, and strictly locally languages are regular, whereas non-regular languages of the other types mentioned above exist.

We set

$$\mathcal{G} = \{FIN, MON, COMB, DEF, RDEF, GDEF, NIL, CIRC, SUF\}$$
$$\cup \{UF, SF, ORD, SLT\} \cup \{SLT_k \mid k \geq 1\}.$$

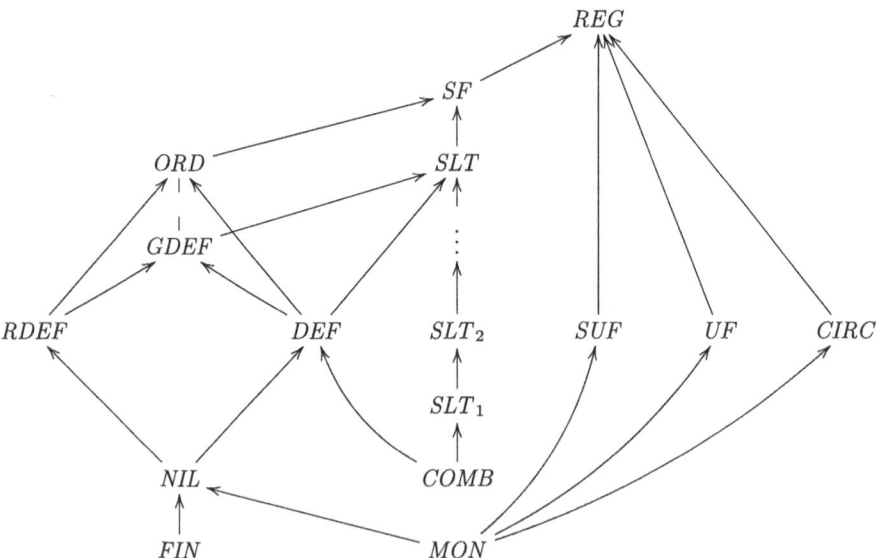

Fig. 1. Hierarchy of subregular languages (an arrow from X to Y denotes $X \subset Y$, a dashed line denotes an unknown relation between the connected families, and if two families are not connected by a directed path then they are incomparable)

The relations between families of $\mathcal{G}$ are investigated, e.g., in [18, 27], and their set-theoretic relations are given in Fig. 1.

2.2 Context-Free Grammars with Control Languages and Appearance Checking

A context-free grammar is specified as a quadruple $G = (N, T, P, S)$ where N and T are disjoint alphabets of nonterminals and terminals, respectively, P is a finite subset of $N \times (N \cup T)^*$, and S is an element of N. We set $V = N \cup T$. The elements of P are called rules or productions. Instead of $p = (A, w) \in P$ we shall use the notation $p = A \rightarrow w$. For a derivation step using the rule p, we write $x \underset{p}{\Longrightarrow} y$. The set of all sentential forms generated by G is denoted by $\mathrm{sf}(G)$.

A context-free grammar with control language and appearance checking is a triple (G, F, R) where $G = (N, T, P, S)$ is a context-free grammar, F is a subset of P, and R is a regular language over P called the control language.

The application of the rule $p = A \rightarrow w$ to a word x in appearance checking mode is defined as follows:

- If x contains an occurrence of A, i.e., $x = x_1 A x_2$, then the word $y = x_1 w x_2$ is generated, that means, $x \underset{p}{\overset{ac}{\Longrightarrow}} y$ (in this case, we say that p is effectively applied); and
- if A does not occur in x and $p \in F$, then we can skip the rule without changing the sentential form x, that means, $x \underset{p}{\overset{ac}{\Longrightarrow}} x$.

Intuitively, we check whether A appears in x, and we apply the rule in the positive case, whereas we skip the rule if it is not applicable but in F.

For a derivation

$$x \underset{p_1}{\overset{ac}{\Longrightarrow}} r_1 \underset{p_2}{\overset{ac}{\Longrightarrow}} r_2 \underset{p_3}{\overset{ac}{\Longrightarrow}} \cdots \underset{p_k}{\overset{ac}{\Longrightarrow}} x_k = y,$$

we also write

$$x \underset{p_1 p_2 \cdots p_k}{\overset{ac}{\Longrightarrow}} y.$$

The language $L^{ac}(G, F, R)$ consists of all words $z \in T^*$ such that there is a derivation $S \underset{p_1 p_2 \cdots p_k}{\overset{ac}{\Longrightarrow}} z$ with $p_1 p_2 \ldots p_k \in R$.

If we choose $F = \emptyset$, then all rules have to be applied effectively. We say that the grammar is without appearance checking. We shortly write $x \underset{p_1 p_2 \cdots p_k}{\Longrightarrow} y$. The language $L^{ac}(G, \emptyset, R)$ consists of all words $z \in T^*$ such that there is a derivation $S \underset{p_1 p_2 \cdots p_k}{\Longrightarrow} z$ with $p_1 p_2 \ldots p_k \in R$. We shortly write $L(G, R)$ instead of $L^{ac}(G, \emptyset, R)$.

For a family X of languages, we define $\mathcal{L}^{ac}(X)$ and $\mathcal{L}(X)$ as the families of all languages which can be generated by grammars (G, F, R) and (G, R), respectively, where G is a context-free grammar and R is a control language belonging to X.

By definition,

$$\mathcal{L}(X) \subseteq \mathcal{L}^{ac}(X) \tag{1}$$

holds.

Example 1. Let $G = (\{S, A, U\}, \{a\}, \{p_1, p_2, p_3, p_4, p_5\}, S)$ be a context-free grammar where

$$p_1 = S \to AA, \ p_2 = S \to U, \ p_3 = A \to S, \ p_4 = A \to U, \ p_5 = S \to a.$$

Then the grammar $(G, \{p_2, p_4\}, (\{p_1\}^*\{p_2\}\{p_3\}^*\{p_4\})^*\{p_5\}^*)$ generates the language $\{a^{2^n} \mid n \geq 1\}$. This can be seen as follows: We consider S^r for some $r \geq 1$ (note that we start with $r = 1$). We now apply sometimes the rule p_1 or the rule p_5. Assume that we apply k times p_1. Then we have to apply p_2. If $k < r$, then p_2 can effectively be used, and we introduce the non-replaceable letter U, i.e., we cannot derive a terminal word. If $k = r$, we have produced A^{2r}, and have to apply p_2 in appearance checking mode. Then we replace using p_3 some As by S. Again, this has to be done $2r$ times, since U is derived otherwise. Thus, we obtain S^{2r}. If we apply p_5, then we have to replace all Ss by a to get a terminal word. Therefore, any derivation has the form

$$S \xrightarrow[p_1 p_2 p_3^2 p_4]{ac} S^2 \xrightarrow[p_1^2 p_2 p_3^4 p_4]{ac} S^4 \Longrightarrow \cdots \xrightarrow[p_1^{2^s} p_2 p_3^{2^{s+1}} p_4]{ac} S^{2^{s+1}} \Longrightarrow \cdots \Longrightarrow S^{2^n} \xrightarrow[p_5^{2^n}]{ac} a^{2^n}.$$

It is well-known that $\mathcal{L}^{ac}(REG) = RE$ (see [11, 23]).

The following statement holds by the definitions.

Lemma 1. *If $X_1 \subseteq X_2$ for two language families X_1 and X_2, then the relation $\mathcal{L}^{ac}(X_1) \subseteq \mathcal{L}^{ac}(X_2)$ holds.*

3   Results

We start with finite control languages.

Lemma 2. *We have $\mathcal{L}^{ac}(FIN) = FIN$.*

Proof. Let $L \in \mathcal{L}^{ac}(FIN)$. Then $L = L(G, F, R)$ for some context-free grammar $G = (N, T, P, S)$, some subset $F \subseteq P$, and some regular set $R = \{q_1, q_2, \ldots q_m\}$ where $q_i \in P^*$ for $1 \leq i \leq m$. The sets $L_i = \{z \mid S \xRightarrow[q_i]{ac} z\}$ are finite for $1 \leq i \leq m$. Hence $L = \bigcup_{i=1}^m L_i$ is also finite. This proves $\mathcal{L}^{ac}(FIN) \subseteq FIN$.

Let $L = \{w_1, w_2, \ldots, w_n\}$ be a finite set of words over T. Then the triple $(G, \emptyset, P)$ with $G = (\{S\}, T, \{S \to w_i \mid 1 \leq i \leq n\}, S)$ generates L. Therefore, $FIN \subseteq \mathcal{L}^{ac}(FIN)$ holds, too.

We now consider strongly locally 1-testable control languages.

Lemma 3. *Each language in $\mathcal{L}^{ac}(SLT_1)$ is context-free.*

Proof. Let $L = L(G, F, R)$ for a grammar $G = (N, T, P, S)$, a subset $F \subseteq P$, and a control language $R = AB^*C \cup (A \cap C) \in SLT_1$, where A, B, C are subsets of P.

Because words in $A \cap C$ generate a finite and thus context-free language, it is sufficient to show that $L(G, F, AB^*C)$ is context-free. Let

$$\alpha_0 \overset{ac}{\underset{p_1}{\Longrightarrow}} \alpha_1 \overset{ac}{\underset{p_2}{\Longrightarrow}} \alpha_2 \overset{ac}{\underset{p_3}{\Longrightarrow}} \quad \cdots \quad \overset{ac}{\underset{p_{n-1}}{\Longrightarrow}} \quad \alpha_{n-1} \overset{ac}{\underset{p_n}{\Longrightarrow}} \alpha_n$$

be a derivation in G with $p_1, p_2, \ldots, p_n \in B$. Moreover, let $p_{i_1}, p_{i_2}, \ldots, p_{i_k}$ be the rules which are not skipped in that derivation. Then it holds that

$$\alpha_0 \underset{p_{i_1}}{\Longrightarrow} \alpha_{i_1} \underset{p_{i_2}}{\Longrightarrow} \alpha_{i_2} \underset{p_{i_3}}{\Longrightarrow} \quad \cdots \quad \underset{p_{i_k}}{\Longrightarrow} \alpha_{i_k} = \alpha_n,$$

that is, we obtain the same word if we only apply the rules which are not skipped. Because $p_{i_1}, p_{i_2}, \ldots, p_{i_k}$ are all in B, we obtain that, for any derivation $\alpha \overset{ac}{\underset{q}{\Longrightarrow}} \beta$ with $q \in B^*$, there is a derivation $\alpha \underset{q'}{\Longrightarrow} \beta$ with $q' \in B^*$.

Therefore, we can - without loss of generality - assume that any terminating derivation in G has the form

$$S \overset{ac}{\underset{p_0}{\Longrightarrow}} \alpha_1 \underset{q'}{\Longrightarrow} \alpha_2 \overset{ac}{\underset{p_1}{\Longrightarrow}} w \in T^* \tag{2}$$

with $p_0 \in A$, $q' \in B^*$, and $p_1 \in C$.

We now discuss four cases according to the situations whether the rules of A or C are effectively used or not.

Case 1: Let R_1 be the set of all words in $L(G)$ with a derivation (2) where p_0 and p_1 are skipped.

Then we get $S = \alpha_1$ and $w = \alpha_2$. Thus the derivation $S = \alpha_1 \underset{q'}{\Longrightarrow} \alpha_2 = w$ can be realized by a derivation in the context-free grammar $G_1 = (N, T, B, S)$. Conversely, if we have a derivation $S \underset{q''}{\Longrightarrow} z$ in G_1, then all rules of q'' are in B, and, consequently, $S \overset{ac}{\underset{p_0}{\Longrightarrow}} S \underset{q''}{\Longrightarrow} z \overset{ac}{\underset{p_1}{\Longrightarrow}} z$ is a derivation in G where p_0 and p_1 are skipped. Thus, $R_1 = L(G_1)$ holds.

Case 2: Let R_2 be the set of all words in $L(G)$ with a derivation (2) where p_0 is skipped and p_1 is effectively applied.

Then we have $S = \alpha_1$ and $\alpha_2 = \alpha_2' D \alpha_2''$, $p_1 = D \to u \in T^*$, and $w = \alpha_2' u \alpha_2''$.

Let N' be the set of all nonterminals D' such that $D' \to u' \in T^*$ is a rule of C. We consider $L_2' = \text{sf}(G_1) \cap T^* N' T^*$. It is well-known that $\text{sf}(G_1)$ is a context-free language. By the closure of the family of context-free languages under intersection with regular sets, we get that L_2' is context-free. We now define the substitution $\tau : (N' \cup T)^* \to T^*$ by $\tau(D') = \{u_1, u_2, \ldots, u_n\}$ for $D' \in N'$, where $D' \to u_i \in T^*$, $1 \leq i \leq n$, are all rules of C with left-hand side D', and $\tau(a) = \{a\}$ for $a \in T$. Let $L_2 = \tau(L_2')$. Since context-free languages are closed under substitutions, L_2 is context-free. Obviously, $w \in L_2$.

Conversely, let $z \in L_2$. Then there are a derivation $S \underset{q''}{\Longrightarrow} \alpha_3 D' \alpha_4$ in G_1 (i.e., all rules of q'' belong to B) with $\alpha_3, \alpha_4 \in T^*$, $D' \in N'$, and a rule $D' \to u' \in C$, and $z = \alpha_3 u' \alpha_4$. Now there is a derivation

$$S \overset{ac}{\underset{p_0}{\Longrightarrow}} S \underset{q''}{\Longrightarrow} \alpha_3 D' \alpha_4 \underset{p'}{\Longrightarrow} \alpha_3 u' \alpha_4 = z$$

in G where $p' = D' \to u' \in C$. Hence, $z \in R_2$.

Therefore, $R_2 = L_2$ holds.

Case 3: Let R_3 be the set of all words in $L(G)$ with a derivation (2) where p_1 is skipped and p_0 is effectively applied.

Then $\alpha_2 = w$. Obviously, the left hand side of p_0 is S. Let Q be the set of rules in A with the left-hand side S. Then we construct the context-free grammar $G_3 = (N \cup \{S'\}, T, B \cup \{S' \to u \mid S \to u \in Q\}, S')$ where S' is a new symbol. Then $w \in L(G_3)$.

Conversely, for $z \in L(G_3)$, let $S' \Longrightarrow z$ be a derivation of z in G_3. Then this derivation starts with a rule $p = S' \to u$ with $S \to u \in Q \subseteq A$. Moreover, since rules with S' at the left-hand side cannot be applied in the sequel, we obtain that the derivation has the form $S' \underset{p}{\Longrightarrow} u \underset{q'}{\Longrightarrow} z$ with $q' \in B^*$. Because there is a rule $p' = S \to u \in A$ and this rule can be effectively applied to S, we obtain the derivation $S \underset{p'}{\Longrightarrow} u \underset{q'}{\Longrightarrow} z$ in G. Since z is a terminal word, we can apply all rules of $F \cap C$ in appearance checking mode to z. Since p_1 belongs to $F \cap C$, we get the derivation $S \underset{p'}{\Longrightarrow} u \underset{q'}{\Longrightarrow} z \overset{ac}{\underset{p_1}{\Longrightarrow}} z$. This proves $z \in R_3$.

Hence, we obtain $L(G_3) = R_3$.

Case 4: Let R_4 be the set of all words in $L(G)$ with a derivation (2) where p_0 and p_1 are effectively applied.

Using the notations of the Cases 2 and 3, we construct the context-free set $L_4 = \tau(\mathrm{sf}(G_3) \cap T^* N' T^*)$. As in the cases before, we can show that $R_4 = L_4$.

Because $L(G) = R_1 \cup R_2 \cup R_3 \cup R_4 = L(G_1) \cup L_2 \cup L(G_3) \cup L_4$, $L(G)$ is the union of four context-free languages, and thus $L(G)$ is context-free.

We now show an analogous result for definite languages.

Lemma 4. *Each language in $\mathcal{L}^{ac}(DEF)$ is context-free.*

Proof. Let $L \in \mathcal{L}^{ac}(DEF)$. Then $L = L^{ac}(G, F, R)$ holds for a context-free grammar $G = (N, T, P, S)$, a subset F of P, and $R = A \cup P^* B$ where $A \subseteq P^*$ and $B \subseteq P^*$ are finite sets. Because

$$L = L^{ac}(G, F, R) = L^{ac}(G, F, A) \cup L^{ac}(G, F, P^* B),$$

it is sufficient to prove that $L^{ac}(G, F, A)$ and $L^{ac}(G, F, P^* B)$ are context-free. Since a finite set A can only derive a finite set of words, $L^{ac}(G, F, A)$ is finite and thus context-free. We now show that $L^{ac}(G, F, P^* B)$ is context-free, too.

Assume that $\lambda \in B$. Then we get $L^{ac}(G, F, P^*) \subseteq L^{ac}(G, F, P^* B)$. Because each word in $P^* B$ is in P^*, we also have $L^{ac}(G, F, P^* B) \subseteq L^{ac}(G, F, P^*)$. Consequently, $L^{ac}(G, F, P^* B) = L^{ac}(G, F, P^*)$ holds. As in the preceding proof, we can show that, for any derivation $S \overset{ac}{\underset{q}{\Longrightarrow}} z$ in (G, F, R), there is a derivation $S \underset{q'}{\Longrightarrow} z$ (q' is the scattered subsequence of q which contains the rules of q which are effectively applied). Thus, we get $L^{ac}(G, F, P^*) = L(G, P^*)$. Furthermore, since P^* allows any sequence of rules, we obtain $L(G, P^*) = L(G)$. Therefore, $L^{ac}(G, F, P^* B)$ is context-free.

Let us assume that B contains a sequence s such that all rules in s belong to F. If $z \in L(G)$, then we have the derivation $S \underset{t}{\Longrightarrow} z \overset{ac}{\underset{s}{\Longrightarrow}} z$ for some sequence

$t \in P^*$. Hence, we have $z \in L^{ac}(G, F, P^*B)$. Thus, $L(G) \subseteq L^{ac}(G, F, P^*B)$ holds. On the other hand, we have as above $L^{ac}(G, F, P^*B) \subseteq L(G, P^*) = L(G)$. Consequently, we obtain $L^{ac}(G, F, P^*B) = L(G)$, which proves the context-freeness of $L^{ac}(G, F, P^*B)$.

We now assume that B only contains non-empty words and each word in B contains at least one rule not in F. Then there is a finite set Q of pairs of words (u, u') such that $u \in N^+$, $u' \in T^*$, and $u \overset{ac}{\underset{x}{\Longrightarrow}} u'$ for some word $x \in B$ hold. Let $u = A_1 A_2 \ldots A_{k_u}$ for some k_u. Obviously, each letter A occurring in u is transformed in a unique word z_A by this derivation such that $z_{A_1} z_{A_2} \ldots z_{A_{k_u}} = u'$.

We now introduce new letters $A_{u, u', i}$, $(u, u') \in Q$, $1 \leq i \leq k_u$, in order to store the relation to u and u' as well as the position of A in u. Moreover, let h be the homomorphism defined by $h(x) = x$ for $x \in T$ and $h(A_{u, u', i}) = z_{A_i}$ for $(u, u') \in Q$, $1 \leq i \leq k_u$.

For a letter $A \in N$, let M_A be the set of all letters $A_{u, u', i}$ where A is the i-th letter of u. Let M be the set of nonterminals with a non-empty set M_A. Now, we define the substitution τ by $\tau(A) = M_A$ for $A \in M$ and $\tau(x) = \{x\}$ for $x \in (N \setminus M) \cup T$, and construct the context-free grammar $G' = (N', T, P', S')$ where

$$N' = \{U\} \cup (N \setminus M) \cup \bigcup_{A \in M} M_A,$$

$$P' = \{B' \to B'_1 \ldots B'_t \mid B \to B_1 \ldots B_t \in P, B' \in \tau(B), B'_i \in \tau(B_i), 1 \leq i \leq t\}$$
$$\cup \{S' \to S'' \mid S'' \in \tau(S)\}.$$

Further, we set

$$U = \{x_1 A_{u, u', 1} x_2 A_{u, u', 2} x_3 \ldots A_{u, u', k_u} x_{k_u+1} \mid x_i \in T^*, 1 \leq i \leq k_u+1, (u, u') \in Q\}.$$

Then we have

$$L^{ac}(G, F, P^*B) = h(\mathrm{sf}(G') \cap U).$$

Since the set of sentential forms of a context-free grammar is context-free and by the closure properties of the family of context-free languages, we get that $L^{ac}(G, F, P^*B)$ is context-free.

Lemma 5. *i) Each language in $\mathcal{L}^{ac}(RDEF)$ is context-free.*
ii) Each language in $\mathcal{L}^{ac}(GDEF)$ is context-free.

Proof. i) Let $G = (N, T, P, S)$ be a context-free grammar, $F \subseteq P$, and $R = A \cup BP^*$ be a reverse definite language. Let $\{\alpha_1, \alpha_2, \ldots, \alpha_m\}$ be the set of all terminal words which can be obtained by a derivation $S \overset{ac}{\underset{q}{\Longrightarrow}} \alpha$ with $q \in A$, and let $\{\beta_1, \beta_2, \ldots, \beta_n\}$ be the set of all words which can be obtained by a derivation $S \overset{ac}{\underset{q'}{\Longrightarrow}} \beta$ with $q' \in B$ (by Lemma 2, both languages are finite). Then we obtain $L(G, F, P) = L(G')$ for the context-free grammar

$$G' = (N \cup \{S'\}, T, P \cup \{S' \to \alpha_i \mid 1 \leq i \leq m\} \cup \{S' \to \beta_j \mid 1 \leq j \leq n\}, S')$$

in analogy to the proof of Lemma 3, Case 3.

ii) The proof for generalized definite languages follows by a combination of the proof for reverse definite languages and definite languages in analogy to the proof of Lemma 3, Case 4.

Corollary 1. *We have*

$$CF = \mathcal{L}^{ac}(MON) = \mathcal{L}^{ac}(NIL) = \mathcal{L}^{ac}(COMB) = \mathcal{L}^{ac}(SLT_1)$$
$$= \mathcal{L}^{ac}(DEF) = \mathcal{L}^{ac}(RDEF) = \mathcal{L}^{ac}(GDEF).$$

Proof. By the results of [8], (1), Lemma 1, Lemma 3, Lemma 4, and Lemma 5, we obtain the relations

$$CF = \mathcal{L}(COMB) \subseteq \mathcal{L}^{ac}(COMB) \subseteq \mathcal{L}^{ac}(SLT_1) \subseteq CF$$

and

$$CF = \mathcal{L}(MON) \subseteq \mathcal{L}^{ac}(MON) \subseteq \mathcal{L}^{ac}(NIL) \subseteq \mathcal{L}^{ac}(DEF) \subseteq \mathcal{L}^{ac}(GDEF) \subseteq CF,$$
$$CF \subseteq \mathcal{L}^{ac}(NIL) \subseteq \mathcal{L}^{ac}(RDEF) \subseteq CF,$$

from which the statement of the corollary immediately follows.

Finally, we present some subregular families which are as powerful as the set of all regular languages.

In [8], it was shown that any language generated by a context-free grammar with a regular control language can be generated by a context-free grammar $G = (N, T, P, S)$ and a control language $R = \{p_i q_i \mid 1 \leq i \leq n\}^*$ where all rules q_i, $1 \leq i \leq n$, are pairwise different and $p_i \neq q_j$ for $1 \leq i \leq n$ and $1 \leq j \leq n$. The proof uses a normal form for matrix grammars (for details on matrix grammars, we refer to [11, 23]). Such a normal form exists also for matrix grammars with appearance checking. Thus, the same argumentation holds for grammars with appearance checking, too (F contains some rules of $\{p_i \mid 1 \leq i \leq n\}$). Because R is strictly locally 2-testable as well as ordered as well as union-free (see [8]), we obtain by Lemma 1 the following statement.

Lemma 6. *For each $k \geq 2$, we have*

$$\mathcal{L}^{ac}(REG) = \mathcal{L}^{ac}(ORD) = \mathcal{L}^{ac}(SF) = \mathcal{L}^{ac}(UF) = \mathcal{L}^{ac}(SLT_k) = \mathcal{L}^{ac}(SLT).$$

Lemma 7. *We have $\mathcal{L}^{ac}(REG) = \mathcal{L}^{ac}(SUF)$.*

Proof. By Lemma 1, it is sufficient to prove that $\mathcal{L}^{ac}(REG) \subseteq \mathcal{L}^{ac}(SUF)$.

Let $L \in \mathcal{L}^{ac}(REG)$. Then there is a triple (G, F, R) with a context-free grammar $G = (N, T, P, S)$, a set $F \subseteq P$ and a regular control language $R \subseteq P^*$ such that $L^{ac}(G, F, R) = L$ holds. We now construct the context-free grammar $G' = (N \cup \{S'\}, T, P \cup \{S' \to S\}, S')$. Let $p = S' \to S$. We set $R' = \mathrm{Suf}(\{p\}R) = \{S' \to S\}R \cup \mathrm{Suf}(R)$.

We consider the grammar (G', F, R') with control and appearance checking. Any derivation in G' has the form $S' \overset{ac}{\underset{p}{\Longrightarrow}} S \overset{ac}{\underset{q}{\Longrightarrow}} w$ where q is a word from R. Consequently, $L^{ac}(G', F, R') = L^{ac}(G, F, R) = L$ and $L \in \mathcal{L}^{ac}(SUF)$ because R' is in SUF by definition. This implies $\mathcal{L}^{ac}(REG) \subseteq \mathcal{L}^{ac}(SUF)$.

Lemma 8. *We have $\mathcal{L}^{ac}(REG) = \mathcal{L}^{ac}(CIRC)$.*

Proof. By Lemma 1, it is sufficient to prove that $\mathcal{L}^{ac}(REG) \subseteq \mathcal{L}^{ac}(CIRC)$.

Let $L \in \mathcal{L}^{ac}(REG)$. Then there is a triple (G, F, R) with a context-free grammar $G = (N, T, P, S)$, a set $F \subseteq P$ and a regular control language $R \subseteq P^*$ such that $L^{ac}(G, F, R) = L$ holds. We now construct the context-free grammar $G' = (N \cup \{S'\}, T, P \cup \{S' \to S\}, S')$. Let $p = S' \to S$. We set $R'' = \mathrm{Circ}(\{p\}R)$ and consider the grammar (G', F, R'').

Let $w \in L^{ac}(G, F, R)$. Then there is word $q \in R$ such that $S \overset{ac}{\underset{q}{\Longrightarrow}} w$ in G. Since we have the derivation $S' \overset{ac}{\underset{p}{\Longrightarrow}} S \overset{ac}{\underset{q}{\Longrightarrow}} w$ in G', we obtain $w \in L^{ac}(G', F, R'')$. This implies $L^{ac}(G, F, R) \subseteq L^{ac}(G', F, R'')$.

Let $w' \in L^{ac}(G', F, R'')$. Then there is a sequence $q_1pq_2 \in \mathrm{Circ}(\{p\}R)$ such that $S' \overset{ac}{\underset{q_1pq_2}{\Longrightarrow}} w'$. Since $q_2q_1 \in R$, all rules of q_1 do not have the left-hand side S'. Consequently, all rules of q_1 belong to F and are skipped in the above derivation. Because w' is a terminal word, it contains no non-terminals, $S' \overset{ac}{\underset{p}{\Longrightarrow}} S \overset{ac}{\underset{q_2}{\Longrightarrow}} w \overset{ac}{\underset{q_1}{\Longrightarrow}} w$ is a correct derivation, too (all rules of q_1 are skipped, again). This means that w' can also be derived in G, because $q_2q_1 \in R$. Hence, $L^{ac}(G', F, R'') \subseteq L^{ac}(G, F, R)$.

Combining the two derived inclusions, we get $L^{ac}(G', F, R'') = L^{ac}(G, F, R)$.

Moreover, we obtain $\mathcal{L}^{ac}(REG) \subseteq \mathcal{L}^{ac}(CIRC)$ because R'' is in $CIRC$ by definition.

Summarizing the obtained relations, we obtain the following theorem.

Theorem 1. *The hierarchy shown in Fig. 2 holds.*

$$RE = \mathcal{L}^{ac}(REG) = \mathcal{L}^{ac}(SF) = \mathcal{L}^{ac}(CIRC)$$
$$= \mathcal{L}^{ac}(SUF) = \mathcal{L}^{ac}(UF) = \mathcal{L}^{ac}(ORD)$$
$$= \mathcal{L}^{ac}(SLT_2) = \mathcal{L}^{ac}(SLT_3) = \ldots = \mathcal{L}^{ac}(SLT)$$

$$\uparrow$$

$$CF = \mathcal{L}^{ac}(DEF) = \mathcal{L}^{ac}(RDEF) = \mathcal{L}^{ac}(GDEF)$$
$$= \mathcal{L}^{ac}(COMB) = \mathcal{L}^{ac}(NIL) = \mathcal{L}^{ac}(MON) = \mathcal{L}^{ac}(SLT_1)$$

$$\uparrow$$

$$FIN = \mathcal{L}^{ac}(FIN)$$

Fig. 2. Hierarchy of language families obtained by subregular control languages and appearance checking (an arrow from X to Y denotes $X \subset Y$).

4 Conclusion

We have studied the power of subregular control languages for context-free grammars with appearance checking. We have obtained a hierarchy of three levels (see

Fig. 2), which differs considerably from the hierarchy of subregular language families (see Fig. 1). This is not surprising, because, in cases of other regulation mechanisms, the obtained hierarchy has also only few levels in contrast to the original hierarchy in Fig. 1.

Moreover, in [8], we have considered the hierarchy of families $\mathcal{L}(X)$ for $X \in \mathcal{G}$. Except the equality to RE (it is known that $\mathcal{L}(REG) \subset \mathcal{L}^{ac}(REG) = RE$) - the same hierarchy as in Fig. 2 has been obtained for grammars without appearance and with subregular control languages.

Furthermore, we can discuss non-erasing grammars, i.e., the set of rules does not contain rules of the form $A \rightarrow \lambda$. Using almost the same proofs, the hierarchy of Fig. 2 also holds, if we investigate non-erasing grammars with regular control sets and with or without appearance checking - again without the equality to RE (non-erasing grammars with regular control and without appearance checking cannot generate all recursively enumerable languages; it is an open problem whether non-erasing grammars with regular control languages and appearance checking can generate all recursively enumerable languages).

We note that in case of context-free grammars without appearance checking, we have also considered the family of regular commutative languages $COMM$ consisting of all regular languages L which satisfy that $a_1 \ldots a_n \in L$ implies $a_{i_1} \ldots a_{i_n} \in L$ for all permutations $(i_1, i_2, \ldots, i_n)$ of $\{1, 2, \ldots, n\}$ and all $n \geq 1$. In [8], it has been shown that the family of context-free grammars (without appearance checking) with regular commutative control languages equals the set CF of context-free languages. We do not have a result for context-free grammars with regular commutative control language and appearance checking.

Moreover, we mention that the results for context-free grammars controlled by subregular languages defined by syntactic restrictions given in [5] remain valid in the case with appearance checking, too. (The only critical part is Case ii) of the proof of [5], Theorem 5.2. There one has to show that $L^{ac}(G, F, A^*B)$ is context-free, where A and B are certain sets of rules, and this can be done in analogy to the proof of Lemma 3, Cases 1 and 2.)

In [7], grammars with control by regular ideals and regular codes has been investigated. Here the appearance checking was already considered.

References

1. Bordihn, H., Holzer, M., Kutrib, M.: Determination of finite automata accepting subregular languages. Theoret. Comput. Sci. **410**, 3209–3222 (2009)
2. Brzozowski, J.A.: Regular expression techniques for sequential circuits. Ph.D. thesis, Princeton University, Princeton, NJ, USA (1962)
3. Brzozowski, J.A.: Canonical regular expressions and minimal state graphs of definite events. In: Proceedings of the Symposium on Mathematical Theory of Automata, Microwave Research Institute, Institute Symposia Series, Brooklyn, vol. 12, pp. 529–561 (1963)
4. Dassow, J.: Subregularly controlled derivations: context-free case. Rostock. Math. Kolloq. **34**, 61–70 (1988)

5. Dassow, J.: Subregularly controlled derivations: restrictions by syntactic parameters. In: Martín-Vide, C., Mitrana, V. (eds.) Where Mathematics, Computer Science, Linguistics and Biology Meet, pp. 51–61. Kluwer, Netherlands (2001)
6. Dassow, J.: Grammars with commutative, circular, and locally testable conditions. In: Ésik, Z., Fülöp, Z. (eds.) Automata, Formal Languages, and Related Topics, pp. 27–37. University of Szeged, Szeged (2009)
7. Dassow, J.: Grammars with control by ideals and codes. J. Autom. Lang. Comb. **23**, 143–164 (2018)
8. Dassow, J.: Remarks on context-free grammars with subregular control languages. Theoret. Comput. Sci. **1010**, 114704 (2024)
9. Dassow, J., Manea, F., Truthe, B.: On external contextual grammars with subregular selection languages. Theoret. Comput. Sci. **449**, 64–73 (2012)
10. Dassow, J., Manea, F., Truthe, B.: Networks of evolutionary processors: the power of subregular filters. Acta Informatica **50**, 41–75 (2013)
11. Dassow, J., Păun, G.H.: Regulated Rewriting in Formal Language Theory. Volume 18 of EATCS Monographs in Theoretical Computer Science. Springer, Berlin (1989)
12. Dassow J., Rudolf, St.: Conditional Lindenmayer systems with subregular conditions: the non-extended case. RAIRO – Theor. Inf. Appl. **48**, 127–147 (2014)
13. Gao, Y., Moreira, N., Reis, R., Yu, S.: A survey on operational state complexity. J. Autom. Lang. Comb. **21**, 251–310 (2016)
14. Gécseg, F., Peak, I.: Algebraic Theory of Automata. Academiai Kiado, Budapest (1972)
15. Gill, A., Kou, L.T.: Multiple-entry finite automata. J. Comput. Syst. Sci. **9**, 1–19 (1974)
16. Ginsburg, S., Spanier, E.: Control sets on grammars. Math. Syst. Theor. **2**, 159–177 (1968)
17. Ginzburg, A.: About some properties of definite, reverse-definite and related automata. IEEE Trans. Electron. Comput. **EC-15**, 809–810 (1966)
18. Havel, I.M.: The theory of regular events II. Kybernetika **5**, 520–544 (1969)
19. Jirásková, G., Krausová, M.: Complexity in prefix-free regular languages. In: McQuillan, I., Pighizzini, G., Trost, B. (eds.) Proceedings of 12th Internat. Workshop Descriptional Complexity of Formal Systems, pp. 236–244. University of Saskatchewan, Saaskatoon (2010)
20. Kleene, S.C.: Representation of events in nerve nets and finite automata. In: Shannon, C.E., McCarthy, J. (eds.) Automata Studies, pp. 3–42. Princeton University Press, Princeton (1956)
21. McNaughton, R., Papert, S.: Counter-free Automata. MIT Press, Cambridge, USA (1971)
22. Rozenberg, G., Salomaa, A. (eds.): Handbook of Formal Languages. Springer, Berlin (1997)
23. Salomaa, A.: Formal Languages. Academic Press, New York (1973)
24. Shyr, H.J.: Free Monoids and Languages. Hon Min Book Co., Taichung, Taiwan (1991)
25. Shyr, H.J., Thierrin, G.: Ordered automata and associated languages. Tamsui Oxf. J. Math. Sci. **5**, 9–20 (1974)
26. Starke, P.H.: Abstrakte Automaten. Deutscher Verlag der Wissenschaften, Berlin (1969)
27. Truthe, B.: Generative capacity of contextual grammars with subregular selection languages. Fund. Inform. **180**, 1–28 (2021)

On Pumping Constants and Smallest Grammars for Context-Free Languages

Hermann Gruber[1] and Markus Holzer[2]($\boxtimes$)

[1] Planerio GmbH, Theresienhöhe 11A, 80538 Munich, Germany
h.gruber@planerio.de
[2] Institut für Informatik, Universität Giessen, Arndtstr. 2, 35392 Giessen, Germany
holzer@informatik.uni-giessen.de

Abstract. We study the relationship between the minimal context-free pumping constant of a context-free language and the size of the context-free grammar that generates it. For the size, we consider the sum of the lengths of the right-hand sides of the productions and the total number of symbols to write the productions, including the "$\rightarrow$" symbol in each production; the latter size concept is known in the literature as symbol complexity. We prove tight bounds for both size concepts. Furthermore, we apply our results to some open problems on the symbol complexity of languages. In particular, we show that for the language $L_n = \{a^n\}$ the symbol complexity is at least $6\log_4 n$ and at most $6\log_4 n + O(\frac{\log n}{\log \log n})$.

1 Introduction

Let $G = (N, T, P, S)$ be a *context-free grammar* (CFG), where N and T are disjoint alphabets of *nonterminals* and *terminals*, respectively, $S \in N$ is the *axiom*, and P is a finite set of *productions* of the form $A \rightarrow \alpha$, where $A \in N$ and $\alpha \in (N \cup T)^*$. As usual, the transitive closure of the derivation relation $\Rightarrow_G$ is written as $\Rightarrow_G^*$. If there is no danger of confusion, we simply write $\Rightarrow$ ($\Rightarrow^*$, respectively) instead of $\Rightarrow_G$ ($\Rightarrow_G^*$, respectively). The *language generated* by G is defined as

$$L(G) = \{\, w \in T^* \mid S \Rightarrow_G^* w \,\}.$$

For every context-free language the Bar-Hillel lemma [1] applies, which reads as follows:

Lemma 1. *Let L be a context-free language over Σ. Then, there is a constant p (depending on L) such that the following holds: If $z \in L$ and $|z| \geq p$, then there are words $u, v, w, x, y \in \Sigma^*$ such that $z = uvwxy$, $|vx| \geq 1$, $|vwx| \leq p$, and $uv^t wx^t y \in L$ for $t \geq 0$—it is then said that v and x can be (simultaneously) pumped in z.*

For a context-free language L, let $\mathtt{mpcf}(L)$ denote the minimal number p satisfying the conditions of Lemma 1. We find the following situation for context-free languages, which follows from the proof of the pumping lemma given in [11, Chapter 6]:

M. D. Jiménez López and G. Vaszil (Eds.): Erzsébet Csuhaj-Varjú Festschrift,
LNCS 15840, pp. 54–68, 2025.
https://doi.org/10.1007/978-3-031-97274-4_4

Theorem 2. *Let L be generated by the context-free grammar $G = (N, T, P, S)$. Then*

$$\texttt{mpcf}(L) \leq m^{2n+3},$$

where $n := |N|$ and $m := \max\{\, 2, |\alpha| \mid A \to \alpha \in P \,\}$.

If the given context-free grammar is in Chomsky normal form,[1] the proof in [13] yields the bound $\texttt{mpcf}(L) \leq 2^n$. Notice, however, that the conversion to normal form incurs a size blow-up in the worst case [14].

When considering linear context-free languages, the bound on the minimal pumping constant becomes linear as we will see next. A context-free grammar is said to be *linear context-free* (LIN) if the productions are of the form $A \to \alpha$, where $A \in N$ and $\alpha \in T^*(N \cup \{\varepsilon\})T^*$—here ε refers to the *empty word*. The pumping lemma for linear-context free languages reads like the pumping lemma for context-free languages, but with one exception: instead of $|vwx| \leq p$, now the condition $|uvxy| \leq p$ is required—see [13, page 143, Exercise 6.11]. For a linear context-free language L let $\texttt{mplin}(L)$ denote the minimal number p satisfying the conditions of the pumping lemma for linear context-free languages. The next result was shown in [7, Theorem 6]:

Theorem 3. *Let L be a* linear *context-free language generated by the linear context-free grammar $G = (N, T, P, S)$. Then*

$$\texttt{mplin}(L) \leq (m-1) \cdot n + 2,$$

where $n := |N|$ and $m := \max\{\, |\alpha| \mid A \to \alpha \in P \,\}$.

In the above theorems, the number of nonterminals and the maximal length of right-hand sides of the productions play a crucial *rôle*. Are there any other relations between the minimal pumping constant of a context-free language and some descriptional complexity measure of context-free languages that is closer to the size of the grammar that generates the language in question? We partially answer this question in the forthcoming.

2   Results on Minimal Context-Free Pumping Constants

Several concurrent notions to measure the actual *size* of a context-free grammar have been proposed in the literature, see, e.g., [2,6,8,11,12,15]. The most intuitive ways to measure the size of a context-free grammar, as they appear in textbooks on automata theory, are

1. to count the sum of the lengths of the right-hand sides of the rules, or
2. to count the total number of symbols to write down the rules, including the "$\to$" symbol in each production.

---

[1] A context-free grammar $G = (N, T, P, S)$ is in *Chomsky normal form* if every production is either of the form $A \to a$ or $A \to BC$ or $S \to \varepsilon$, for $A, B, C \in N$ and $a \in T$.

The latter way to measure the size of a context-free grammar facilitates telling apart the start and end of each production, and, originating from [8]. This seems to be the oldest explicit notion of grammar size. The recent literature in the field of descriptional complexity [3,10] refers to this measure as the *symbol complexity* of a context-free grammar. The convention to use the sum of the length of the right-hand sides of the productions has been adopted by papers dealing with the *smallest grammar problem*. In that optimization problem, the task is, given word w, to find a context-free grammar G, such that (i) the grammar G generates the single word w and (ii) the size of G is as small as possible. The first systematic study of grammar-based compression [2] proved that the size of G is always in $\Omega(\log |w|)$; our results below can be seen as an extension of that result to general context-free grammars.

Table 1. OEIS sequences.

	OEIS	Sequence
P. Halmos	A000792 (offset 1)	1, 2, 3, 4, 6, 9, 12, 18, 27, 36, 54, 81, 108, 162, 243, 324, 486, 729, 972, 1458, ...
J. Derbyshire	A193286	1, 2, 3, 4, 5, 6, 7, 9, 12, 16, 20, 25, 30, 36, 48, 64, 80, 100, 125, 150, 192, 256, 320, 400, 500, 625, 768, 1024, 1280, 1600, 2000, 2500, 3125, ...

We start our investigation by determining a tight bound on the minimal context-free pumping constant in terms of the sum of the lengths of the right-hand sides of the grammar. For this, we need some properties of a function ρ which became known as the maximum product function w.r.t. a partition of the number [9], that is, the value $\rho(n)$ is obtained by maximizing the product $\prod_{i=0}^{h} k_i$ of positive integers k_i subject to the condition $\sum_{i=0}^{h} k_i = n$, for $1 \leq k_i \leq n$ with $0 \leq i \leq h$. Moreover, $\rho(n)$ obeys a recursive relation, namely, $\rho(1) = 1$, $\rho(2) = 2$, $\rho(3) = 3$, $\rho(4) = 4$, and $\rho(n) = 3 \cdot \rho(n-3)$, for $n > 4$. For further uses of this function, see sequence A000792 (with offset 1) in "The On-line Encyclopedia of Integer Sequences" (OEIS)—Table 1. This function became also known in graph theory as the Moon-Moser bound [18], see also [17]. For the proofs to come, we define $\rho(0) = 0$, which is different from the convention used for A000792. Then the following statement on the ρ function is immediate: (i) the recurrence is a literal translation of the definition of the ρ function as the maximum value of the product subject to the sum condition, and (ii) the closed formula follows since one takes as many of the k_i's as possible to be 3 and then use one or two 2's only; larger k_i's with $k_i \geq 4$ can be replaced by 2 and $k_i - 2$, since $2(k_i - 2) \geq k_i$ for $k_i \geq 4$, in order to increase the product value. Thus, we obtain the following result.

Lemma 4. *For a positive integer n, let the function $\rho(n)$ be given by the recurrence $\rho(i) = i$ for $0 \leq i \leq 3$, and*

$$\rho(n) = \max_{1 \leq k < n} \{k \cdot \rho(n - k)\} \quad \text{for } n \geq 4.$$

Then

$$\rho(n) = \begin{cases} 0, & \text{for } n = 0 \\ 1, & \text{for } n = 1 \\ 3^{\frac{n}{3}}, & \text{for } n \equiv 0 \pmod 3 \text{ and } n \geq 1 \\ 4 \cdot 3^{\frac{n-4}{3}}, & \text{for } n \equiv 1 \pmod 3 \text{ and } n \geq 4 \\ 2 \cdot 3^{\frac{n-2}{3}}, & \text{for } n \equiv 2 \pmod 3. \end{cases}$$

Also, $\rho(n - k) + k \leq \rho(n)$, for $n \geq 1$, and a positive integer k with $1 \leq k \leq n$. $\square$

Now we are ready for the tight upper bound on the minimal pumping constant of context-free languages in terms of the sum of the lengths of the right-hand sides of the grammar.

Theorem 5. *Let L be generated by the context-free grammar $G = (N, T, P, S)$, where L is not empty. Then*

$$\mathit{mpcf}(L) \leq \rho(m_G) + 1,$$

where $m_G := \sum_{(A \to \alpha) \in P} |\alpha|$ and ρ is the function from Lemma 4. Furthermore, for every $m > 0$, there exists a context-free grammar G_m witnessing that this bound is tight.

Proof. We prove the upper bound using the following statement: Let w be a word in $L(G)$; if w cannot be pumped, then $|w| \leq \rho(m_G)$.

We prove this statement by lexicographic induction on the parameter m_G and the minimum depth of a parse tree T in G for w. If $d(T)$ denotes the depth of parse tree T, then for the base case of the induction we have a grammar G with $m_G = 0$, and a parse tree of depth 1. In the latter, the root is labeled by the start symbol S, and there are $|w| = m_G$ terminal leaves. We obtain $\rho(0) = 0$, thus establishing the base case of the induction.

For the induction step, assume that the claim holds for all grammars G' with $m_{G'} < m_G$ and, in G, for all words admitting a parse tree of depth at most $d-1$. We consider two cases. Consider a parse tree T of depth d for w:

Case 1. There is a path in T from the root to some leaf labeled with a terminal symbol, such that the start symbol S appears at least twice.

The start symbol appears as a label at the root of the parse tree. There is also a proper subtree of T of depth at most $d-1$, whose root is labeled by S. This subtree is parse tree of a word y according to the grammar G, and y is a contiguous subword of w.

Case 1a. Assume $y = w$. Then we have a contradiction, since we chose w as a word not admitting a parse tree of depth less than d.

Case 1b. Otherwise, assume $y \neq w$. Then we can write $w = xyr$ with $|x| > 0$
or $|y| > 0$, and $S \Rightarrow^* xSz$ as well as $S \Rightarrow^* y$. Thus, we have $x^i y z^i \in L(G)$,
for all $i > 0$, and w can be pumped. Similarly, we have a contradiction
also in this subcase.

Case 2. On every path in T from the root to some leaf labeled with a terminal
symbol, the start symbol S appears only once.

There is a production $p = (S \rightarrow \beta)$ that corresponds to the root of the parse
tree and its children.

Case 2a. Right-hand side β contains at least one terminal symbol. Let p'
denote the production obtained from p by deleting the first terminal symbol t on its right-hand side, and let G' denote the grammar obtained from
G by replacing the production p with p'. Then, $m_{G'} = m_G - 1$, and there
is a word w' such that w' is obtained from w by deleting a single letter,
and w' admits a parse tree of depth d according to G'. By the induction
assumption, $|w| = |w'| + 1 \leq \rho(m_G - 1) + 1$. Recall from Lemma 4 that we
have $\rho(m_G - 1) + 1 \leq \rho(m_G)$, thus establishing the bound in this subcase.

Case 2b. Right-hand side β contains only nonterminal symbols. If there are j
occurrences of nonterminals in β, then there are j subtrees of depth at
most $d - 1$ whose leaves spell out a subword of w each. Together these
subwords make up the word w. Notice that neither of the subtrees uses
the variable S, and also not p. If B is the nonterminal label of such a
subtree, it is a parse tree of the context-free grammar

$$G_B = (N \setminus \{S\}, T, P \setminus \{p\}, B).$$

We next show that we can assume $1 \leq j < m_G$: because $|\beta| = j$ and $|\beta| \leq$
m_G, we have $m_G - j \geq 0$. Also, if $j = m_G$, then no terminals can appear on
the right side of any production. It follows that $|w| = 0$. Since $d(T) \geq 2$,
we must have $j \geq 1$. Thus, $1 \leq j < m_G$ if w is not empty.

By the induction assumption, each of the j occurrences of a nonterminal
generates a contiguous substring of w, and each such substring has length
at most $\rho(m_G - j)$. Hence we obtain

$$|w| \leq \sum_{i=1}^{j} \rho(m_G - j), \text{ for some } j \text{ with } 1 \leq j < m_G.$$

Observe, that all summands in the above sum are identical, so we can
rewrite the inequality as $|w| \leq j \cdot \rho(m_G - j)$. In turn, by Lemma 4, we
have $j \cdot \rho(m_G - j) \leq \rho(m_G)$ for each such j. Combining the last two
inequalities yields $|w| \leq \rho(m_G)$ also in this case, and the proof of the
upper estimate is completed.

Regarding the grammars witnessing that the bound is tight, let us first con-
sider an example with $m = 13$. With $n = \lfloor \frac{m}{3} \rfloor + 1 = 5$, grammar G_{13} is given
with variables $A_1, A_2, \ldots A_5$, alphabet $\Sigma = \{a\}$, and productions

$$A_i \rightarrow A_{i+1} A_{i+1} A_{i+1}, \quad \text{for } 1 \leq i \leq 3,$$
$$A_4 \rightarrow A_5 A_5,$$

and

$$A_5 \to aa,$$

and the axiom A_1. The pattern generalizes as follows: grammar G_m has n variables, where $n = \frac{m}{3}$ when m is divisible by 3, and $n = \lfloor \frac{m}{3} \rfloor + 1$ otherwise; of these variables, all but the last two produce 3 symbols each. When $m \equiv 1$ (mod 3) and $m \geq 4$, the last two variables produce only 2 symbols each; when $m \equiv 2$ (mod 3), then the penultimate variable produces 3 symbols, and the last variable produces 2 symbols; when $m \equiv 0 \mod 3$, then also the last two variables produce 3 symbols each. For the edge case $m = 1$, we have a single production that produces a single terminal symbol. It is readily seen that G_m generates a single unary word of length $\rho(m)$. □

Let us quickly consider the case of linear context-free languages. Regarding the sum of the lengths of the right-hand sides of the grammar, we can proceed as in the proof of Theorem 5, but the analysis degenerates to some easy cases. The proof is left as an exercise to the reader; we also note that the new bound implies the previous one from [7, Theorem. 6].

Theorem 6. *Let the language L be generated by the linear context-free grammar $G = (N, T, P, S)$, where L is not empty. Then*

$$mplin(L) \leq m_G + 1,$$

where $m_G := \sum_{(A \to \alpha) \in P} |\alpha|$. Furthermore, for every $m \geq 1$, there exists a linear context-free grammar G_m witnessing that this bound is tight. □

Next let us consider the *symbol complexity* of a grammar, which counts the total number of symbols to write down the rules, including the "→" symbol in each production. As before, we first state a technical lemma, which relates to an integer sequence. The latter is the solution to a recreational mathematical puzzle, described in the following. A text editing software allows for the following "keystroke" actions:

- typing a single character,
- selecting all text (Ctrl+A on Windows and Linux operating systems, Cmd+A for Mac users),
- copying the selection to the clipboard (Ctrl+C on Windows and Linux operating systems, Cmd+C for Mac users), and
- pasting the clipboard contents (Ctrl+V on Windows and Linux operating systems, Cmd+V for Mac users).

The keyboard problem asks, given a positive integer n, for the maximum amount of characters that can be produced using n keystroke actions. Note that the copy command deselects the buffer text, i.e., we perform copying with replacement, which means that the first paste, or simple insertion, after copying, eliminates, overwrites, or otherwise renders obsolete the currently existing text output. For instance, the 11-keystroke sequence $aaaACVVACVa$ (simple character a and select, copy, and paste simplified) outputs 7 characters—the buffer change is depicted by the sequence

$$\varepsilon \to^a a \to^a aa \to^a aaa \to^A aaa \to^C aaa \to^V aaa \to^V aaa\, aaa$$
$$\to^A aaa\, aaa \to^C aaa\, aaa \to^V aaa\, aaa \to^a aaa\, aaa\, a.$$

For 11 keystrokes the maximum amount of characters obtainable is 20—by the keystroke sequence $aaaaaACVVVV$. A solution of the problem can be found in [19], and is named $\sigma(n)$—see Table 1 and for more information consult A193286 in OEIS. The value $\sigma(n)$ is obtained by maximizing the product $\prod_{i=0}^{h} k_i$ of positive integers k_i subject to the condition $\sum_{i=0}^{h} k_i = n - 2h$, where h is the number of copy operations. Moreover, $\sigma(n)$ obeys a recursive relation: we have $\sigma(n) = n$ for $1 \le n \le 7$; a few sporadic values occur with $\sigma(8) = 3^2$, $\sigma(12) = 5^2$, $\sigma(13) = 6 \cdot 5$, $\sigma(19) = 5^3$, $\sigma(20) = 6 \cdot 5^2$, $\sigma(26) = 5^4$, and $\sigma(33) = 5^5$. For all other n, the formula $\sigma(n) = 4 \cdot \sigma(n - 6)$ applies; see [19] for further background and explanation. We obtain the following result (again, we define that $\sigma(0) = 0$):

Lemma 7. *For a positive integer n, let the function $\sigma(n)$ be given by the recurrence $\sigma(n) = n$, for $0 \le n \le 7$, and*

$$\sigma(n) = \max_{1 \le k < n-2} \{k \cdot \sigma(n - k - 2)\}, \quad \text{for } n \ge 8.$$

Then

$$\sigma(n) = \begin{cases} 5^2 \cdot 4^{(n-12)/6}, & \text{for } n \bmod 6 \equiv 0 \text{ and } n \ge 12 \\ 5^3 \cdot 4^{(n-19)/6}, & \text{for } n \bmod 6 \equiv 1 \text{ and } n \ge 19 \\ 5^4 \cdot 4^{(n-26)/6}, & \text{for } n \bmod 6 \equiv 2 \text{ and } n \ge 26 \\ 5^5 \cdot 4^{(n-33)/6}, & \text{for } n \bmod 6 \equiv 3 \text{ and } n \ge 33 \\ 4^{(n+2)/6}, & \text{for } n \bmod 6 \equiv 4 \\ 5 \cdot 4^{(n-5)/6}, & \text{for } n \bmod 6 \equiv 5. \end{cases}$$

The finite number of remaining cases for $\sigma(n)$ can be found in Table 1 under A193286. □

Proof. The recurrence on $\sigma(n)$ is a literal translation of its definition as the maximum product $\prod_{i=0}^{h} k_i$ of positive integers k_i subject to the condition $\sum_{i=0}^{h} k_i = n - 2h$, where h is the number of multiplications used.

Provided n is large enough, we immediately obtain a formula for $\sigma(n)$ for each remainder of n modulo 6 from the original recurrence $\sigma(n) = 4 \cdot \sigma(n - 6)$, together with the sporadic values given above. The tedious details are left to the reader. □

Next we study a recurrence, which looks very similar to the recurrence of σ, with a few slight exceptions:

Theorem 8. *For an integer $n \geq 2$, let the function $\mu(n)$ be given by the recurrence $\mu(2) = 0$, $\mu(3) = 1$, $\mu(4) = 2$, $\mu(5) = 3$, and*

$$\mu(n) = \max\{\, \mu(n-1)+1, \, \max_{2 \leq k \leq n-4}\{k \cdot \mu(n-k-2)\}\,\}, \text{ for } n \geq 6.$$

Then $\mu(n+2) = \sigma(n)$, for $n \geq 0$. In particular, we have

$$\mu(n) = \begin{cases} 5^0 \cdot 4^{n/6}, & \text{for } n \bmod 6 \equiv 0 \text{ and } n \geq 6 \\ 5^1 \cdot 4^{(n-7)/6}, & \text{for } n \bmod 6 \equiv 1 \text{ and } n \geq 7, \\ 5^2 \cdot 4^{(n-14)/6}, & \text{for } n \bmod 6 \equiv 2 \text{ and } n \geq 14 \\ 5^3 \cdot 4^{(n-21)/6}, & \text{for } n \bmod 6 \equiv 3 \text{ and } n \geq 21 \\ 5^4 \cdot 4^{(n-28)/6}, & \text{for } n \bmod 6 \equiv 4 \text{ and } n \geq 28 \\ 5^5 \cdot 4^{(n-35)/6}, & \text{for } n \bmod 6 \equiv 5 \text{ and } n \geq 35. \end{cases}$$

The finite number of remaining cases for $\mu(n)$ can be found in Table 1 under A193286, taking care of the offset by two.

Proof. First, reconsider the recurrence for the σ function as stated in Lemma 7. One observes that $\sigma(n-1)+1 \leq \sigma(n)$, for $n \geq 2$. This is due to the fact that $\sigma(n)$ grows exponentially for $n \geq 33$ and the remaining finite number of cases can be verified by inspecting the appropriate sequence given in Table 1. Thus, for $n \geq 8$, we can safely replace the σ-recurrence with

$$\sigma(n) = \max\{\, \sigma(n-1)+1, \, \max_{1 \leq k < n-2}\{k \cdot \sigma(n-k-2)\}\,\}.$$

Now we are ready to show that $\mu(n+2) = \sigma(n)$, for $n \geq 0$ by induction on n. Easy calculations show that $\mu(n+2) = \sigma(n)$, for $0 \leq n \leq 7$; these are left to the reader. Then, for the induction step, let $n \geq 8$. For μ, the recurrence applies, namely

$$\mu(n+2) = \max\{\, \mu((n+2)-1)+1, \, \max_{2 \leq k \leq (n+2)-4}\{k \cdot \mu((n+2)-k-2)\}\,\}$$

$$= \max\{\, \mu(n+1)+1, \, \max_{2 \leq k \leq n-2}\{k \cdot \mu(n-k)\}\,\}.$$

For the inner maximum, we first show that the range for the variable k can be extended to include $k = 1$ without altering the value of the maximum: By induction, we know that μ is strictly monotonically increasing for values up to $n-1$, because of the corresponding property of σ. Thus,

$$2 \cdot \mu(n-2) \geq 2 \cdot (\mu(n-1)+1) > 1 \cdot \mu(n-1),$$

and hence

$$\max_{2 \leq k \leq n-2}\{k \cdot \mu(n-k)\} = \max_{1 \leq k \leq n-2}\{k \cdot \mu(n-k)\}.$$

The term $\max_{1 \leq k \leq n-2}\{k \cdot \mu(n-k)\}$, when spelled out, reads as

$$\max\{\, 1 \cdot \mu(n-1), 2 \cdot \mu(n-2), \ldots, (n-3) \cdot \mu(3), (n-2) \cdot \mu(2)\,\}.$$

Since $\mu(2) = 0$ by definition, this simplifies to $\max_{1 \leq k \leq n-3}\{k \cdot \mu(n-k)\}$. Then, by the induction hypothesis, the μ-terms can be replaced by appropriate σ-terms. Hence, the term is $\max_{1 \leq k \leq n-3}\{k \cdot \sigma(n-k-2)\}$. Next, we combine this term with the outer maximum, which means that

$$\mu(n+2) = \max\{\,\mu(n+1)+1, \max_{1 \leq k \leq n-2}\{k \cdot \mu(n-k)\}\,\}$$

$$= \max\{\,\sigma(n-1)+1, \max_{1 \leq k \leq n-3}\{k \cdot \sigma(n-k-2)\}\,\}$$

$$= \sigma(n),$$

where we have applied the alternative recurrence for σ with two nested maximum operations. This completes the induction proof.

To finish the proof of the theorem, evaluating the formula for σ from Lemma 7 at $n-2$ somewhat magically reveals a pattern:

$$\mu(n) = \sigma(n-2) = \begin{cases} 5^0 \cdot 4^{n/6}, & \text{for } n \bmod 6 \equiv 0 \\ 5^1 \cdot 4^{(n-7)/6}, & \text{for } n \bmod 6 \equiv 1 \text{ and } n \geq 7, \\ 5^2 \cdot 4^{(n-14)/6}, & \text{for } n \bmod 6 \equiv 2 \text{ and } n \geq 14 \\ 5^3 \cdot 4^{(n-21)/6}, & \text{for } n \bmod 6 \equiv 3 \text{ and } n \geq 21 \\ 5^4 \cdot 4^{(n-28)/6}, & \text{for } n \bmod 6 \equiv 4 \text{ and } n \geq 28 \\ 5^5 \cdot 4^{(n-35)/6}, & \text{for } n \bmod 6 \equiv 5 \text{ and } n \geq 35, \end{cases}$$

and the proof is completed.   □

Observe, that the pattern mentioned above simplifies to

$$\mu(n) = 5^{n \bmod 6} \cdot 4^{(n-n_0)/6} \text{ for all } n \geq n_0, \text{ with } n_0 = 7 \cdot (n \bmod 6) \quad (1)$$

and will be later used in order to obtain a lower bound on the symbol complexity of the language $L_n = \{a^n\}$ in Theorem 13.

Now, we are ready to estimate the minimal context-free pumping constant in terms of the symbol complexity of the underlying context-free grammar.

Theorem 9. *Let L be generated by the context-free grammar $G = (N, T, P, S)$, where L is not empty. Then*

$$mpcf(L) \leq \mu(s_G) + 1,$$

where $s_G := \sum_{(A \to \alpha) \in P}(2 + |\alpha|)$ and μ is the function from Theorem 8. Furthermore, for every $s \geq 2$, there exists a context-free grammar G_s witnessing that this bound is tight.

Proof. For the upper bound, the proof runs essentially along the same lines as the proof of Theorem 5, but instead of the parameter m_G, we express the bound in terms of s_G.

In **Case 2b** of the proof, some care has to be taken. If the right-hand side β of the production $p = (S \to \beta)$ consists of a single variable A, then let G' denote the grammar obtained from G by removing p and using A as the start symbol. The grammar G' has $s_G - 3$ symbols, and generates the same word w with a parse tree of lower depth.

So, the interesting subcase of **Case 2b** that remains is $|\beta| \geq 2$. Here, we estimate $|\beta| \leq s_G - 4$, taking the arrow symbol and the left-hand side of the production p into account, as well as the fact that, in **Case 2b**, there is at least one other production different from p. We note for later reference that estimate $2 \leq |\beta| \leq s_G - 4$ implies that this subcase can only appear for $s_G \geq 6$. Also, the production p accounts for $|\beta| + 2$ symbols, so the recurrent bound changes to $|w| \leq j \cdot \sigma(s_G - 2 - j)$, with $2 \leq j \leq s_G - 4$. Altogether, we obtain the following recurrence, with start value $\mu(2) = 0$:

$$\mu(s) = \begin{cases} 0, & \text{if } s = 2 \\ \mu(s-1) + 1, & \text{if } 3 \leq s \leq 5, \\ \max\{\,\mu(s-1) + 1, \max_{2 \leq j \leq s-4}\{j \cdot \mu(s-2-j)\}\,\}, & \text{if } s \geq 6, \end{cases}$$

obtaining the recurrence already studied in Theorem 8.

For the lower bound, we can construct a context-free grammar G_s generating a single unary word, where the lengths of the right-hand sides are as in the factorization of $\sigma(s)$ given in the formula. $\square$

For linear context-free grammars, the bound is again very simple—the tight bound is attained by grammars with a single production. The straightforward proof is omitted.

Theorem 10. *Let the language L be generated by the linear context-free grammar $G = (N, T, P, S)$, where L is not empty. Then*

$$mplin(L) \leq s_G - 1,$$

where $s_G := \sum_{(A \to \alpha) \in P}(2 + |\alpha|)$. Furthermore, for every $s \geq 2$, there exists a linear context-free grammar G_s witnessing that this bound is tight. $\square$

3   More on the Symbol Complexity of Languages and Operations

In this section, we apply these new insights to questions regarding descriptional complexity of context-free languages and language operations. In [3], results are presented which show how the required number of variables, productions and symbols can behave under the operations union, concatenation and star. The recurring question is the following: what is the range of complexities that can be attained by applying a language operation to languages of complexity m and n? We make this more precise for the symbol complexity under the concatenation operation. Following [3] define

$$g_{\cdot}^{\mathrm{symb}}(m, n) = \{\,\mathrm{symb}(L_1 \cdot L_2) \mid \mathrm{symb}(L_1) = m \text{ and } \mathrm{symb}(L_2) = n\,\},$$

where $\mathrm{symb}(L)$ refers to the symbol complexity of L, which is the minimum value among the symbol complexity of all context-free grammars generating L. Note that $g^{\mathrm{symb}}(m, n) = g^{\mathrm{symb}}(n, m)$ for all m and n.

Compared to the number of variables [5] or productions [4], the symbol complexity of context-free languages seems to be more difficult to tackle. For example, although it is known that all languages of symbol complexity 3 consist of a single word of length 1, there are gaps in the known values for $g^{\mathrm{symb}}(3, n)$, see [10, pp. 106f.]—see Table 2.

Table 2. Symbol complexity of concatenation.

n	3	4	5	6	≥ 7
$g^{\mathrm{symb}}(3, n)$	$\{4\}$	$\{5\}$	$\{6, 7\}$	$7 \in \cdot$ $\cdot \not\ni 0, 1, \ldots, 6, 14, 15, \ldots$	$\cdot \not\ni 0, 1, \ldots, 6, n + 8, n + 9, \ldots$

Let $L_n = \{a^n\}$, for $n \geq 0$. With the help of this language we can prove the following result:

Theorem 11. *For $n \geq 2$, we have $g^{\mathrm{symb}}(3, n) \ni n + 1$.*

Proof. The cases $n \leq 6$ are treated in [10], so we assume $n \geq 7$. Consider the unary singleton languages $L_k = \{a^k\}$, for $k \geq 1$. Then by Theorem 9, we have $\mathrm{symb}(L_{\mu(n)}) = n$, and in particular $\mathrm{symb}(L_1) = 3$. Again by Theorem 9, the concatenation of these two languages cannot be generated with n symbols. On the other hand, as observed in [8], we have $\mathrm{symb}(L_{k+1}) \leq \mathrm{symb}(L_k) + 1$, for all $k \geq 0$, thus $\mathrm{symb}(L_{\mu(n)+1}) = n + 1$, as desired.   □

With the knowledge of $\mathrm{symb}(L_{\mu(n)})$ and $\mathrm{symb}(L_{\mu(n)+1})$, one can sporadically fill other gaps in the known values of $g^{\mathrm{symb}}(m, n)$—in particular when m and n are small.

Theorem 12. *For $m, n \geq 3$ with $m + n \leq 12$, we have $g^{\mathrm{symb}}(m, n) \ni m + n - 2$.*

Proof. For $1 \leq k \leq 7$, we have $\mathrm{symb}(L_k) = k + 2$. For $k = 8$, we have $\mu(9) + 1 = 8$, which implies that $\mathrm{symb}(L_k) = k + 2$ also in that case. Thus, we can use L_{m-2} and L_{n-2} as witness languages—their concatenation L_{m+n-4} requires $m + n - 2$ symbols.   □

Only one of the values in the above theorem, namely $g^{\mathrm{symb}}(4, 5) \ni 7$, had been previously determined in [10]. To give a final example, we evaluate $\mathrm{symb}(L_4) = 6$, $\mathrm{symb}(L_8) = \mathrm{symb}(L_9) = 10$, $\mathrm{symb}(L_{12}) = 11$ and $\mathrm{symb}(L_{13}) = 12$, to obtain $g^{\mathrm{symb}}(6, 10) \supseteq \{11, 12\}$.

In the remainder of this section we are interested in the question, what is the symbol complexity of $L_n = \{a^n\}$ in general? An exact characterization may be out of reach. In [2], a clever construction is given, which, among other ingredients, works by recursively tripling the word length. However, in that paper, the goal is to minimize the sum of lengths of the right-hand sides in the grammar. For symbol complexity, the strategy needs to be adapted, so that it is based on quadrupling.

Theorem 13. *Let $n \geq 1$ be an integer and $L_n = \{a^n\}$. Then*

$$6 \log_4 n \leq symb(L_n) \leq 6 \log_4 n + O\left(\frac{\log n}{\log \log n}\right).$$

Proof. The lower bound can be derived from Eq. 1 and Theorem 9 for large enough s: the minimum size is attained when $\mu(s) = n$ for some s. Then

$$n = 5^{s \bmod 6} \cdot 4^{(s-s_0)/6} \text{ with } s_0 = 7 \cdot (s \bmod 6),$$

for large enough s. By applying the logarithm in base 4 to the above formula, with $r = s \bmod 6$, we obtain:

$$\log_4(n) = (\log_4 5) \cdot r + \frac{s - 7r}{6}.$$

Multiplying by six and solving for s results in

$$s = 6 \log_4(n) - (6 \log_4 5) \cdot r + 7r = 6 \log_4(n) + (7 - \underbrace{6 \log_4 5}_{\approx 6.958}) \cdot r.$$

The right-hand side is minimal when $r = 0$, so $s \geq 6 \log_4(n)$, which is the desired lower bound.

For the upper bound, the algorithm is analogous to the proof of [2, Theorem. 11]. Let b be a power 4, that is, $b = 4^j$, to be fixed later. The idea is to represent n in base b as $n = \sum_{i=0}^{t} d_i b^i$, or merely, using Horner's rule,

$$n = (((d_t b + d_{t-1})b + d_{t_2})b + \cdots + d_1)b + d_0.$$

Here, $t = \lfloor \log_b n \rfloor$.

First, we introduce nonterminals $T_1, T_2, \ldots, T_{b-1}$ with productions $T_1 \to a$ and $T_{i+1} \to aT_i$, for $1 \leq i < b - 1$, so we can generate strings of each short length at the cost of at most $4b$ symbols, without the need for extra symbols in the construction to come.

We prove by induction on n that for $n \geq 1$, we can generate a^n with at most $(6j + 8)t$ additional symbols—in addition to those productions generating short strings, which we just have introduced. The cases with $n \leq b - 1$ are readily verified, since $t = 0$ then, and we need no additional symbols in that case.

Now, assume the claim holds for all integers up to $n - 1$. Let $q = \lfloor n/b \rfloor$ and $r = n \bmod b$, then $n = bq + r$ and $t - 1 = \lfloor \log_b q \rfloor$. Using the inductive hypothesis, there is a grammar G_q generating a^q with $(6j + 8)(t - 1)$ additional symbols. Let $G_q = (N_q, \{a\}, P_q, S_q)$, where the set of nonterminals N_q contains already $T_1, T_2, \ldots, T_{b-1}$ and the set of productions P_q the corresponding T_i rules as described above.

We construct the context-free grammar $G_n = (N_n, \{a\}, P_n, S_n)$ with

$$N_n = N_q \cup \{X_1, X_2, \ldots, X_j\} \cup \{S_n\},$$

where $X_1, X_2, \ldots, X_j$ and S_n are new pairwise different nonterminals not contained in N_q. Moreover P_n contains all rules from P_q and in addition

$$S_n \to X_j T_r,$$
$$X_i \to X_{i-1} X_{i-1} X_{i-1} X_{i-1}, \text{ for } 2 \le i \le j$$

as well as

$$X_1 \to S_q.$$

Then, the variable X_j generates a unary word of length $q \cdot 4^j$, and the nonterminal S_n is responsible for adding length r to this. In the induction step, we introduced at most $4 + 6j + 4 = 6j + 8$ new symbols, as desired.

Altogether, the grammar thus constructed requires at most $4b + (6j + 8)t$ symbols. With $b = 4^j$ and $t \le \log_b n$, we obtain

$$\texttt{symb}(G_n) \le 4^{j+1} + 6j \log_{4^j} n + 8 \log_{4^j} n$$
$$= 4^{j+1} + 6 \log_4 n + \frac{8}{j} \log_4 n.$$

Setting $j = \frac{1}{2} \lfloor \log_4 \log_4 n \rfloor$, this evaluates to $6 \log_4 n + O(\frac{\log n}{\log \log n})$ as desired. $\square$

Notice that in the above proof, we have $j > 1$ only for $n \ge 4^{4^4} = 2^{512}$, which is approximately 1.3×10^{154}.

Another interesting aspect is that the grammar constructed in the proof of [2, Theorem. 11] has a number of $\log_3(n) + o(\log n)$ productions, and the sum of the lengths of the right-hand sides is $3 \cdot \log_3(n)$. This accounts for a symbol complexity of $5 \cdot \log_3(n) + o(\log n)$, which is off the optimal bound by a factor(!) of roughly $\frac{5 \cdot \log_3 n}{6 \cdot \log_4 n} \approx 1.05$. *Vice versa*, let us count the sum of the right-hand sides of the grammar we constructed in Theorem 13: the sum is $4 \cdot \log_4 n + o(\log n)$, whereas the optimal bound is approximately $3 \cdot \log_3 n$, as proved in [2, Theorem. 11]. Regarding the sum of the right-hand sides, our new grammar is off the optimal bound by a factor of $\frac{4 \cdot \log_4 n}{3 \cdot \log_3 n} \approx 1.06$. This nicely illustrates how already a small variation in the definition of *size* of a context-free grammar can largely affect what kinds of grammars we consider optimal: will a strategy based on tripling the word length, or rather, one based on quadrupling, yield the smallest grammar?

We observe a similar discrepancy when restricting to grammars in Chomsky normal form, as done, e.g., in [16]. Let us again consider the sum of the right-hand sides. It is plausible that a smallest grammar G in Chomsky normal form for L_n has $m_G = 1 + 2 \cdot \log_2 n$ when n is a power of two, and $\frac{2 \cdot \log_2 n}{3 \cdot \log_3 n} \approx 1.06$.

Acknowledgment. Thanks to Christian Rauch for his comments on an earlier draft of this paper. Moreover, the authors thank the anonymous referees for their helpful comments that improved the presentation and quality of this paper.

References

1. Bar-Hillel, Y., Perles, M., Shamir, E.: On formal properties of simple phrase structure grammars. Zeitschrift für Phonetik, Sprachwissenschaft und Kommunikationsforschung **14**, 143–177 (1961). https://doi.org/10.1524/stuf.1961.14.14.143
2. Charikar, M., et al.: The smallest grammar problem. IEEE Trans. Inf. Theory **51**(7), 2554–2576 (2005). https://doi.org/10.1109/TIT.2005.850116
3. Dassow, J.: Descriptional complexity and operations – two non-classical cases. In: Pighizzini, G., Câmpeanu, C. (eds.) DCFS 2017. LNCS, vol. 10316, pp. 33–44. Springer, Cham (2017). https://doi.org/10.1007/978-3-319-60252-3_3
4. Dassow, J., Harbich, R.: Production complexity of some operations on context-free languages. In: Kutrib, M., Moreira, N., Reis, R. (eds.) DCFS 2012. LNCS, vol. 7386, pp. 141–154. Springer, Heidelberg (2012). https://doi.org/10.1007/978-3-642-31623-4_11
5. Dassow, J., Stiebe, R.: Nonterminal complexity of some operations on context-free languages. Fund. Inform. **83**(1–2), 35–49 (2008). https://doi.org/10.3233/FUN-2008-831-205
6. Ginsburg, S., Lynch, N.: Size complexity in context-free grammars forms. J. ACM **23**(4), 582–598 (1976). https://doi.org/10.1145/321556.321560
7. Gruber, H., Holzer, M., Rauch, C.: The pumping lemma for context-free languages is undecidable. In: Day, J.D., Manea, F. (eds.) Proceedings of the 28th International Conference on Developments in Language Theory. LNCS, vol. 14791, pp. 141–155. Springer, Göttingen, Germany, August 2024. https://doi.org/10.1007/978-3-031-66159-4_11
8. Gruska, J.: On the size of context-free grammars. Kybernetika **8**(3), 213–218 (1972)
9. Halmos, P.: Problems for Mathematicians, Young and Old. No. 12 in The Dolciani Mathematical Expositions. Mathematical Association of America (1991)
10. Harbich, R.: Regel- und Symbolkomplexität kontextfreier Sprachen unter ausgewählten Operationen. Ph.D. thesis, Otto-von-Guericke University Magdeburg, Germany (2019). https://doi.org/10.25673/32915
11. Harrison, M.A.: Introduction to Formal Language Theory. Addison-Wesley (1978)
12. Harrison, M.A., Yehudai, A.: Eliminating null rules in linear time. Comput. J. **24**(2), 156–161 (1981). https://doi.org/10.1093/comjnl/24.2.156
13. Hopcroft, J.E., Ullman, J.D.: Introduction to Automata Theory, Languages and Computation. Addison-Wesley (1979)
14. Lange, M., Leiß, H.: To CNF or not to CNF? An efficient yet presentable version of the CYK algorithm. Informatica Didactica **8** (2009)
15. Mengel, S., Vinall-Smeeth, H.: A lower bound on unambiguous context free grammars via communication complexity. Proc. ACM Manag. Data **3**(2), 1–19 (2025). https://doi.org/10.1145/3725225
16. Mieno, T., Inenaga, S., Horiyama, T.: RePair grammars are the smallest grammars for Fibonacci words. In: Bannai, H., Holub, J. (eds.) Proceedings of the 33rd Annual Symposium on Combinatorial Pattern Matching. Leibniz International Proceedings in Informatics, vol. 223, pp. 26:1–26:17. Schloss Dagstuhl–Leibniz-Zentrum für Informatik (2022). https://doi.org/10.4230/LIPICS.CPM.2022.26
17. Miller, R.E., Muller, D.E.: A problem of maximum consistent subsets. Research Report RC-240, IBM Research Center, Yorktown Heights, New York, USA, March 1960
18. Moon, J.W., Moser, L.: On cliques in graphs. Israel J. Math. **3**, 23–25 (1965). https://doi.org/10.1007/BF02760024

19. Rowell, J.T.: Solution sequences for the keyboard problem and its generalizations. J. Integer Sequences **18**(10) (2015)

Centralized Versions of Jumping Finite Automata

Alexander Meduna$^{(\boxtimes)}$ and Zdeněk Foltýn

Department of Information Systems, Faculty of Information Technology, Brno
University of Technology, Božetěchova 1/2, 612 66 Brno, Czech Republic
meduna@fit.vutbr.cz, xfolty20@stud.fit.vutbr.cz

Abstract. The present paper introduces centralized versions of jumping
finite automata and gives the principal reason for their introduction in
terms of today's discontinuous computation in practice. In essence, a
centralized version, C, works just like the original uncentralized version
of these automata except that C contains a special central symbol, #,
whose single occurrence is always inserted into an input word, w. C
performs a jump in such a way that it replaces a subword containing #
with one #. If, by making a sequence of jumps in this centralized way,
it eventually wipes outall w with # as the only symbol unerased, C
accepts w; the set of all accepted words in this way is the language
of C. This paper shows that the language family resulting from these
centralized versions coincides with that of linear languages. In addition,
this paper defines several special cases of these centralized versions and
demonstrates their equivalences to special cases of linear grammars, such
as minimal and even linear grammars. Consequently, in terms of the
language theory, all the variety of centralized jumping finite automata
can be seen as automaton-based counterparts to linear grammars and
their special cases.

Keywords: Discontinuous computation · Jumping finite automata ·
Centralized versions · Linear grammars and languages · Special cases ·
Identities between language families

1 Introduction

From a historical perspective, most computational methods developed in the
previous century were designed for strictly continuous information processing
simply because no other way of computation existed at that time. Accordingly,
their formalizations, usually based upon grammars or automata, reflect this way
of computation as well. That is, their formal models work on words, representing the information being processed, in a strictly continuous left-to-right,
symbol-by-symbol manner. Today's information methods, however, often work
in a fundamentally different way because they perform their computations discontinuously. Indeed, within a discontinuous running process, a computational
step may be performed somewhere on the left within the information, while the

© The Author(s), under exclusive license to Springer Nature Switzerland AG 2025
M. D. Jiménez López and G. Vaszil (Eds.): Erzsébet Csuhaj-Varjú Festschrift,
LNCS 15840, pp. 69–84, 2025.
https://doi.org/10.1007/978-3-031-97274-4_5

very next computational step is executed far away from it to the right. Before the next step is carried out, the process jumps over a large portion of the information to another position for execution. Of course, classical last-century formal models, which operate on words strictly continuously, can hardly provide the theory of computation with adequate formalizations of discontinuous information processing. Consequently, to formalize this modern computation more adequately, the theory of computation has recently adapted classical formal models in such a way that they also work discontinuously on input words. Indeed, this theory has introduced new versions of formal models, generally referred to as *jumping grammars and automata* (see [1]). Perhaps most importantly, *jumping finite automata* (see [2]) have been introduced as discontinuously working counterparts to classical finite automata, which fulfill a crucial role in both theoretical and practical aspects of computer science. These jumping versions of finite automata represent the central topic of the present paper.

To give an intuitive insight into jumping finite automata, we first recall the notion of a classical finite automaton, A, and that of its jumping version, J; in addition, we sketch their essential difference. Conceptually, A, introduced many decades ago in [3], consists of an input tape, a read head, and a finite state control. The input tape is divided into squares, each containing one symbol of an input word. The symbol under the read head is the current input symbol. The finite control is represented by a finite set of states together with a control relation, which is usually specified as a set of computational rules. A operates by making a sequence of moves. Each move is made according to a computational rule that describes how the current state is changed and whether the current input symbol is read. If the symbol is read, the read head is shifted precisely one square to the right. A has one state defined as the start state, and some states are designated as final states. If A can read a word by making a sequence of moves from the start state to a final state, A accepts this word; otherwise, A rejects it. J is conceptualized exactly as A, but it works slightly differently because it does not read the input string in a symbol-by-symbol left-to-right way; otherwise, it operates in the same manner. More precisely, after reading a symbol, J can jump over an utterly unlimited portion of the tape in either direction and continue making jumps from there. Once an occurrence of a symbol is read on the tape, it is erased so it cannot be re-read again later during its computation.

We are now ready to explain the key purpose and subject of this paper. Compared to A, J obviously reflects the completely discontinuous way of computation more accurately, which is likely why the theory of computation has recently dedicated numerous studies to their investigation, an up-to-2024 summary of which can be found in [1]. Nevertheless, today's computer science frequently employs discontinuous computational methods in a somewhat centralized manner. Since J performs its jumps in an utterly unrestricted way, it can hardly serve as an adequate model for this centralized form of discontinuous information processing. To provide computer science with a more properly designed formalization of this processing, based on J, the present paper introduces and investigates its centralized version, C – the principal subject of this paper.

Quite broadly speaking, C formalizes discontinuous information processing just like J, but its computation is performed at the central part of the information being processed. More formally, this central part is represented by a special central symbol, #, whose single occurrence always appears in the input word that represents the information. C starts its computation with an input word w that contains one occurrence of # inserted anywhere into w. As opposed to J, which performs jumps in an utterly unrestricted manner, C always performs a jump by replacing a subword containing # with a single occurrence of #. If, by making a sequence of jumps in this way, C eventually erases all the symbols of w while # remains the only symbol left unerased, C accepts w. The set of all words accepted in this way forms the language of C. Based on several natural restrictions, a variety of special cases of C is considered in this paper. Some restrictions are placed on the components of C, such as reducing the number of states to one. Others are concerned with the way C performs computations around #, such as evenly distributed jumps around #.

As its fundamental result, the paper shows that the language family resulting from the centralized jumping finite automata coincides with that generated by linear languages (see Corollary 2). Furthermore, it demonstrates several equivalences between special cases of C and proper subfamilies of the linear language families, such as the minimal and even linear language families (see Theorems 5 and 6). Consequently, in terms of formal language theory, these newly introduced versions of C actually represent new automaton-based counterparts to these subfamilies.

The present paper is organized as follows. Section 2 recalls all the terminology needed in this paper. Section 3 defines various centralized versions of jumping finite automata that are discussed later. Section 4 presents the fundamental results achieved in this paper; most importantly, it demonstrates that their basic versions and linear grammars are equivalent. Section 5 establishes several equivalences between special cases of these automata and special cases of linear grammars. Finally, Sect. 6 summarizes the present study, links its concepts and results to the previous results in the formal language theory, and suggests five open problem areas closely related to its subject.

As already pointed out above, the present study as a whole is motivated and inspired by a realistic viewpoint at modern methods working in a discontinuously computational way. Therefore, throughout the paper, we give all constructive proof parts directly as algorithms, generally entitled as *Algorithm X: Name* (for example, *Algorithm 1: Conversion from CGJFA to ε-free CGJFA*), in order to emphasize their straightforward way of implementation and use in practice.

2   Preliminaries

This section gives the basic terminology used throughout this paper.

For any set Q, let $|Q|$ denote its cardinality. For an alphabet Σ (a nonempty finite set), let Σ^* and Σ^+ denote the free monoid and free semigroup over Σ under concatenation, respectively. The identity element of Σ^* is denoted by ε.

For any string $x \in \Sigma^*$, its length is denoted by $|x|$. Let $x = a_1 a_2 \ldots a_n$, where $a_i \in \Sigma$ for all $1 \le i \le n = |x|$ (note that $n = 0$ if and only if $x = \varepsilon$). The *reversal* of x, denoted by x^R, is defined as $x^R = a_n a_{n-1} \ldots a_1$.

A *grammar* is a quadruple $G = (N, T, P, S)$, where N is a finite set of non-terminals, T is a finite set of terminals with $N \cap T = \emptyset$, $P \subseteq T^* N T^* \times (T \cup N)^*$ is a finite set of productions, and $S \in N$ is the start symbol.

A grammar G is called *context-free* if each production is of the form (A, α) for some $A \in N$ and $\alpha \in (T \cup N)^*$. We write $A \to \alpha$ to denote $(A, \alpha) \in P$. G is *linear* if every production is either of the form $A \to xBy$ or $A \to w$, where $A, B \in N$ and $x, y, w \in T^*$. A linear grammar is *even* if every rule $A \to xBy$ satisfies $|x| = |y|$. A linear grammar is *minimal* if $|N| = 1$.

The binary *derivation relation* $\Rightarrow$ over $(N \cup T)^*$ is defined as follows: if $u, v \in (N \cup T)^*$ and $A \to \alpha \in P$, then $uAv \Rightarrow u\alpha v$. The relation $\Rightarrow$ is extended to $\Rightarrow^m$ (for $m \ge 0$), $\Rightarrow^+$, and $\Rightarrow^*$. A *sentential form* of G is any string in $(N \cup T)^*$ that can be derived from the start symbol S using a finite number of derivation steps. The language generated by G, denoted $L(G)$, is:

$$L(G) = \{w \in T^* \mid S \Rightarrow^* w\}.$$

The families of languages generated by linear, minimal, and even linear grammars are denoted by **LIN**, **MIN**, and **EVEN**, respectively.

In general, two language models, such as grammars or automata, are said to be equivalent if they generate the same language.

3   Definitions

First, this section recalls the notion of a general jumping finite automaton (see [2]). Then, it introduces the central notions of this paper – that of a centralized general jumping finite automaton along with some of their special cases.

Definition 1. *A general jumping finite automaton (GJFA) is a quintuple* $M = (Q, \Sigma, R, s, F)$, *where:*

- Q *is a finite set of states;*
- Σ *is a finite alphabet, such that* $\Sigma \cap Q = \emptyset$;
- $R \subseteq Q \times \Sigma^* \times Q$ *is a finite rule set;*
- $s \in Q$ *is the starting state;*
- $F \subseteq Q$ *is the set of final states.*

A configuration of M *is any string in* $\Sigma^* Q \Sigma^*$. *The binary* jumping relation, *denoted* $\curvearrowright$, *is defined as follows: for any* $x, x', y, y' \in \Sigma^*$ *where* $xy = x'y'$, *and* $(q, w, p) \in R$, M *makes a* jump *from* $xqwy$ *to* $x'py'$, *written:*

$$xqwy \curvearrowright x'py'.$$

Extending $\curvearrowright$ *to* $\curvearrowright^i$ $(i \ge 0)$, $\curvearrowright^*$, *and* $\curvearrowright^+$ *in the usual manner, the language of* M *is defined as:*

$$L(M) = \{uv \mid u, v \in \Sigma^*, usv \curvearrowright^* f \text{ for some } f \in F\}.$$

Definition 2. *Let M be a GJFA, and let n be a non-negative integer. Then n is called the* degree *of M if, for every rule $(q, w, p) \in R$, it holds that $|w| \leq n$. Specifically, M is a* jumping finite automaton *(JFA) if its degree is 1. Moreover, M is said to be* ε-free *if every rule $(q, w, p) \in R$ satisfies $|w| \geq 1$.*

Next, we define the central notion of a centralized general jumping finite automaton.

Definition 3. *A* centralized general jumping finite automaton *(CGJFA) is a quintuple $M = (Q, \Sigma, R, \#, F)$, where Q, Σ, and F have the same meaning as in definition of GJFA (see Definition 1); $\#$ is a* central symbol, *such that $\# \notin Q \cup \Sigma$; and $R \subseteq (\{\#\} \cup Q) \times \Sigma^* \{\#\} \Sigma^* \times Q$ is finite.*

A configuration *of M is any member of $(\{\#\} \cup Q) \times \Sigma^* \{\#\} \Sigma^*$. Let K be the set of all configurations of M. We define a binary relation, denoted by $\curvearrowright_\#$, over K as follows: for any $x, y \in \Sigma^*$ and any rule $(q, w, p) \in R$, M makes a* centralized jump *$(q, xwy) \curvearrowright_\# (p, x \# y)$. Extend $\curvearrowright_\#$ to $\curvearrowright_\#^i$ (for $i \geq 0$), $\curvearrowright_\#^*$, and $\curvearrowright_\#^+$ in the usual manner.*

The language *of M, denoted by $L(M)$, is defined as:*

$$L(M) = \{xy \mid x, y \in \Sigma^*, (\#, x \# y) \curvearrowright_\#^* (f, \#) \text{ for some } f \in F\}.$$

The elements of R are referred to as rules. *Every rule $(q, w, p) \in R$ is written as*

$$(q, w) \rightarrow p$$

in what follows. For brevity, we often label $(q, w) \rightarrow p$ as $r : (q, w) \rightarrow p$ by unique label r, and we simply refer to it as r – that is, by its rule label. A rule of the form $(\#, w) \rightarrow p$ is called a starting rule. *A rule of the form $(q, w) \rightarrow p$, where $q \in Q$, is called a* non-starting rule. *Furthermore, if a non-starting rule is of the form $(q, \#) \rightarrow p$, we call it an* ε-rule.

A CGJFA M is said to be ε-free *if and only if it contains no ε-rules.*

Definition 4. *Let M be a CGJFA, and let n be a non-negative integer. Then n is called the* degree *of M if, for every rule $(p, x \# y) \rightarrow q \in R$, it holds that $|xy| \leq n$. Specifically, M is called a* centralized jumping finite automaton *(CJFA) if its degree is 1.*

It is worth noting that if a CGJFA is of degree n, for some $n \geq 0$, then it is also of degree m, for any $m \geq n$.

Example 1. In a simple and straightforward way, we sketch a potential application of CJFAs in practice. More specifically, we outline how they may serve a useful role in scientific fields dealing with palindromically symmetric sequences.

As an example, consider musicology. Retrogradations—melodic lines that are the reverse of a previously stated sequence of notes—have been widely used throughout the history of music, from medieval canons through compositions by Bartók and Schoenberg, up to modern electronic music (see [4–6], and Section 12.2 in [7]).

To illustrate, consider Joseph Haydn's famous *Symphony No. 47 in G major*, which is, not surprisingly, nicknamed "the Palindrome." In the third movement, a minuet and trio, the second half of the minuet is the same as the first but backwards; the second half of the ensuing trio similarly reflects the first half, and then the minuet is repeated.

In a strictly mathematical way, the retrogradational musical form and its generation can be easily formalized by CJFAs in the following way. Let Σ be the set of all notes under consideration, and define the language L as the set of all musical phrases followed by their retrograde reversals:

$$L = \{ww^R \mid w \in \Sigma^*\}.$$

The language L is recognized by the following CJFA M:

$$M = (\{q\}, \Sigma, \{(\#, \#) \to q\} \cup \{(q, a\#a) \to q \mid a \in \Sigma\}, \#, \{q\})$$

From a more general standpoint, it is evident that CGJFAs and CJFAs can efficiently handle most other palindrome-based symmetries encountered in science. For instance, in genetics, they can describe nucleotide sequences followed by their complementary strands. Similarly, CJFAs can model palindrome-like structures found in fractals in mathematics, backmasking in audio recording techniques, and chiastic structures in literary analysis.

On the other hand, it is also evident that the original, non-centralized versions of GJFAs and JFAs cannot effectively model such symmetries, as they lack the ability to process input relative to a fixed central reference.

3.1   Denotation of Language Families Accepted by CGJFAs

Throughout, we use **CGJFA**, **CGJFA**$_{\varepsilon\text{-free}}$, **CJFA**, and **CJFA**$_{\varepsilon\text{-free}}$ to denote the families of languages accepted by CGJFAs, ε-free CGJFAs, CJFAs, and ε-free CJFAs, respectively.

4   Results

Definition 5. *The ε-closure of a state $q \in Q$, denoted by ε-closure(q), is the set of all states $q' \in Q$ such that q' is reachable from q using only ε-rules, preserving the tape's content. Formally,*

$$\varepsilon\text{-}closure(q) = \{q' \in Q \mid (q, x\#y) \curvearrowright_{\#}^* (q', x\#y) \text{ for all } x, y \in \Sigma^*\}.$$

Theorem 1. *For any CGJFA M, there exists an ε-free CGJFA M' such that $L(M') = L(M)$. Moreover, if M has degree n, then M' also has degree n.*

Proof. First, we present Algorithm 1, which transforms any CGJFA M into an equivalent ε-free CGJFA M', while preserving its degrees. We then formally verify its correctness.

Algorithm 1: Conversion from CGJFA to ε-free CGJFA

Input : CGJFA $M = (Q, \Sigma, R, \#, F)$
Output: ε-free CGJFA $M' = (Q, \Sigma, R', \#, F')$ such that $L(M') = L(M)$

begin

    // Copy all starting rules
    $R' := \{r \mid r : (\#, x\#y) \to s \in R \text{ where } x, y \in \Sigma^*, s \in Q\}$

    // Mark states as final if they reach a final state via ε-rules
    $F' := \{q \mid q \in Q \text{ and } \varepsilon\text{-closure}(q) \cap F \neq \emptyset\}$

    for $q \in Q$ **do**
        // Propagate non-ε-rules from the ε-closure
        $R' := R' \cup \{(q, x\#y) \to p \mid q' \in \varepsilon\text{-closure}(q), (q', x\#y) \to p \in R, xy \neq \varepsilon\}$
    end

end

Observe that no ε-rules are introduced into R. Notably, starting rules of the form $(\#, \#) \to q$ do not qualify as ε-rules. Since the algorithm only reuses strings that already appear in some rules of R, all valid degrees of M remain valid in M'.

Consider an accepted string $w \in L(M)$. Let $u, x, y, v \in \Sigma^*$ such that $w = uxyv$, where xy is processed using the starting rule $(\#, x\#y) \to s$ for some $s \in Q$, and uv is the remaining portion of the input. Let p denote the first state reached after processing all symbols of uv. The acceptance sequence of w in M can then be expressed as

$$(\#, ux\#yv) \curvearrowright_\# (s, u\#v) \curvearrowright_\#^* (p, \#) \curvearrowright_\#^* (f, \#)$$

for some $f \in F$.

Since all starting rules were preserved, both automata behave identically during the first jump. Consequently, $(\#, ux\#yv) \curvearrowright_\# (s, u\#v)$ in M if and only if it is possible in M'.

We now establish that M can perform $(s, u\#v) \curvearrowright_\#^* (p, \#)$ if and only if M' can. First, consider the edge case where $u = v = \varepsilon$. In this scenario, the first state entered after processing the entire tape is simply s, so $p = s$. As a result, the transition reduces to the trivial case, $(s, \#) \curvearrowright_\#^* (s, \#)$, for both automata.

Next, consider the case where $(s, u\#v) \curvearrowright_\#^+ (p, \#)$ in M with $uv \neq \varepsilon$. During this sequence of jumps, M must have applied $n \geq 1$ non-ε-rules of the form

$$(q_i, u_i\#v_i) \to p_i,$$

where $q_i, p_i \in Q$, $u_i, v_i \in \Sigma^*$, and $u_i v_i \neq \varepsilon$ for all $1 \leq i \leq n$. Consequently, we can express:

$$uv = u_n \cdots u_1 v_1 \cdots v_n.$$

Since the first state entered after processing all symbols of uv is p_n, we have $p = p_n$. Defining $p_0 = s$, we observe that M transitions from $p_0 = s$ to $p_n = p$

while processing uv through the sequence

$$(p_{i-1}u'_iu_i\#v_iv'_i) \curvearrowright_\#^* (q_i, u_i\#v_i) \curvearrowright_\# (p_i, \#).$$

for all $1 \le i \le n$, where $u'_i, v'_i \in \Sigma^*$ represent the remaining input after reading u_iv_i.

As each q_i belongs to ε-closure(p_{i-1}) and $(q_i, u_i\#v_i) \to p_i \in R$ with $u_iv_i \ne \varepsilon$, the for-loop in the algorithm guarantees that

$$(p_{i-1}, u_i\#v_i) \to p_i$$

is included in R'. Consequently, M' transitions from $p_0 = s$ to $p_n = p$ by chaining $(p_{i-1}, u_i\#v_i) \to p_i$ for all $1 \le i \le n$, thereby processing uv.

To establish the reverse direction, consider a rule $(q, x\#y) \to p$ included in R', where $q \in Q$ and $x, y \in \Sigma^*$. By construction, there must exist a state $q' \in Q$ such that

$$(q, x\#y) \curvearrowright_\#^* (q', x\#y) \curvearrowright_\# (p, \#)$$

in M. Therefore, if $(q, ux\#yv) \curvearrowright_\# (p, u\#v)$ occurs in M', then $(q, ux\#yv) \curvearrowright_\#^+ (p, u\#v)$ must be possible in M.

In the final stage of acceptance, $(p, \#) \curvearrowright_\#^* (f, \#)$, automaton M reaches a final state using zero or more ε-jumps. This implies that $f \in \varepsilon$-closure(p). The last step of the algorithm ensures that p is marked as a final state in M', and M' accepts uv from p. Conversely, a state f' is added to F' if and only if M can transition from f' to final state in F without modifying the input. Thus, the language recognized by M' remains unchanged.

Therefore, $L(M) = L(M')$. Consequently, we have demonstrated that for an arbitrary CGJFA M, there exists an ε-free CGJFA M' such that $L(M') = L(M)$. It is also clear that M and M' have the same degree. In other words, we have proved that Theorem 1 holds true.   □

The following theorem demonstrates how to turn an arbitrary CGJFA to an equivalent CJFA. Consequently, CGJFAs and CJFAs have the same power.

Theorem 2. *For any CGJFA M, there exists a CJFA M', such that $L(M) = L(M')$.*

Proof. First, we present the Algorithm 2, which converts any CGJFA M into CJFA M'. Then we formally verify the algorithm's correctness.

To begin, observe that the algorithm populates R' exclusively with ε-rules and rules containing exactly one symbol from the input alphabet. Hence, the resulting automaton M' is of degree 1, meaning M' is a CJFA.

To show that $L(M) \subseteq L(M')$, consider how M transitions from some $q_\# \in Q \cup \{\#\}$ to $p \in Q$ using a rule

$$r: (q_\#, x\#y) \to p \in R,$$

while removing $x, y \in \Sigma^*$ from the tape. Since Algorithm 2 replaces each such rule with a sequence of transitions that process x and y symbol by symbol, we argue that M' can simulate this jump step by step.

Algorithm 2: Conversion from CGJFA to CJFA

Input   : CGJFA $M = (Q, \Sigma, R, \#, F)$
Output: CJFA $M' = (Q', \Sigma, R', \#, F)$ such that $L(M') = L(M)$

begin

   Set $R' := \emptyset, \quad Q' := Q$

   forall the $(q_\#, x\#y) \to p \in R$, *where* $q_\# \in Q \cup \{\#\}$, $p \in Q$, $x, y \in \Sigma^*$ **do**

      Let $n := |x|, \quad m := |y|, \quad r_0 := q_\#$

      // Decompose x and y into symbols
      Express $x = a_n \ldots a_1, \quad y = b_1 \ldots b_m$

      if $n + m > 0$ **then**

         Introduce new states $r_1, \ldots, r_{n+m}$, where $r_i \notin Q$ for all
         $1 \le i \le n + m$
         Add $r_1, \ldots, r_{n+m}$ to Q'

         for $k := 1$ **to** $n + m$ **do**

            if $i \le n$ **then**

               Add $(r_{k-1}, a_k\#) \to r_k$ to R' *// Process left substring x*

            else

               Add $(r_{k-1}, \#b_{k-n}) \to r_k$ to R' *// Process right substring y*
            end

         end

      end

      // Finalize transition to p
      Add $(r_{n+m}, \#) \to p$ to R'

   end

end

In the edge case where $x = y = \varepsilon$, we have $n + m = 0$, and the body of the for-loop is skipped, leading directly to the last step, where $(q_\#, \#) \to p$ is introduced into R'.

Otherwise, for each symbol of xy, a new state is introduced into Q'. Subsequently, for each $1 \le i \le |xy|$, the algorithm adds a rule that jumps from the previous state r_{i-1} to r_i while reading the corresponding symbol c_i from the tape. First, the symbols of the left substring x are processed, from the innermost to the outermost symbol. The behavior is then mirrored for y. Since we set $r_0 = q_\#$, it follows that M' can use the newly introduced rules to transition from $q_\#$ to the final state of the sequence, $r_{|xy|}$, while processing xy symbol by symbol. After completely erasing xy, M' jumps to p using the rule introduced at the end of the for-loop. Since this holds for any transition in M, we conclude that $L(M) \subseteq L(M')$.

To establish the opposite inclusion, $L(M') \subseteq L(M)$, consider how the rules of M' are constructed. Each transition sequence in M' corresponds uniquely to a rule $r \in R$ of M. Since the states introduced by Algorithm 2 are uniquely associated with a single rule, M' can transition from $q_\#$ to p only by following the sequence of intermediate states assigned to that rule. This forces M' to process symbols exactly as M would have, and no branching can occur within a transition sequence corresponding to a single rule r. Branching is only possible after reaching a state that belongs to the original automaton M, ensuring that each computation path in M' simulates a valid computation in M. Since the final state set F is shared by both automata, it is impossible for M' to accept a string that M would not have accepted. Thus, we conclude that $L(M) = L(M')$. □

Algorithms 1 and 2 act as powerful conversion tools, enabling the transformation of any CGJFA into a CJFA, as well as their respective ε-free versions. This leads us to the following corollary.

Corollary 1. $CGJFA = CGJFA_{\varepsilon\text{-free}} = CJFA = CJFA_{\varepsilon\text{-free}}$.

Proof. The following inclusions hold by definition, as the left-hand side is a special case of the right-hand side:

1. $\mathbf{CGJFA}_{\varepsilon\text{-free}} \subseteq \mathbf{CGJFA}$,
2. $\mathbf{CJFA} \subseteq \mathbf{CGJFA}$,
3. $\mathbf{CJFA}_{\varepsilon\text{-free}} \subseteq \mathbf{CJFA}$.

By Theorem 1, we have $\mathbf{CGJFA} \subseteq \mathbf{CGJFA}_{\varepsilon\text{-free}}$. Note that Algorithm 1 preserves the degrees of the input CGJFA. This implies that when the algorithm is applied to a CJFA, the result will be an ε-free CJFA, leading to the inclusion $\mathbf{CJFA} \subseteq \mathbf{CJFA}_{\varepsilon\text{-free}}$. Finally, by Theorem 2, we obtain $\mathbf{CGJFA} \subseteq \mathbf{CJFA}$. □

In the rest of this section, we show that $\mathbf{CGJFA} = \mathbf{LIN}$.

Lemma 1. *For any CGJFA M, there exists an equivalent CGJFA M' such that M' has exactly one final state.*

Proof. We construct M' by modifying M as follows: First, we introduce a new state f to the state set Q and redefine the final state set as $F = \{f\}$. Next, for each original final state $f' \in F$ of M, we add an ε-rule $(f', \#) \to f$ to the rule set R. This transformation ensures that all previous final states lead to a unique final state while preserving the language recognized by M. □

Theorem 3. *For any CGJFA M, there exists a linear grammar G such that $L(M) = L(G)$.*

Proof. Without loss of generality, assume that M has a single final state f (see Lemma 1). We present Algorithm 3, which converts M into an equivalent linear grammar G. A formal verification of its correctness follows.

We argue that the linear grammar G mirrors the behavior of M. Instead of erasing the input string as M does, G reconstructs it in reverse order of steps, ensuring that both recognize the same language.

Algorithm 3: Conversion of a CGJFA to a linear grammar

Input : CGJFA $M = (Q, \Sigma, R, \#, \{f\})$ with a single final state f
Output: Linear grammar $G = (N, T, P, f)$ such that $L(G) = L(M)$

begin

    Let $N := Q$, $T := \Sigma$

    for $(q, x\#y) \to p \in R$, where $x, y \in \Sigma^*$ and $q, p \in Q$ **do**
        // Notice that p and q are nonterminals in G
        Add production $p \to xqy$ to P
    end

    for $(\#, m\#n) \to p \in R$, where $m, n \in \Sigma^*$ and $p \in Q$ **do**
        Add production $p \to mn$ to P
    end

end

Since M has to begin an accepting computation by using some starting rule $(\#, m\#n) \to s$, $m, n \in \Sigma^*$, $s \in Q$, and finalize by ending up in the final state f, any string $w \in L(M)$ must be erased according to the sequence:

$$(\#, um\#nv) \curvearrowright_\# (s, u\#v) \curvearrowright_\#^* (f, \#)$$

for some $u, v \in \Sigma^*$, where $w = umnv$.

Now consider how Algorithm 3 constructs P. For any rule $(q, x\#y) \to p \in R$ that M uses to erase xy from the tape while transitioning from q to p, the algorithm introduces the production $p \to xqy$ in G. This allows G to reconstruct xy while shifting the derivation from the nonterminal p to q, mirroring the corresponding transition in M.

Observe that the position of the central symbol $\#$ in M corresponds to the position of the nonterminal in G during derivations. Since f is the start symbol of G, it can derive:

$$f \Rightarrow usv.$$

Finally, since $(\#, m\#n) \to s$, the production $s \to mn$ was introduced to P by the second for-loop and therefore $f \Rightarrow usv \Rightarrow umnv = w$. Thus, every string accepted by M is generated by G, proving that $L(M) \subseteq L(G)$.

To establish the opposite inclusion, $L(G) \subseteq L(M)$, observe that every production in G was created directly from a transition rule in M. If G can derive a string w from f, then it must have followed a sequence of productions that correspond exactly to a sequence of jumps in M, but in reverse order, and must have used the production $s \to mn$ to finalize the derivation, which corresponds to the starting rule M would have used when it starts its computation. Since each derivation step in G corresponds to a valid transition in M, the automaton must be able to erase w, starting from $\#$ and reaching its final state f. Hence, we conclude that $L(M) = L(G)$. □

Theorem 4. *For any linear grammar G, there exists a CGJFA M such that $L(G) = L(M)$.*

Proof. First, we present Algorithm 4, which converts any linear grammar into an equivalent CGJFA. Then, we formally verify its correctness.

Algorithm 4: Conversion of a linear grammar to a CGJFA

Input   : Linear grammar $G = (N, T, P, S)$
Output: CGJFA $M = (Q, \Sigma, R, \#, \{S\})$ such that $L(M) = L(G)$

begin
  Set $Q := N$, $\Sigma := T$, $F := \{S\}$

  forall the $p \in P$ **do**
    if p *is of the form* $A \to xBy$ *where* $x, y \in T^*$, $A, B \in N$ **then**
      | Add $(B, x\#y) \to A$ to R
    else if p *is of the form* $A \to w$ *where* $w \in T^*$, $A \in N$ **then**
      | Add $(\#, \#w) \to A$ to R
    end
  end
end

Analogously to the proof of Theorem 3, we argue that the behavior of M simulates that of G, but in reverse.

Consider any string $w \in L(G)$. Then there exists a derivation of the form:

$$S \Rightarrow^* uEv \Rightarrow umv$$

for some $E \in N$ and $u, v, m \in \Sigma^*$, where $w = umv$.

Each step in the sequence $S \Rightarrow^* uEv$ corresponds to a production $A \to xBy$, where $A, B \in N$ and $x, y \in T^*$. The algorithm introduces the rule $(B, x\#y) \to A$ into R, allowing M to transition from B to A while erasing x and y from around the central symbol $\#$.

Thus, for the sequence $S \Rightarrow^* uEv$, M performs $(E, u\#v) \curvearrowright_\#^* (S, \#)$. Using the final production $E \to m \in P$, where $E \in N$ and $m \in T^*$, G derives $uEv \Rightarrow umv$. The algorithm, therefore, introduced the starting rule $(\#, \#m) \to E$ to R, ensuring that M transitions as follows:

$$(\#, u\#mv) \curvearrowright_\# (E, u\#v) \curvearrowright_\#^* (S, \#).$$

Since S is the final state of M, $w = umv$ is accepted, proving that $L(G) \subseteq L(M)$.

To establish $L(M) \subseteq L(G)$, consider a string $w \in L(M)$. Since all starting rules introduced are of the form $(\#, \#m) \to A$ for some $A \in Q$ and $m \in \Sigma^*$, there exist $u, v \in \Sigma^*$ such that $w = umv$ and

$$(\#, u\#mv) \curvearrowright_\# (A, u\#v) \curvearrowright_\#^* (S, \#).$$

By the construction of Algorithm 4, for any rule $(B, x\#y) \to C \in R$, where $B, C \in Q$ and $x, y \in \Sigma^*$, a corresponding production $A \to xBy$ must have existed in P. Hence, the sequence of rules used during the jumps $(A, u\#v) \curvearrowright_\#^* (S, \#)$ corresponds to a sequence of productions that derives $S \Rightarrow^* uAv$.

Finally, since $(\#, \#m) \to A$ is in R, the set P must contain the production $A \to m$, meaning that

$$S \Rightarrow^* uAv \Rightarrow umv$$

is a valid derivation in G. Hence, $w = umv \in L(G)$, and we conclude that $L(M) = L(G)$.   □

Having established algorithms for converting between CGJFAs and linear grammars, we immediately obtain the following corollary.

Corollary 2. LIN = CGJFA

Proof. This follows directly from Theorems 3 and 4.   □

5   Specialized Versions of CGJFAs

Definition 6. *Let $M = (Q, \Sigma, R, \#, F)$ be a CGJFA. If $|Q| = 1$, then M is called a one-state centralized general jumping finite automaton (OSCGJFA). Without loss of generality, we refer to the single state as q. We denote the family of languages generated by OSCGJFAs as* **OSCGJFA**.

Theorem 5. MIN = OSCGJFA

Proof. This follows directly from Theorems 3 and 4, along with Algorithms 3 and 4.

A linear grammar is minimal if and only if it has a single nonterminal. Algorithm 3 constructs a grammar by copying the unique state q from an OSCGJFA into the nonterminal set N of G without introducing additional nonterminals. Since M has only one state, it can have at most one final state. If $F = \emptyset$, then $L(M) = \emptyset$, which aligns with any minimal grammar that lacks a production of the form $A \to w$. Thus, the algorithm correctly transforms OSCGJFAs with $F = \{q\}$ into minimal grammars, proving **OSCGJFA $\subseteq$ MIN**.

Conversely, Algorithm 4 transforms any minimal grammar into a CGJFA while preserving its single nonterminal as its only state. Hence, every minimal grammar corresponds to an OSCGJFA, establishing **MIN $\subseteq$ OSCGJFA**.   □

Definition 7. *Let $M = (Q, \Sigma, R, \#, F)$ be a CGJFA. If, for every non-starting rule $(q, x\#y) \to p$ it holds that $|x| = |y|$, then M is called a balanced centralized general jumping finite automaton (BCGJFA). We denote the family of languages generated by BCGJFAs as* **BCGJFA**.

Theorem 6. EVEN = BCGJFA

Proof. This follows directly from Theorems 3 and 4, along with Algorithms 3 and 4.

Algorithm 4 converts an even linear grammar into a CGJFA by introducing, for each production $A \to xBy$, a rule $(B, x\#y) \to A$ into R. Since $|x| = |y|$ holds for every production in an even linear grammar, the resulting CGJFA satisfies the balance condition. Thus, **EVEN $\subseteq$ BCGJFA**.

Conversely, if M is a balanced CGJFA, Algorithm 3 constructs a linear grammar G such that every newly introduced rule of the form $A \to xBy$ satisfies $|x| = |y|$. Thus, G is an even linear grammar, proving **BCGJFA $\subseteq$ EVEN**. □

6   Conclusion

To summarize the present study, we have introduced and studied CGJFAs and CJFAs as new centralized versions of GJFAs and JFAs, respectively. In essence, CGJFAs and CJFAs work just like their originals, except that they contain a special central symbol, #, whose single occurrence is always inserted into an input word w. They perform their jumps in such a way that they replace a subword containing # with one #. If, by making a sequence of jumps in this way, they erase all the symbols of w but #, they accept w.

We have demonstrated that the language family accepted by CGJFAs and CJFAs and that of linear languages are identical. In addition, we have introduced several special cases of CGJFAs and CJFAs and demonstrated their equivalences to special cases of linear grammars.

It is worth pointing out that formal language theory has achieved many other characterizations of the linear language family and its subfamilies. In fact, the first such characterizations were established decades ago, for instance in [8] and [9, Section 5.7]. More recently, several other characterizations have been introduced in the 21st century (see [10,11]).

Most likely, certain special versions of jumping finite automata are closely related to special cases of Watson-Crick finite automata, which have been the subject of intensive study in recent years. Specifically, the special version corresponding to **MIN** (see Definition 6) is equivalent to stateless (no-state) $5' \to 3'$ Watson-Crick finite automata (see [12]), while the balanced version (see Definition 7) corresponds to both-head stepping sensing $5' \to 3'$ Watson-Crick automata (see [13]).

Although we have established several fundamental results concerning CGJFAs, CJFAs, and their restricted versions (see Sects. 4 and 5), there still remain many open problem areas to study. Next, we suggest five of them:

1. Investigate more classical topics of automata theory, such as minimization, in terms of these newly introduced automata and their restricted versions.
2. Conceptualize and investigate pushdown versions of CGJFAs and CJFAs by analogy with the extension of finite automata to pushdown automata via pushdown stacks.

Without defining them rigorously here, it is evident that these pushdown versions can accept certain non-context-free languages, such as $a^n b^n c^n$. Indeed, take any $a^n b^n c^n$, where n is a non-negative integer. Starting from a configuration in which # is placed in front of the first occurrence of b, the automaton repeatedly replaces #b with #, pushing each b onto a stack; once all bs are erased, it replaces a#c with # while popping b's from the stack. The automaton accepts if and only if both the tape and the stack are empty. What is their precise power? Does there exist a well-known language family they characterize?

3. In [14], Csuhaj-Varju et al. introduced grammar systems. In a similar way, introduce systems of CGJFAs and CJFAs and study their properties.

4. Introduce and study regulated versions of CGJFAs and CJFAs by analogy with classical regulated automata (see [15]).

5. In detail, study a relation between all the automata considered in this paper and Watson-Crick Finite Automata, including all their special cases.

Acknowledgement. This work was supported by the BUT FIT-S-23-8209 grant. The authors thank both referees for useful suggestions concerning the first version of this study. Alexander Meduna's deep thanks go to Prof. Erzsebet Csuhaj-Varjú for her constant encouragement and inspiring ideas over the past few decades; köszönöm, Erzsi.

References

1. Meduna, A., Křivka, Z.: Jumping Computation: Updating Automata and Grammars for Discontinuous Information Processing. CRC Press, Boca Raton (2024)

2. Meduna, A., Zemek, P.: Jumping finite automata. Int. J. Found. Comput. Sci. **23**(7), 1555–1578 (2012). https://doi.org/10.1142/S0129054112500244

3. McCulloch, W.S., Pitts, W.: A logical calculus of the ideas immanent in nervous activity. Bull. Math. Biophys. **5**(4), 115–133 (1943). https://doi.org/10.1007/BF02478259

4. Grant, M.J.: Serial Music, Serial Aesthetics: Compositional Theory in Post-war Europe. Cambridge University Press, Cambridge (2001)

5. Morgan, R.P.: Symmetrical form and common-practice tonality. Music Theory Spectr. **20**(1), 1–47 (1998). https://doi.org/10.2307/746155

6. Fauvel, J., Flood, R., Wilson, J.R. (eds.): Music and Mathematics: From Pythagoras to Fractals. Oxford University Press, New York (2006)

7. Meduna, A., Kožár, T.: Automata: Theory, Trends, and Applications. World Scientific, Singapore (2023). https://doi.org/10.1142/13464

8. Rosenberg, A.L.: A machine realization of the linear context-free languages. Inf. Control **10**(2), 175–188 (1967). https://doi.org/10.1016/S0019-9958(67)80006-8

9. Harrison, M.A.: Introduction to Formal Language Theory. Addison-Wesley, New York (1978)

10. Loukanova, R.: Linear context-free languages. In: Theoretical Aspects of Computing - ICTAC 2007. LNCS, vol. 4711, pp. 351–365. Springer, Heidelberg (2007)

11. Nagy, B.: On $5' \to 3'$ sensing Watson-Crick finite automata. In: DNA Computing - DNA 2007. LNCS, vol. 4848, pp. 256–262. Springer, Heidelberg (2008)

12. Nagy, B.: On language classes accepted by stateless $5' \to 3'$ Watson-Crick finite automata. Annales Mathematicae et Informaticae **58**, 110–120 (2023). https://doi.org/10.33039/ami.2023.08.004
13. Nagy, B.: $5' \to 3'$ Sensing Watson-Crick finite automata. In: Sequence and Genome Analysis II – Methods and Applications, pp. 39–56. iConcept Press (2010)
14. Csuhaj-Varjú, E., Dassow, J., Kelemen, J., Păun, G.: Grammar Systems: A Grammatical Approach to Distribution and Cooperation. Routledge, London (1994). https://doi.org/10.4324/9781315075617
15. Meduna, A., Zemek, P.: Regulated Grammars and Automata. Springer, New York (2014). https://doi.org/10.1007/978-1-4939-0369-6

On Pushdown CD-Systems of Regular Grammars

Benedek Nagy[1,2]([✉]) [iD]

[1] Department of Mathematics, Faculty of Arts and Sciences, Eastern Mediterranean University, Famagusta, North Cyprus, Mersin-10, Turkey
nbenedek.inf@gmail.com
[2] Department of Computer Science, Faculty of Informatics, Eszterházy Károly Catholic University, Eger, Hungary

Abstract. It is known and straightforward to show that cooperative distributed (CD) systems of regular grammars can generate only regular languages independently of the mode of cooperation (e.g., $*, t, \leq k$, $= k, \geq k$ for $k \in \mathbb{N}$, $k > 0$). In this paper CD-systems of regular grammars are shown such that the next active component is chosen by the help of an external pushdown storage. We show that these systems can generate exactly the context-free languages. Moreover, based on this fact, a strong relation to fractal automata is given.

Keywords: CD-systems · Pushdown automata · Context-free languages · Fractal automata

1 Introduction

The theory of regular and context-free languages is one of the most basic and most important fundamental fields of theoretical computer science. The field is fairly old, the basic concepts and results are from the middle of the last century (see, for instance, [6,7,16]).

Regular grammars generate regular languages, and they are accepted by finite automata. Context-free grammars generate a wider class, namely the family of context-free languages, and these languages are accepted by nondeterministic pushdown automata.

Cooperative distributed systems (CD-systems) of some simple formal computing devices are widely used to simulate cooperating systems and their power [1–5]. These systems of grammars can be used in various modes of generation/computation based on various conditions when a component finishes its task before other component becomes active. CD-systems of (stateless, deterministic) restarting automata with window size one were investigated in [11,15] based on =1 mode of computation. These systems are also known as finite automata with translucent letters [12]. As expected, in several cases, CD-systems are much more expressive than their component grammars/automata themselves. However this is not the case at regular grammars. The generating power of regular grammars

M. D. Jiménez López and G. Vaszil (Eds.): Erzsébet Csuhaj-Varjú Festschrift,
LNCS 15840, pp. 85–102, 2025.
https://doi.org/10.1007/978-3-031-97274-4_6

remains the same even several of them are contained in a CD-system independently of the mode of the distributed cooperative computation (using the usual modes, see Sect. 3). A generalisation of the mentioned CD-systems of restarting automata was investigated in [13,14], where a pushdown store helps to choose the next active component of the computation. These PDCD-systems are also interpreted as pushdown automata with translucent letters. In this paper, based on the same idea, we investigate a natural extension of CD-systems of regular grammars using an external pushdown store.

The structure of the paper is as follows. In the next section we recall some preliminaries and present some basic definitions. In Sect. 3, we recall the CD-systems of generative grammars concentrating on regular grammars. In Sect. 4, we define pushdown CD-systems (PDCD-systems) of regular grammars and prove that their generating power coincide with the context-free languages. We also show a graphical representation of PDCD-systems working in mode t in Sect. 5: these representations are, in fact, the fractal automata: infinite state models that accept the context-free languages [8–10]. Some closure remarks and open problems close the paper.

2   Basic Definitions and Preliminaries

It is assumed that the reader is familiar with the basic concepts of formal languages and automata (see, for instance, [7,16] for any unexplained concepts).

First some notions about Chomsky-type grammars and generated languages are recalled and our notations are given.

We use Σ for a finite nonempty alphabet and ε to denote the empty word. For any word u we will write $|u|$ for its length, i.e., the number of letters it contains. Further, $\Sigma^{\leq k}$ denotes the set of all words over Σ having length at most k.

A grammar is a construct $G = (N, \Sigma, S, H)$, where N, Σ are the nonterminal and terminal alphabets, with $N \cap \Sigma = \emptyset$; they are finite sets. Further, $S \in N$ is a special symbol, called initial letter and H, the set of derivation rules (or productions), is a finite set of pairs, where a pair uses to be written in the form $v \to w$ with $v \in (N \cup \Sigma)^* N (N \cup \Sigma)^*$ and $w \in (N \cup \Sigma)^*$. The language generated by a grammar G is the set of terminal words which can be derived from the initial letter: $L(G) = \{ w \mid S \Rightarrow^* w \text{ with } w \in \Sigma^* \}$.

Depending on the possible structures of the derivation rules, various classes of grammars and, thus, various classes of generated languages are defined, such as, context-sensitive, context-free, and regular ones. They form a proper hierarchy, the Chomsky hierarchy.

We recall only the definition of regular and context-free grammars:

- a grammar is regular if each of its rules is in one of the forms $A \to v$, $A \to vB$, where $A, B \in N$ and $v \in \Sigma \cup \{\varepsilon\}$.
- a grammar is context-free if each of its rules is in the form $A \to v$, where $A \in N$ and $v \in (N \cup \Sigma)^*$.

Two generating and/or accepting devices (i.e., grammars and automata, respectively) are called equivalent if they generate/accept the same language.

The regular grammars can easily be translated to finite automata that accept the same language. The context-free languages are accepted by nondeterministic pushdown automata.

A pushdown automaton is a tuple $PDA = (Q, q_0, Q_a, \Sigma, \Gamma, \bot, \delta)$, where Q is a finite set, the set of states, $q_0 \in Q$ is the initial state, $Q_a \subseteq Q$ is the set of accepting (or final) states, Σ is the (tape) alphabet, Γ is the stack alphabet, $\bot \notin \Gamma$ is the (non-erasable) bottom marker of the pushdown stack and δ is the transition mapping of the form $\delta : Q \times (\Sigma \cup \{\varepsilon\}) \times (\Gamma \cup \{\bot\}) \to 2^{Q \times (\Gamma \cup \{\bot\})^*}$ as follows: $\delta(q, a, V) \subseteq 2^{Q \times \Gamma^{\leq 2}}$ where $q \in Q, a \in \Sigma \cup \{\varepsilon\}$ and $V \in \Gamma$, while $\delta(q, a, \bot) \subseteq 2^{Q \times (\bot \cdot \Gamma^{\leq 2})}$.

A configuration of PDA consists of three parts: (u, q, U), where u is the remaining part of the input, q is the actual state and $U \in \bot \cdot \Gamma^*$ is the actual content of the stack. The work starts in the initial configuration $(w, q_0, \bot)$. A configuration is changed to a new configuration according to an allowed transition described by δ: $(q', V') \in \delta(q, a, V)$ meaning that in state q PDA can read the input letter a (nothing is read in case $a = \varepsilon$) if symbol V was on the top of the stack (rightmost symbol of U in the actual configuration), and by this transition the state of PDA is switched to q' and symbol V is replaced by the symbol(s of) V' in the stack. A configuration is an accepting configuration if it is of the form $(\varepsilon, q, \bot)$. If PDA can reach an accepting configuration from its initial configuration with an input word w, then w is accepted by PDA. The set of accepted words forms the accepted language $L(PDA)$.

The model we have just described able to accept exactly the class of context-free languages. We note here that there are various models of pushdown automata that characterize the class of context-free languages, e.g., pushdown automata accepting by final (accepting) states (having accepting configurations of the form (ε, q, U) with $q \in Q_a$ and $U \in (\bot \cdot \Gamma^*)$), pushdown automata accepting by empty stack (the model that we have described first), pushdown automata accepting by final state and empty stack (having accepting configurations of the form $(\varepsilon, q, \bot)$ where $q \in Q_a$), stateless pushdown automata, etc.

3 CD-Systems of Regular Grammars

A cooperative distributed system (CD-system) of (regular) grammars is a system of order n $(n \geq 1)$: $CD = (N, \Sigma, S, (H_1, \ldots, H_n))$, where (N, Σ, S, H_i) are (regular) grammars, the components of the system, i.e., the sets $H_1, \ldots, H_n$ are finite sets of (regular) derivation rules. The work of these systems are defined in various modes: For every $i \in \{1, \ldots, n\}$ the derivation of the i-th component in

1. *-mode is denoted by $\Rightarrow_i^*$ and defined as follows: $p \Rightarrow_i^* q$ if and only if q can be derived from p by using only productions of H_i.
2. terminating mode is denoted by $\Rightarrow_i^t$ and defined as follows: $p \Rightarrow_i^t q$ if and only if $p \Rightarrow_i^* q$ and there is no $r \in (N \cup \Sigma)^*$ such that $q \Rightarrow_i^* r$ and $q \neq r$.

3. k steps (k is a positive integer) is denoted by $\Rightarrow_i^{=k}$ and defined as follows: $p \Rightarrow_i^{=k} q$ if and only if there are $r_0, r_1, \ldots, r_k \in (N \cup \Sigma)^*$ such that $p = r_0, q = r_k$ and for every j ($0 \leq j \leq k - 1$) $r_j \Rightarrow_i r_{j+1}$ is fulfilled (r_{j+1} can be derived from r_j by applying a rule of H_i once).

4. at most k steps (k is a positive integer) is denoted by $\Rightarrow_i^{\leq k}$ and defined as follows: $p \Rightarrow_i^{\leq k} q$ if and only if $p \Rightarrow_i^{=j} q$ for some value $j \leq k$.

5. at least k steps (k is a positive integer) is denoted by $\Rightarrow_i^{\geq k}$ and defined as follows: $p \Rightarrow_i^{\geq k} q$ if and only if $p \Rightarrow_i^{=j} q$ for some value $j \geq k$.

The generated language of a CD-system of (regular) grammars in mode $f \in \{*, t\} \cup \{= k, \leq k, \geq k \mid k \in \mathbb{N}, k > 0\}$ is defined as $L(CD)_f = \{w \in \Sigma^* \mid S \Rightarrow_{i_1}^f w_1 \Rightarrow_{i_2}^f w_2 \cdots \Rightarrow_{i_m}^f w_m = w, m \geq 1, 1 \leq i_j \leq n, 1 \leq j \leq m\}$.

Proposition 1. *The class of languages that is generated by regular grammars in mode $f \in \{*, t\} \cup \{= k, \leq k, \geq k \mid k \in \mathbb{N}, k > 0\}$ is exactly the class of regular languages.*

Having a CD-system of regular grammars the generating power remains the same (independently of the mode of cooperation). It can be proven by introducing various new nonterminals referring to nonterminals of various components grammars. Because lack of space we do not give further details on this process.

4 PDCD-Systems of Regular Grammars

Now let us define a kind of extension of the CD-systems of regular grammars. In [13,14] pushdown CD-systems of very simple restarting automata were investigated (in = 1 mode of cooperation), in this paper we do a similar extension for the regular grammars allowing several types of cooperation modes.

Definition 1. *A PDCD-system of (regular) grammars is a system of order n ($n \geq 1$) $PDCD = (N, \Sigma, S, (H_1, \ldots, H_n), \Gamma, \bot, \delta)$, where $N, \Sigma, S, (H_1, \ldots, H_n)$ are the same as at CD-systems of (regular) grammars: they form the components of the system; further, Γ is a finite set of symbols (used as a stack alphabet), $\bot \notin \Gamma$ is the bottom marker of the pushdown store and $\delta : \{1, \ldots, n\} \times (\Gamma \cup \{\bot\}) \to 2^{\{1,\ldots,n\} \times (\Gamma \cup \{\bot\})^*}$ is the (nondeterministic) successor relation. For every pair $(j, V) \in \{1, \ldots, n\} \times \Gamma$ the value of $\delta(j, V)$ is a subset of $\{1, \ldots, n\} \times \Gamma^{\leq 2}$ and for every pair of the form $(j, \bot)$ with $j \in \{1, \ldots, n\}$ the value of $\delta(j, \bot)$ is a subset of $\{1, \ldots, n\} \times (\bot \cdot \Gamma^{\leq 2})$ (we use the leftmost letter as the bottom of the stack, consequently the rightmost letter is its top symbol).*

The configuration of the PDCD-system is a triplet containing the sentential form, the index of the active component (with its stopping condition) and the content of the pushdown stack.

Let the mode of the computation $f \in \{*, t\} \cup \{= k, \leq k, \geq k \mid k \in \mathbb{N}, k > 0\}$ be fixed. Further, let, initially, the pushdown stack be empty (containing only the non-erasable bottom marker $\perp$). In PDCD-systems, any component having production of the form $S \to v$ ($v \in (N \cup \Sigma)^*$) can start the computation (it is chosen nondeterministically), let it be, say component i_0. Thus, the initial configuration is $(S, (i_0, f), \perp)$.

In derivation steps the sentential form is changed as the applied derivation rule describes. The derivation mode can be changed, i.e., at modes $f \in \{= k, \leq k, \geq k \mid k > 0\}$ it changes to $= k - 1, \leq k - 1, \geq k - 1$, respectively. Furthermore, the modes $\leq k, \geq 0$ and $*$ can be changed to $= 0$ nondeterministically after any derivation step. Moreover the mode t switches to $= 0$ if there is no applicable production in the active component for the actual sentential form (as we give some more details later on). (We note here that w.l.o.g we assume that there is no production of the form $A \to A$ in a PDCD-system that is used in mode t, as this would make a trap not to allow finishing the derivation.) A component finishes its task if the actual configuration shows $= 0$ or ≤ 0 mode.

When i_0 finishes its task in mode f (the configuration is $(w, (i_0, f'), \perp)$ with $w \in (N \cup \Sigma)^*$, and $f' \in \{= 0, \leq 0\}$), then the index of the next active component is chosen by using the set $\delta(i_0, \perp)$ and the stack is modified accordingly, e.g., if $(i_1, \perp U) \in \delta(i_0, \perp)$, then component i_1 becomes active and the stack content is modified to $\perp U$ (where $U \in \Gamma^*$). The stack is used only when the next active component is determined.

Then component i_1 is working in mode f (the originally fixed derivation mode), and when it finishes its task the next component is chosen by using the set $\delta(i_1, V)$, where V is the rightmost letter of $\perp U$, etc.

As we have mentioned, in mode t, the mode may switch to $= 0$. This happen when the following condition holds. Let the active component be i. If there is no nonterminal in w in the actual configuration $(w, (i, t), U)$, with $w \in \Sigma^*$ and $U \in \perp \Gamma^*$ or there is no production with the nonterminal, let us say A, which is the only nonterminal of the actual configuration $(wA, (i, t), U)$ (with $w \in \Sigma^*$ and $U \in \perp \Gamma^*$) and there is no production in H_i with A on its left hand side. In these cases, the configuration is switched to $(w, (i, = 0), U)$ and $(wA, (i, = 0), U)$, respectively.

In general, when the configuration is $(w, (i, f'), \perp U)$ with $w \in (N \cup \Sigma)^*$, and $f' \in \{= 0, \leq 0\}$, then the next configuration is $(w, (i', f), U')$ where $(i', V'') \in \delta(i, V')$ and V' is the rightmost symbol of $\perp U = VV'$ with $V \in \{\varepsilon\} \cup \perp \Gamma^*$, and $U' = VV''$ if $V \neq \varepsilon$ and $U' = V''$ if $V = \varepsilon$.

A configuration $(w, (i, f'), U)$ is called finishing configuration if $w \in \Sigma^*$, $f' \in \{= 0, \leq 0\}$ and $U = \perp$ for some index $i \in \{1, \ldots, n\}$.

The generated language of a PDCD-system $PDCD$ in mode f is given by the set of words $L(PDCD) = \{w \in \Sigma^* \mid$ there is a finishing configuration $(w, (i, f'), \perp)$ for some $i \in \{1, \ldots, n\}\}$.

Let us see an example for a PDCD-system.

Example 1. Let $PDCD = (\{S, A, B, D, E, F\}, \{1, 0, [,], +, -, *\}, S, (H_1, H_2, H_3, H_4, H_5, H_6, H_7), \{D, E\}, \perp, \delta)$, where the components contain the following rules:

$$H_1: \qquad H_2: \qquad H_3: \qquad H_4:$$
$$S \to 0F, \qquad S \to [D, \qquad D \to S, \qquad B \to +E,$$
$$S \to 1A, \qquad\qquad\qquad E \to S, \qquad B \to -E,$$
$$A \to 1A, \qquad\qquad\qquad\qquad\qquad\qquad B \to *E,$$
$$A \to 0A, \qquad H_5: \qquad H_6: \qquad H_7:$$
$$A \to F, \qquad B \to \varepsilon, \qquad B \to]F, \qquad F \to B;$$

further δ is defined as follows

$$\delta(1, \perp) = \{(7, \perp)\}, \qquad \delta(1, D) = \{(7, D)\}, \qquad \delta(1, E) = \{(7, E)\},$$
$$\delta(2, \perp) = \{(3, \perp D)\}, \qquad \delta(2, D) = \{(3, DD)\}, \qquad \delta(2, E) = \{(3, ED)\},$$
$$\delta(3, \perp) = \{\}, \qquad \delta(3, D) = \{(1, D), (2, D)\}, \qquad \delta(3, E) = \{(1, E), (2, E)\},$$
$$\delta(4, \perp) = \{(3, \perp E)\}, \qquad \delta(4, D) = \{(3, DE)\}, \qquad \delta(4, E) = \{(3, EE)\},$$
$$\delta(5, \perp) = \{\}, \qquad \delta(5, D) = \{\}, \qquad \delta(5, E) = \{\},$$
$$\delta(6, \perp) = \{(7, \perp)\}, \qquad \delta(6, D) = \{(7, D)\}, \qquad \delta(6, E) = \{(7, E)\},$$
$$\delta(7, \perp) = \{(5, \perp)\}, \qquad \delta(7, D) = \{(4, \varepsilon)\}, \qquad \delta(7, E) = \{(6, \varepsilon)\}.$$

The language generated by this system in mode t is the context-free language having fully bracketed expressions (using brackets [and]) with binary nonnegative integers using binary operations $+$, $-$ and $*$.

The derivation may start with the work of component 1 or 2. Actually, component 2 is opening a bracket ([) and then a D is pushed into the stack, while the derivation continues with component 3 and then by component 1 or 2. Component 1 derives a binary integer and then component 7 is used: depending on the top symbol of the pushdown stack the derivation is finished (empty stack) by component 5, or continued by an operation sign (at the case when D is in the top) by component 4, or by a closing bracket (], when E is the top symbol) by component 6, and so forth. An example derivation is as follows:

$(S, (2, t), \perp) \Rightarrow ([D, (2, t), \perp) \Rightarrow ([D, (2 = 0), \perp) \Rightarrow$

$([D, (3, t), \perp D) \Rightarrow ([S, (3, t), \perp D) \Rightarrow ([S, (3, = 0), \perp D) \Rightarrow$

$([S, (2, t), \perp D) \Rightarrow ([[D, (2, t), \perp D) \Rightarrow ([[D, (2, = 0), \perp D) \Rightarrow$

$([[D, (3, t), \perp DD) \Rightarrow ([[S, (3, t), \perp DD) \Rightarrow ([[S, (3, = 0), \perp DD) \Rightarrow$

$([[S, (1, t), \perp DD) \Rightarrow ([[1A, (1, t), \perp DD) \Rightarrow ([[11A, (1, t), \perp DD) \Rightarrow^* ([[11F, (1, = 0), \perp DD) \Rightarrow$

$([[11F, (7, t), \perp DD) \Rightarrow^* ([[11B, (4, t), \perp D) \Rightarrow^* ([[11 - E, (3, t), \perp DE) \Rightarrow^*$

$([[11 - S, (1, t), \perp DE) \Rightarrow ([[11 - 1A, (1, t), \perp DE) \Rightarrow ([[11 - 10A, (1, t), \perp DE) \Rightarrow^*$

$([[11 - 10F, (7, t), \perp DE) \Rightarrow^* ([[11 - 10B, (6, t), \perp D) \Rightarrow^* ([[11 - 10]F, (7, t), \perp D) \Rightarrow^*$

$([[11 - 10]B, (4, t), \perp) \Rightarrow^* ([[11 - 10] * E, (3, t), \perp E) \Rightarrow^* ([[11 - 10] * S, (2, t), \perp E) \Rightarrow^*$

$([[11 - 10] * [D, (3, t), \perp ED) \Rightarrow^* ([[11 - 10] * [S, (1, t), \perp ED) \Rightarrow^* ([[11 - 10] * [100F, (7, t), \perp ED) \Rightarrow^*$

$([[11 - 10] * [100B, (4, t), \perp E) \Rightarrow^* ([[11 - 10] * [100 + E, (3, t), \perp EE) \Rightarrow^*$

$([[11 - 10] * [100 + S, (1, t), \perp EE) \Rightarrow^* ([[11 - 10] * [100 + 0F, (7, t), \perp EE) \Rightarrow^*$

$([[11 - 10] * [100 + 0B, (6, t), \perp E) \Rightarrow^* ([[11 - 10] * [100 + 0]F, (7, t), \perp E) \Rightarrow^*$

$([[11 - 10] * [100 + 0]B, (6, t), \perp) \Rightarrow^* ([[11 - 10] * [100 + 0]F, (7, t), \perp) \Rightarrow^*$

$[[11 - 10] * [100 + 0]]B, (5, t), \perp) \Rightarrow^* ([[11 - 10] * [100 + 0]], (5, = 0), \perp),$

This is a finishing configuration by generating $[[11 - 10] * [100 + 0]]$.

In the remaining part of the section we present results about the generative power of PDCD-systems of regular grammars.

Note that it is allowed by our definition that the same component works on the sentential form in two consecutive turns (i.e., $(i, U) \in \delta(i, V)$ is allowed). Of course, it may not make sense in mode t, but in other modes it may make sense. On the other hand, actually, the same generating power can be achieved without allowing these generations by adding, for instance, identical components that could work by turns.

Further, we prove equivalence relations among systems used in various generating modes. In the proof of our first result we use a somewhat related idea as the one we have just mentioned.

Theorem 1. *The language family that can be generated by PDCD-systems of regular grammars in mode $= 1$ is the same as the language family that can be generated by PDCD-systems of regular grammars in mode $*$.*

Proof. Both directions of the proof go by simulation. Let

$$PDCD = (N, \Sigma, S, (H_1, H_2, \ldots, H_n), \Gamma, \bot, \delta)$$

be a system that is used to generate language L in mode $=1$. Then, one can construct the system

$$PDCD' = (N', \Sigma, S_1, (H'_1, H''_1, H'_2, H''_2, \ldots, H'_n, H''_n), \Gamma, \bot, \delta')$$

in the following way: Let $N' = \{A, A' \mid A \in N\}$ and for the j-th component $(1 \leq j \leq n)$ let $H'_j = \{A \to aB' \mid A \to aB \in H_j$ for $A, B \in N, a \in \Sigma \cup \{\varepsilon\}\} \cup \{A \to a \mid A \to a \in H_j$ for $A \in N, a \in \Sigma \cup \{\varepsilon\}\}$ and $H''_j = H' \cup \{A' \to aB \mid A \to aB \in H_j$ for $A, B \in N, a \in \Sigma \cup \{\varepsilon\}\} \cup \{A' \to a \mid A \to a \in H_j$ for $A \in N, a \in \Sigma \cup \{\varepsilon\}\}$. The successor relation δ' is defined in such a way that it allows to use primed and doubleprimed components in an alternating way: $\delta'(j', V) = \{(m'', U) \mid (m, U) \in \delta(j, V)\}$ and $\delta'(j'', V) = \{(m', U) \mid (m, U) \in \delta(j, V)\}$. Thus, in any of the component grammars of $PDCD'$ there cannot be two consecutive derivation steps, hence mode $= 1$ is equivalent to mode $*$.

For the other direction, let us have $PDCD = (N, \Sigma, S, (H_1, \ldots, H_n), \Gamma, \bot, \delta)$ be a system that is used to generate language L in mode $*$. To generate the same language in mode $= 1$, let us use the modified system

$$PDCD' = (N, \Sigma, S, (H_1, \ldots, H_n), \Gamma, \bot, \delta'),$$

where $\delta'(i, U) = \delta(i, U) \cup \{(i, U)\}$, in this way allowing to use the same component more than once consecutively.   □

In fact, the mode ≥ 1 is equivalent to the mode $*$, as there is no real condition given for the number of derivation steps in a component grammar, it can be any positive integer (of course depending also on the component grammar itself similarly as at mode $*$). Hence, from the previous theorem we have the following:

Corollary 1. *The language family that can be generated by PDCD-systems of regular grammars in mode $= 1$ is the same as the language family that can be generated by PDCD-systems of regular grammars in mode ≥ 1.*

Theorem 2. *The language family that can be generated by PDCD-systems of regular grammars in mode = 1 is the same as the language family that can be generated by PDCD-systems of regular grammars in mode ≤ k for any value of k > 0.*

Proof. Actually, the construction we had in the second part of the proof of Theorem 1 suffices also to show that mode = 1 can be simulated by ≤ k (with any positive integer k), since in that PDCD-systems, there could be exactly one derivation step in any component before switching to other component, and therefore the derivations in mode = 1 and mode ≤ k are exactly the same.

To prove the other direction, consider

$$PDCD = (N, \Sigma, S, (H_1, \ldots, H_n), \Gamma, \bot, \delta),$$

a system that is used to generate language L in mode $\leq k$. Let us construct the system

$$PDCD' = (N, \Sigma, S, (H_1^1, \ldots, H_1^k, \ldots, H_n^1, \ldots, H_n^k), \Gamma, \bot, \delta')$$

be defined in the following way. Let

$$H_j^i = \{A \rightarrow aB \mid A \rightarrow aB \in H_j \text{ for } A, B \in N, a \in \Sigma \cup \{\varepsilon\}\}$$

for every $1 \leq i \leq k$ and $1 \leq j \leq n$. Further, let δ' be defined in the following way:

$$\delta'(j^\ell, V) = \{(m^1, U) \mid (m, U) \in \delta(j, V)\} \cup \{(j^{\ell+1}, V)\} \text{ if } \ell < k$$

and

$$\delta'(j^k, V) = \{(m^1, U) \mid (m, U) \in \delta(j, V)\}.$$

By this construction the components $H_j^1, \ldots, H_j^k$ in mode = 1 simulate stepwise the work of the original component H_j in mode $\leq k$, since it could be that each of these components will be used one after the other, or after any, the derivation may continues with the component H_i^1 corresponding to the component H_i of the original system $PDCD$ working after component i.

Therefore $PDCD'$ in mode = 1 is equivalent to $PDCD$ in mode $\leq k$.   □

Let us consider now the working modes = k and $\geq k$ for $k > 1$.

Theorem 3. *The language family that can be generated by PDCD-systems of regular grammars in mode = 1 is the same as the language family that can be generated by PDCD-systems of regular grammars in mode = k for any value of k > 1.*

Proof. Let

$$PDCD = (N, \Sigma, S, (H_1, \ldots, H_n), \Gamma, \bot, \delta)$$

be a system that is used to generate language L in mode = 1. Then one can construct the system

$$PDCD' = (N', \Sigma, S_1, (H_1', \ldots, H_n'), \Gamma, \bot, \delta)$$

in the following way: Let $N' = \{A_i \mid A \in N, 1 \leq i \leq k\}$ and $H = \{A_i \to A_{i+1} \mid A \in N, 1 \leq i \leq k-1\}$. For the j-th component $(1 \leq j \leq n)$ let

$$H'_j = H \cup \{A_k \to aB_1 \mid A \to aB \in H_j \text{ for } A, B \in N, a \in \Sigma \cup \{\varepsilon\}\}$$

$$\cup \ \{A_k \to a \mid A \to a \in H_j \text{ for } A \in N, a \in \Sigma \cup \{\varepsilon\}\}.$$

Now, based on the construction, it can be shown that $PDCD'$ in mode $= k$ can simulate exactly the same computations as the ones can be done by $PDCD$ in mode $= 1$: a component in the first $k - 1$ steps just counting from 1 till $k - 1$ by the index of the actual nonterminal, and by the k-th step it simulates the derivation step of the original system.

Now, for the other direction, let

$$PDCD = (N, \Sigma, S, (H_1, \dots, H_n), \Gamma, \bot, \delta)$$

be a system that is used to generate language L in mode $= k$ (for a fixed $k > 1$). Then let

$$PDCD' = (N', \Sigma, S^1, (H_1^1, \dots, H_1^k, \dots, H_n^1, \dots, H_n^k), \Gamma, \bot, \delta')$$

be defined in the following way. Let $N' = \{A^i \mid A \in N, 1 \leq i \leq k\}$. Let

$$H_j^i = \{A^i \to aB^{i+1} \mid A \to aB \in H_j \text{ for } A, B \in N, a \in \Sigma \cup \{\varepsilon\}\}$$

for every $1 \leq i < k$ and $1 \leq j \leq n$ and

$$H_j^k = \{A^k \to aB^1 \mid A \to aB \in H_k\} \cup \{A^k \to a \mid A \to a \in H_k\}$$

for every $1 \leq j \leq n$.
Further let δ' be defined in the following way: $\delta'(j^i, V) = \{(j^{i+1}, V)\}$ for every $1 \leq j \leq n$, $1 \leq i < k$ and $V \in \Gamma \cup \{\bot\}$; and $\delta'(j^k, V) = \{(m^1, U) \mid (m, U) \in \delta(j, V)\}$.

By this construction, the components $H_j^1, \dots, H_j^k$ in mode $= 1$ simulate stepwise the work of the original component H_j in mode $= k$. Therefore $PDCD'$ in mode $= 1$ is equivalent to $PDCD$ in mode $= k$. Hence the proof.   □

By modifying the previous proof we can also state the next theorem.

Theorem 4. *The language family that can be generated by PDCD-systems of regular grammars in mode $= 1$ is the same as the language family that can be generated by PDCD-systems of regular grammars in mode $\geq k$ (for any fixed $k > 1$).*

Proof. Let $k > 0$ be fixed. The first direction is to show that every PDCD-system of regular grammars working in mode $= 1$ has an equivalent system working in mode $\geq k$. Actually, the mode $\geq k$, can be used if in each component there could be exactly k derivation steps, and thus, the construction shown in the first part of the proof of Theorem 3 can also be used here.

Now, we show that PDCD-systems working in mode $\geq k$ can be simulated by systems working in mode $= 1$. Let

$$PDCD = (N, \Sigma, S, (H_1, \ldots, H_n), \Gamma, \perp, \delta)$$

be a system that is used to generate language L in mode $\geq k$. Then let

$$PDCD' = (N', \Sigma, S^1, (H_1^1, \ldots, H_1^k, \ldots, H_n^1, \ldots, H_n^k), \Gamma, \perp, \delta')$$

be defined as follows: Let $N' = \{A^i \mid A \in N, 1 \leq i \leq k\}$. Let

$$H_j^i = \{A^i \to aB^{i+1} \mid A \to aB \in H_j \text{ for } A, B \in N, a \in \Sigma \cup \{\varepsilon\}\}$$

for every $1 \leq i < k$ and $1 \leq j \leq n$ and

$$H_j^k = \{A^k \to aB^k, A^k \to aB^1 \mid A \to aB \in H_k\} \cup \{A^k \to a \mid A \to a \in H_k\}$$

for every $1 \leq j \leq n$.
Further let δ' be defined in the following way: $\delta'(j^i, V) = \{(j^{i+1}, V)\}$ for every $1 \leq j \leq n$, $1 \leq i < k$ and $V \in \Gamma \cup \{\perp\}$; and $\delta'(j^k, V) = \{(m^1, U) \mid (m, U) \in \delta(j, V)\} \cup \{(j^k, V)\}$.

By this construction, the components $H_j^1, \ldots, H_j^k$ in mode $= 1$ simulate stepwise the work of the original component H_j in mode $\geq k$ since H_j^k can be used several times. Therefore $PDCD'$ in mode $= 1$ is equivalent to $PDCD$ in mode $\geq k$. Thus, the statement of the theorem is proven.   □

Now we are ready to state one of our main results.

Theorem 5. *The language family that can be generated by PDCD-systems of regular grammars in mode $= 1$ is exactly the class of context-free languages.*

Proof. The proof is constructive in both directions. First we show that every context-free language can be generated by PDCD-systems of regular grammars in mode $= 1$ computations. Let L be a context-free language, and thus, let

$$PDA = (\{1, \ldots, n\}, 1, \{n\}, \Sigma, \Gamma, \perp, \delta)$$

be a pushdown automaton that accepts it by final state and empty stack, with an appropriate number of states (here, w.l.o.g., numbers are used to name the states and there is only one final state). Let us construct a PDCD-system as follows: let

$$PDCD = (\{A_1, \ldots, A_n\}, \Sigma, A_1, (H_1, \ldots, H_n), \Gamma, \perp, \delta'),$$

where the sets of productions and the successor relation are defined as follows: If $(j, U) \in \delta(i, a, V)$ $(1 \leq i, j \leq n, a \in \Sigma \cup \{\varepsilon\}, U \in (\Gamma \cup \{\perp\})^*, V \in \Gamma \cup \{\perp\})$, then let $(j, U) \in \delta'(i, V)$ and $A_i \to aA_j \in H_i$. Further, let $A_n \to \varepsilon \in H_n$. Then $PDCD$ simulates PDA: every transition of PDA is done in two steps: first a derivation rule is applied (referring to the reading from the tape) and then, by the successor relation, the stack operation is simulated. Finally, $PDCD$ can finish a derivation by the component H_n when PDA reaches its accepting state n and also the stack is empty at that time.

Now, let us prove that only context-free languages can be generated by PDCD-systems of regular grammars in mode $= 1$. Thus, let

$$PDCD = (N, \Sigma, S, (H_1, \ldots, H_n), \Gamma, \bot, \delta)$$

be given. We construct a pushdown automaton

$$PDA = (Q, q_0, \{q_f\}, \Sigma, \Gamma, \bot, \delta')$$

accepting a language with its accepting state q_f that equivalent to $PDCD$. Let $Q = \{q_0, q_f\} \cup (\{1, \ldots, n\} \times N)$ be the set of states. Further, let δ' be given in the following way:

-   $((i, S), \bot) \in \delta'(q_0, \varepsilon, \bot)$ for every $1 \leq i \leq n$;
-   $((j, B), U) \in \delta'((i, A), a, V)$ if $A \to aB \in H_i$ $(A, B \in N, a \in \Sigma \cup \{\varepsilon\})$ and $(j, U) \in \delta(i, V)$ $(V \in \Gamma \cup \{\bot\}, U \in (\Gamma \cup \{\bot\})^*, 1 \leq i, j \leq n)$;
-   $(q_f, \bot) \in \delta'((i, A), a, \bot)$ if $A \to a \in H_i$ (with $A \in N, a \in \Sigma \cup \{\varepsilon\}, 1 \leq i \leq n)$.

A state (i, A) denotes that component i is active and nonterminal A appears in the actual sentential form. The accepting state q_f is reached when the stack becomes empty and there is no nonterminal in the sentential form, i.e., when a successful derivation is simulated. In this way PDA simulates the work of $PDCD$ in mode $= 1$, and accepts the language that $PDCD$ generates in mode $= 1$. The equivalence stated in the theorem is proven.   □

5   Fractal Automata and Mode t Derivations

As the class of context-free languages is accepted by the class of pop–no-change–push (shortly, pnp) pushdown automaton, we recall this concept (for more details, see, e.g., [10]).

A pushdown automaton is a pnp pushdown automaton, if it uses only three types of restricted transitions:

-   pop operation: the top element is popped out from the stack and the next state depends on that symbol as well;
-   no change: in this transition the stack is not used, the next state does not depend on the stack contents, and the stack has not been changed during this transition;
-   push operation: a new element is pushed to the stack and the next state is independent of the earlier stack contents.

One may consider this type of automata as a kind of normal form for pushdown automata.

Now, let us consider PDCD-systems of regular grammars working in mode t.

Theorem 6. *The language family that can be generated by PDCD-systems of regular grammars in mode t is exactly the class of context-free languages.*

Proof. In the first part of the proof we present that PDCD-systems working in mode $= 1$ (that are equivalent to context-free grammars and to pushdown automata by Theorem 5) can be simulated by PDCD-systems working in mode t. Actually in the first part of the proof of Theorem 4 we have constructed the system $PDCD'$ that works in modes $= k, \geq k$ and t similarly, and thus it generates the same language as the original system in mode $= 1$.

Now, let us prove the other direction, i.e., that PDCD-systems in working mode t cannot generate more than the class of context-free languages. Because the lack of space we describe mainly the idea of this part of the proof.

Let us check what is the condition for a component to terminate. A component is a regular grammar, and thus the derivation terminates if and only if the actual sentential form has not a nonterminal that occurs on the left-hand-side of any rule of the component. More precisely, there are two mutual disjoint cases: if the derivation finishes without any nonterminal in the sentential form (this e.g. could happen at successful derivations), or the nonterminal of the sentential form is such a nonterminal from which the derivation cannot be continued in that component. Since the component is a regular grammar, in any case, a regular language describes this terminating derivation: for component i, let the regular language $R_{i,A}^0$ (that may be empty) be the language that can be generated by terminating mode without having nonterminal at the end of the derivation, starting from nonterminal A; and similarly the regular language $R_{i,A}^0(B)$ (that may be empty) describes the language that can be generated by terminating mode having nonterminal B in the sentential form at the end of this terminating derivation starting from nonterminal A. Regular languages can be accepted by finite automata, and also by pushdown automata without changing the stack content (for any $V \in \Gamma \cup \{\bot\}$ the transition mapping pop and push back the same symbol at every transition). Thus one may construct a pushdown automaton PDA such that it is able to simulate the work of a component, and then by using/changing the stack, it can simulate the successor relation (in a similar manner as it is described in the construction at the second part of the proof of Theorem 5), then simulates the next active component and so on. This PDA accepts the same language as the original PDCD-system generates in mode t. $\square$

Further, based on the pnp normal form for pushdown automata, one can construct a PDCD-system generating every context-free language in mode t such that the successor relation works as one of the following cases for every component i:

- $(j, \varepsilon) \in \delta(i, V)$ for every $V \in \Gamma \cup \{\bot\}$, j may depend on the value of V (pop);
- $(j, V) \in \delta(i, V)$ for every $V \in \Gamma \cup \{\bot\}$ and j does not depend on the value of V (no change);
- $(j, VV') \in \delta(i, V)$ for every $V \in \Gamma \cup \{\bot\}$, $V' \in \Gamma$, j does not depend on the value of V (push).

In a PDCD-system satisfying the above condition there are three possibilities to use the stack: either the topmost symbol is popped and the next component is chosen by the information stored in that symbol, or a new symbol is pushed to the stack (the symbol that was on the top before is left in the stack without used) or, in some cases we may not use the stack at all (neither pop, nor push is used, and the next active component is chosen without the information in the stack).

A fractal automaton is a (usually) infinite state automaton that is built up by finitely many types of subautomata (we denote the types by $\alpha, ..., \gamma$, etc.) in a recursive manner. A subautomation is similar to a nondeterministic finite automaton (maybe with ε-transitions) with a sole accepting state, but some of its states may be replaced by (maybe another type) subautomata, we refer to those as recursion states. For each recursion state a subautomaton type is assigned and we replace it by an occurrence of that type subautomata. Also the sets of states of any two subautomata of different type are disjoint. When a subautomaton is embedded instead of a recursion state (we refer to it as an occurrence of the subautomaton), then the transition to this recursion state (in a computation) actually, reaches the initial state of the embedded subautomaton, and transition from this recursion state is applied when the computation has reached the accepting state of the embedded subautomaton. Thus, there could be (even infinitely) many occurrences of a subautomaton in the fractal automaton, and one of the occurrences of a subautomaton also plays the role of the main subautomaton, starting the computation. We give it formally based on [10].

Definition 2. *A fractal automaton is a tuple $FRA = (Q, \Sigma, \Lambda, \delta, s, f)$ with the (infinite) set of states Q, the (input) alphabet Σ, the label alphabet Λ, the transition function $\delta : Q \times (\Sigma \cup \{\varepsilon\}) \to 2^Q$ (only to finite subsets of Q), the initial and the final states $s, f \in Q$, respectively, they are standard states.*

Further, the label alphabet Λ contains two disjoint finite sets $\Lambda = \Lambda_a \cup \Lambda_n$. Λ_n contains the names of the standard states. The symbols of Λ_a denote the recursion states. $x \in \Lambda$ identifies both the subautomaton type and the state in it (either it is a standard or a recursion state). Let Λ_a^γ and Λ_n^γ denote the sets of recursion and standard states of a type γ subautomaton, respectively. Every state of the fractal automaton $q \in Q$ is identified by its label of the form $u \cdot p$ from the set $\Lambda_a^* \Lambda_n$ ($u \in \Lambda_a^*, p \in \Lambda_n$). The set of states is defined in an iterative way. Let

- *$Q_0 = \Lambda_n^\alpha \cup \{J \mid J \in \Lambda_a^\alpha\}$ for the type α of the main subautomaton. Thus, states labeled by elements of Λ_n^α having address with $u = \varepsilon$ and they are located in the main subautomaton, a specific occurrence of type α that is not embedded to any subautomaton.*
- *Starting from the set Q_i the set Q_{i+1} is obtained as follows. $Q_{i+1} = (Q_i \cap \Lambda_a^* \Lambda_n) \cup \{uJp \mid u \in \Lambda_a^*, J \in \Lambda_a, uJ \in Q_i, p \in \Lambda_n^\gamma$, where γ is the type associated to $J\} \cup \{uJK \mid u \in \Lambda_a^*, J \in \Lambda_a, uJ \in Q_i, K \in \Lambda_a^\gamma$, where γ is the type associated to $J\}$.*

With this infinite process, in the limit, one obtains the infinite set of states $Q = \lim_{i \to \infty} Q_i$.

The transition function δ is defined as follows.

- *For two states $up, ur \in Q$, let $up \in \delta(ur, b)$ with $u \in \Lambda_a^*$, $p, r \in \Lambda_n^\alpha$, $b \in \Sigma \cup \{\varepsilon\}$ if the transition $p \in \delta(r, b)$ was in the subautomaton type α between two standard states.*
- *$uJp \in \delta(ur, b)$ with $u \in \Lambda_a^*$, $J \in \Lambda_a$, $r \in \Lambda_n^\alpha$, $p \in \Lambda_n^\beta$, $b \in \Sigma \cup \{\varepsilon\}$ if in the subautomaton of type α there is a transition from a standard state r with b to the recursion state J for which a type β subautomaton is assigned and its initial state is p (assuming $uJp, ur \in Q$).*
- *$up \in \delta(uJr, b)$ with $u \in \Lambda_a^*$, $J \in \Lambda_a$, $r \in \Lambda_n^\beta$, $p \in \Lambda_n^\alpha$, $b \in \Sigma \cup \{\varepsilon\}$ if r is the final state of the type β subautomaton and in the type α subautomaton there is a transition from the recursion state J (with an assigned type β subautomaton) to the state p with b (assuming $up, uJr \in Q$).*

Thus, (usually) $Q \subset \Lambda_a^* \Lambda_n$ is restricted to contain only valid states that can be reached from s by the transition function for some input words.

A fractal automaton works in a similar way as a finite automaton (the only difference is that the former has an infinite number of states), thus the computations, the accepting computations and the accepted language are defined analogously. Moreover, for every word $w \in \Sigma^*$ there is a value $i \geq 0$ such that its acceptance can be decided using the finite set Q_i instead of the infinite set Q. Even if the set of states Q is infinite, there is a convenient way to address the states of a fractal automaton.

Further, we show that the fractal automata can also be seen as special graphical (diagrammatic) representations of PDCD-systems of regular grammars working in mode t.

Let $PDCD = (N, \Sigma, S, (H_1, \ldots, H_n), \Gamma, \bot, \delta)$ working in mode t have stack operations pop, no change and push. Consider $FRA = (Q, \Sigma, \Lambda, \delta', q_0, q_a)$ with the set of states Q, the initial and accepting states $q_0, q_a \in Q$, respectively, the (input) alphabet Σ, the label alphabet Λ and the transition function δ' : $Q \times (\Sigma \cup \{\varepsilon\}) \to 2^Q$. Further, let $\Lambda = \Gamma \cup \{q_0, q_a\} \cup \{1, \ldots, n\} \times N$ and $Q = (\Gamma^* \cdot (\{1, \ldots, n\} \times N)) \cup \{q_0, q_a\}$.

Let $\delta(q_0, \varepsilon) = \{(i, S) \mid 1 \leq i \leq n\}$, $U \cdot (i, B) \in \delta((U \cdot (i, A), a)$ (where $U \in \Gamma^*$, $A, B \in N$ and $a \in \Sigma \cup \{\varepsilon\}$) if $A \to aB \in H_i$.

Further, let $UVV'(j, A) \in \delta'((UV(i, A), \varepsilon)$ if $(j, VV') \in \delta(i, V)$ and there is no rule of the form $A \to u$ in H_i with $U \in \Gamma^*, V, V' \in \Gamma, A \in N, u \in (\Sigma \cup N)^*$; in case $V = \bot$, i.e., if $(j, \bot V') \in \delta(i, \bot)$, then $V'(j, A) \in \delta'((i, A))$); push of V' to the stack, stepping into a recursion in the fractal automaton.

Then, let $U(j, A) \in \delta'(UV(i, A), \varepsilon)$ if $(j, \varepsilon) \in \delta(i, V)$ and there is no rule of the form $A \to u$ in H_i (pop V from the stack, coming out from a recursion in the fractal automaton).

Let $UV(j, A) \in \delta'(UV(i, A), \varepsilon)$ if $(j, V) \in \delta(i, V)$ and there is no rule of the form $A \to u$ in H_i (case of no change of the stack).

Finally, let $q_a \in \delta'((i, A), a)$ if $A \to a \in H_i$ ($a \in \Sigma \cup \{\varepsilon\}, A \in N$).

Usually, only those states of the system are used that are reachable from q_0. FRA is a fractal automaton that is equivalent to $PDCD$, i.e., accepts the same language that is generated by $PCCD$ in mode t.

The states of the fractal automata are addressed by finite length words, actually, a state label is corresponding to the content of the stack and the only nonterminal of the actual sentential form of the derivation reaching the actual state together with the active component.

Remark 1. If the order of the PDCD-system is 1, then in mode t the pushdown stack cannot be used, and thus the fractal automaton of the system is a finite automaton accepting the regular language generated by the only component of the system.

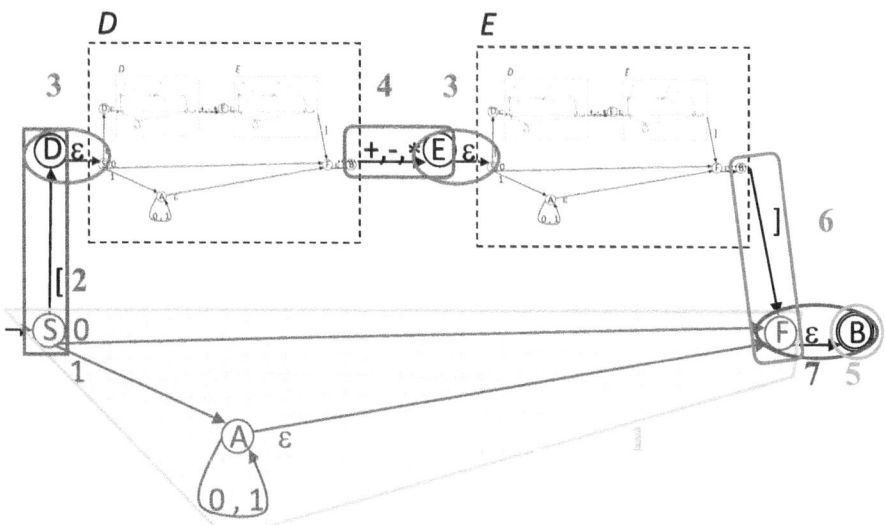

Fig. 1. Fractal automaton accepting a non-regular context-free language, the colored parts show the represented component grammars. Colored numbers refer to the index of the component. For brevity, q_0, q_a and transitions $\delta(q_0, \varepsilon) = \{(1, S), (2, S)\}$ and $\delta((5, B), \varepsilon) = \{q_a\}$ are not shown.

Now let us see the fractal automaton that is based on the PDCD-system shown in Example 1. Figure 1 shows the fractal automaton that accepts this context-free language. Rectangles are representing the occurrences of the embedded subautomata into recursion states, i.e., they separate the states having different label addresses from Γ^*. One could observe that, there is a sole type and there are two recursion states. The states of the fractal automaton can be addressed by strings from $\Gamma^* \cdot (\{1, \ldots, 7\} \times N)$. Actually, in this example, all the component grammars appear already in the main subautomaton, i.e., they are used already when the stack contains only ⊥. Therefore, we can highlight with colors the parts that refers to the various component grammars (shown in Fig. 1), this colored number and the nonterminal written in the state together is an element of Λ_n. In the example the Italic version of D and E are in Λ_a.

In our example every rectangle is self-similar to the original automaton, as we use only one type. In the general case, it can happen that some rectangles (subautomata) differ from each other. In this case, there may be component grammars that do not appear in the main subautomaton.

For every context-free language there is a finite number of types of sub-automata. Usually, each component grammar is connected to specific area of a subautomaton (rectangle), and appears in all the (maybe infinitely many) occurrences of the given rectangle (subautomaton).

The derivation of Example 1 can be represented by a walk as an accepting computation of the corresponding fractal automaton as it is shown in Fig. 2.

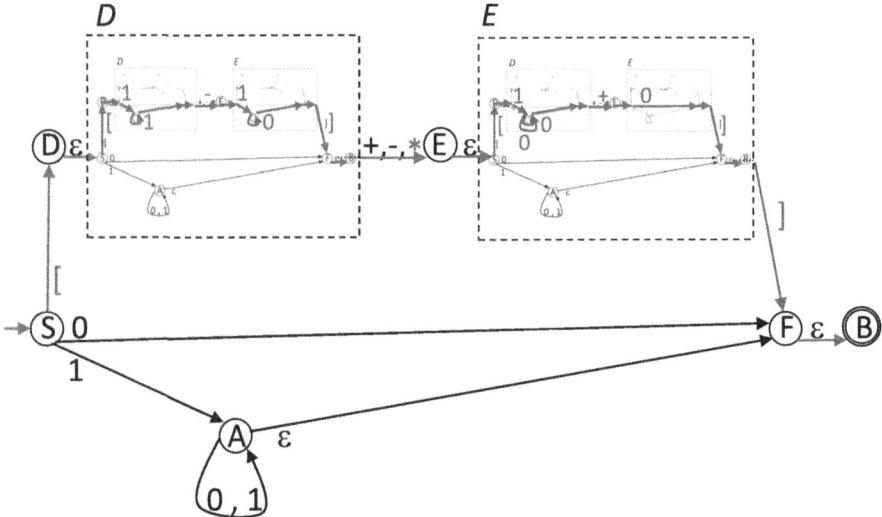

Fig. 2. A computation in the fractal automaton is represented by a walk from its start to its end: $[[11 - 10] * [100 + 0]]$ is accepted by FRA with the shown computation.

Observing the work of these automata we can state the following fact.

Remark 2. For any context-free languages (that is not the empty language) the fractal automaton accepting the language must have at least one recursion-free accepting path, i.e. there is a word of the language that is accepted without recursion.

6   Conclusions, Open Problems

PDCD-systems of regular grammars are presented in this paper. It was shown, that using any of the usual modes of derivations, the PDCD-systems of regular grammars are able to generate exactly the context-free languages. Based on PDCD-systems working in mode t, a graphical representation of context-free languages is given by a shown relation to fractal automata that have a self-similar property by recursion.

An interesting question for future research is to investigate the PDCD-systems of a more general class of grammars, e.g., context-free grammars. Since CD-systems of context-free grammars are themselves much more powerful than context-free grammars (e.g., in mode t the class of ET0L languages can be generated), it is an interesting question whether an additional pushdown storage can increase further their generating power. It would also be interesting to check whether PDCD-systems of regular grammars with some combined or hybrid modes of derivations are able to generate some non context-free languages.

Some interesting open questions about the fractal automata are also arisen, for instance, from descriptional complexity point of view, e.g., what the minimal number of mutually different rectangle diagrams is needed to describe a given context-free language (we know that it is one for regular languages, but it can be one for some non-regular context-free languages also as we have shown with our example).

References

1. Csuhaj-Varjú, E., Dassow, J., Kelemen, J., Păun, G.: Grammar Systems. A Grammatical Approach to Distribution and Cooperation. Gordon and Breach, London (1994)
2. Csuhaj-Varjú, E.: Grammar systems. In: Martin-Vide, C., Mitrana V., Păun, Gh. (eds.): Formal Languages and Applications, chap. 14, pp. 275–310. Springer, Heidelberg (2004)
3. Dassow, J., Păun, G.: Regulated rewriting in formal language theory. In: (EATCS Monographs on Theoretical Computer Science 18). Springer, Berlin (1989)
4. Dassow, J., Păun, G., Rozenberg, G.: Grammar systems. In: [16], vol. 2, chap. 4, pp. 155–213
5. Herendi, T., Nagy, B.: Parallel Approach of Algorithms. Typotex, Budapest (2013)
6. Hopcroft, J.E., Ullmann, J.D.: Introduction to Automata Theory, Languages, and Computation. Addison-Wesley, Reading (1979)
7. Horváth, G., Nagy, B.: Formal Languages and Automata Theory. Typotex, Budapest (2014)
8. Nagy, B.: Graphical representations of context-free languages. In: Dwyer, T., Purchase, H., Delaney, A. (eds.) Diagrammatic Representation and Inference (Diagrams 2014), LNCS, vol. 8578, pp. 48–50. Springer, Heidelberg (2014). https://doi.org/10.1007/978-3-662-44043-8_7
9. Nagy, B.: From finite automata to fractal automata – the power of recursion. In: Durand-Lose, J., Vaszil, G. (eds.) Proceedings of the 9th International Conference Machines, Computations, and Universality (MCU 2022). LNCS, vol. 13419, pp. 109–125. Springer (2022). https://doi.org/10.1007/978-3-031-13502-6_8
10. Nagy, B.: Fractal automata: recursion in context-free and in deterministic and linear context-free languages. Int. J. Found. Comput. Sci., 1–32 (2025). https://doi.org/10.1142/S0129054125450017

11. Nagy, B., Otto, F.: CD-systems of stateless deterministic R(1)-automata accept all rational trace languages. In: Dediu, A.H., Fernau, H., Martin-Vide, C. (eds.) LATA 2010. LNCS, vol. 6031, pp. 463–474. Springer, Berlin (2010). https://doi.org/10.1007/978-3-642-13089-2_39

12. Nagy, B., Otto, F.: Finite-state acceptors with translucent letters. In: Bel-Enguix, G., Dahl, V., Ortega De La Puente, A. (eds.) ICAART 2011 - 3rd International Conference on Agents and Artificial Intelligence, BILC 2011, Proceedings of the of 1st International Workshop on AI Methods for Interdisciplinary Research in Language and Biology, pp. 3–13, SciTePress, Portugal (2011)

13. Nagy, B., Otto, F.: An automata-theoretical characterization of context-free trace languages. In: Cerná, I., Gyimóthy, T., Hromkovic, J., Jefferey, K., Královic, R., Vukolic, M., Wolf, S. (eds.) SOFSEM 2011. LNCS, vol. 6543, pp. 406–417. Springer, Heidelberg (2011). https://doi.org/10.1007/978-3-642-18381-2_34

14. Nagy, B., Otto, F.: CD-systems of stateless deterministic R(1)-automata governed by an external pushdown store. RAIRO Theoret. Inform. Appl. RAIRO-ITA **45**, 413–448 (2011). https://doi.org/10.1051/ita/2011123

15. Nagy, B., Otto, F.: On CD-systems of stateless deterministic R-automata with window size one. J. Comput. Syst. Sci. JCSS **78**, 780–806 (2012). https://doi.org/10.1016/j.jcss.2011.12.009

16. Rozenberg, G., Salomaa, A. (eds.): Handbook of Formal Languages, vol. 3. Springer, Heidelberg (1997)

Parallel Accepting Colonies: Computational Power and Deterministic Parsing

Petr Sosík and Lucie Ciencialová(✉)

Institute of Computer Science, Faculty of Philosophy and Science in Opava,
Silesian University in Opava, Opava, Czech Republic
{petr.sosik,lucie.ciencialova}@fpf.slu.cz

Abstract. In the framework of formal languages, colonies are understood as teams of simple rewriting agents acting on strings of symbols. They were introduced as formal devices generating sets of strings (i.e., formal languages) from a given axiom. We study variants of colonies acting as parallel language acceptors, i.e., characterizing formal languages by their reduction to the axiom. We first show that the class of languages these colonies accept in the weakly competitive mode strictly contains the class of context-free languages. Then we focus on their possible applications in parallel parsing of formal languages. We construct a class of restricted parallel accepting colonies for which there exists a deterministic parsing algorithm working in polynomial time.

Keywords: Grammar system · parallel colony · deterministic parsing

1 Introduction

Over the decades, many mechanisms have been explored that utilize both generative and accepting approaches to problems in formal languages and automata theory. Most of these mechanisms are based on a sequential approach, but there are also systems that operate in parallel, offering potential advantages in computational efficiency and modeling complex processes. Grammar systems are distributed computing models that explore various aspects of cooperation and communication in language generation in a sequential and also in a parallel manner. Each grammar operates on a string that represents an environment, making grammar systems a suitable formalization for decentralized or distributed systems of agents in artificial intelligence. The study of grammar systems began in the 1990s, driven by the motivation behind blackboard architectures. The concept of cooperating distributed (CD) grammar systems was introduced in [4,6]. The early models within grammar systems theory were primarily inspired by distributed artificial intelligence. CD grammar systems were designed as a syntactic model of blackboard-based problem-solving architectures, in which multiple independent agents collaborate by modifying a shared blackboard that represents the current state of the problem solving process. In a CD grammar system,

M. D. Jiménez López and G. Vaszil (Eds.): Erzsébet Csuhaj-Varjú Festschrift,
LNCS 15840, pp. 103–116, 2025.
https://doi.org/10.1007/978-3-031-97274-4_7

generative grammars act as agents, and a string represents the global database. Agents sequentially modify the string according to their cooperation strategy, thus contributing to the solution of a problem and the generation of a terminal word. These systems demonstrate that even simple grammars with basic cooperation can generate complex languages. For an overview, see [5,8]. While CD grammar systems use sequential rewriting, parallel communicating grammar systems (PCGS) [12] introduce parallelism, allowing grammars to operate on their own strings in parallel and communicating by exchanging strings upon request. The language of the system consists of words produced by the master component. In [1] the authors deal with the accepting mode of PCGS and show that all types of accepting PCGS define recursively enumerable languages, even without λ rules. In [2] generating PCGS were examined and it was shown that non-returning context-free PCGS generate context-sensitive languages and can be recognized in linear space.

The model of colony, introduced in [9], is inspired by the behaviour of reactive agents in robotics. Like CD and PC grammar systems, it consists of multiple agents/components that work together and are represented by finite languages. The system includes an environment component represented by a string, which remains passive and only changes through the actions of the components. Since there is no predefined strategy, each grammar acts whenever possible, with conflicts resolved non-deterministically. The language of a colony is the set of all possible (terminal) strings of the environment. Various derivation modes and acceptance styles have been explored (see [3,10]). Despite using simple regular grammars, colonies exhibit emergent behaviour and can generate large language classes. Key differences arise from the number of components that act in one step, distinguishing sequential, parallel, and team-based models. For additional derivation modes and results on different terminal alphabets, see [9–11]. In parallel colonies, introduced in [7], multiple components can be active at the same time, following the principle that all components capable of operating on the current string must do so simultaneously. A component is considered active if its start symbol appears in the environment. Each active component must rewrite one occurrence of its start symbol. If all components have distinct start symbols, no conflicts arise. However, when components share the same start symbol and there are insufficient occurrences in the environment, competition conflicts must be resolved, resulting in several different derivation modes [7].

This paper deals with parallel colonies working in the accepting mode (i.e., as language acceptors), where the components consume substrings of the processed string and replace them by their starting symbols. After fixing elements of the formal language theory in Sect. 2, Sect. 3 defines variants and behavior of parallel accepting colonies. In Sect. 4 we establish a new result about classes of languages accepted by these colonies. In Sect. 5 we show that there exists an efficient parallel deterministic algorithm for parsing of languages of these colonies, suggesting possible applications relevant to programming languages. Section 6 discusses open problems and concludes the paper.

2   Formal Prerequisites

In this section, we review necessary elements of the formal language theory. The reader is referred to the monograph [13] for a general overview. For a finite alphabet V we denote by V^* the free monoid generated by V under the operation of catenation. Catenation of strings x_1, x_2 is denoted $x_1 x_2$, the empty string is denoted by λ, $V^+ = V^* - \{\lambda\}$. Let L_1 and L_2 subsets of V^*. Their catenation will be denoted as $L_1 \cdot L_2 = \{x_1 x_2 | x_1 \in L_1, \ x_2 \in L_2\}$.

For $x \in V^*$ and $a \in V$, $|x|_a$ denotes the number of occurrences of a in x. For $U \subseteq V$ we denote $|x|_U = \sum_{a \in U} |x|_a$. Similarly, let $w \in V^+$, $L \subseteq V^+$, then we denote

$$|x|_w = \max\{n \geq 0 \mid x = x_0 w x_1 w \ldots w x_n, \ x_0, \ldots, x_n \in V^*\},$$

$$|x|_L = \max\{n \geq 0 \mid x = x_0 w_1 x_1 w_2 \ldots w_n x_n; \ w_1, \ldots w_n \in L, \ x_0, \ldots, x_n \in V^*\}.$$

A context-free grammar (CFG) is defined as a tuple $G = (N, T, P, S)$, where N is a finite set of nonterminal symbols, T is a finite set of terminal symbols disjoint from N, P is a finite set of production rules of the form $A \to \alpha$, where A is a nonterminal symbol and $\alpha \in (N \cup T)^*$, and S is a distinguished start symbol from V.

A derivation step in a CFG is the process of replacing a nonterminal in a string by the right-hand side of one of its production rules. If a string γ_1 contains a nonterminal A and there exists a production rule $A \to \alpha$, then replacing A with α in γ_1 produces a new string γ_2, which is written as $\gamma_1 \Rightarrow \gamma_2$. A derivation is a sequence of derivation steps that starts from the start symbol and produces a terminal string.

A leftmost derivation in a context-free grammar is a derivation where, at each step, the leftmost nonterminal in the current string is replaced using a production rule. Leftmost derivations are particularly useful in parsing as they provide a structured way of analyzing the syntactic construction of a string.

A context-free grammar is in Greibach Normal Form (GNF) if every production rule has the form $A \to a\alpha$, where $A \in N$, $a \in T$, and $\alpha \in N^*$. The only exception is that the start symbol may produce the empty string λ if and only if the language contains λ. This normal form ensures that every derivation step immediately produces one terminal symbol.

A k-limited *ET0L*system abbreviated as *klET0L* system is a quintuple $G = (V, V_T, \{P_1, P_2, \ldots, P_r\}, \omega, k)$ where V_T is a nonempty subset (terminal alphabet) of the alphabet V, $\omega \in V^+$ and each so-called table P_i is a finite subset of $V \times V^+$ which satisfies the condition that for each $a \in V$ there is a word $w_a \in V^*$ such that $a \to w_a \in P_i$ such that each P_i defines a finite substitution $\sigma_i : V \to 2^{V^*}$. G is called propagating if no table contains an erasing production $a \to \lambda$. According to G, $x \Rightarrow y$ (for $x, y \in V^*$) iff there is a table P_i and partitions $x = x_0 \alpha_1 x_1 \ldots \alpha_n x_n$, $y = x_0 \beta_1 x_1 \ldots \beta_n x_n$ such that $\alpha_r \to \beta_r \in P_i$ for each $1 \leq r \leq n$ and, for each $a \in V$, $k_a = |\{r : \alpha_r = a\}| \leq k$ where $k_a < k$ implies that a is not contained in $x_0 x_1 \ldots x_n$. The language generated by a *klET0L* system G is $L_{gen}(G) = \{w \in V_T^* \mid \omega \Rightarrow^* w\}$. For $k = 1$, let us denote the class of

languages of 1-limited extended tabled interactionless Lindenmayer systems by
1lET0L.

A matrix grammar is an ordered quadruple $G = (N, T, M, S)$, where N, T,
and S are exactly as in the definition of a generative grammar but M is a finite
set of finite nonempty sequences whose elements production rules of the form
$\alpha \to \beta$, where $\alpha \in (N \cup T) * N(N \cup T)*$ and $\beta \in (N \cup T)*$. The sequences
are referred to as matrices and written $m = [\alpha_1 \to \beta_1, \ldots, \alpha_r \to \beta_r]$, $r \geq 1$.
Let F be the collection of all productions appearing in the matrices m of
a matrix grammar G and F_1 a subset of F. A binary relation $\Rightarrow_{ac}$ (which
depends on G and F_1) on the set $(N \cup T)^*$ is defined as follows: For any
$u, v \in (N \cup T)^*$, $u \Rightarrow_{ac} v$ holds iff there exists an integer $r \geq 1$ and
words $u_1, \ldots u_{r+1}$, $\alpha_1, \ldots, \alpha_r$, $\beta_1, \ldots, \beta_r$, $x_1, \ldots, x_r$, $y_1, \ldots, y_r$,
over $(N \cup T)^*$ such that (1) $u_1 = u$, $u_{r+1} = v$, (2) the matrix $m = [\alpha_1 \to$
$\beta_1, \ldots, \alpha_r \to \beta_r] \in M$ and (3) for every $i \in \{1, 2, \ldots, r\}$ either $u_i = x_i \alpha_i y_i$ and
$u_{i+1} = x_i \beta_i y_i$ or else production $\alpha_i \to \beta_i \in F_i$, α_i is not a subword of u_i, and
$u_i = u_{i+1}$. The language generated by G with appearance checking for produc-
tions in F_1 is defined by $L_{ac}(G, F_1) = \{w \in T^* \mid S \Rightarrow_{ac}^* w\}$. Let us denote the
class of languages of matrix grammar using context-free productions without
λ–productions with appearance checking by MAT_{ac}.

Please consult [13] for more details.

3   Parallel Accepting Colonies

Definition 1. *A colony of degree* n; $n \geq 0$ *is a construct*

$$C = (N, T, (S_1, F_1), \ldots, (S_n, F_n), S), \quad where$$

- N *is a finite nonempty set called the set of nonterminals of* C
- T *is a finite nonempty set called the set of terminals of* C
- (S_i, F_i), $1 \leq i \leq n$, *is called a component of* C; $S_i \in N$ *is a start symbol of
  the component;* $F_i \subseteq (T \cup N - \{S_i\})^*$ *is a finite language*
- $S = S_i$ *for some* i, $1 \leq i \leq n$, *is called the start symbol of* C.

For a given colony C we denote $V = N \cup T$, the total alphabet of the colony,
and $F = F_1 \cup F_2 \cup \cdots \cup F_n$. Parallel colonies can work both in generating and
accepting mode. For the definition of generating mode and examples, the reader
is referred to [7]. Parallel accepting colonies were introduced analogously in [14].

Definition 2 ([14]). *Let* $C = (N, T, (S_1, F_1), \ldots, (S_n, F_n), S)$ *be a colony and
let* $x, y \in V^*$, *where* V *is the total alphabet of* C.

1. *We say that* C *accepts strings in parallel* without competition, *when the
   derivation step is defined as follows:* $y \xRightarrow{\text{acc}}_n x$ *iff*
   (a) $x = x_1 S_{i_1} x_2 S_{i_2} \ldots x_k S_{i_k} x_{k+1}$, $x_j \in V^*$, $1 \leq j \leq k + 1$;
       $y = x_1 z_{i_1} x_2 z_{i_2} \ldots x_k z_{i_k} x_{k+1}$; $z_{i_j} \in F_{i_j}$, $1 \leq j \leq k$;
   (b) $i_u \neq i_v$ *for all* $u \neq v$, $1 \leq u, v \leq k$.

2. *We say that C accepts strings in parallel with the weak competition when the derivation step is defined as follows: $y \stackrel{acc}{\Longrightarrow}_w x$ iff $y \stackrel{acc}{\Longrightarrow}_n x$ and, moreover,*
   (c) $|x_p|_{F_m} = 0$ for each j, i, $1 \le j \le k+1$; $1 \le i \le n$; $i \notin \{i_1, i_2, \ldots, i_k\}$.
3. *We say that C accepts strings in parallel with the strong competition when the derivation step is defined as follows: $y \stackrel{acc}{\Longrightarrow}_s x$ iff $y \stackrel{acc}{\Longrightarrow}_n x$ and, moreover,*
   (d) if $|y|_w > 0$ for some $w \in F_i$, $1 \le i \le n$, then there is j, $1 \le j \le k$, such that $i_j = i$.

Informally, in the weak competition mode, a component (S_i, F_i) can be inactive only if it cannot be used to rewrite any of the intact substrings $x_1, \ldots, x_{k+1}$ of y. In the strong competition mode, a component (S_i, F_i) must be used in the derivation step whenever F_i contains a substring of the processed string y. If it cannot be used (e.g., due to competition with other components attempting to rewrite an overlapping part of y), then the derivation is blocked. Instead of no competition, weak competition, or strong competition, respectively, we will say for brevity that C works in a competition mode n, w, or s, respectively.

Definition 3. *The language accepted by a colony C in parallel in a competition mode $m \in \{n, w, s\}$ is the set*

$$L_m^{acc}(C) = \{w \mid w \stackrel{acc}{\Longrightarrow}_m^* S, \ w \in T^*\},$$

where $\stackrel{acc}{\Longrightarrow}_m^*$ denotes the reflexive and transitive closure of $\stackrel{acc}{\Longrightarrow}_m$.

We denote COL_m^{acc} the class of languages accepted by colonies in parallel in competition mode $m \in \{n, w, s\}$. Analogously, due to [7], we denote the classes of languages generated by parallel colonies in modes $m \in \{n, w, s\}$ by COL_m^{gen}.

Example 1. Consider the language $L = \{a^n b^n c^n \mid n \ge 1\}$, which is known to be neither in CF nor in COL_w^{gen}.

(a) $L_s^{acc}(C) = L$ for the following colony:

$C \ = \ (\{S, X, Y, X', Y', Z\}, \{a, b, c\}, (S, \{abc, XY, aXbYc\}), (X, \{X'\}), (Y, \{Y'\}), \ (X', \{aab, aaXb\}), (Y', \{bcc, bYcc\}), (Z, \{XbYcc, XbbYccc, aaXbY, aaa XbbY\}), S).$

(b) $L_w^{acc}(C) = L$ for the following colony:

$C \ = \ (\{S, X, Y, X', Y', Z\}, \{a, b, c\}, (S, \{abc, XY, aXbYc\}), (X, \{X'\}), (Y, \{Y'\}), (X', \{aab, aaXb\}), (Y', \{bcc, bYcc\}), (Z, \{X, Y\}), S).$

In both cases, components associated with S, X, Y, X', Y' guarantee that the processed string must be of the form $a^i b^j c^k$ such that $i + k = 2j$. The last component blocks the derivation in the case $i \ne k$; hence, the string is accepted only for $i = j = k$.

4   Generative Power of Accepting Colonies

Lemma 1. $COL_n^{acc} = CF$.

Proof. Consider a context-free grammar $G = (N, T, P, S)$. Construct a parallel accepting colony $C = (N, T, (S_1, F_1), \ldots, (S_n, F_n), S)$, $n = |N|$, with components (S_i, F_i) for each $S_i \in N$ such that $F_i = \{y \mid (A \to y) \in P\}$. Clearly, a terminal string can be generated by G *iff* it can be accepted by C using one component in each step, i.e., without parallelism. Conversely, any derivation of C can be reversely and sequentially mirrored in G. Hence, $L(G) = L_n^{acc}(C)$. Analogously, to any parallel accepting colony, one can construct a context-free grammar generating the language accepted by the colony without competition.

Summarizing the results in [7,10,14], together with Lemma 1 and Example 1, we can establish the following relations:

$$COL_n^{gen} = COL_n^{acc} = CF$$

$$CF \subset COL_w^{gen} \subset 1lET0L, \quad CF \subset COL_s^{gen} \subseteq MAT_{ac}$$

$$COL_s^{gen} \setminus COL_w^{gen} \neq \emptyset, \quad COL_w^{acc} \setminus COL_w^{gen} \neq \emptyset$$

$$COL_w^{acc} \subseteq CS, \quad COL_s^{acc} \subseteq CS$$

The relation of the classes CF and COL_w^{acc} remained open in [14]. Here we establish a proper inclusion.

Theorem 1. $CF \subseteq COL_w^{acc}$.

Proof. Let $G = (N, T, P, S)$ be a context-free grammar in Greibach normal form and denote $T = \{a_1, a_2, \ldots, a_k\}$, $N = \{B_1, \ldots, B_n\}$, where $k, n \geq 1$. Let $\{A_1, \ldots, A_k\}$, $\{A'_1, \ldots, A'_k\}$, $\{B'_1, \ldots, B'_n\}$ be sets of new nonterminals that are not in N.

Let σ be an injective coding such that $\sigma(a_i) = A_i$ for each i, $1 \leq i \leq k$, and $\sigma(B_i) = B'_i$ for each i, $1 \leq i \leq n$. Consider a colony

$$\begin{aligned}
C = (&N \cup \{A_1, \ldots, A_k\} \cup \{A'_1, \ldots, A'_k\} \cup \{B'_1, \ldots, B'_n\}, T, \\
&(B_1, F_1), \ldots, (B_n, F_n), (B'_1, \{B_1\}), \ldots, (B'_n, \{B_n\}) \\
&(A_1, \{a_1, A'_1\}), \ldots, (A_k, \{a_k, A'_k\}), (A'_1, \{A_1\}), \ldots, (A'_k, \{A_k\}), S),
\end{aligned}$$

where $F_i = \{\sigma(\alpha) \mid (B_i \to \alpha) \in P\}$ for each i, $1 \leq i \leq n$. We will show that $L(G) = L_w^{acc}(C)$.

(i) $L(G) \subseteq L_w^{acc}(C)$: Consider a leftmost derivation

$$S \Longrightarrow a_{i_1}\beta_1 \Longrightarrow a_{i_1}a_{i_2}\beta_2 \Longrightarrow \ldots \Longrightarrow a_{i_1} \ldots a_{i_m}\beta_m = w \qquad (1)$$

in G for some $w \in T^*$, $a_{i_j} \in T$, $\beta_j \in N^*$, $1 \leq j \leq m$. Clearly $\beta_m = \lambda$. w can be reduced to S by C in the following way:

(a) At the first step, only the components $(A_1, \{a_1, A_1'\}), \ldots, (A_k, \{a_k, A_k'\})$ can be used and one occurrence of each terminal symbol a_i in w is rewritten to $\sigma(a_i)$. Assume, without loss of generality, that the rightmost occurrence of each terminal is rewritten by C, so that w adopts the form $b_1 \ldots b_{m-1} A_{i_m}$, where $b_j \in \{a_{i_j}, A_{i_j}\}$ for each j, $1 \le j < m$.

(b) Induction hypothesis: let, after simulation of $m - \ell$ steps of the derivation (1) in reverse order, the string derived by C have the form

$$y = b_1 \ldots b_{\ell-1} A_{i_\ell} \beta_\ell, \quad 1 \le \ell \le m,$$

where $b_j \in \{a_{i_j}, A_{i_j}, A_{i_j}'\}$ for each j, $1 \le j < \ell$, and $\beta_\ell \in \sigma(N^*)$. Moreover, let $|y|_{A_i} \le 1$, $|y|_{A_i'} \le 1$ for each i, $1 \le i \le k$. By (1), P must contain a rule allowing for the derivation $\beta_{\ell-1} \Longrightarrow a_{i_\ell} \beta_\ell$. Then C it must contain a component such that C can take the derivation step

$$y = b_1 \ldots b_{\ell-1} A_{i_\ell} \beta_\ell \stackrel{\text{acc}}{\Longrightarrow}_w b_1' \ldots b_{\ell-1}' \beta_{\ell-1} = x,$$

where $b_j' \in \{a_{i_j}, A_{i_j}, A_{i_j}'\}$ for each j, $1 \le j < \ell$, and $\beta_{\ell-1} \in N \cdot \sigma(N^*)$. Moreover, $|x|_{A_i} \le 1$, $|x|_{A_i'} \le 1$ for each i, $1 \le i \le k$. During this step
* each occurrence of A_i in y except A_{i_ℓ} is rewritten to A_i';
* each occurrence of A_i' in y is rewritten to A_i;
* other unused components $(A_i, \{a_i, A_i'\})$ rewrite rightmost occurrences of a_i to A_i;
* this is a correct step in weak competition mode, since no other component of C can be active.

(c) In the next step of C :
* the prefix letter B of $\beta_{\ell-1}$ is rewritten to B';
* each occurrence of A_i in x is rewritten to A_i';
* each occurrence of A_i' in x is rewritten to A_i;
* again this is a correct step in weak competition mode.
Finally, if now $b_{\ell-1}' \ne A_{\ell-1}$ (and hence $b_{\ell-1}' = A_{\ell-1}'$), another step is performed, exchanging again each A_i for A_i' and vice versa.

(d) By induction, steps (b) and (c) can be iterated until S is derived from w.

(ii) $L_w^{acc}(C) \subseteq L(G)$: Assume that there exists a derivation $w \stackrel{\text{acc}}{\Longrightarrow}_w^* S$ in C, for some $w \in T^*$. The derivation must contain a sequence of actions of components (B_i, F_i), as the remaining components only apply (reverse) coding σ. Each action of such a component of C can be reversely simulated by a rule of G, and hence $S \Longrightarrow_G^* w$.

Together with Example 1 we have

Corollary 1. $CF \subset COL_w^{acc}$.

5   Deterministic Parsing in Parallel Colonies

The following definition fixes the intuitive concept of a derivation tree of parallel colony very similarly as in the case of CF grammars.

Definition 4. *Let* $C = (N, T, (S_1, F_1), \ldots, (S_n, F_n), S)$ *be a parallel accepting colony in a competition mode* $m \in \{n, w, s\}$. *Let* $y \in V^*$ *be a string such that* $y \overset{acc}{\underset{m}{\Longrightarrow}}{}^* S$. *A derivation tree of* y *is the oriented tree* T_y *with labelled nodes, whose frontier labels form* y *(from left to right) and for which the following holds:*

- *if* $y = S$, *then* T *consists of one node labelled* S;
- *otherwise there is* $w \in V^*$ *such that* $y \overset{acc}{\underset{m}{\Longrightarrow}} w \overset{acc}{\underset{m}{\Longrightarrow}}{}^* S$ *and*

$$w = x_1 S_{i_1} x_2 S_{i_2} \ldots x_k S_{i_k} x_{k+1}, \ x_j \in V^*, \ 1 \le j \le k+1,$$

$$y = x_1 z_{i_1} x_2 z_{i_2} \ldots x_k z_{i_k} x_{k+1}, \ z_{i_j} \in F_{i_j}, \ 1 \le j \le k.$$

Let T_w *be a derivation tree of* w, *then* T_y *is constructed from* T_w *by adding children forming* z_{i_j} *to each leaf* S_{i_j}, $1 \le j \le k$.

Lemma 2. *Let* $C = (N, T, (S_1, F_1), \ldots, (S_n, F_n), S)$ *be a parallel colony in a competition mode* $m \in \{n, w, s\}$ *and let* $w \in V^*$ *be a string such that* $w \overset{acc}{\underset{m}{\Longrightarrow}}{}^+ S$. *For each nonempty substring* $v \in V^+$ *of* w *there is a* $y \in F$ *such that at least one of the following conditions holds:*

(i) $w = \alpha y \beta = \alpha \gamma v \delta \beta$;
(ii) $w = \alpha \gamma y \delta \beta = \alpha v \beta$;
(iii) $w = \alpha \gamma y \beta = \alpha v \delta \beta$, *where* $|\gamma| < |v|$ *and* $|\delta| < |y|$;
(iv) $w = \alpha y \delta \beta = \alpha \gamma v \beta$, *where* $|\gamma| < |y|$ *and* $|\delta| < |v|$;

for some $\alpha, \beta, \gamma, \delta \in V^*$.

Proof. Recall that we denoted $F = F_1 \cup F_2 \cup \cdots \cup F_n$. Let T be the derivation tree of w in C, and let $d(v)$ be the depth (distance from the root) of a node v in T. Simple variants of cases (i)–(iv) of the lemma are illustrated in Fig. 1. Assume that there is a nonempty substring $v \in V^+$ of w such that none of the cases (i)–(iv) hold for any $y \in F$. Then $|v| \ge 2$ (otherwise the case (i) occurred) and we can write $v = axb$ for some $a, b \in V$, $x \in V^*$. Moreover, a and b have different parent nodes in T (otherwise one of the cases (i), (ii) occurred). Then there must be a node c in x such that $d(c) > d(a)$ and $d(c) > d(b)$, otherwise one of the cases (iii), (iv) occurred. Hence v contains a substring $c_1 c_2 \ldots c_k$, $k \ge 3$, such that $d(c_1) < d(c_2) = \cdots = d(c_{k-1}) > d(c_k)$. This implies that the case (ii) occurs – a contradiction.

Lemma 3. *Let* $C = (N, T, (S_1, F_1), \ldots, (S_n, F_n), S)$ *be a parallel colony in a competition mode* $m \in \{n, w, s\}$, *and let* $w \in V^*$ *be a string such that* $w \overset{acc}{\underset{m}{\Longrightarrow}}$ $z \overset{acc}{\underset{m}{\Longrightarrow}}{}^* S$, $w \overset{acc}{\underset{m}{\Longrightarrow}} x$ *and not* $x \overset{acc}{\underset{m}{\Longrightarrow}}{}^* S$ *for some* $x, z \in V^*$. *Then there are* $v \in F_i$, $y \in F_j$ *for some* i, j, $1 \le i, j \le n$, *where either* $S_i \ne S_j$ *or* $v \ne y$, *such that at least one of the following conditions holds:*

(a) $w = \alpha y \beta = \alpha \gamma v \delta \beta$;
(b) $w = \alpha \gamma y \beta = \alpha v \delta \beta$, $|\gamma| < |v|$ *and* $|\delta| < |y|$;

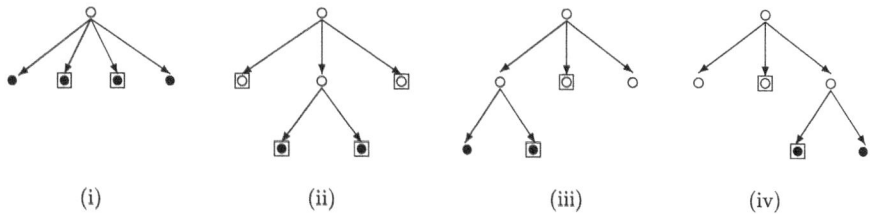

Fig. 1. An example of the cases (i)–(iv) from Lemma 2. The filled circles denote sub-words of y, the squares denote subwords of v.

for some $\alpha, \beta, \gamma, \delta \in V^*$.

Proof. Consider an arbitrary $v \in F_i$ for some i, $1 \le i \le n$, such that the reduction of v to S_i is used in the derivation $w \overset{\text{acc}}{\Longrightarrow}_m x$. Since $w \overset{\text{acc}}{\Longrightarrow}{}^*_m S$, due to Lemma 2 there exists an $y \in F_j$ for some j, $1 \le j \le n$ satisfying the conditions (i)–(iv) of Lemma 2. Since the order of S_i and S_j in the statement of the lemma is arbitrary, and hence strings v and y may be freely exchanged, the conditions (i) and (ii) of Lemma 2 are equivalent to our condition (a), and the conditions (iii) and (iv) are equivalent to our condition (b).

Moreover, if for each such v and y both $S_i = S_j$ and $v = y$ hold, then the steps $w \overset{\text{acc}}{\Longrightarrow}_m z$ and $w \overset{\text{acc}}{\Longrightarrow}_m x$ would be identical, which contradicts the assumption that $z \overset{\text{acc}}{\Longrightarrow}{}^*_m S$ and not $x \overset{\text{acc}}{\Longrightarrow}{}^*_m S$.

Before introducing restrictions on colonies that guarantee deterministic parallel parsing, function FIRST, LAST, FOLLOW and BEFORE must be defined analogously like in the classical parsing theory.

Definition 5. *Let $C = (N, T, (S_1, F_1), \dots, (S_n, F_n), S)$ be a colony, $\alpha \in V^*$, $A \in N$ and $k \ge 0$. We define*

$$\text{FIRST}_k(\alpha) = \{x \mid x\beta \overset{\text{acc}}{\Longrightarrow}{}^*_n \alpha;\ \beta, x \in V^*,\ |x| = k\} \cup \{x \mid x \overset{\text{acc}}{\Longrightarrow}{}^*_n \alpha;\ x \in V^*,\ |x| < k\}$$

$$\text{LAST}_k(\alpha) = \{x \mid \beta x \overset{\text{acc}}{\Longrightarrow}{}^*_n \alpha;\ \beta, x \in V^*,\ |x| = k\} \cup \{x \mid x \overset{\text{acc}}{\Longrightarrow}{}^*_n \alpha;\ x \in V^*,\ |x| < k\}$$

$$\text{BEFORE}_k(A) = \{x \mid \alpha x A \beta \overset{\text{acc}}{\Longrightarrow}{}^*_n S;\ \alpha, \beta, x \in V^*,\ |x| = k\} \cup \{x \mid x A \beta \overset{\text{acc}}{\Longrightarrow}{}^*_n S;\ \beta, x \in V^*,\ |x| < k\}$$

$$\text{FOLLOW}_k(A) = \{x \mid \alpha A x \beta \overset{\text{acc}}{\Longrightarrow}{}^*_n S;\ \alpha, \beta, x \in V^*,\ |x| = k\} \cup \{x \mid \alpha A x \overset{\text{acc}}{\Longrightarrow}{}^*_n S;\ \alpha, x \in V^*,\ |x| < k\}$$

Definition 6. *Let $C = (N, T, (S_1, F_1), \dots, (S_n, F_n), S)$ be a colony. We say that C is (k, ℓ) deterministic, if for each $x \in F_i$, $y \in F_j$ such that either $S_i \ne S_j$ or $x \ne y$ the following holds:*

(i) if $x = \alpha\beta$, $y = \beta\gamma$ for some $\beta \in V^+$, $\alpha, \gamma \in V^*$, then either

$$\mathrm{BEFORE}_k(S_j) \cap \mathrm{LAST}_k(\mathrm{BEFORE}_k(S_i) \cdot \{\alpha\}) = \emptyset, \ or \qquad (2)$$

$$\mathrm{FOLLOW}_\ell(S_i) \cap \mathrm{FIRST}_\ell(\{\gamma\} \cdot \mathrm{FOLLOW}_\ell(S_j)) = \emptyset; \qquad (3)$$

(ii) if $x = \beta$, $y = \alpha\beta\gamma$ for some $\beta \in V^+$, $\alpha, \gamma \in V^*$, then either

$$\mathrm{BEFORE}_k(S_i) \cap \mathrm{LAST}_k(\mathrm{BEFORE}_k(S_j) \cdot \{\alpha\}) = \emptyset, \ or \qquad (4)$$

$$\mathrm{FOLLOW}_\ell(S_i) \cap \mathrm{FIRST}_\ell(\{\gamma\} \cdot \mathrm{FOLLOW}_\ell(S_j)) = \emptyset. \qquad (5)$$

Intuitively, let a string $z \in V^*$ contain a substring uvw such that $v \in F_j$ and $u \in \mathrm{BEFORE}_k(S_j)$ for some component (S_j, F_j) of the colony. Let further the rewriting of v to S_j be a part of the derivation $z \overset{acc}{\Longrightarrow}{}^* S$. Then the condition (2) ensures that there is no other component (S_i, F_i) of C, $i \neq j$, which could also act on z and rewrite its part overlapping with v. Hence, to decide whether v should be overwritten by (S_j, F_j), it is enough to check whether the string u of length at most k placed left to v is in $\mathrm{BEFORE}_k(S_j)$. Analogously, condition (3) applies similarly to the string w of length at most ℓ placed right to v.

Algorithm 1. Parsing with (k, ℓ) deterministic parallel accepting colony

Denote $C = (N, T, (S_1, F_1), \ldots, (S_n, F_n), S)$ a (k, ℓ) deterministic colony and $w \in V^*$ an analysed string. Consider an arbitrary competition mode $m \in \{n, w, s\}$. Initially, let all the components of C and all the symbols of w be unmarked.

1. Find an unmarked substring y of w such that $y \in F_i$ for some unmarked component (S_i, F_i) and the following holds:
   - $w = \alpha x y z \beta$ for some $\alpha, \beta, x, z \in V^*$;
   - $|x| = k$ or $|x| < k$ and $\alpha = \epsilon$;
   - $|z| = \ell$ or $|z| < \ell$ and $\beta = \epsilon$;
   - $x \in \mathrm{BEFORE}_k(S_i)$ and $z \in \mathrm{FOLLOW}_\ell(S_i)$.
2. Mark the component (S_i, F_i) and all the symbols of y as used.
3. Repeat steps 1 and 2 until no further such y can be found (with a parallel hardware these steps can be done in parallel).
4. Check whether the parallel reduction of all marked y's to the corresponding S_i's represents a correct derivation step due to the chosen competition mode m. If not, break the parsing process.
5. Replace each marked y by the corresponding S_i. Unmark all symbols and all components.
6. Repeat steps 1–5 until $w = S$ or until no further derivation step can be done.

Theorem 2. *Let $C = (N, T, (S_1, F_1), \ldots, (S_n, F_n), S)$ be a (k, ℓ) deterministic parallel colony in a competition mode $m \in \{n, w, s\}$. Let $w \overset{\mathrm{acc}}{\Longrightarrow}{}^{*}_{m} S$ and $w \overset{\mathrm{acc}}{\Longrightarrow}_{m} x$ for some $w, x \in V^*$, the step $w \overset{\mathrm{acc}}{\Longrightarrow}_{m} x$ being done according to Algorithm 1. Then $x \overset{\mathrm{acc}}{\Longrightarrow}{}^{*}_{m} S$.*

Proof. For an arbitrary $\alpha \in V^*$, $k, \ell \geq 0$ we denote

$$\mathrm{left}_\ell(\alpha) = \begin{cases} \beta & \text{if there are } \beta, \gamma \in V^* \text{ such that } \alpha = \beta\gamma, \ |\beta| = \ell; \\ \alpha & \text{otherwise;} \end{cases}$$

$$\mathrm{right}_k(\alpha) = \begin{cases} \beta & \text{if there are } \beta, \gamma \in V^* \text{ such that } \alpha = \gamma\beta, \ |\beta| = k; \\ \alpha & \text{otherwise.} \end{cases}$$

Assume, by contradiction, that there is $x \in V^*$ such that $w \overset{\mathrm{acc}}{\Longrightarrow}_{m} x$ and not $x \overset{\mathrm{acc}}{\Longrightarrow}{}^{*}_{m} S$. Then, by Lemma 3, there must be $v, y \in F$ such that at least one of the conditions (a), (b) from this lemma holds.

(a) Assume that $w = \alpha y\beta = \alpha\gamma v\delta\beta$, where $v, y, \alpha, \beta, \gamma, \delta$ are specified in Lemma 3. Then necessarily

$$\mathrm{right}_k(\alpha) \in \mathrm{BEFORE}_k(S_j), \tag{6}$$
$$\mathrm{right}_k(\alpha\gamma) \in \mathrm{BEFORE}_k(S_i), \tag{7}$$
$$\mathrm{left}_\ell(\beta) \in \mathrm{FOLLOW}_\ell(S_j), \tag{8}$$
$$\mathrm{left}_\ell(\delta\beta) \in \mathrm{FOLLOW}_\ell(S_i). \tag{9}$$

From (6) and (8) we can obtain

$$\mathrm{right}_k(\alpha\gamma) \in \mathrm{LAST}_k(\mathrm{BEFORE}_k(S_j) \cdot \{\gamma\}),$$
$$\mathrm{left}_\ell(\delta\beta) \in \mathrm{FIRST}_\ell(\{\delta\} \cdot \mathrm{FOLLOW}_\ell(S_j)).$$

Together with (7) and (9) we have

$$\mathrm{BEFORE}_k(S_i) \cap \mathrm{LAST}_k(\mathrm{BEFORE}_k(S_j) \cdot \{\gamma\}) \neq \emptyset,$$
$$\mathrm{FOLLOW}_\ell(S_i) \cap \mathrm{FIRST}_\ell(\{\delta\} \cdot \mathrm{FOLLOW}_\ell(S_j)) \neq \emptyset,$$

which contradicts the condition (ii) of Definition 6 and hence the colony C would not be (k, ℓ) deterministic, a contradiction.

(b) Assume that $w = \alpha\gamma y\beta = \alpha v\delta\beta$, with $|\gamma| < |v|$ and $|\delta| < |y|$; then a derivation analogous to the case (a) above leads to a conflict with the condition (i) of Definition 6, hence again the colony C would not be (k, ℓ) deterministic, a contradiction.

Corollary 2. *Let $C = (N, T, (S_1, F_1), \ldots, (S_n, F_n), S)$ be a (k, ℓ) deterministic parallel colony working in any mode $m \in \{n, w, s\}$. For a given $w \in L(C)$ the Algorithm 1 reduces w to S and produces its derivation tree. For a given $w \notin L(C)$ the algorithm stops without reduction to S.*

For a colony $C = (N, T, (S_1, F_1), \ldots, (S_n, F_n), S)$, define its size $S(C)$ as the sum of the lengths of all strings in $F_1, \ldots, F_n$.

Theorem 3. *Algorithm 1 with an input (C, w), for a (k, ℓ) is a deterministic parallel colony $C = (N, T, (S_1, F_1), \ldots, (S_n, F_n), S)$, computes one derivation step of C in deterministic polynomial time with respect to $S(C)$, $|w|$, k and ℓ.*

Proof. Assume that the sets $\text{BEFORE}_k(S_i)$ and $\text{FOLLOW}_\ell(S_i)$ are precomputed for each component (S_i, F_i), $1 \leq i \leq n$, and stored in an efficient way, such as a tree or a sorted list. The sizes of these two sets are $\mathcal{O}(s^k)$ and $\mathcal{O}(s^\ell)$, respectively, where s is the size of the colony alphabet. One can assume, without loss of generality, that $s = \mathcal{O}(S(C))$. One derivation step of C is calculated by phases 1–5 of the Algorithm 1.

- Checking the condition $x \in \text{BEFORE}_k(S_i)$ and $z \in \text{FOLLOW}_\ell(S_i)$ in phase 1 of the algorithm for a chosen string $y \in F_i$ takes time $\mathcal{O}(k + \ell)$, as the searching of these sorted sets can be done in logarithmic time w.r.t. their sizes.
- As steps 1, 2, 3 of the algorithm are repeated, in the worst case, for all strings $y \in F_i$, $1 \leq i \leq n$, and for all their positions in w, the total time is $\mathcal{O}(S(C) \cdot |w| \cdot (k + \ell))$.
- Phase 4 requires checking of the presence of all strings $y \in F_i$, $1 \leq i \leq n$, in w, taking time $\mathcal{O}(S(C) \cdot |w|)$.
- Phase 5 can be completed in time $\mathcal{O}(S(C) + |w|)$.

The total time of phases 1–5 is thus $\mathcal{O}(S(C) \cdot |w| \cdot (k + \ell))$.

6   Conclusion and Open Problems

In this paper, we have shown that parallel accepting colonies in weakly competitive mode can accept a strictly larger class of languages than context-free languages. Weakly and strongly accepting colonies are both subsets of the class of context-sensitive languages. A tight upper bound of the classes COL_w^{acc} and COL_s^{acc} remains to be examined, as well as the relation of the class COL_s^{acc} to CF.

We also constructed classes $COL_m^{\text{acc}}(k, \ell)$ of parallel accepting colonies, for either none, weak, or strong competition mode m, with a deterministic parsing algorithm that runs in polynomial time. The characterization of these classes remains open and is a subject of further research. Obviously, $COL_m^{\text{acc}}(k, \ell) \subseteq COL_m^{\text{acc}}$, $m \in \{n, w, s\}$, but probably not conversely. We hypothesize that these classes are incomparable with CF for any $k, \ell \geq 0$. Simultaneously, we conjecture that these classes are large enough to be able to cover many formal languages with practical applications, namely the core parts of programming languages. Many current parsing systems (e.g., GLR, Earley, or CYK parsers) operate sequentially and handle ambiguity via complex backtracking or memoization strategies. The integration of the deterministic parallel colony model - either directly or via a hybrid approach—could improve their efficiency, particularly in deterministic substructures or in pre-processing stages. Moreover, existing parsing frameworks could leverage this theorem to parallelize certain grammar fragments, thereby optimizing performance without sacrificing correctness.

Acknowledgement. We would like to express our sincere gratitude to Erzsébet Csuhaj-Varjú for her outstanding support and professional dedication throughout our research. Her insightful contributions, stimulating discussions, and valuable ideas have significantly enriched our work. We are particularly grateful for her patience in listening to our questions and her clarity in explaining complex concepts.

The research was supported by the Silesian University in Opava under the Student Funding Plan, project SGS/9/2024.

Disclosure of Interests. The authors have no competing interests to declare that are relevant to the content of this article.

References

1. Bordihn, H., Dassow, J., Vaszil, Gy.: Grammar systems as language analyzers and recursively enumerable languages. In: Fundamentals of Computation Theory, pp. 136–147. Springer, Heidelberg (1999)
2. Bruda, S.: On the computational complexity of context-free Parallel Communicating Grammar Systems. In: Păun, G., Salomaa, A. (eds.) New Trends in Formal Languages. LNCS, vol. 1218, pp. 256–266. Springer, Heidelberg (1997). https://doi.org/10.1007/3-540-62844-4_18
3. Csuhaj-Varjú, E.: Colonies: a multi-agent approach to language generation. In: Extended Finite State Models of Language, pp. 208–225. Cambridge University Press (1999)
4. Csuhaj-Varjú, E., Dassow, J.: On cooperating-distributed grammar systems J. Inform. Process. Cybernet. **26**, 49–63 (1990)
5. Csuhaj-Varjú, E., Dassow, J., Kelemen, J., Păun, Gh.: Grammar Systems. Gordon & Breach (1994)
6. Csuhaj-Varju, E., Kelemen, J.: Cooperating grammar systems: a syntactical framework for blackboard model of problem solving. In: Proceedings of the AIICSR 1989, pp. 121–127 (1989)
7. Dassow, J., Kelemen, J., Păun, Gh.: On parallelism in colonies. Cybernet. Syst. **24**, 37–49 (1993)
8. Dassow, J., Păun, Gh., Rozenberg, G.: Grammar systems. In: Handbook of Formal Languages, pp. 155—214. Springer, Berlin (1997)
9. Kelemen, J., Kelemenová, A.: A grammar-theoretic treatment of multiagent systems. Cybern. Syst. **23**, 621–633 (1992)
10. Kelemenová, A., Csuhaj-Varjú, E.: Languages of colonies. Theoret. Comput. Sci. **134**, 119–130 (1994)
11. Kelemenová, A., Kelemen, J.: From colonies to eco(grammar)systems: an overview. In: Karhumäki, J., Maurer, H., Rozenberg, G. (eds.) Results and Trends in Theoretical Computer Science, vol. 812, pp. 213–231. Springer (1994)
12. Paun, Gh., Santean, L.: Parallel communicating grammar systems: the regular case. Ann. Univ. Bucharest Ser. Matem.-Inform. **38**, 55–63 (1989)

13. Salomaa, A., Rozenberg, G. (eds.): Handbook of Formal Languages. Springer, Berlin (1997)
14. Sosík, P.: Parallel accepting colonies and neural networks. In: Păun, Gh., Salomaa, A. (eds.) Grammatical Models of Multi-agent Systems, pp. 144–156. Gordon and Breach, London (1999)

Networks of Language Processors

Unconventional Computational Models for Distributed Networks: Results and Perspectives

Katalin Anna Lazár[✉]

Department of Algorithms and their Applications, Faculty of Informatics, ELTE
Eötvös Loránd University, Pázmány Péter sétány 1/c, Budapest 1117, Hungary
lazarkati@inf.elte.hu

Abstract. This paper aims to provide a systematic and coherent overview of advances in computational modeling within the framework of grammar systems theory. In grammar systems theory, grammars can be interpreted as agents, while the generated language describes the behavior of the system. The agents collectively shape the complexity and emergent properties of the system, which go beyond the scope of individual dynamics. Such emergent phenomena, considered as computational results, require an understanding of the limitations of these computations. We consider Internet crawlers searching for novel information on the World Wide Web, network clustering, peer-to-peer networks, and string assembly in distributed environments. First, we review the results concerning the computational capabilities of the devised constructs, which can be viewed as language-generating devices. Special emphasis is placed on certain variants, namely eco-grammar systems and networks of language processors, including networks of evolutionary processors. In addition, this paper shows how the NP-complete Hamiltonian Path Problem can be solved efficiently in linear time using networks of evolutionary processors. Finally, prospective avenues for future research are proposed to inspire further exploration in this area.

Keywords: Eco-grammar systems · Networks of language processors · Networks of evolutionary processors · computational completeness and efficiency

1 Introduction

In grammar systems theory, the behavior of an agent is not just a predefined set of actions, but rather an emergent property that arises from its complex and dynamic interactions with its environment [7]. This perspective reframes our understanding of formal languages as sequences of symbols that encapsulate, at a symbolic level, the behavior of complex systems composed of cooperating and communicating agents. The properties of the system are determined by the individual and collective behavior of its agents. In particular, their cooperation

M. D. Jiménez López and G. Vaszil (Eds.): Erzsébet Csuhaj-Varjú Festschrift,
LNCS 15840, pp. 119–134, 2025.
https://doi.org/10.1007/978-3-031-97274-4_8

can give rise to emergent properties at the macroscopic level, a phenomenon that transcends the individual dynamics of the components themselves. Such emergent properties can be interpreted as the results of computation. An unconventional perspective through the lens of grammar systems provides a robust framework for exploring these boundaries from a theoretical point of view.

In this paper, we focus on eco-grammar systems and networks of language processors, including evolutionary processors from a modeling perspective. We review the results published in [10, 16–23].

An eco-grammar system aims to model the interplay between the environment and the agents in complex systems such as ecosystems. In the original model [6, 8], both the environment and the agents have internal representations, and the interaction between the different components of the system is quite complex. This led to the development of simple eco-grammar systems where agents neither evolve nor do their actions on the environment depend on the state of the system.

Networks of language processors were initially conceptualized to provide a parallel and distributed framework for symbolic processing [9]. They consist of multiple language-identifying devices or components placed at the nodes of a virtual graph. The components alternately perform rewriting and communication steps to process strings. Successful communication depends on whether the strings satisfy the context conditions imposed by the filters. A special variant of networks of language processors is the network of evolutionary processors (NEP) [4]. A NEP consists of evolutionary processors that perform specific point mutations-insertions, deletions, or substitutions-on strings. In hybrid NEPs (HNEPs) [24], each node has its own mode of operation, and filters are defined by random context conditions (as opposed to NEPs where filters are regular languages). NEPs can be viewed as biological computational models: the rewriting operations can be interpreted as mutations and the filtering process as selection.

2   Preliminaries

We assume that the reader is familiar with basic concepts of formal language theory; for further details, see [25].

Let V be an alphabet. The set of all words over V is denoted by V^*, while V^+ represents the set of all nonempty words, i.e., $V^+ = V^* \setminus \{\lambda\}$, where λ is the empty string.

Let U denote the set (the universe) of objects. A multiset is a pair $M = (V, f)$, where V is an arbitrary (not necessarily finite) set of objects of U and $f : U \to \mathbb{N}_0$ is a mapping that assigns multiplicity to each object such that if $a \notin V$, then $f(a) = 0$. The support of $M = (V, f)$ is defined by $supp(M) = \{a \in V \mid f(a) \geq 1\}$. M is a finite multiset if $supp(M)$ is finite. The set of all finite multisets over the set V is denoted by V°.

A context condition ϱ over V^* is defined as a computable mapping $\varrho : V^* \to \{\text{true}, \text{false}\}$. We divide ϱ into two types:

1. **reg**: A regular context condition over V^* given by a regular language $L \subseteq V^*$. Here, $\varrho(\omega) = $ true if $\omega \in L$, and $\varrho(\omega) = $ false otherwise.
2. **rc**: A random context condition over V^* specified by a pair (Q, R), where $Q, R \subseteq V$. In this case, $\varrho(\omega) = $ true if $\omega \in V^*$ contains all elements of Q and excludes all elements of R, otherwise $\varrho(\omega) = $ false. Note that Q and R can be empty, in which case the context check is omitted. Q is referred to as the *permitting*, and R as the *forbidding* context.

The families of languages generated by regular, context-free, context-sensitive, and phrase structure grammars are denoted by $\mathcal{L}(\text{REG})$, $\mathcal{L}(\text{CF})$, $\mathcal{L}(\text{CS})$, and $\mathcal{L}(\text{RE})$, respectively.

The language family produced by 0L systems is denoted by $\mathcal{L}(0L)$. A deterministic 0L system is called a D0L system. If the axiom is replaced by a finite language, then we have an F0L (FD0L) system with a finite number of axioms, referred to as an F0L (FD0L) system. $\mathcal{L}(T0L)$ represents the language family generated by T0L systems.

3   Eco-Foraging Systems

First, we model the behavior of Internet crawlers searching for novel information using eco-foraging systems, a variant of eco-grammar systems, as proposed in [16,18,21,23]. These crawlers compete and collaborate as they navigate the Web. Discoveries made by one crawler can serve as contextual input for others, speeding up the search process. Each crawler curates a prioritized list of the most promising URLs, called a *weblog*, which is updated periodically. High weblog scores indicate clusters of relevant documents, making them strategic starting points for searches. The sequence of URLs visited between updates forms a path. Crawlers are tasked with finding novel documents, adhering to temporal constraints, or addressing different topics, a feature termed *topic specificity*. Our model consists of two main components: the web environment and the agents (crawlers).

Definition 1. *A web environment with n foragers, where $n \geq 1$, is formally defined by $E = (V_E, T'_E, \mathcal{P}_E)$ such that*

- V_E *is a finite alphabet, representing the alphabet of the web environment, whose elements are the web pages that can be modified by the joint actions of the crawlers and the web environment itself; $V_E = V_M \cup T'_E \cup V_N \cup \bar{V}_N$, with $V_N = \bigcup_{i=1}^{n} N_i$ and $\bar{V}_N = \bigcup_{i=1}^{n} N_i^{(i)}$, where*
  - V_M *denotes a finite set of marker symbols that characterize the work of the web environment,*
  - $N_i = \{X_{i,1}, \dots, X_{i,s_i}\}$ *and* $N_i^{(i)} = \{X_{i,1}^{(i)}, \dots, X_{i,s_i}^{(i)}\}$, $1 \leq s_i$, $1 \leq i \leq n$, *are finite alphabets, the identifiable web pages and those explicitly visited by the i-th crawler,*
  - $T_E = \bigcup_{j=1}^{k} N_{i_j}$, *are the web pages that should be visited by the crawlers, and for some k, $1 \leq k \leq n$, $\{i_1, \dots, i_k\} \subseteq \{1, \dots, n\}$,*

- $T'_E = \{Z' \mid Z \in T_E\}$, are the web pages that were actually recognized by the crawlers and reinforced later by the environment,
- V_M, T'_E, V_N, and $\bar{V}_N$, are pairwise disjoint sets,

- $\mathcal{P}_E = \{P_{E_1}, \ldots, P_{E_r}\}$, where P_{E_q}, $1 \leq q \leq r$, is a finite set of evolution rules of the following forms:
  - $Y \to \alpha$, where $Y \in V_N, \alpha \in V_N^*$, describes an update of a non-visited web page, including the insertion of new web page(s) into the environment, the deletion, or substitution of some part of the environmental state,
  - $Z^{(i)} \to \beta$, where $Z^{(i)} \in N_i^{(i)}$, $1 \leq i \leq n$, and $\beta \in V_N^* \cup V_N^* Z^{(i)} V_N^*$, corresponds to the removal of a visited web page or its (identical) rewriting, possibly accompanied by the insertion of additional web pages,
  - $Z^{(j)} \to Z'$, $Z' \to Z'$, where $Z^{(j)} \in N_j^{(j)}$, $1 \leq j \leq n$, $N_j \subseteq T_E$, $Z' \in T'_E$ and $Z \in T_E$, is the reinforcement of a visited web page by the environment,
  - $U \to \gamma$, where $U \in V_M$ and $\gamma \in V_N^* V_M^* V_N^*$ describes the modification of elements within V_M and/or the insertion of new web pages.

In addition, any set of rules contained within $\mathcal{P}_E$ is said to be complete; that is, for any $c \in V_E$, there exists at least one applicable rule within each P_{E_q}, where $1 \leq q \leq r$.

The crawlers are represented as programmed grammar schemes, with the programmed feature defining crawler itineraries (paths).

Definition 2. A programmed eco-foraging system with appearance checking (a $FEG_{PR_{ac}}$ system) of degree n, $n \geq 1$, is a construct $\Gamma = (E, A_1, \ldots, A_n, c_{init})$, such that

- $E = (V_E, T'_E, \mathcal{P}_E)$ represents the web environment (see Definition 1),
- $A_i = (N_i \cup N_i^{(i)}, S_i, R_i)$, $1 \leq i \leq n$, is the i-th crawler, a programmed grammar scheme with appearance checking, where
  - $N_i \cup N_i^{(i)}$ is the nonterminal alphabet of the i-th crawler (see Definition 1),
  - $S_i \in N_i$ is the start symbol of the i-th crawler, corresponding to the initial web page to be visited by the crawler,
  - R_i is a finite set of triplets of the following forms:
    * $(l_{i,1} : S_i \to S_i^{(i)}, \sigma_i(l_{i,1}), \psi_i(l_{i,1}))$, where $\sigma_i(l_{i,1}) \subseteq \{l_{i,1}, \ldots, l_{i,s_i}\}$, and $\psi_i(l_{i,1}) = \{l_{i,1}\}$, is called the initial rule of the i-th crawler,
    * $(l_{i,k} : X_{i,k} \to X_{i,k}^{(i)}, \sigma_i(l_{i,k}), \psi_i(l_{i,k}))$, where $X_{i,k} \in N_i \setminus \{S_i\}$, $X_{i,k}^{(i)} \in N_i^{(i)} \setminus \{S_i^{(i)}\}$, $2 \leq k \leq s_i$, with $\sigma_i(l_{i,k}) \subseteq \{l_{i,1}, \ldots, l_{i,s_i}\}$, and $\psi_i(l_{i,k}) \subseteq \{h_{i,2}, \ldots, h_{i,s_i}\}$ (the i-th crawler attempts to visit a web page that has not yet been discovered), or
    * $(h_{i,k} : X_{i,k}^{(i)} \to X_{i,k}^{(i)}, \sigma_i(h_{i,k}), \psi_i(h_{i,k}))$, where $X_{i,k}^{(i)} \in N_i^{(i)} \setminus \{S_i^{(i)}\}$, $2 \leq k \leq s_i$ (the i-th crawler revisits a previously discovered web page), with $\sigma_i(h_{i,k}) \subseteq \{l_{i,1}, \ldots, l_{i,s_i}\}$, and $\psi_i(h_{i,k}) \subseteq \{h_{i,2}, \ldots, h_{i,s_i}\}$, where
  - $Label(R_i) = \{l_{i,1}, \ldots, l_{i,s_i}, h_{i,2}, \ldots, h_{i,s_i}\}$ is the set of labels of the rules in R_i.

– $c_{init} = (l_{1,1}, \ldots, l_{n,1}; \omega_{init})$ *is called the initial configuration of* Γ*, where* $l_{i,1}$ *is the label of the initial rule of the* i*-th crawler,* $1 \le i \le n$, $\omega_{init} = z_1 S_{j_1} z_2 \ldots z_k S_{j_k} z_{k+1}$, $S_{j_h} \in N_{j_h}, z_l \in V_E^*, 1 \le h \le k, 1 \le l \le k+1$, *and for some* k, $0 \le k \le n$, *it holds that* $\{j_1, \ldots, j_k\} \subseteq \{1, \ldots, n\}$. *The string* ω_{init} *is referred to as the initial state of the web environment of* Γ*, or equivalently, the initial environmental state.*

The programmed grammar schemes determine the selection of the subsequent rules based on the previous ones. Crawlers prioritize unvisited web pages. If they fail to identify a new page, they move on to a previously identified page. The initial state of the web environment, referred to as ω_{init}, indicates that not all agents are able to start their work. When crawlers start their search, they have to apply their initial rules.

Definition 3. *Let* $\Gamma = (E, A_1, \ldots, A_n, c_{init})$ *be a* $\mathrm{FEG}_{\mathrm{PR}_{ac}}$ *system of degree* n, *where* $n \ge 1$. *An* $(n+1)$*-tuple* $c = (k_1, \ldots, k_n; \omega_E)$, *where* $k_i \in Label(R_i)$, *for* $1 \le i \le n$, *and* $\omega_E \in V_E^*$, *is referred to as a configuration of* Γ. *The string* ω_E *is the state of the web environment of* Γ *in configuration* c, *and is alternatively referred to as the environmental state in configuration* c.

Definition 4. *Let* $\Gamma = (E, A_1, \ldots, A_n, c_{init})$ *be a* $\mathrm{FEG}_{\mathrm{PR}_{ac}}$ *system of degree* n, *where* $n \ge 1$. *Let* $c_1 = (k_1, \ldots, k_n; \omega_E)$ *and* $c_2 = (k_1', \ldots, k_n'; \omega_E')$ *be two configurations of* Γ. *We say that* c_1 *directly derives* c_2 *in* Γ*, denoted by* $c_1 \Longrightarrow_\Gamma c_2$*, if the following conditions are satisfied:*

1. $\omega_E = u_1 \alpha_{i_1} u_2 \ldots u_k \alpha_{i_k} u_{k+1}$ *and* $\omega_E'' = u_1 \beta_{i_1} u_2 \ldots u_k \beta_{i_k} u_{k+1}$, *where for some* k, $0 \le k \le n$, *it holds that* $\{i_1, \ldots, i_k\} \subseteq \{1, \ldots, n\}$, $\alpha_{i_j} \in N_j \cup N_j^{(j)}$, *and* $\beta_{i_j} \in N_j^{(j)}$, *for* $1 \le j \le k$, *and* $u_h \in V_E^*$, $1 \le h \le k+1$,
2. $(k_{i_j} : \alpha_{i_j} \to \beta_{i_j}, \sigma(k_{i_j}), \psi(k_{i_j})) \in R_{i_j}$ *and* $k_{i_j}' \in \sigma(k_{i_j})$, *for* $1 \le j \le k$,
3. *there is no* $m \in \{1, \ldots, n\} \setminus \{i_1, \ldots, i_k\}$, *such that* $(k_m : \alpha_m \to \beta_m, \sigma(k_m), \psi(k_m)) \in R_m$ *can be applied to* $u_1 u_2 \ldots u_{k+1}$,
4. $k_m' \in \psi(k_m)$ *for* $m \in \{1, \ldots, n\} \setminus \{i_1, \ldots, i_k\}$,
5. $\omega_E' = v_1 \beta_{i_1} v_2 \ldots v_k \beta_{i_k} v_{k+1}$, *where* $u_1 \ldots u_{k+1} \Longrightarrow v_1 \ldots v_{k+1}$ *is a 0L rewriting according to some* P_{E_q}, $1 \le q \le r$, $P_{E_q} \in \mathcal{P}_E$.

The action rules of the crawlers and the rule set of the web environment jointly determine the next state of the web environment. The actions performed by the crawlers take precedence over the evolution rules of the web environment, and these actions must be carried out simultaneously. The transitive (and reflexive) closure of $\Longrightarrow_\Gamma$ is denoted by $\Longrightarrow_\Gamma^+ (\Longrightarrow_\Gamma^*)$.

Definition 5. *The language generated by an* $\mathrm{FEG}_{\mathrm{PR}_{ac}}$ *system* $\Gamma = (E, A_1, \ldots, A_n, c_{init})$ *is defined by* $L(\Gamma) = \{u \mid c_{init} = (l_{1,1}, \ldots, l_{n,1}; \omega) \Longrightarrow_\Gamma^* (k_1, \ldots, k_n; u), u \in T_E'^*\}$.

$\mathcal{L}(\text{FEG}_{\text{PR}_{ac}})$ denotes the class of languages generated by $\text{FEG}_{\text{PR}_{ac}}$ systems. The class of recursively enumerable languages is equivalent to the class of languages generated by programmed eco-foraging systems with appearance checking, as demonstrated in [21]. This means that crawlers can identify any computable set of environmental states.

Theorem 1. $\mathcal{L}(\text{RE}) = \mathcal{L}(\text{FEG}_{\text{PR}_{ac}})$.

To keep track of the aging of the web environment, a lifetime parameter can be assigned to each web page. During the crawling process, certain web pages may become obsolete, and consequently unrecognizable for crawlers. To address this phenomenon, we introduced programmed eco-foraging systems with time and appearance checking feature. We have shown that the language generated by these systems corresponds exactly to the language family defined by unordered scattered context grammars of finite index [21]. It can be concluded that the imposed time constraint leads to a smaller class of languages, and thus reduces the effectiveness of the cooperation.

4   Formation of Network Clusters

We study the behavior of interacting and cooperating agents involved in the formation of hierarchical network structures. The agents operate in a dynamically evolving problem space corresponding to the environment. The state of the environment is jointly shaped by the agents' actions and its own evolution. In the proposed model, agents are organized into clusters, which are represented as dynamic teams. We extend the concept of dynamic team constitution introduced in [11] and, to this end, revisit the notion of simple eco-grammar systems.

Definition 6. *A simple eco-grammar system (a SEG system) with n agents, $n \geq 1$, is a construct $\Gamma = (V_E, P_E, R_1, \ldots, R_n, \omega)$, where*

- *V_E is a finite alphabet, the alphabet of the system,*
- *P_E is a finite and complete set of pure context-free rules over V_E (i.e. rules of the form $a \to \alpha$ with $a \in V_E$, $\alpha \in V_E^*$, and for each $a \in V_E$, there is a rule $a \to \alpha$ in P_E), the set of developmental rules of the environment,*
- *$R_i, 1 \leq i \leq n$, is a finite set of pure context-free rules over V_E, the set of action rules of the i-th agent,*
- *$\omega \in V_E^+$ is the axiom, the initial state of the environment.*

A string over V_E is the environmental state. A SEG system functions through the change of environmental states, altered by the action rules of the agents and by the developmental rules of the environment. A team in a SEG system is a set of agents, and the derivation mode is defined as follows:

Definition 7. *For a SEG system $\Gamma = (V, P_E, R_1, \ldots, R_n, \omega_E)$, a team $\mathcal{T} = \{R_{i_1}, \ldots, R_{i_s}\}$, and two environmental states ω, ω', we define the direct derivation step (written by $\omega \models_{\mathcal{T}} \omega'$) as follows:*

- $\omega_E = x_1 a_1 x_2 \ldots x_s a_s x_{s+1}$ and $\omega'_E = y_1 z_1 y_2 \ldots y_s z_s y_{s+1}$, for some s, $1 \le s \le n$, $a_h \in V_E$, $x_j, y_j, z_h \in V_E^*$, $1 \le h \le s$, $1 \le j \le s+1$,
- $a_h \to z_h \in R_{i_h}$, $\{i_1, \ldots, i_h\} \subseteq \{1, \ldots, n\}$, $1 \le h \le s$,
- $y_j = x_j$ is either the empty word, or $x_j \Rightarrow_{P_E} y_j$, $1 \le j \le s+1$, is a 0L rewriting.

We defined the level of competence/excitation of an agent relative to the environmental state. This level represents the number of different symbols in the environmental state that the agent is capable of replacing. In [16,20], we introduced three modes of team constitution to illustrate cluster formation scenarios in dynamic environments.

- $d^{\Diamond q}$-mode, for $q \in \mathbb{N}_0$, and $\Diamond \in \{\le, =, \ge\}$: those agents whose levels of competence/excitation differ by at most/exactly/at least q, belong to the same team.
- $c^{\Diamond q}$-mode, for $q \in \mathbb{N}_0$, and $\Diamond \in \{\le, =, \ge\}$: an agent qualifies for team membership if it is competent with respect to the state of the environment and the cardinality of the set of symbols on the left side of its rules differs from its level of competence/excitation by at most/exactly/at least q.
- $t^{\triangle V_B}$-mode, for $\emptyset \ne V_B, V_C \subseteq V$, $V_B \triangle V_C$, where V is the alphabet of the environment and $\triangle \in \{\subseteq, =, \supseteq\}$: an agent is a member of the team, if it is competent with respect to the environmental string and the string obtained from the environmental string through the deletion of the letters not belonging to all the subsets of a given subset V_B/to a given subset V_B/to all the sets that contain a given subset V_B, is an element of the set of non-empty strings that can be produced by using the set of symbols appearing on the left side of the rules of the given agent.

Definition 8. *For a SEG system $\Gamma = (V, P_E, R_1, \ldots, R_n, \omega_E)$, and two environmental states ω, ω', we say that ω directly derives ω' in Γ in team derivation mode α, where $\alpha \in \{d^{\Diamond q}, c^{\Diamond q}, t^{\triangle V_B} \mid \Diamond \in \{\le, =, \ge\}, \triangle \in \{\subseteq, =, \supseteq\}, q \in \mathbb{N}_0, \emptyset \ne V_B \subseteq V\}$, denoted by $\omega \overset{\alpha}{\Longrightarrow}_\Gamma \omega'$, if either $\omega \models_T \omega'$ for some team T formed according to condition α in Γ, or, if such a team does not exist, then $\omega \Longrightarrow_{P_E} \omega'$.*

The language of a SEG system is the set of all environmental states that can be reached from the initial configuration by a sequence of direct derivation steps.

The class of languages generated by SEG systems with at most n agents using team derivation mode α is denoted by $\mathcal{L}(\mathrm{SEG}(n, \alpha))$, where $\alpha \in \{d^{\Diamond q}, c^{\Diamond q} \mid \Diamond \in \{\le, =, \ge\}, q \in \mathbb{N}_0\}$. For an alphabet V and for some $\emptyset \ne V_B \subseteq V$, $\triangle \in \{\subseteq, =, \supseteq\}$, we denote by $\mathcal{L}(\mathrm{SEG}(n, t^{\triangle V_B}))$ the class of languages produced by SEG systems with at most n agents employing team derivation mode $t^{\triangle V_B}$. By definition we consider a 0L system to be a SEG system with no agent. Furthermore, we set $\mathcal{L}(\mathrm{SEG}(\alpha)) = \bigcup_{n \ge 0} \mathcal{L}(\mathrm{SEG}(n, \alpha))$, $\alpha \in \{d^{\Diamond q}, c^{\Diamond q} \mid \Diamond \in \{\le, =, \ge\}, q \in \mathbb{N}_0\}$ and $\mathcal{L}(\mathrm{SEG}(t^{\triangle V_B})) = \bigcup_{n > 0} \mathcal{L}(\mathrm{SEG}(n, t^{\triangle V_B}))$ for some $\emptyset \ne V_B \subseteq V$, $\triangle \in \{\subseteq, =, \supseteq\}$.

4.1   The Power of Team Cooperation

We infer the difficulty of the problem that agents can solve given the different team constitution modes from the language classes that these systems are able to generate. The language hierarchies induced by the number of agents are infinite:

Theorem 2. *Language hierarchies* $\mathcal{L}(\mathrm{SEG}(n-1,c^{\Diamond q})) \subseteq \mathcal{L}(\mathrm{SEG}(n,c^{\Diamond q}))$, $\Diamond \in \{\leq,=,\geq\}$, $q \geq 0$, *and* $\mathcal{L}(\mathrm{SEG}(n-1,\alpha)) \subseteq \mathcal{L}(\mathrm{SEG}(n,\alpha))$, *where* $n \geq 2$, $\alpha \in \{d^{=0}, d^{\geq 0}, d^{\leq q}, d^{\geq 1} \mid q \geq 0\}$, *are infinite.*

The families of languages defined by SEG systems operating in different team modes are incomparable to the family of regular and context-free languages.

Theorem 3. *The following statements can be verified:*

- *for each* $\vartheta \in \{d^{\Diamond q}, c^{\Diamond q} \mid \Diamond \in \{\leq,=,\geq\}, q \in \mathbb{N}_0\}$, *the family* $\mathcal{L}(\mathrm{SEG}(\vartheta))$ *is incomparable with* $\mathcal{L}(\mathrm{REG})$ *and* $\mathcal{L}(\mathrm{CF})$;
- *for each alphabet* V *with* $\mathrm{card}(V) \geq 2$, *there exists* V_B, $\emptyset \neq V_B \subseteq V$, *such that the family* $\mathcal{L}(\mathrm{SEG}(t^{\triangle V_B}))$, $\triangle \in \{\subseteq, =, \supseteq\}$, *is incomparable with* $\mathcal{L}(\mathrm{REG})$ *and* $\mathcal{L}(\mathrm{CF})$.

The families of languages generated by SEG systems working in certain team modes are incomparable to the family of T0L languages.

Theorem 4. *The claims set forth below are valid:*

- *for each* $\alpha \in \{d^{\Diamond q}, c^{\Diamond q} \mid \Diamond \in \{\leq,=,\geq\}, q \in \mathbb{N}_0\}$, $\mathcal{L}(\mathrm{SEG}(\alpha))$ *and* $\mathcal{L}(\mathrm{T0L})$ *are incomparable;*
- *for each alphabet* V, *there exists* V_B, $\emptyset \neq V_B \subseteq V$, *such that* $\mathcal{L}(\mathrm{SEG}(t^{\triangle V_B}))$, $\triangle \in \{\subseteq, =, \supseteq\}$, *and* $\mathcal{L}(\mathrm{T0L})$ *are incomparable.*

However, any recursively enumerable language can be represented by simple eco-grammar systems, where the active teams are organized according to different conditions of team constitution. The following theorems hold:

Theorem 5. *A language* L *over an alphabet* T *is recursively enumerable, if and only if it can be obtained as* $L = L' \cap T^*$ *for some* $L' \in \mathcal{L}(\mathrm{SEG}(\alpha))$, *where* $\alpha \in \{d^{=q}, c^{=q}, c^{\leq q} \mid q \in \mathbb{N}\}$.

Theorem 6. *For any recursively enumerable language* $L \subseteq T^*$, *there exists a* SEG *system* $\Gamma = (V, P_E, R_1, \ldots, R_m, \omega_E)$, $m \geq 1$, *and* V_B, $\emptyset \neq V_B \subseteq V$, *such that* $L = L' \cap T^*$ *holds, where* $L' \in \mathcal{L}(\mathrm{SEG}(\alpha))$, $\alpha \in \{t^{=V_B}, t^{\supseteq V_B}\}$.

These results demonstrate that the cooperation of teams may lead to quite a large computational power.

5   P2P Networks

In peer-to-peer (P2P) networks, participants, called peers, have equal status, allowing them to act either as service requesters (client role) or service providers (server role). These peers autonomously organize themselves into peer groups, which are collections of peers that collectively agree on a shared set of services. Both peers and peer groups are capable of offering network services, whose availability is advertised. Communication between peers is facilitated by the exchange of messages through pipes. In order to model P2P networks, we employ a network of parallel multiset string processors, as proposed in [22].

Definition 9. *A network of parallel multiset string processors with teams of collective (team/peer group level) and individual (component/peer level) filtering (a $\mathrm{T_{ci}NPMP_{FOL}}$ system) of degree n, $n \geq 1$, is a construct $\Gamma = (V, (t_1, \Theta_1, \Xi_1), \ldots, (t_n, \Theta_n, \Xi_n))$, where*

- *V is an alphabet, the alphabet of the system,*
- *$t_i = \{c_{i,1}, \ldots, c_{i,r_i}\}, 1 \leq i \leq n, r_i \geq 1$, is the i-th team (peer group), where*
  - *$c_{i,j} = (P_{i,j}, F_{i,j}, \Psi_{i,j}, \Upsilon_{i,j}), 1 \leq i \leq n, 1 \leq j \leq r_i$, is the (i,j)-th component (peer) of the network, where*
    - *$P_{i,j}, 1 \leq i \leq n, 1 \leq j \leq r_i$, is a finite and complete set of pure context-free rules over V (i.e. rules of the form $A \rightarrow \alpha$ with $A \in V$, $\alpha \in V^*$ and for each $A \in V$, there is a rule $A \rightarrow \alpha$ in $P_{i,j}$), the production set of the (i,j)-th component,*
    - *$F_{i,j} \in V^\circ$, $1 \leq i \leq n$, $1 \leq j \leq r_i$, is a non-empty finite multiset of strings (advertisements or messages), representing axioms of the (i,j)-th component, and*
    - *$\Psi_{i,j} = \{\psi_{i,j_1}, \ldots, \psi_{i,j_{s_{i,j}}}\}, \Upsilon_{i,j} = \{v_{i,j_1}, \ldots, v_{i,j_{o_{i,j}}}\}, 1 \leq i \leq n, 1 \leq j \leq r_i$, where $\psi_{i,j_k}, v_{i,j_l}, 1 \leq k \leq s_{i,j}, 1 \leq l \leq o_{i,j}$, are context conditions over V^*, the exit filter and entrance filter, respectively, of the (i,j)-th component.*
- *$\Theta_i = \{\theta_{i1}, \ldots, \theta_{ip_i}\}, \Xi_i = \{\xi_{i1}, \ldots, \xi_{iq_i}\}, 1 \leq i \leq n$, where $\theta_{ij}, \xi_{ik}, 1 \leq j \leq p_i, 1 \leq k \leq q_i$, are context conditions over V^*, called an exit filter and an entrance filter, respectively, of the i-th team.*

We use multiset string processors as components because in P2P networks, multiple copies of advertisements or messages may exist on peers, with each recipient retrieving its own copy. For advertisements, filters θ_{ij} and ξ_{ik} regulate access at the collective/team level (peer group information filtering), while filters ψ_{i,j_k} and v_{i,j_l} restrict access to advertisements specific to the components of a given team (individual/peer level filtering).

In the case of messages, filters θ_{ij} and ξ_{ik} act as pipe endpoints - designated as an output pipe (sender) and input pipe (receiver) at the collective/team level. Similarly, filters ψ_{i,j_k} and v_{i,j_l} act as pipe endpoints for message transfer at the individual/peer level.

We distinguish different classes of $T_{ci}NPMP$ systems according to the types of the filters and the types of the production sets. The class of $T_{ci}NPMP$ systems with (X)-type collective and (Y)-type individual filters, where $X, Y \in \{reg, rc\}$ and $Z \in \{0L, D0L, F0L, \ldots\}$ are denoted by $T_{c_X i_Y}NPMP_Z$.

The $T_{ci}NPMP_{F0L}$ system functions by changing its states.

Definition 10. *By a state (or configuration) of a $T_{ci}NPMP_{F0L}$ system $\Gamma = (V, (t_1, \Theta_1, \Xi_1), \ldots, (t_n, \Theta_n, \Xi_n))$, $n \geq 1$, we mean a tuple $s = (M_{1,1}, \ldots, M_{1,r_1}, \ldots, M_{n,1}, \ldots, M_{n,r_n})$, where $M_{i,j} \in V^{\circ}$, $1 \leq i \leq n, 1 \leq j \leq r_i$, is called the state of the (i, j)-th component and represents the multiset of strings present at component (i, j) at that step. We call $s_0 = (F_{1,1}, \ldots, F_{1,r_1}, \ldots, F_{n,1}, \ldots, F_{n,r_n})$ the initial state of the system.*

Definition 11. *(Configuration transition).* *Let $\Gamma = (V, (t_1, \Theta_1, \Xi_1), \ldots, (t_n, \Theta_n, \Xi_n))$, $n \geq 1$, be a $T_{ci}NPMP_{F0L}$ system (see Definition 9). Let $s_1 = (M_{1,1}, \ldots, M_{1,r_1}, \ldots, M_{n,1}, \ldots, M_{n,r_n})$ and $s_2 = (M'_{1,1}, \ldots, M'_{1,r_1}, \ldots, M'_{n,1}, \ldots, M'_{n,r_n})$ be two states of Γ. We say that*

1. *s_2 is derived from s_1 by a rewriting step in Γ, written as $s_1 \Rightarrow s_2$, if a new string is obtained from each string in a parallel manner (by the application of Lindenmayer rules) in each multiset of strings.*
2. *s_2 is derived from s_1 by a communication step in Γ, written as $s_1 \vdash s_2$, if the new collections of strings sent from the current multiset of strings of the nodes, either via the filters of the teams, the components, or both, satisfy the context conditions described by the given filters. A new multiset of strings at a node consists of all strings that are able to pass the exit filter of the sender and the entrance filter of the receiver.*

Parallel rewriting rules are used to describe the modification of a message or an advertisement. Components share string copies available to them.

A component can request access to a message in the following scenarios: (i) collective information filtering (accessible to any team member), (ii) individual information filtering (team-specific access), or (iii) both, depending on the context conditions met.

Message delivery occurs through: (i) pipes connecting components from different teams (collective filtering), (ii) pipes connecting team members (individual filtering), or (iii) both, as specified by the context conditions.

By a computation C in Γ we mean a sequence of states $s_0, s_1, \ldots$, where $s_k \Rightarrow s_{k+1}$, if $k = 2j, j \geq 0$, and $s_k \vdash s_{k+1}$, if $k = 2j + 1, j \geq 0$.

5.1   Information Dynamics

This formalism makes it possible to enforce access control and analyze information dynamics in P2P networks. Filters regulate strings (advertisements and messages) that specify what can be shared, sent, or received, thus controlling the flow of information.

Population growth and communication functions characterize the accumulated data and information flow between peers using collective or individual information filtering. The population growth function quantifies the growth of information within the network, at nodes, or during communication. These functions also help identify malfunctioning peers that are failing to communicate or congesting the network.

We have established the connection between the growth of the number of strings present during computation at the components of $T_{c_{rc}i_{rc}}NPMP_{FD0L}$ systems and the growth functions of D0L systems [17,19,22]. Using the theory of D0L systems, we can obtain that the population growth function of our network is either exponential or polynomially bounded, which is decidable. This result guarantees that the access control model specified by the filters reaches a decision. Second, the alphabets of words generated by the D0L system form an almost periodic sequence. As a consequence, the function of these P2P networks leads to information saturation after some time. When the system reaches the state of saturation, all the disclosed information can be evaluated, i.e., the peers cannot disclose any additional information according to the current access control specification. Finally, for any two $T_{c_{rc}i_{rc}}NPMP_{FD0L}$ systems, the sequence and language equivalence problems are decidable. In practice, this means that for any two P2P networks, it is decidable whether they function in the same way in terms of information dynamics. In other words, we can determine whether two networks accumulate or transmit information in the same order.

6   String Assembly in Networks

Self-assembly refers to the autonomous aggregation of simple entities into complex structures. We investigated the properties of a formal language-theoretic operation that models the linear self-assembly of partially overlapping DNA strands. This operation, called overlap assembly, combines input strands xy and yz that share a non-empty overlap y to produce the output xyz. Originally introduced as the (self-)assembly of strings and languages [12], our study emphasizes dynamic self-assembly over distributed and separated regions, each governed by different assembly rules. We incorporated a novel communication mechanism within networks of evolutionary processors (NEPs), appending filtered communicated strings via different variants of the overlap operation [10].

We defined variants of the overlap operation in which the length of the overlap is bounded. Let V be an alphabet and let $x, y \in V^*$. For $x, y \in V^+$ and $k \geq 0$, let the k-overlap of x and y be $x \bar{\odot}_k y = \{x'zy' \mid x = x'z, y = zy', |z| = k\}$. For $x, y \in V^*$ and $xy = yx = x$, we define $x \bar{\odot}_k y = y \bar{\odot}_k x = \{x\}$.

For $x, y \in V^+$, the maximal overlap (abbreviated as max-overlap) is defined as $x \bar{\odot}_{max} y = \{x'zy' \mid x = x'z, y = zy'$ and there are no words $z', x'', y'' \in V^*$ such that z is a proper subword of z', $x = x''z'$, $y = z'y''\}$. For $x, y \in V^*$ and $xy = yx = x$, we define $x \bar{\odot}_{max} y = y \bar{\odot}_{max} x = \{x\}$.

For two languages $L_1, L_2 \subseteq V^*$ and for operation $\bar{\odot}_\alpha$, where $\alpha \in \{max\} \cup \{k \mid k \geq 0\}$ let $L_1 \bar{\odot}_\alpha L_2 = \bigcup_{x_1 \in L_1, x_2 \in L_2} x_1 \bar{\odot}_\alpha x_2$.

For languages $L_1, L_2, \ldots, L_n \subseteq V^*$, $n \geq 2$ and for $\bar{\odot}_\alpha$, where $\alpha \in \{max\} \cup \{k \mid k \geq 0\}$, we recursively define $L_1 \bar{\odot}_\alpha \ldots \bar{\odot}_\alpha L_n$ as follows: for $1 \leq j \leq n - 1$, $L_1 \bar{\odot}_\alpha \ldots \bar{\odot}_\alpha L_{j+1} = u \bar{\odot}_\alpha L_{j+1}$, where $u = L_1 \bar{\odot}_\alpha \ldots \bar{\odot}_\alpha L_j$.

The new model of NEPs differs from the original in the way it communicates. Analogously to the standard case, the (hybrid) evolutionary processors at each node perform point mutations on the strings available to them. These point mutation rules include substitution, deletion, and insertion rules.

We say that a rule $a \to b$, where $a, b \in V \cup \{\lambda\}$ and V is an alphabet, is a substitution rule, if both a and b are different from λ. The rule $a \to b$, where $a, b \in V \cup \{\lambda\}$, is a deletion rule, if $a \neq \lambda$ and $b = \lambda$, and it is an insertion rule, if $a = \lambda$ and $b \neq \lambda$. The set of all substitution, deletion and insertion rules over V is denoted by Sub_V, Del_V, and Ins_V, respectively.

Given a rule p, as above and a word $w \in V^*$, we define the actions of p on w as follows:

- If $p \equiv a \to b \in Sub_V$, then

$$p(w) = \begin{cases} \{ubv \mid \exists u, v \in V^* \text{ such that } w = uav\}, \\ \{w\} \text{ otherwise.} \end{cases}$$

- If $r \equiv a \to \lambda \in Del_V$, then

$$p(w) = \begin{cases} \{uv \mid \exists u, v \in V^* \text{ such that } w = uav\}, \\ \{w\} \text{ otherwise.} \end{cases}$$

- If $p \equiv \lambda \to a \in Ins_V$, then $p(w) = \{uav \mid w = uv, u, v \in V^*\}$.

Let $u, v \in V^*$ and let $R \subseteq Sub_V \cup Ins_V \cup R \subseteq Del_V$. We say that v is directly derived from u by R, denoted by $u \Longrightarrow_R v$, if v can be obtained from u by an action of some rule $p \in R$. The transitive reflexive closure of the relation $\Longrightarrow_R$ is denoted by $\Longrightarrow_R^*$.

A pair $M = (V, R)$, where V is an alphabet and $R \subseteq Sub_V$ or $R \subseteq Ins_V$ or $R \subseteq Del_V$ is a finite set of point mutation rules over V, is called an evolutionary processor. If $R \subseteq (Sub_V \cup Ins_V \cup Del_V)$, that is, the finite set of point mutation rules may have more than one type of point mutation rules, then we speak of a hybrid evolutionary processor.

Definition 12. *A network of evolutionary processors with string assembly (an ASMNEP, for short) of degree n, $n \geq 1$, is a construct*

$$\Pi = (V, (A_1, R_1, I_1, O_1), \ldots, (A_n, R_n, I_n, O_n), i_o),$$

where $1 \leq i_o \leq n$, and

- *V is a finite alphabet, called the alphabet of Π,*
- *(A_i, R_i, I_i, O_i), $1 \leq i \leq n$, is the i-th node (component) of Π, where*
  - *$A_i \subseteq V^*$ is the finite set of the axioms of the component,*
  - *R_i is a finite set of point mutation rules over V,*
  - *I_i is a regular language, $I_i \subseteq V^*$, called the input filter of the i-th node,*

- O_i is a regular language, $O_i \subseteq V^*$, called the output filter of the i-th node, and
  - i_o is the label of the output node.

ASMNEPs work by directly changing their states. A state or configuration of an ASMNEP of degree n is represented as a n-tuple of languages, where the i-th language denotes the set of strings present at node i at a given moment. The initial state of the ASMNEP corresponds to the n-tuple of its axioms.

Definition 13. Let $\Pi = (V, (A_1, R_1, I_1, O_1), \ldots, (A_n, R_n, I_n, O_n), i_o)$, $n \geq 1$, be an ASMNEP. By a state (a configuration) of Π we mean an n-tuple $C = (L_1 \ldots, L_n)$ where $L_i \subseteq V^*$, $1 \leq i \leq n$. L_i called the state of the i-th component. The initial state (configuration) of Π is $C_0 = (A_1, \ldots, A_n)$.

Definition 14. Let $\Pi = (V, (A_1, R_1, I_1, O_1), \ldots, (A_n, R_n, I_n, O_n), i_o)$, $n \geq 1$, be an ASMNEP and let $C_1 = (L_1, \ldots, L_n)$ and $C_2 = (L'_1, \ldots, L'_n)$ be two states of Π. We say that C_2 is obtained from C_1 by a direct derivation step in Π in the communication mode α, where $\alpha = \{max\} \cup \{k \mid k \geq 0\}$, written as

$$(L_1 \ldots, L_n) \vdash_{\Pi,\alpha} (L'_1, \ldots, L'_n),$$

if we have

$$L'_i = \begin{cases} I_i \cap L'' & \text{if } I_i \cap L'' \neq \emptyset, \\ A_i & \text{otherwise,} \end{cases}$$

where

$$L'' = \bigcup_{\{j_1, \ldots, j_n\} = \{1, \ldots, n\}} \Delta_{j_1} \bar{\odot}_\alpha \cdots \bar{\odot}_\alpha \Delta_{j_n},$$

$$\Delta_{i_j} = \begin{cases} \bar{L}_{i_j} \cap O_{i_j} & \text{if } \bar{L}_{i_j} \cap O_{i_j} \neq \emptyset, \\ \{\lambda\} & \text{otherwise,} \end{cases}$$

and

$$\bar{L}_i = \{w \mid u \Longrightarrow^*_{R_i} w, u \in L_i\}, 1 \leq i \leq n.$$

First, the components perform point mutations on each string available to them. Then, if a string successfully passes the output filter of the evolutionary processor, it is assembled in the environment according to the specific variation of the overlap operation. In effect, the assembled new strings are overlaps of strings sent to the environment by the nodes, and all these strings originate from different source nodes. If a copy of the new strings obtained passes the input filter of a node, the string is added to the set of strings of that node. If the node does not receive a string, it returns to its set of axioms.

The transitive reflexive closure of $\vdash_{\Pi,\alpha}$ is denoted by $\vdash^*_{\Pi,\alpha}$. A sequence of direct derivation steps (starting from the initial state) is called a derivation in Π. The language of an ASMNEP Π is the set of strings that appear in a state of the output node during the derivation.

Definition 15. *Let* $\Pi = (V, (A_1, R_1, I_1, O_1), \ldots, (A_n, R_n, I_n, O_n), i_0)$, $n \geq 1$, *be an ASMNEP. The language generated by Π in the communication mode α, where $\alpha \in \{max\} \cup \{k \mid k \geq 0\}$ is $L_\alpha(\Pi) = \{w \in L'_{i_0} \mid (A_1, \ldots, A_n) \vdash^*_{\Pi,\alpha} (L'_1, \ldots, L'_n)\}$.*

6.1   The Power and Efficiency of ASMNEPs

We verified that these three-node networks are computationally complete devices and that they can efficiently solve NP-complete problems [10]. Specifically, we considered a well-known NP-complete problem, the Hamiltonian Path Problem (HPP), and showed that it can be solved in constant time by ASMNEPs.

Theorem 7. *Any recursively enumerable language L can be generated by an ASMNEP Π with three components working in communication mode α, where $\alpha \in \{max, 0, 1\}$. Furthermore, the components of Π have no insertion rule.*

Theorem 8. *For any directed graph γ, we can effectively give an ASMNEP Π that decides in communication mode $\alpha \in \{max\} \cup \{k \mid k \geq 0\}$ whether or not γ contains a Hamiltonian path. Moreover, if γ has a Hamiltonian path, then the representation of the path is unique.*

7   Conclusions

The previous summary illustrates how the properties of various distributed networks can be approached using tools from grammar system theory. Eco-grammar systems and networks of evolutionary processors have been studied extensively in recent years [1,2,14]. Eco-grammar systems are a promising way to explore the complex interplay between computational models and ecological phenomena. Future research could focus on improving their ability to simulate diverse emergent computations within ecosystems, providing insight into cooperative and competitive behaviors that mirror natural ecosystems. For networks of evolutionary processors, one promising direction is to extend the overlap operations used during communication steps [3,5,13]. Another interesting avenue is to remove input and output filtering constraints and implement free filters to evaluate how such changes affect both the generative power and the efficiency of the model. In addition, imposing constraints on the communication graphs-limiting interactions between evolutionary processors-may provide insights into the balance between structural constraints and computational completeness. Exploring these possibilities may also reveal new methods for efficiently solving NP-complete problems.

Disclosure of Interests. The author has no competing interests to declare that are relevant to the content of this article.

References

1. Alhazov, A.: Developments in networks of evolutionary processors. Comput. Sci. J. Moldova **21**(1), 3–35 (2013)
2. Alhazov, A., Freund, R., Rogozhin, V., Rogozhin, Y.: Computational completeness of complete, star-like, and linear hybrid networks of evolutionary processors with a small number of processors. Nat. Comput. **15**(1), 51–68 (2016). https://doi.org/10.1007/s11047-015-9534-1
3. Bottoni, P., Labella, A., Manca, V., Mitrana, V.: Superposition based on Watson-Crick-like complementarity. Theory Comput. Syst. **39**(4), 503–524 (2006)
4. Castellanos, J., Martín-Vide, C., Mitrana, V., Sempere, J.M.: Networks of evolutionary processors. Acta Informatica **39**(6–7), 517–529 (2003)
5. Cheptea, D., Martín-Vide, C., Mitrana, V.: A new operation on words suggested by DNA biochemistry: hairpin completion. Transv. Comput., 216–228 (2006)
6. Csuhaj-Varjú, E.: Eco-grammar systems: recent results and perspectives. In: Păun, G. (ed.) Artificial Life: Grammatical Models, pp. 79–103. Black Sea University Press, Bucharest (1995)
7. Csuhaj-Varjú, E., Dassow, J., Kelemen, J., Păun, Gh.: Grammar systems. In: A Grammatical Approach on Distribution and Cooperation. Gordon and Breach, London, UK (1994)
8. Csuhaj-Varjú, E., Kelemen, J., Kelemenová, A., Păun, Gh.: Eco–grammar systems: a grammatical framework for studying lifelike interactions. Artif. Life **3**, 1–28 (1997)
9. Csuhaj-Varjú, E., Salomaa, A.: Networks of parallel language processors. In: New Trends in Formal Languages, Control, Cooperation and Combinatorics. LNCS, vol. 1218, pp. 299–318. Springer (1997)
10. Csuhaj-Varjú, E., Lázár, K.A.: String assembly in networks of evolutionary processors. J. Autom. Lang. Comb. **21**(1–2), 37–50 (2016)
11. Csuhaj-Varjú, E., Mitrana, V.: Dynamical teams in eco grammar systems. Fund. Inform **44**, 83 94 (2000)
12. Csuhaj-Varjú, E., Petre, I., Vaszil, Gy.: Self-assembly of strings and languages. Theoret. Comput. Sci. **374**(1), 74–81 (2007)
13. Enaganti, S.K., Ibarra, O.H., Kari, L., Kopecki, S.: On the overlap assembly of strings and languages. Nat. Comput. **16**(1), 175–185 (2016). https://doi.org/10.1007/s11047-015-9538-x
14. Kelemenová, A.: Variants of grammar systems: motivations and problems. In: ITAT, pp. 9–15 (2020)
15. Kobayashi, S., Mitrana, V., Păun, Gh., Rozenberg, G.: Formal properties of PA-matching. Theoret. Comput. Sci. **262**(1–2), 117–131 (2001)
16. Lázár, K.A.: A bridge between self-organizing networks and grammar systems theory. Int. J. Found. Comput. Sci. **24**(4), 501–517 (2013)
17. Lázár, K. A.: A computational model of XACML-based access control management in distributed networks. In: Beckmann, A., Csuhaj-Varjú, E., Meer, K. (eds.) Proceedings of the 10th Conference on Computability in Europe (CiE 2014). LNCS, vol. 8493, pp. 265–274. Springer, Cham (2014)
18. Lázár, K.A.: A formal language theoretic approach to distributed computing on dynamic networks. Adv. Complex Syst. **13**(3), 253–280 (2010)
19. Lázár, K.A., Farkas, Cs.: Security in $T_{ct}NMP$ systems. In: Proceedings of the 5th International Workshop on Security in Information Systems (WOSIS 2007), pp. 95–104. INSTICC Press, Portugal (2007)

20. Lázár, K.A., Csuhaj-Varjú, E., Lőrincz, A.: Dynamically formed clusters of agents in eco-grammar systems. Int. J. Found. Comput. Sci. **20**(2), 293–311 (2009)
21. Lázár, K.A., Csuhaj-Varjú, E., Lőrincz, A.: On eco-foraging systems. Rom. J. Inf. Sci. Technol. **13**(3), 279–309 (2010)
22. Lázár, K., Csuhaj-Varjú, E., Lőrincz, A.: Peer-to-peer networks: a language theoretic approach. Comput. Inform. **27**, 403–422 (2008)
23. Lőrincz, A., Lázár, K.A., Palotai, Zs.: Efficiency of goal-oriented communicating agents in different graph topologies: a study with Internet crawlers. Physica A **378**(1), 127–134 (2007)
24. Martín-Vide, C., Mitrana, V., Pérez-Jiménez, M.J., Sancho-Caparrini, F.: Hybrid networks of evolutionary processors. In: Cantú-Paz, E., et al. (eds.) GECCO 2003. LNCS, vol. 2723, pp. 401–412. Springer, Heidelberg (2003). https://doi.org/10.1007/3-540-45105-6_49
25. Rozenberg, G., Salomaa, A. (eds.): Handbook of Formal Languages. Springer (1997)

On the Number of Evolutionary Processors in Networks with Length-Driven Communication

Bianca Truthe[✉]

Justus-Liebig-Universität Gießen, Institut für Informatik, Arndtstr. 2, 35392 Gießen, Germany
bianca.truthe@informatik.uni-giessen.de

Abstract. Recently, a new variant of networks of evolutionary processors has been introduced by Erzsébet Csuhaj-Varjú and Pramod Kumar Sethy in the Journal of Membrane Computing ('Length-driven communication in networks of evolutionary processors'). In this variant, the filtering of words before communication is based on whether their length in the current node increases, decreases, or remains unchanged in the preceding evolutionary step. It was shown there that any recursively enumerable language is generated by a hybrid network of evolutionary processors with this new communication mode. The network constructed has eight nodes and simulates a phrase structure grammar in Penttonen normal form. In the present paper, we improve this result by showing that seven nodes are sufficient for generating any recursively enumerable language by such a kind of networks.

1 Introduction

Networks of language processors have be introduced by Erzsébet Csuhaj-Varjú and Arto Salomaa in [2] motivated by machines with processors working in parallel. They are characterized by processors which perform rewriting steps on words and communicate with each other by sending the obtained words to the other nodes; the communication is controlled by finite automata which decide which words can be sent and received by the nodes. In the paper [1], Juan Castellanos, Carlos Martín-Vide, Victor Mitrana and José M. Sempere restricted the rewriting steps to local mutations known from the evolution of DNA strands, i.e., insertions, deletions, and substitutions of letters, and the corresponding networks are called networks of evolutionary processors. They have shown that such networks are computationally complete, i.e., they are able to generate all recursively enumerable languages.

Since then, many variants of networks have been introduced and studied. In the first paper regarding evolutionary processors [1], deletion and insertion

M. D. Jiménez López and G. Vaszil (Eds.): Erzsébet Csuhaj-Varjú Festschrift,
LNCS 15840, pp. 135–153, 2025.
https://doi.org/10.1007/978-3-031-97274-4_9

rules could be applied only at the ends of a word whereas substitutions took place at arbitrary positions. So, to each rule, a mode was assigned (r-mode for application at the right end of a word, l-mode for application at the left end of a word, and $*$-mode for an arbitrary position). Later, variants were investigated where also substitution rules could be restricted to either end a the word or where also insertion or deletion rules could be applied at arbitrary positions. If the processors are all specialized in the same type of operation (insertion, deletion, or substitution) and the same mode (r, l, or $*$), one speaks about hybrid networks of evolutionary networks. All these networks can be seen as language generating or accepting device. In generating networks, every node has a finite initial set of axioms to start with; a designated node works as the output node (exactly those words over some terminal alphabet which are present at some time in this node belong to the generated language). In accepting networks, there are two designated nodes, namely the input node and the output node. The input node starts its computation with an input word; all other nodes have no words to process in the beginning. As soon as the output node contains a word, the original input word is accepted. So, the language accepted by such a network is the set of all input words for which there is a computation which leads to a word in the output node. In [6], it was shown for accepting hybrid networks of evolutionary processors that they are also computationally complete. A survey regardings different kinds of models with computational completeness is given in [10].

Recently, a new variant of networks of evolutionary processors has been introduced by Erzsébet Csuhaj-Varjú and Pramod Kumar Sethy [3]. In this variant, the filtering of words before communication is based on whether their length in current node increases, decreases, or remains unchanged in the preceding evolutionary step. It was shown there that any recursively enumerable language is generated by a hybrid network of evolutionary processors with this new communication mode. The network constructed has eight nodes and simulates a phrase structure grammar in Penttonen normal form.

In the present paper, we improve this result by showing that seven nodes are sufficient for generating any recursively enumerable language by such a kind of networks. We simulate a phrase structure grammar in Kuroda normal form which is more general than Penttonen normal form with respect to the kind of rules and therefore maybe better in terms of descriptional complexity. The specialization to the Penttonen normal form would not improve the result here.

2   Definitions

We assume that the reader is familiar with the basic concepts of formal language theory (see e.g. [9]). We only recall here some notations used in the paper.

An alphabet is a finite and nonempty set of symbols. The set of all words over some alphabet V is denoted by V^*; the empty word is denoted by λ.

A phrase structure grammar is a quadruple $G = (N, T, P, S)$ where N and T are alphabets (the elements of N are called non-terminal symbols; the elements of T are called terminal symbols), P is a finite set of production rules which are written in the form $\alpha \to \beta$ with $\alpha \in (N \cup T)^* \setminus T^*$ and $\beta \in (N \cup T)^*$, and $S \in N$ is called the axiom. A grammar is in Kuroda normal form [5] if each of its production rules has one of the following forms:

$$AB \to CD, \ A \to CD, \ A \to x, \text{ where } A, B, C, D \in N, \ x \in N \cup T \cup \{\lambda\}.$$

A grammar is in Penttonen normal form [7] if it is in Kuroda normal form and every non-context-free rule has the form $AB \to AC$ with $A, B, C \in N$.

Given an alphabet V, we say that a rule $a \to b$ with $a, b \in V \cup \{\lambda\}$ is a substitution rule if both a and b are not λ; it is a deletion rule if $a \neq \lambda$ and $b = \lambda$; it is an insertion rule if $a = \lambda$ and $b \neq \lambda$.

For a rule, it is possible to require that the rule is applied only at the left end or at the right end of a word. For a rule $a \to b$, we write

$$a \xrightarrow{l} b \quad \text{or} \quad a \xrightarrow{r} b$$

if the rule should only be applied at the left or right end, respectively. In the literature, these restrictions usually do not exist for substitution rules. However, in this new variant of networks of evolutionary processors [3], it seems to be essential that also substitutions can be controlled to take place at one of the ends of a word because a substitution at a 'wrong' place cannot be discovered by the filters. So, we allow this restriction for substitution rules also here in this paper. However, in [4], a technique was used which allows substitutions everywhere and which tests the correctness of the position by a successful deletion and later insertion. This technique seems to be applicable also here but maybe for the price of more nodes. This question will remain open for future research.

The general application mode (operation may take place everywhere in a word) is denoted by $*$. We define the following results of the application of a rule $p = a \to b$ working in mode $*$ to a word w as

$$p(w) = \begin{cases} \{\, ubv \mid w = uav \,\}, & \text{if } a \text{ is a subword of } w, \\ \{w\}, & \text{otherwise.} \end{cases}$$

For a rule $p = a \xrightarrow{x} b$ applied in mode $x \in \{l, r\}$, we also define

$$p(w) = \begin{cases} \{\, ub \mid w = ua \,\}, & \text{if } a \text{ is suffix of } w \text{ and } x = r, \\ \{\, bu \mid w = au \,\}, & \text{if } a \text{ is prefix of } w \text{ and } x = l, \\ \{w\}, & \text{otherwise.} \end{cases}$$

In order to emphasize the mode $x \in \{*, l, r\}$ of a rule $p = a \xrightarrow{x} b$, we also write p_x. For a rule p, a finite set M of rules, and a language L, we define

$$p(L) = \bigcup_{w \in L} p(w) \quad \text{and} \quad M(L) = \bigcup_{p \in M} p(L).$$

For an alphabet V, we denote by Sub_V, Sub_V^l, Sub_V^r, Del_V, Del_V^l, Del_V^r, Ins_V, Ins_V^l, and Ins_V^r, the set of all substitution rules for arbitrary positions, substitution rules for the left end, substitution rules for the right end, deletion rules for arbitrary positions, deletion rules for the left end, deletion rules for the right end, insertion rules for arbitrary positions, insertion rules for the left end, and insertion rules for the right end, respectively, over the alphabet V.

We say that a rule $p = a \to b \in M$ is applicable to a string $w \in V^*$ in the application mode $x \in \{*, l, r\}$, if a is a subword (if $x = *$), a suffix (if $x = r$), or a prefix (if $x = l$) of the word w. We define

$$\mathrm{App}(w, M, x) = \{ \, p \in M \mid p \text{ is applicable to } w \text{ in mode } x \, \}.$$

In what follows, we shall refer to the rewriting operations defined above as evolutionary operations or mutation rules since they may be viewed as linguistic formulations of local DNA mutations.

Example 1. Let $w = aba$ be a word and

$$M = \left\{ a \to c, b \to c, a \xrightarrow{l} d, b \xrightarrow{r} c \right\}$$

be a set mutation rules. The rule $p = a \to c$ derives the word w to the word cba and to the word abc (but not the word cbc – a rule is applied only at one position). The rule $p = b \to c$ derives the word w to the word aca. The rule $p = a \xrightarrow{l} d$ derives the word w to the word dba (the rule p is applied only at the left word of the word since the application mode is l). The rule $p = b \xrightarrow{r} c$ yields the word w because the rule is applied only at the right end of the word but the left-hand side b of the rule is not a suffix of the word w and, hence, this rules cannot be applied. Thus, $M(\{w\}) = \{cba, abc, aca, dba, aba\}$. A parallel application of different rules to a word is also not allowed, therefore, for instance $dca \notin M(\{w\})$. Furthermore,

$$\mathrm{App}(w, M, *) = \{a \to c, b \to c\},$$
$$\mathrm{App}(w, M, l) = \left\{ a \xrightarrow{l} d \right\},$$
$$\mathrm{App}(w, M, r) = \emptyset.$$

We now define networks of evolutionary processors with communication based on comparison of lengths of strings for generating languages (similar networks can be defined for accepting languages).

Definition 1. *A generating network of evolutionary processors (of size n) with communication based on comparison of lengths of strings is an $(n + 4)$-tuple*

$$\mathcal{N} = (V, O, N_1, N_2, \ldots, N_n, E, n_o)$$

where

- V is an alphabet (called the working alphabet of the network),
- O is an alphabet (called the output alphabet of the network),
- for $1 \leq i \leq n$, there is a processor $N_i = (A_i, M_i, \alpha_i, \varrho_i)$ where
  - A_i is a finite subset of V^* (the language of axioms, from where the processing starts in this processor),
  - $\alpha_i \in \{*, l, r\}$ is the application mode of this node,
  - M_i is a set of evolutionary rules of a certain type, i.e., $M_i \subseteq \mathrm{Sub}_V^{\alpha_i}$ or $M_i \subseteq \mathrm{Del}_V^{\alpha_i}$ or $M_i \subseteq \mathrm{Ins}_V^{\alpha_i}$,
  - $\varrho_i \in \{(>), (<), (=), (\hat{=})\}$ is the communication mode of this node,
- E is a subset of $\{1, 2, \ldots, n\} \times \{1, 2, \ldots, n\}$, and
- n_o is a natural number from the set $\{1, 2, \ldots, n\}$; the processor N_{n_o} is called the output node of the network.

Before we define the generated language of such a network, we briefly describe how it works. The underlying structure of a network is a graph consisting of some, say n, nodes $N_1, N_2, \ldots, N_n$ (called processors) and edges given by E such that there is a directed edge from node N_k to node N_i if and only if $(k, i) \in E$. Any processor N_i consists of a set A_i of start words (axioms) and a set M_i of evolutionary rules (also called mutation rules) which are all of the same type (substitution, deletion, or insertion) and which are all applied in the same mode α_i. We say that N_i is a substitution node or a deletion node or an insertion node if $M_i \subseteq \mathrm{Sub}_V^{\alpha_i}$ or $M_i \subseteq \mathrm{Del}_V^{\alpha_i}$ or $M_i \subseteq \mathrm{Ins}_V^{\alpha_i}$, respectively. The communication mode ϱ_i controls which words 'survive' (leave the node and are communicated to an adjacent node).

With any node N_i and any time moment $t \geq 0$, we associate a set $C_t(i)$ of words (the words contained in the node N_i at time t). Initially, N_i contains the words of A_i (its axioms). In a so-called evolutionary step, from $C_t(i)$ all words of the set $M_i(C_t(i))$ are derived. After an evolutionary step, a communication step follows. Which words are communicated by a node N_i, is controlled by the communication mode ϱ_i of this node. Let $w \in C_t(i)$ for some odd number $t \geq 0$ be a word in node N_i after an evolutionary step. In the case of $\varrho_i = (>)$, the word w will be sent out from node N_i if it was obtained by an insertion rule which increases the length (w is longer than the word where it was derived from). In the case of $\varrho_i = (<)$, the word w will be sent out from node N_i if it was obtained by a deletion rule which decreases the length (w is shorter than the word where it was derived from). In the case of $\varrho_i = (=)$, the word w will be sent out from node N_i if it was obtained by a substitution rule which maintains the length and which was really applied (if $w \in p_{\alpha_i}(u)$ for some word $u \in C_{t-1}(i)$, $p_{\alpha_i} \in \mathrm{Sub}_V^{\alpha_i}$, and $p_{\alpha_i} \in \mathrm{App}(u, M, \alpha_i)$). In the case of $\varrho_i = (\hat{=})$, then the word w will be sent out from node N_i if it was present in the node already before the evolutionary step ($w \in C_{t-1}(i)$) and no rule was applicable ($\mathrm{App}(w, M, \alpha_i) = \emptyset$). Words which are not selected for being sent out by the mode ϱ_i, vanish from the node and from the entire network. This is in contrast to other definitions of networks of evolutionary processors where non-communicated words remain in the node where they are and take place in the next evolutionary step. The words which are sent out from node N_i move along every edge of the underlying graph which leads from node N_i to an adjacent node N_k. So, the language $C_{t+1}(i)$ of node N_i after a communication step consists of all words which have been communicated by a node N_k with $(k, i) \in E$.

We now define the steps of the computation of a network and the resulting language formally.

Definition 2. *Let $\mathcal{N}$ by a network as defined in Definition 1.*

1. *A configuration C of $\mathcal{N}$ is an n-tuple $C = (C(1), C(2), \ldots, C(n))$ where $C(i)$ is a subset of V^* for $1 \le i \le n$.*
2. *Let $C = (C(1), C(2), \ldots, C(n))$, $C^{\mathrm{ev}} = (C^{\mathrm{ev}}(1), C^{\mathrm{ev}}(2), \ldots, C^{\mathrm{ev}}(n))$, and $C^{\mathrm{com}} = (C^{\mathrm{com}}(1), C^{\mathrm{com}}(2), \ldots, C^{\mathrm{com}}(n))$ be three configurations of $\mathcal{N}$.*
   - *We say that C derives C^{ev} in one evolutionary step $(C \Longrightarrow C^{\mathrm{ev}})$ if $C^{\mathrm{ev}}(i) = M_i(C(i))$ for $1 \le i \le n$.*
   - *The set $\mathrm{Com}(C^{\mathrm{ev}}(i), i)$ of all words which are to be communicated by node N_i after an evolutionary step which produced the set $C^{\mathrm{ev}}(i)$ in this node is defined by*

$$
\mathrm{Com}(C^{\mathrm{ev}}(i), i) = \begin{cases} \{\, w \mid \exists u \in C(i) \ \exists p_{\alpha_i} \in \mathrm{App}(u, M_i, \alpha_i) : w \in p_{\alpha_i}(u) \,\}, \\ \quad \text{if } \varrho_i \in \{(>), (<), (=)\}, \\ \{\, w \mid w \in C(i) \text{ and } \mathrm{App}(w, M_i, \alpha_i) = \emptyset \,\}, \\ \quad \text{if } \varrho_i \in \{(\hat{=})\}. \end{cases}
$$

   - *We say that C^{ev} derives C^{com} in one communication step $(C^{\mathrm{ev}} \vdash C^{\mathrm{com}})$ if, for $1 \le i \le n$,*

$$
C^{\mathrm{com}}(i) = \bigcup_{(k,i) \in E} \mathrm{Com}(C^{\mathrm{ev}}(k), k).
$$

3. *The computation of $\mathcal{N}$ is a sequence of configurations*

$$
C_t = (C_t(1), C_t(2), \ldots, C_t(n)), \ \text{for } t \ge 0,
$$

   such that
   - *$C_0 = (A_1, A_2, \ldots, A_n)$,*
   - *for any $t \ge 0$, C_{2t} derives C_{2t+1} in one evolutionary step:*

$$
C_{2t} \Longrightarrow C_{2t+1},
$$

   - *for any $t \ge 0$, C_{2t+1} derives C_{2t+2} in one communication step:*

$$
C_{2t+1} \vdash C_{2t+2}.
$$

The relations $\Longrightarrow$ and $\vdash$ are also defined for $V^* \times V^*$:
For any two words $u \in V^*$ and $v \in V^*$, we say that

- *u is derived to v in an evolutionary step (u $\Longrightarrow$ v) if there are t $\geq$ 0 and i with $1 \leq i \leq n$ such that $u \in C_{2t}(i)$ and $v \in C_{2t+1}(i)$ and*
- *u is derived to v in a communication step (u $\vdash$ v) if there are t $\geq$ 0 as well as i and k with $1 \leq i \leq n$, $1 \leq k \leq n$, and $(i,k) \in E$ such that $u \in C_{2t+1}(i)$ and $v \in C_{2t+2}(k)$.*

4. *The language $L(\mathcal{N})$ generated by $\mathcal{N}$ with output alphabet O is defined as*

$$L(\mathcal{N}) = \bigcup_{t \geq 0}(C_t(n_o) \cap O)$$

where $C_t = (C_t(1), C_t(2), \ldots, C_t(n))$ with $t \geq 0$ is the computation of $\mathcal{N}$.

The computation starts with an evolutionary step and then communication steps and evolutionary steps are alternately performed. In contrast to other network models, the filtering of words for the communication is not achieved by checking for structural properties of the words but simply by the fact that the words have been generated in the preceding evolutionary step or that no rule could be applied. Therefore, we also have a terminal alphabet called the output alphabet in this new model. The language generated consists of all words over the output alphabet which are in the output node N_{n_o} at some moment t with $t \geq 0$.

If, in a network $\mathcal{N}$, every node has the application mode $*$, then cN is called network of evolutionary processors with communication based on length comparison, clNEP for short. If different modes occur, then $\mathcal{N}$ is called a hybrid network of evolutionary processors with communication based on length comparison, clHNEP for short.

3 Results

In [3], it was shown that clHNEPs are computationally complete by constructing a clHNEP with eight nodes which simulates a phrase structure grammar in Penttonen normal form. We use here the same idea and construct a clHNEP with seven nodes which simulates a phrase structure grammar in Kuroda normal form which is more general with respect to the description of rules. A specialization to Penttonen normal form does not improve the result based on the idea used here.

3.1 Preliminary Considerations

We use here a kind of 'rotation and simulation method' as already used and described in [4] which is also used in [3]. The idea roots back to Post rewriting rules, introduced in [8].

For simulating rules with more than one symbol on the left-hand or right-hand side, it is necessary to detect two consecutive letters in a word in the network. In general, this can be achieved by filtering with regular or even special regular grammars. Such a filtering is not possible in the model used here.

However, the ends of a word can be detected to some extent. Therefore, we chose the Kuroda or even Penttonen normal form to simulate because every side of every rule has at most two symbols. In order to get such two consecutive symbols at the ends of a word, the word is rotated until the first letter of the subword is at the right end of the word and the second letter is at the left end of the word. Those positions can be checked by deletion and insertion nodes where the operations take place at the ends of a word only. The first and last letter of the input word are not consecutive. In order to separate these letters during the rotation, the unique letter # will be used as a separator.

For example, let $AB \rightarrow CD$ be a rule of the grammar under consideration where A, B, C, and D are non-terminal symbols and let $\#uABv$ be a word to which the rule should be applied, then the word is first rotated to the word $Bv\#uA$ and then the end letters A and B are replaced by C and D, respectively, yielding the word $Dv\#uC$ which can further be rotated to the word $\#uCDv$. Context-free rules are simulated in a similar way.

The rotation of a letter x from the right end to the left end of a (possibly already rotated) word can be achieved in the same way as if we would simulate the application of the 'rule' $x\lambda \rightarrow \lambda x$ as described above for $AB \rightarrow CD$ where $A = D = x$ and $B = C = \lambda$. Since x is not changed but only moved to the other end of the word, it does not matter of which type the symbol x is (non-terminal, terminal, or marker). A word $\lambda v\#ux$ is transformed into the word $xv\#u\lambda$ and $\lambda uv\#$ is transformed to $\#uv\lambda$).

3.2   Construction of a Simulating Network

Let L be a recursively enumerable language and $G = (N, T, P, S)$ a grammar in Kuroda normal form which generates the language L. We will construct a clHNEP $\mathcal{N}$ which simulates the derivation process of the grammar G. Let Σ be the union of the sets N and T and let its elements be denoted by $\sigma_1, \sigma_2, \ldots, \sigma_s$. Let # be a new symbol (not belonging to the alphabet Σ). We set $\sigma_{s+1} = \#$. This symbol will serve as the separator between the actual beginning and end of the word after a rotation. Further, let $\Sigma_\# = \Sigma \cup \{\#\}$.

We first collect the different kinds of rules of P. Let

$$P_0 = \{\, A \rightarrow \lambda \mid A \rightarrow \lambda \in P \,\},$$
$$P_1 = \{\, A \rightarrow x \mid A \in N, x \in N \cup T, A \rightarrow x \in P \,\},$$
$$P_2 = \{\, A \rightarrow BC \mid \{A, B, C\} \subseteq N, A \rightarrow BC \in P \,\},$$
$$P_3 = \{\, AB \rightarrow CD \mid \{A, B, C, D\} \subseteq N, AB \rightarrow CD \in P \,\}.$$

Let

$$a_1 = |P_1| \text{ and } s_1 = a_1$$

be the number of the rules of P with only one symbol on the right-hand side and let $p_1, \ldots, p_{s_1}$ be these rules.

Let

$$a_2 = |P_2|$$

be the number of the rules of P with one non-terminal on the left-hand side and two non-terminals on the right-hand side, let $s_2 = s_1 + a_2$, and let $p_{s_1+1}, \ldots, p_{s_2}$ be these rules.

Let

$$a_3 = |P_3|$$

be the number of the rules of P which have two non-terminals on every side, let $s_3 = s_2 + a_3$, and let $p_{s_2+1}, \ldots, p_{s_3}$ be these rules.

Let

$$a_4 = |\{ x\lambda \to \lambda x \mid x \in \Sigma_\# \}|$$

be the number of the 'rotation rules'. Then $a_4 = s+1$. Further, let $s_4 = s_3 + a_4$.

We introduce four functions l_1, l_2, r_1, and r_2 which assign to each rule index i with $1 \le i \le s_4$ the first symbol of the left-hand side of rule p_i, the second symbol of the left-hand side of rule p_i (λ if not present), the second symbol from right of the right-hand side of rule p_i (λ if there is only one symbol), the first symbol from right of the right-hand side of rule p_i, respectively:

$$l_1 : \{1, 2, \ldots, s_4\} \to \Sigma_\#,$$
$$l_2 : \{1, 2, \ldots, s_4\} \to N \cup \{\lambda\},$$
$$r_1 : \{1, 2, \ldots, s_4\} \to N \cup \{\lambda\},$$
$$r_2 : \{1, 2, \ldots, s_4\} \to \Sigma_\#$$

where, in case of $1 \le i \le s_1$ and $p_i = A \to x$,

$$l_1(i) = A, \quad l_2(i) = \lambda, \quad r_1(i) = \lambda, \quad r_2(i) = x,$$

in case of $s_1 + 1 < i \le s_2$ and $p_i = A \to BC$,

$$l_1(i) = A, \quad l_2(i) = \lambda, \quad r_1(i) = B, \quad r_2(i) = C,$$

in case of $s_2 + 1 \le i \le s_3$ and $p_i = AB \to CD$,

$$l_1(i) = A, \quad l_2(i) = B, \quad r_1(i) = C, \quad r_2(i) = D,$$

and in case of $s_3 + 1 \le i \le s_4$,

$$l_1(i) = \sigma_{i-s_3}, \quad l_2(i) = \lambda, \quad r_1(i) = \lambda, \quad r_2(i) = \sigma_{i-s_3}.$$

We now construct the mentioned network $\mathcal{N}$ with seven nodes which will be defined below and which are connected as shown in the picture (Fig. 1).

As the alphabet of the network, we set

$$V = \Sigma_\# \cup \{\text{\_}, \bot\}$$
$$\cup \{ [l_1(i)]_{i,j} \mid 1 \le i \le s_4, 0 \le j \le i \}$$
$$\cup \{ \langle r_2(i) \rangle_{i,j} \mid 1 \le i \le s_4, 0 \le j \le i \}.$$

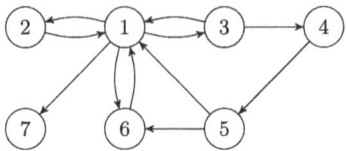

Fig. 1. Network for Simulation

The output alphabet of the network is the terminal alphabet T of the simulated grammar G. The network is now defined as

$$\mathcal{N} = (V, T, N_1, N_2, \ldots, N_7, E, 7)$$

where $N_1, \ldots, N_7$ are the nodes which will be defined below (with N_7 being the output node) and

$$E = \{(1,2),(1,3),(1,6),(1,7),(2,1),(3,1),(3,4),(4,5),(5,1),(5,6),(6,1)\}$$

is the set of edges as shown in Fig. 1.

Let the nodes be $N_i = (A_i, M_i, \alpha_i, \varrho_i)$ for $1 \leq i \leq 7$. The node N_1 is in some sense the start node: It is the only node which has an axiom. This axiom corresponds to the start symbol S of the simulated grammar G. Therefore, we set $A_1 = \{\#S\}$ and $A_i = \emptyset$ for $2 \leq i \leq 7$. Further, we set

$$\alpha_1 = r,$$
$$M_1 = \{\# \to \bot\} \cup \{A \to {}_\sqcup \mid A \to \lambda \in P_0\}$$
$$\cup \{l_1(i) \to [l_1(i)]_{i,i} \mid 1 \leq i \leq s_4\},$$
$$\cup \{[l_1(i)]_{i,j} \to [l_1(i)]_{i,j-1} \mid 1 \leq i \leq s_4, 1 \leq j \leq i\},$$
$$\varrho_1 = (=).$$

This node initiates the simulation of a rule of the grammar G, the rotation of the symbol from the right end to the left end of a word, or the finalization. The simulation of the erasing rules of P_0 is initiated by replacing the symbol which is to be deleted by a 'dummy' symbol which is really deleted by a deletion node (N_6). The simulation of the other rules and the rotation are initiated by marking the first symbol of the left-hand side of a rule or the symbol which is to be rotated to the other end of the word. This marking $[\cdot]_{i,i}$ contains information about which end of the word is effected (right end of the word, therefore, rectangular brackets) and about which rule is chosen for simulation. For a correct simulation, at the other end of the word, the same rule has to be chosen. In order to ensure this in a network whose number of nodes does not depend on the number of rules, both ends are calculated down until one reaches zero. If the other end reaches zero after the same number of steps, then at both ends, the same rule was chosen. In order not to forget the number of this rule, it is stored twice (one for keeping this information, one for decrementing). A similar marking will be used at the other end of a word (see nodes N_2 and N_3).

The node N_2 is used when a new symbol is needed at the left end of a word. This is the case when $l_2(i) = \lambda$ (but $r_2(i) \neq \lambda$). Therefore, we set

$$\alpha_2 = l,$$
$$M_2 = \{ \lambda \to \langle r_2(i) \rangle_{i,i} \mid 1 \leq i \leq s_1 \text{ or } s_2 + 1 \leq i \leq s_4 \},$$
$$\varrho_2 = (>).$$

Although such rules can always be applied when a word is present in this node, inserting more than one such symbol will produce a word which cannot be derived to a word in the output node. This will be shown the proof of correctness (Lemma 2).

The node N_3 is used when an existing symbol at the left end of a word has to be changed. This is the case when $l_2(i) \neq \lambda$ (and $r_2(i) \neq \lambda$) as well as during the simulation or rotation when calculating down at this end. Therefore, we set

$$\alpha_3 = l,$$
$$M_3 = \{ l_2(i) \to \langle r_2(i) \rangle_{i,i} \mid s_1 + 1 \leq i \leq s_2 \}$$
$$\cup \{ \langle r_2(i) \rangle_{i,j} \to \langle r_2(i) \rangle_{i,j-1} \mid 1 \leq i \leq s_4, 1 \leq j \leq i \},$$
$$\varrho_3 = (=).$$

The nodes N_4 and N_5 are used for detecting whether the process of decrementing at both ends finishes after the same number of steps (in the affirmative case, both zero markings can be replaced and the word survives, otherwise, there is only one zero marking which can be replaced but another one which cannot, so the word will not be communicated and vanishes). The node N_4 is for the right end of the word, hence, the base symbol $l_1(i)$ has to be replaced by $r_1(i)$. Since $r_1(i)$ can be λ or a non-terminal symbol from N, we use the same trick as in node N_1: If $r_1(i) - \lambda$, then $[l_1(i)]_{i,0}$ is substituted by the blank symbol $\textvisiblespace$ (which is later deleted by node N_6). The node N_5 is for the left end of the word, where the base symbol is already $r_2(i)$. So, in this node, the marked symbol is substituted by its base symbol. We set

$$\alpha_4 = r,$$
$$M_4 = \{ [l_1(i)]_{i,0} \to r_1(i) \mid s_1 + 1 \leq i \leq s_3 \}$$
$$\cup \{ [l_1(i)]_{i,0} \to \textvisiblespace \mid 1 \leq i \leq s_1 \text{ or } s_3 + 1 \leq i \leq s_4 \},$$
$$\varrho_4 = (=),$$
$$\alpha_5 = l,$$
$$M_5 = \{ \langle r_2(i) \rangle_{i,0} \to r_2(i) \mid 1 \leq i \leq s_4 \},$$
$$\varrho_5 = (=).$$

The node N_6 is for finishing the simulation of an erasing rule or the rotation by deleting the right-most symbol of the word but only if it has been marked as a blank symbol before. Hence, we set

$$\alpha_6 = r,$$
$$M_6 = \{ \_ \to \lambda \},$$
$$\varrho_6 = (<).$$

The node N_7 serves as the output node. Every terminal word over the output alphabet which is contained in this node at some time belongs to the language generated. On the other hand, every word in the language generated is at some time in this node and it is over the alphabet. In node N_1, the finalization was initiated with the rule $\# \to \bot$. In node N_7, it is finished by deleting this symbol $\bot$. This node does not have outgoing edges because, without the separator symbol, wrong simulations would be possible leading to terminal words which are not generated by the grammar G. This is also the reason, why the deleting nodes N_6 and N_7 cannot be joined. For node N_7, we set

$$\alpha_7 = r,$$
$$M_7 = \{ \bot \to \lambda \},$$
$$\varrho_7 = (<).$$

Since this node has no outgoing edge, the communication mode can by arbitrary.

3.3   Proof of Correctness

In this section, we prove that the network $\mathcal{N}$ constructed in the previous section indeed simulates the given grammar G. We first show that every word in the language $L(G)$ is generated by the clHNEP $\mathcal{N}$ and then that every word generated by the network $\mathcal{N}$ is also generated by the grammar G. From both results, we obtain the equivalence of both models.

Lemma 1. *Let G be a phrase structure grammar in Kuroda normal form and $\mathcal{N}$ be the network constructed above depending on the grammar G. Then, every word generated by G is also generated by $\mathcal{N}$: $L(G) \subseteq L(\mathcal{N})$.*

Proof. Let $G = (N, T, P, S)$ be a grammar in Kuroda normal form and $\mathcal{N}$ be the clHNEP for the grammar G with $\mathcal{N} = (V, T, N_1, N_2, \ldots, N_7, E, 7)$ as constructed above. Further, as in the construction, let $\#$ by a symbol which is neither a nonterminal nor a terminal symbol, $\Sigma = N \cup T$, and $\Sigma_\# = \Sigma \cup \{\#\}$. We will show that if $w \in \Sigma^*$ is a sentential form of G, then $\#w \in C_{2t}(1)$ for some $t \geq 0$. For the start symbol S of the grammar G, this holds since $\#S \in A_1$ and, therefore, $\#S \in C_0(1)$.

Before we show that this holds for an arbitrary sentential form, too, we show that a word $ux \in \Sigma_\#^*$ can be rotated to the word xu in the network (starting and ending in the same node N_1 and before an evolutionary step). Let $u \in \Sigma_\#^*$

be a word and $x \in \Sigma_\#$ be a symbol such that $ux \in C_{2t}(1)$ for some $t \geq 0$. Then there is a computation such that

$$u[x]_{i,i} \in C_{2t+1}(1) \cap C_{2t+2}(2),$$
$$\langle x \rangle_{i,i} u[x]_{i,i} \in C_{2t+3}(2) \cap C_{2t+4}(1),$$
$$\langle x \rangle_{i,i} u[x]_{i,i-1} \in C_{2t+5}(1) \cap C_{2t+6}(3),$$
$$\langle x \rangle_{i,i-1} u[x]_{i,i-1} \in C_{2t+7}(3) \cap C_{2t+8}(1)$$

which continues to

$$\langle x \rangle_{i,1} u[x]_{i,1} \in C_{2t+3+4(i-1)}(3) \cap C_{2t+3+4(i-1)+1}(1),$$
$$\langle x \rangle_{i,1} u[x]_{i,0} \in C_{2t+4i+1}(1) \cap C_{2t+4i+2}(3),$$
$$\langle x \rangle_{i,0} u[x]_{i,0} \in C_{2t+4i+3}(3) \cap C_{2t+4i+4}(4)$$

and finally to

$$\langle x \rangle_{i,0} u_\lrcorner \in C_{2t+4i+5}(4) \cap C_{2t+4i+6}(5),$$
$$xu_\lrcorner \in C_{2t+4i+7}(5) \cap C_{2t+4i+8}(6),$$
$$xu \in C_{2t+4i+9}(6) \cap C_{2t+4i+10}(1).$$

Now, let w_1 be a sentential form of G such that $\#w_1 \in C_{2t}(1)$ for some $t \geq 0$ and let w_2 be a sentential form directly derived from w_1. There is a rule $p \in P$ such that $w_1 \Longrightarrow_p w_2$. We distinguish the following cases.

1. $p \in P_0$: In this case, there are a non-terminal symbol A such that $p = A \to \lambda$ and letters $x_1, x_2, \ldots, x_m$ with $m \geq 0$ such that $w_1 = x_1 \ldots x_k A x_{k+1} \ldots x_m$ and $w_2 = x_1 \ldots x_k x_{k+1} \ldots x_m$. Since $\#w_1 \in C_{2t}(1)$, after some rotations, we have $x_{k+1} \ldots x_m \# x_1 \ldots x_k A \in C_{2t'}(1)$. The computation continues to

$$x_{k+1} \ldots x_m \# x_1 \ldots x_k \lrcorner \in C_{2t'+1}(1) \cap C_{2t'+2}(6) \text{ and}$$
$$x_{k+1} k + 1 \ldots x_m \# x_1 \ldots x_k \in C_{2t'+3}(6) \cap C_{2t'+4}(1).$$

After further rotations, we obtain $\#x_1 \ldots x_k x_{k+1} \ldots x_m = \#w_2 \in C_{2t''}(1)$.

2. $p \in P_1$: In this case, there are a non-terminal symbol A and a symbol $x \in \Sigma$ such that $p = A \to x$ and letters $x_1, x_2, \ldots, x_m$ with $m \geq 0$ such that $w_1 = x_1 \ldots x_k A x_{k+1} \ldots x_m$ and $w_2 = x_1 \ldots x_k x x_{k+1} \ldots x_m$. Similarly to the rotation, the computation leads in node N_1 from $\#w_1$ to the words $x_{k+1} \ldots x_m \# x_1 \ldots x_k A$, $x x_{k+1} \ldots x_m \# x_1 \ldots x_k$, and $\#x_1 \ldots x_k x x_{k+1} \ldots x_m$.

3. $p \in P_2$: In this case, there are three non-terminal symbols A, B, and C such that $p = A \to BC$ and letters $x_1, x_2, \ldots, x_m$ with $m \geq 0$ such that $w_1 = x_1 \ldots x_k A x_{k+1} \ldots x_m$ and $w_2 = x_1 \ldots x_k BC x_{k+1} \ldots x_m$. The computation continues to $x_{k+1} \ldots x_m \# x_1 \ldots x_k A$ and $x_{k+1} \ldots x_m \# x_1 \ldots x_k [A]_{i,i}$ in N_1 and

further to

$$x_{k+1} \ldots x_m \# x_1 \ldots x_k [A]_{i,i} \in C_{2t}(2),$$
$$\langle C \rangle_{i,i} x_{k+1} \ldots x_m \# x_1 \ldots x_k [A]_{i,i} \in C_{2t+1}(2) \cap C_{2t+2}(1),$$
$$\langle C \rangle_{i,i} x_{k+1} \ldots x_m \# x_1 \ldots x_k [A]_{i,i-1} \in C_{2t+3}(1) \cap C_{2t+4}(3),$$
$$\langle C \rangle_{i,i-1} x_{k+1} \ldots x_m \# x_1 \ldots x_k [A]_{i,i-1} \in C_{2t+5}(3) \cap C_{2t+6}(1),$$

$$\vdots$$

$$\langle C \rangle_{i,0} x_{k+1} \ldots x_m \# x_1 \ldots x_k [A]_{i,0} \in C_{2t'-1}(3) \cap C_{2t'}(4),$$
$$\langle C \rangle_{i,0} x_{k+1} \ldots x_m \# x_1 \ldots x_k B \in C_{2t'+1}(4) \cap C_{2t'+2}(5),$$
$$C x_{k+1} \ldots x_m \# x_1 \ldots x_k B \in C_{2t'+3}(5) \cap C_{2t'+4}(1),$$

and finally to $\# x_1 \ldots x_k BC x_{k+1} \ldots x_m \in C_{2t''}(1)$.

4. $p \in P_3$: In this case, there are four non-terminal symbols A, B, C, and D such that $p = AB \to CD$ and letters $x_1, x_2, \ldots, x_m$ with $m \geq 0$ such that $w_1 = x_1 \ldots x_k AB x_{k+1} \ldots x_m$ and $w_2 = x_1 \ldots x_k CD x_{k+1} \ldots x_m$. The computation runs as in the previous case with the exception that

$$B x_{k+1} \ldots x_m \# x_1 \ldots x_k [A]_{i,i} \in C_{2t}(3),$$
$$\langle D \rangle_{i,i} x_{k+1} \ldots x_m \# x_1 \ldots x_k [A]_{i,i} \in C_{2t+1}(3) \cap C_{2t+2}(1),$$
$$\langle D \rangle_{i,0} x_{k+1} \ldots x_m \# x_1 \ldots x_k C \in C_{2t'+1}(4) \cap C_{2t'+2}(5),$$

and finally $\# x_1 \ldots x_k CD x_{k+1} \ldots x_m \in C_{2t''}(1)$.

Let now w be a word of $L(G)$. Then $\# w \in C_{2t}(1)$ according to the considerations above. The computation continues to $\perp w \in C_{2t+1}(1) \cap C_{2t+2}(7)$. In N_7, the word evolves to w which is a word over the output alphabet O. Since N_7 is the output node, we now have that $w \in L(\mathcal{N})$.   □

The proof in the other direction is more complex since 'dead end' computations have to be handled as well. The idea is to show that any successful computation (which generates a word over the output alphabet) has a path as demonstrated in the proof of the previous lemma which corresponds to a derivation in the grammar G.

Lemma 2. *Let G be a phrase structure grammar in Kuroda normal form and $\mathcal{N}$ be the network constructed above depending on the grammar G. Then, every word generated by $\mathcal{N}$ is also generated by G: $L(\mathcal{N}) \subseteq L(G)$.*

Proof. Let $w \in L(\mathcal{N})$ be a word generated by the network (being at some time in the output node N_7). Then there is a computation C starting in node N_1 with the axiom $\# S$ (no other node has an axiom) which finally leads to the word $w \in T$. The only rule for replacing or deleting the symbol $\#$ in the entire network is the rule $\# \to \perp$ in node N_1. The only rule for replacing or deleting the symbol $\perp$ in the entire network is the rule $\perp \to \lambda$ in node N_7. This node has no axioms, only one incoming edge, and no outgoing edges. Hence, any computation from $\#S$ to w is a computation from $\#S \in C_0(1)$ to the word $w\# \in C_{2t}(1)$ which continues as $w\# \Longrightarrow w\bot \in C_{2t+1}(1) \vdash w\bot \in C_{2t+2}(7) \Longrightarrow w$.

The network contains five elementary cycles; all of them contain the node N_1. The maximal length is also five. Hence, after at most five communication steps, the current word of the considered computation C is again in node N_1. Let us consider a word $\tilde{w} = v\#u \in C_{2k}(1)$ for some number k with $0 \le k < t$ where $uv \in \Sigma^*$ is a sentential form of the grammar G and which occurs during the computation C. We now show that the next word over the alphabet $\Sigma_\#$ in node N_1 is also a sentential form of the grammar G up to rotation.

Since the computation continues, a rule of M_1 is applicable to the word $v\#u$. We distinguish the following cases according to the type of rule which is applied:

1. $\# \to \bot$: In this case, we have $u = \lambda$. The word $v\bot \in C_{2k+1}(1)$ is communicated to the nodes N_2, N_3, N_6, and N_7.
   - In the node N_2, a rule is applied and the word is sent back to node N_1. There, no rule can be applied and the computation ends without arriving at the word w.
   - In the node N_3, it might be that a rule is applied, otherwise the computation ends. After an application, the word is sent back to node N_1 where again the computation stops and it is sent also to node N_4 where no rule can be applied, so the computation ends in this case, too.
   - In the node N_6, no rule can be applied and the computation stops.
   - In the node N_7, the end marker $\bot$ is deleted. If the remaining word $v \in C_{2k+3}(7)$ is a terminal word from T^*, then it is generated and the computation stops, otherwise, the computation also stops. Since $k < t$, the computation does not continue to the situation that $w \in C_{2t+3}(7)$.
   Since in all cases, the computation stops prematurely, the rule $\# \to \bot$ is not applied to the word $\tilde{w}$.
2. $A \to \textvisiblespace$: In this case, we have $u = u'A$ for some word $u' \in \Sigma$. The word $v\#u'\textvisiblespace \in C_{2k+1}(1)$ is communicated to the nodes N_2, N_3, N_6, and N_7. Regarding nodes N_2 and N_3, we have the same situation as before. In node N_7, the word is not changed. It does not belong to the generated language because it is not from the set T^*. In the node N_6, the symbol $\textvisiblespace$ is deleted and the word returns to node N_1. Hence, $v\#u' \in C_{2k+4}(1) \cap \Sigma_\#$. Furthermore, the word $u'Av$ is a sentential form of G and $A \to \lambda \in P_0$. Therefore, also $u'v$ is a sentential form of G.
3. $l_1(i) \to [l_1(i)]_{i,i}$ for some i with $1 \le i \le s_4$: In node N_6 or N_7, a rule cannot be applied. So, the computations stops. In node N_2, a symbol $\langle r_2(j) \rangle_{j,j}$ is inserted for a number j with $1 \le j \le s_1$ or $s_2 + 1 \le j \le s_4$. In node N_3, the symbol at the left end of the word is substituted by $\langle r_2(j) \rangle_{j,j}$ if it is $l_2(j)$ for some number j with $s_1 + 1 \le j \le s_2$, otherwise, the computation ends. After being communicated to node N_4, the computation stops because $i > 0$. Hence, in both cases, the word returns to node N_1. During the following cycles, the computation will never continue in the nodes N_6 and N_7 because their rules cannot be applied at the right end of the word. The same holds for node N_4 when it receives a word from node N_3 until the counter at the right end is

zero. So, for a while the words swing between node N_1 on the one side and node N_2 and node N_3 on the other side. In node N_1, the symbol at the right end of the word is counted down. In node N_3, the symbol at the left end of the word is counted down. There are three cases for a word

$$\langle r_2(j)\rangle_{j,k_j} v' \# u'[l_1(i)]_{i,k_i} \in C_{2k+4(i-k_i+1)}(1) \tag{1}$$

with $1 \le k_i \le i$ and $1 \le k_j \le j$ such that $k_i = 1$ or $k_j = 1$:

– $k_i = 1$ and $k_j > 1$: The computation continues as

$$\langle r_2(j)\rangle_{j,k_j} v' \# u'[l_1(i)]_{i,1} \in C_{2k+4i}(1)$$
$$\Longrightarrow \langle r_2(j)\rangle_{j,k_j} v' \# u'[l_1(i)]_{i,0} \in C_{2k+4i+1}(1)$$
$$\vdash \langle r_2(j)\rangle_{j,k_j} v' \# u'[l_1(i)]_{i,0} \in C_{2k+4i+2}(2) \cap C_{2k+4i+2}(3).$$

Then, the following happens:
- In node N_2, a symbol $\langle r_2(k)\rangle_{k,k}$ is inserted for a number k with $1 \le k \le s_1$ or $s_2 + 1 \le k \le s_4$. But then back in node N_1, the computation stops because there is no rule which can be applied at the right end.
- In node N_3, the word changes to $\langle r_2(j)\rangle_{j,k_j-1} v' \# u'[l_1(i)]_{i,0}$. Back to node N_1, the computation stops. In node N_4, the symbol at the right end is substituted. But then, in node N_5, the computation stops because $k_j - 1 > 0$.

Hence, the computation does not lead to the word w if, for the rule numbers i and j chosen, it holds $i < j$.

– $k_j = 1$ and $k_i > 1$: The computation continues as

$$\langle r_2(j)\rangle_{j,1} v' \# u'[l_1(i)]_{i,k_i} \in C_{2k+4(i-k_i+1)}(1)$$
$$\Longrightarrow \langle r_2(j)\rangle_{j,1} v' \# u'[l_1(i)]_{i,k_i-1} \in C_{2k+4(i-k_i+1)+1}(1)$$
$$\vdash \langle r_2(j)\rangle_{j,1} v' \# u'[l_1(i)]_{i,k_i-1} \in C_{2k+4(i-k_i+1)+2}(2) \cap C_{2k+4(i-k_i+1)+2}(3).$$

Then, the following happens:
- In node N_2, a symbol $\langle r_2(k)\rangle_{k,k}$ is inserted for a number k with $1 \le k \le s_1$ or $s_2 + 1 \le k \le s_4$. Going back to node N_1, the computation continues again until the counter at one of the ends has reached one and then, we have again one of these cases here.
- In node N_3, the word changes to $\langle r_2(j)\rangle_{j,0} v' \# u'[l_1(i)]_{i,k_i-1}$.
  * Going back to node N_1, the computation continues between the nodes N_1 and N_2 (in node N_3, no rule can be applied anymore) until the counter at the right end reaches zero. Then the computation stops because, in node N_1, no rule can be applied.
  * In node N_4, the computation stops as well because $k_i - 1 > 0$.

Hence, the computation does not lead to the word w if, for the rule numbers i and j chosen, it holds $i > j$.

– $k_i = k_j = 1$: The computation continues as

$$\langle r_2(j)\rangle_{j,1} v' \# u'[l_1(i)]_{i,1} \in C_{2k+4i}(1)$$
$$\Longrightarrow \langle r_2(j)\rangle_{j,1} v' \# u'[l_1(i)]_{i,0} \in C_{2k+4i+1}(1)$$
$$\vdash \langle r_2(j)\rangle_{j,1} v' \# u'[l_1(i)]_{i,0} \in C_{2k+4i+2}(2) \cap C_{2k+4i+2}(3).$$

Then, the following happens:

- In node N_2, a symbol $\langle r_2(k)\rangle_{k,k}$ is inserted for a number k with $1 \leq k \leq s_1$ or $s_2+1 \leq k \leq s_4$. But then back in node N_1, the computation stops because there is no rule which can be applied.
- In node N_3, the word changes to $\langle r_2(j)\rangle_{j,0}v'\#u'[l_1(i)]_{i,0}$. Back in node N_1, the computation stops. In node N_4, the symbol $[l_1(i)]_{i,0}$ at the right end is substituted by $r_1(i)$ if $r_1(i) \neq \lambda$ or $\_$ if $r_1(i) = \lambda$. Further, in node N_5, the symbol $\langle r_2(j)\rangle_{j,0}$ at the left end is substituted by $r_2(j)$. Then, the word is communicated to the nodes N_1 and N_6. If the symbol at the right end is $\_$, then the computation stops in node N_1 but the symbol is deleted in node N_6 and then the word continues to node N_1. If the symbol at the right end is not $\_$, then the computation stops in node N_6 but the word is also in node N_1 where the computation continues.

The word in node N_1 is now $r_2(j)v'\#u'r_1(i)$. There are two cases:

- The word v' contains at least one symbol $\langle r_2(l)\rangle_{l,k_l}$ for a number l with $1 \leq l \leq s_4$. Then, at some time, after the first such symbol has been inserted by node N_2 or produced by substitution in node N_3, another symbol of this kind has been inserted by node N_2. This means that counting down at the left end was disturbed and the computation should stop without generating a word in the output node N_7. Indeed, this symbol can never be deleted again which can be seen as follows: In the cycle of N_1 and node N_2, only more symbols of this kind are introduced. In the cycle of N_1 and node N_3, also no symbol of the subword v' is affected because the symbol $\langle r_2(l)\rangle_{l,k_l}$ is not at the left end of the word. Neither is this symbol affected by the other nodes N_4 to N_7. What could happen is that all the symbols to the right of the symbol $\langle r_2(l)\rangle_{l,k_l}$ are rotated such that this symbol reaches the right end of the word. But then the computation stops in node N_1 because no rule can be applied (this is the reason why the symbols at the right end are marked by $[\cdot]$ and the symbols originating from the left end are marked differently by $\langle\cdot\rangle$).
- The word v' does not contain a symbol $\langle r_2(l)\rangle_{l,k_l}$ with $1 \leq l \leq s_4$. In this case, both ends were counted down alternatingly in the nodes N_1 and N_3. Hence, from $k_i = k_j$, it follows $i = j$. The word $l_2(i)v'\#u'l_1(i) \in C_{2k}(1)$ is derived to the word

$$r_2(i)v'\#u'r_1(i) \in C_{2k+4(i+1)+h}(1)$$

where $h = 0$ if $r_1(i) \neq \lambda$ (the computation did not involve node N_6) and $h = 2$ if $r_1(i) = \lambda$ (the computation went through node N_6). Furthermore, the word belongs to the set $\Sigma_\#$ as the first word in the computation after $v\#u$ and it holds $u'l_1(i)l_2(i)v' = u'r_1(i)r_2(i)v'$ if $s_3 + 1 \leq i \leq s_4$ (if i corresponds to a rotation rule) or $u'l_1(i)l_2(i)v' \Longrightarrow_G u'r_1(i)r_2(i)v'$ is a derivation in the grammar G (if i is the number of a rule in P). In both cases, the word derived in the network is a sentential form of G.

Hence, the computation only leads to the word w if, for the rule numbers i and j chosen, it holds $i = j$ and not more than one marker is introduced at the left end of the word.

If the computation continues from $\tilde{w}$ to w, then the next word after $\tilde{w}$ in the node N_1 which belongs to $\Sigma_{\#}^*$ is a sentential form of the grammar G.

Hence, for any computation from $\#S \in C_0(1)$ to the word $w\# \in C_{2t}(1)$, there is a sequence $(w_0, w_1, \ldots, w_m)$ of words $w_i \in \Sigma^*$ with $0 \le i \le m$ for some $m > 0$ where $w_0 = S$ and $w_m = w$ such that, for each word w_i, there are two words $w_{i,1}$ and $w_{i,2}$ with $w_i = w_{i,1} w_{i,2}$ and $w_{i,2}\#w_{i,1} \in C_{2t_i}(1)$ during the computation. Furthermore, we have that $t_0 < t_1 < \cdots < t_m$ and each word w_i is a sentential form of the grammar G. Hence, the is also the derivation $S = w_0 \Longrightarrow^* w_1 \Longrightarrow^* \cdots \Longrightarrow^* w_m = w$ in G. Thus, every word which is generated by the network $\mathcal{N}$ is also generated by the grammar G, which proves the relation $L(\mathcal{N}) \subseteq L(G)$. $\square$

With Lemma 1, we have the relation $L(G) \subseteq L(\mathcal{N})$. With Lemma 2, we have the other relation $L(\mathcal{N}) \subseteq L(G)$. Together, we obtain the equality $L(G) = L(\mathcal{N})$. Since for any recursively enumerable language, there is a grammar in Kuroda normal form (according to [5]) which we have used for the construction, we have shown the computational completeness of hybrid networks of evolutionary processors with communication based on length comparison. Moreover, the size of seven nodes is sufficient.

Theorem 1. *For any recursively enumerable language L, there exists a hybrid network of evolutionary processors with communication based on length comparison (clHNEP) $\mathcal{N}$ of size 7 generating the language L.*

Proof. The construction in Sect. 3.2 shows such a network $\mathcal{N}$ and how to construct it from a phrase structure grammar G in Kuroda normal form generating the language L. From the Lemmas 1 and 2, one can conclude that $L(G) = L(\mathcal{N})$. Hence, the constructed network $\mathcal{N}$ is equivalent to the grammar G. $\square$

4   Conclusion

It seems that the constructed clHNEP is optimal with respect to size in terms of the number of nodes because the 'appearance checking' which we need can be performed only at the ends of a word and it can be done only by mutation operations not by just looking at it. Hence, we need a node for substitutions on the right end, a node for substitutions at the left end, an insertion node for increasing the length of a sentential form, a deletion node for decreasing the length, and an output node (a symbol marking the end or beginning of a word is needed but is must be deleted to obtain a terminal word; after this deletion, it must not circulate anymore in the network, so this cannot be handled by a 'processing' deletion node). In our construction, there are two more nodes for checking whether the counting down at both ends needed the same time. For this, the other nodes could not be used because then they could perform any of the operations (the counting end or further counting depending on the symbol being present at the respective end of the word), so they could not block the computation which is needed in order to continue only if the rules at both ends were chosen equally. Maybe, the substitution nodes can be replaced by insertion and deletion nodes but this would certainly increase the number of nodes. This is not a proof but only a conjecture which gives some ideas for future research.

As already mentioned, we believe that it is possible to construct a clHNEP for any recursively enumerable language where all substitution nodes work in the $*$-mode (such that the l-mode and r-mode are only used for insertion and deletion nodes). But also this needs to be studied and proved.

A further extension of research leads to accepting networks of evolutionary processors. The investigations on similar models show that the results are often the same in terms of computational capacity but, nevertheless, there are some differences which required other proofs.

References

1. Castellanos, J., Martín-Vide, C., Mitrana, V., Sempere, J.M.: Solving NP-complete problems with networks of evolutionary processors. In: IWANN 2001: Proceedings of the 6th International Work-Conference on Artificial and Natural Neural Networks. LNCS, vol. 2084, pp. 621–628. Springer, Berlin (2001)
2. Csuhaj-Varjú, E., Salomaa, A.: Networks of parallel language processors. In: Păun, G., Salomaa, A. (eds.) New Trends in Formal Languages. LNCS, vol. 1218, pp. 299–318. Springer, Heidelberg (1997). https://doi.org/10.1007/3-540-62844-4_22
3. Csuhaj Varjú, E., Sethy, P.K.: Length-driven communication in networks of evolutionary processors. J. Membr. Comput. (2025). https://doi.org/10.1007/s41965-025-00184-1
4. Dassow, J., Manea, F., Truthe, B.: On the power of accepting networks of evolutionary processors with special topologies and random context filters. Fund. Inform. **136**(1–2), 1–35 (2015)
5. Kuroda, S.Y.: Classes of languages and linear-bounded automata. Inf. Control **7**(2), 207–223 (1964)
6. Margenstern, M., Mitrana, V., Pérez-Jiménez, M.J.: Accepting hybrid networks of evolutionary processors. In: Ferretti, C., Mauri, G., Zandron, C. (eds.) DNA Computing, 10th International Workshop on DNA Computing, DNA 10, Milan, Italy, 7–10 June 2004, Revised Selected Papers. LNCS, vol. 3384, pp. 235–246. Springer (2004)
7. Penttonen, M.: One-sided and two-sided context in formal grammars. Inf. Control **25**, 371–392 (1974)
8. Post, E.L.: Formal reductions of the general combinatorial decision problem. Am. J. Math. **65**(2), 197–215 (1943)
9. Rozenberg, G., Salomaa, A. (eds.): Handbook of Formal Languages. Springer, Berlin (1997)
10. Truthe, B.: A survey on computationally complete accepting and generating networks of evolutionary processors. In: Durand-Lose, J., Vaszil, G. (eds.) Machines, Computations, and Universality, 9th International Conference, MCU 2022, Debrecen, Hungary, 31 August–2 September 2022, Proceedings. LNCS, vol. 13419, pp. 12–26. Springer (2022)

Bio-inspired Models and Membrane Systems

Variants of Tissue P Systems with Prescribed Teams of Channel Rules

Artiom Alhazov[1] , Rudolf Freund[2(✉)] , Sergiu Ivanov[3] , Marion Oswald[2] ,
and Sergey Verlan[4]

[1] Vladimir Andrunachievici Institute of Mathematics and Computer Science, State
University of Moldova, Academiei 5, 2028 Chișinău, Moldova
artiom@math.md
[2] Faculty of Informatics, TU Wien, Favoritenstraße 9–11, 1040 Wien, Austria
rudi@emcc.at, marion.oswald@tuwien.ac.at
[3] IBISC, Univ. Évry, Paris-Saclay University, 23, boulevard de France, 91034 Évry,
France
sergiu.ivanov@ibisc.univ-evry.fr
[4] Univ. Paris Est Creteil, LACL, 94010, 61, av. Général de Gaulle, Creteil, France
verlan@u-pec.fr

Abstract. In this paper we consider tissue P systems with prescribed
teams of channel rules, with the application of the channel rules possibly
depending on some given condition. A channel rule opens a channel from
one cell to another one for one object to pass through it, and the channel
is only open for one step. A *team of channel rules* then is a multiset
of such channel rules. We especially investigate two variants of how the
rules in the teams can be applied: in the *enforcing mode*, the opened
channel has to be used by the object it has been opened for, whereas
in the *permitting mode* an open channel has to be used if possible, but
can also remain unused if no object exists which could pass through.
We show how multiset grammars using evolution rules equipped with
random context conditions can easily be simulated by teams of channel
rules, as well as how variants of purely communicating (tissue) P systems
can be interpreted in this framework of tissue P systems with prescribed
teams of channel rules. Moreover, we prove computational completeness
results for various models of purely communicating (tissue) P systems,
often based on already proven results, some even with all channel rules
working the enforcing mode without applicability conditions. We also
show how computations on strings can be carried out by tissue P systems
with prescribed teams of channel rules. Finally, we also discuss how these
systems allow for "going beyond Turing".

Keywords: channel rules · prescribed teams · tissue P systems ·
antiport rules · symport rules · minimal communication rules ·
applicability conditions · computational completeness · derivation
modes

M. D. Jiménez López and G. Vaszil (Eds.): Erzsébet Csuhaj-Varjú Festschrift,
LNCS 15840, pp. 157–178, 2025.
https://doi.org/10.1007/978-3-031-97274-4_10

1 Introduction

Membrane (P) systems were introduced at the end of the last millenium in [35] as a model of computing based on multiset-rewriting, inspired by the hierarchical membrane structure and the functioning of the living cell, where the molecules/objects evolve in parallel. This area of biologically motivated computing has emerged in a fascinating way during the last 25 years. Many interesting variants as well as a lot of applications of these theoretical models have been investigated by scientists all over the world, e.g., see [36] and [37]. For actual information, we refer to the *P systems webpage* [41] as well as to the issues of the *Bulletin of the International Membrane Computing Society* and of the *Journal of Membrane Computing*.

When P systems operate on multisets of objects with non-cooperative rules, their power (even) when working in the maximally parallel derivation mode is rather restricted; for example, the multiset language $\{b^{2^n} \mid n \in \mathbb{N}\}$ cannot be obtained by halting computations. On the other hand, cooperative rules easily allow specific variants of P systems to yield computational completeness. Yet also other different variants of cooperation between objects and rules have been investigated, for example, control mechanisms as graph-controlled and matrix grammars, mostly used in the sequential derivation mode, for example see [27]. In matrix grammars, rules are grouped into sequences (called matrices), which have to be applied in the given order one after another. In a less strict variant the rules are given as a set of rules, so-called *prescribed teams*, where the rules can be applied in any order, see [11]. In contrast to the original model, in which the rules of a team can be applied together only sequentially, in [2], simple P systems (i.e., consisting of only one mebrane region) working with prescribed teams of sets of rules were investigated. There a *team* was defined as a set of multisets of rules, where each multiset of rules has assigned (i) its own applicability condition and (ii) its own derivation mode in which the rules in this multiset have to be applied together, and based on one of these teams a suitable multiset of rules to be applied to the underlying configuration is constructed. In [5], such prescribed teams are working on different objects.

In contrast to these previous papers on using prescribed teams, especially see [2], we here consider tissue P systems and not only simple P systems (consisting of only one mebrane region) as well as pure communication rules, which we call *channel rules*. A channel rule just for one derivation step opens a channel for one object to pass from one cell to another cell. Moreover, teams now are considered as multisets of channel rules which are applied either sequentially or in the maximally parallel derivation mode.

Variants of (tissue) P systems using channels between their cells have already been considered in various earlier papers. For example, in [24] P systems (with a hierarchical communication structure) with activated/prohibited membrane channels were considered, with channels between membrane regions opened for multisets of objects to pass through by activating finite multisets if not prohibited by finite prohibiting multisets. The accepting variant of these system, i.e., the P automata variant, then was considered in [26], showing how any recursively enumerable string language can be accepted by such P automata. In [30] tissue P systems with channel states were considered, where states were controlling the passage of objects between cells.

Specific variants of purely communicating (tissue) P systems have been considered already at the early stage of the emerging area of membrane systems. In 2002, P systems with symport and antiport rules were introduced in [34]. A first overview on the main results for P systems with symport and antiport rules was given in [6]. Another special variant of purely communicating P systems was considered in [39]. Generalized communicating P systems were introduced in [40]. Further new results for these variants can be found, for example, in [17,18]. A more recent short overview on communicating P systems is given in [10].

In this paper we start with the general definition of tissue P systems as described in the formal framework for static P systems, see [31], and show how channel rules can be interpreted within this framework. A prescribed team in the model presented in this paper then consists of a multiset of channel rules. For the application of these teams we will restrict ourselves to the two very basic modes, i.e., the maximally parallel and the sequential derivation mode. For (the definition of) other derivation modes, we refer to the formal framework for static P systems, see [31], or for those defined recently to [1,3,4,7].

We then introduce the model of a *tissue P system with teams of multisets of channel rules* (a *TPPTCS* for short), and two special variants of how the channel rules in the teams, i.e., in the multisets of channel rules, have to be applied: in the *enforcing mode*, an opened channel has to be used by an object it has been opened for (*enforcing channel rule*), whereas in the *permitting mode* an opened channel has to be used if possible, but can also remain unused if no object exists which could pass through (*permitting channel rule*). We emphasize that when applying a team, all the enforcing channel rules in the team must be used, whereas in the permitting mode, channel rules may remain unused if not enough objects exist to use them. As derivation modes for TPPTCSs, we only consider the sequential and the maximally parallel derivation mode.

As a first result we show how multiset grammars using evolution rules equipped with random context conditions can be simulated by TPPTCSs with three cells using teams of enforcing and permitting channel rules in the sequential derivation mode. Then we give three different proofs how register machines can be simulated by TPPTCSs using only enforcing channel rules or also permitting channel rules, both in the sequential and the maximally parallel derivation mode.

Moreover, we show how generalized communicating P systems with minimal communication rules, e.g., see [17,18,40], can be interpreted within our model of TPPTCSs only using enforcing channel rules in the maximally parallel derivation mode. Based on these results, we immediately obtain several computational completeness results for TPPTCSs working in the maximally parallel mode and with all channel rules working in the enforcing mode.

Finally, we show how computations on strings can be carried out by TPPTCSs and also discuss how these systems allow for "going beyond Turing".

The (rest of the) paper is organized as follows: To keep the paper self-contained, in Sect. 2 we recall the basic definitions from formal language theory. In the succeeding section, the general definition of tissue P systems and the basic derivation modes taken into consideration in our paper are defined. Then in Sect. 4, *tissue P systems with prescribed teams of channel rules* (*TPPTCSs* for short) are defined and a small depictive example is given; moreover, we show multiset grammars using evolution rules equipped with random context conditions can be simulated by TPPTCSs. In Sect. 5 we give three different proofs how register machines can be simulated by TPPTCSs. Based on these results, we establish several computational completeness results in Sect. 6. Moreover, we explain how specific variants of purely communicating (tissue) P systems, especially the variants of generalized communicating P systems with minimal communication rules, can be implemented within our model of TPPTCSs and in that way how several computational completeness results can be deduced for TPPTCSs working in the maximally parallel mode and with all channel rules working in the enforcing mode. In Sect. 7 we explain how the model of TPPTCSs can be extended to be able to make computations on strings. Finally we discuss how these systems allow for "going beyond Turing". An overview on the results obtained in this paper and ideas for future research conclude the paper in Sect. 9.

2   Definitions

In this section we mention some notions required for our definitions and results to keep the paper self-contained.

For an alphabet V, a finite non-empty set of abstract symbols, the free monoid generated by V under the operation of concatenation, i.e., the set containing all possible strings over V, is denoted by V^*. The empty string is denoted by λ, and $V^* \backslash \{\lambda\}$ is denoted by V^+. By $\mathbb{N}$ we denote the set of all non-negative integers, by $\mathbb{N}^k$ the set of all vectors with k components of non-negative integers.

Let V be a (finite) set, $V = \{a_1, \dots, a_k\}$. A *finite multiset* M over V is a mapping $M : V \to \mathbb{N}$, i.e., for each $a \in V$, $M(a)$ specifies the number of occurrences of a in M. A finite multiset M over V can also be represented by any string x that contains exactly $M(a_i)$ symbols a_i for all $1 \le i \le k$, e.g., by $a^{M(a_1)} \dots a^{M(a_k)}$, or else by the set $\{a^{M(a_i)} \mid 1 \le i \le k\}$. The *support* of M is the set $supp(M) = \{a \in V \mid M(a) \ge 1\}$. The set of all finite multisets over the set V is denoted by $\langle V, \mathbb{N} \rangle$. The *empty multiset* is represented by λ as the empty string. The cardinality of a set or multiset M is denoted by $|M|$.

We may also consider mappings M of the form $M : V \to \mathbb{N}_\infty$, where $\mathbb{N}_\infty = \mathbb{N} \cup \{\infty\}$, i.e., elements of M may have an infinite multiplicity; we shall call such multisets where $M(a_i) = \infty$ for at least one i, $1 \le i \le k$, infinite multisets. The set of all such multisets M over V with $M : V \to \mathbb{N}_\infty$ is denoted by $\langle V, \mathbb{N}_\infty \rangle$. For $W \subseteq V$, W^∞ denotes the infinite multiset with $W(a) = \infty$ for all $a \in W$. Let x and y be two multisets over V, i.e., from $\langle V, \mathbb{N} \rangle$ or $\langle V, \mathbb{N}_\infty \rangle$. Then x is called a *submultiset* of y, written $x \le y$ or $x \subseteq y$, if and only if $x(a) \le y(a)$ for all $a \in V$; if, moreover, $x(a) < y(a)$ for some $a \in V$, then x is called a *strict submultiset* of y. Observe that for all $n \in \mathbb{N}$, $n + \infty = \infty$, and $\infty - n = \infty$. The *sum* of x and y, denoted by $x + y$ or $x \cup y$, is a multiset z such that $z(a) = x(a) + y(a)$ for all $a \in V$. The *difference* of two multisets x and y, denoted by $x - y$, provided that $y \subseteq x$, is the multiset z with $z(a) = x(a) - y(a)$ for all $a \in V$. Observe that in the following, when taking the sum or the difference of two multisets x and y from $\langle V, \mathbb{N}_\infty \rangle$, we shall always assume $\{x(a), y(a)\} \cap \mathbb{N} \neq \emptyset$. If $X = (x_1, \ldots, x_m)$ and $Y = (y_1, \ldots, y_m)$ are vectors of multisets over V, then $X \leq Y$ if and only if $x_j \subseteq y_j$ for all j, $1 \leq j \leq m$; in the same way, sum and difference of vectors of multisets are defined by taking the sum and the difference, respectively, in each component.

NREG and NRE denote the families of regular and of recursively enumerable sets of natural numbers; PsREG and PsRE denote the families of regular and of recursively enumerable sets of vectors of natural numbers.

For further notions and results in formal language theory we refer to textbooks like [19] and [38].

2.1   Register Machines

Register machines are well-known universal devices for computing on (or generating or accepting) sets of vectors of natural numbers. The following definitions are given as in previous papers, e.g., see [1].

Definition 1. *A* register machine *is a construct* $M = (m, B, l_0, l_h, P)$ *where*

- m *is the number of registers,*
- B *is the set of labels for the instructions in* P,
- P *is the set of instructions bijectively labeled by elements of* B,
- $l_0 \in B$ *is the initial label, and*
- $l_h \in B$ *is the final label.*

The instructions of M *can be of the following forms:*

- $p : (ADD(r), q, s); p \in B \setminus \{l_h\}$, $q, s \in B$, $1 \leq r \leq m$.
  Increase the value of register r *by one, and non-deterministically jump to instruction* q *or* s.
- $p : (SUB(r), q, s); p \in B \setminus \{l_h\}$, $q, s \in B$, $1 \leq r \leq m$.
  If the value of register r *is not zero then decrease the value of register* r *by one (*decrement *case) and jump to instruction* q, *otherwise jump to instruction* s (zero-test *case*).
- $l_h : HALT$. *Stop the execution of the register machine.*
  The register machine halts if and only if it reaches the HALT-instruction.

A configuration *of a register machine is described by the contents of each register and by the value of the current label, which indicates the next instruction to be executed.* M *is called* deterministic *if the ADD-instructions all are of the form* $p : (ADD(r), q)$.

Throughout the paper, B_{ADD} *denotes the set of labels of ADD-instructions* $p : (ADD(r), q, s)$ *of arbitrary registers* r. $B_{SUB(r)}$ *denotes the set of labels of all*

SUB-instructions $p : (SUB(r), q, s)$ *of a decrementable register* r *and* B_{SUB} *the set of all SUB-instructions .*

Moreover, for any $p \in B \setminus \{l_h\}$, $Reg(p)$ *denotes the register affected by the ADD- or SUB-instruction labeled by* p; *for the sake of completeness, in addition* $Reg(l_h) = 1$ *is taken.*

It is known that register machines are computationally complete, e.g., see [33], i.e., register machines characterize NRE ($PsRE$), the families of recursively enumerable sets of (vectors of) natural numbers. Hence, register machines are a convenient model to be compared with models dealing with (sets of) numbers directly instead of strings. For useful results on the computational power of register machines, we refer to [33].

3 Tissue P Systems

Very often, specific variants of P systems working on multisets can be reduced to a model of multiset rewriting within just one membrane region by applying the well-known flattening process, which means that computations in a P system with an arbitrary (static) membrane structure can be simulated in a P system with only one membrane region, e.g., see [22]. Yet as the model considered in this paper relies on pure communication of objects between cells, we have to consider a model based on the concept of tissue P systems. The following definition of a tissue P system follows the definition of a *network of cells* as used in the *Formal Framework for Static (Tissue) P Systems*, see [31].

Definition 2. *A* tissue P system *of degree* $n \geq 1$ *is a construct*

$$\Pi = (n, V, \Sigma, w, Inf, \mathcal{R}, \delta) \quad \text{where}$$

- n *is the number of cells in* Π,
- V *is the alphabet of* objects;
- $\Sigma \subseteq V$ *is the alphabet of* terminal objects;
- $w = (w_1, \ldots, w_n)$, *with* $w_i \in \langle V, \mathbb{N} \rangle$, $1 \leq i \leq n$, *being the finite multiset of objects initially assigned to cell* i;
- $Inf = (Inf_1, \ldots, Inf_n)$, *with* $Inf_i \subseteq V$, $1 \leq i \leq n$, *being the set of objects available infinitely often in cell* i;
- $\mathcal{R}$ *is a finite set of* interaction rules *over* V *of the form* $(K, X \rightarrow Y)$ *with* $X = (x_1, \ldots, x_n)$, $Y = (y_1, \ldots, y_n)$, $x_i, y_i \in \langle V, \mathbb{N} \rangle$, $1 \leq i \leq n$, *and* K *being an applicability condition;*
- δ *is the* derivation mode.

Definition 3. *A* configuration C *of* Π *is an* n-tuple of multisets over V $(u'_1, \ldots, u'_n)$ *with* $u'_i \in \mathbb{N}_\infty$, $1 \leq i \leq n$; *in the following,* C *will also be described by its finite part* C_f *only, i.e., by* $(u_1, \ldots, u_n)$ *satisfying* $u'_i = u_i \cup Inf_i^\infty$ *and* $u_i \cap Inf_i = \emptyset$, $1 \leq i \leq n$.

The set of all multisets of rules applicable to C in the derivation mode δ is denoted by $Appl(\Pi, C, \delta)$. A computation in Π using the derivation mode δ is a sequence of configurations $(C_0, C_1, \dots)$ where C_{i+1} is obtained from C_i by applying the rules in $\mathcal{R}$ in the derivation mode δ. A halting computation ends with a configuration to which no multiset of rules is applicable any more in the derivation mode δ.

The applicability condition K in a rule $(K, X \to Y)$ in the most general case can be any computable feature of the underlying configuration. Usually we can restrict ourselves to vectors of regular multisets $(E_1, \dots, E_n)$, which check whether the finite multiset u_i is in E_i for all $1 \leq i \leq n$. A special subcase for the E_i is the variant of *random context* conditions given by two sets (P_i, Q_i), $P_i, Q_i \subseteq V$, where P_i is the set of *permitting contexts* and Q_i is the set of *forbidden contexts* in cell i, $1 \leq i \leq n$; all elements from P_i must be in u_i and none from Q_i is allowed to be in u_i. A rule $(K, X \to Y)$ is called *applicable* to a configuration $(u'_1, \dots, u'_n)$ if it fulfills the applicability condition K and $X \subseteq (u'_1, \dots, u'_n)$; the result of applying this rule is $((u'_1, \dots, u'_n) - X) + Y$. The set of all rules applicable to a configuration C is defined by $Appl(\Pi, C)$.

An algorithm how to compute the set $Appl(\Pi, C, \delta)$ of multisets of rules applicable to the configuration C in the derivation mode δ is explained in more detail in [31]. For short, a multiset of rules R' over $\mathcal{R}$ is in $Appl(\Pi, C, \delta)$ if

- for each of the rules $(K, X \to Y)$ in R' the applicability condition K is fulfilled and
- it can bind the necessary objects in each cell i given by the finite multiset of objects available in cell i as well as from Inf_i^∞;
- alltogether the rules in R' fulfill the requirements given by the derivation mode δ.

Definition 4. *(Basic derivation modes)*

- *For the asynchronous derivation mode (asyn),*

$$Appl(\Pi, C, asyn) = Appl(\Pi, C).$$

- *For the sequential derivation mode (sequ),*

$$Appl(\Pi, C, sequ) = \{R \in Appl(\Pi, C) \mid |R| = 1\}.$$

i.e., any multiset of rules $R \in Appl(\Pi, C, sequ)$ contains exactly one rule.
- *For the maximally parallel derivation mode (max),*

$$Appl(\Pi, C, max) = \{R \in Appl(\Pi, C) \mid$$
$$\text{there is no } R' \in Appl(\Pi, C)$$
$$\text{such that } R' \supset R\},$$

i.e., in the maximally parallel derivation mode we only select multisets of rules R which are not extendable. In this derivation mode we have to avoid rules not involving an object with only a finite multiplicity.

For further derivation modes, we, for example, refer to [3,4].

3.1   Computations in a Tissue P System

The tissue P system continues with applying multisets of rules according to the given derivation mode until there remain no applicable rules, i.e., as usual, we consider *halting computations*.

We may generate or accept or even compute functions or relations. The inputs/outputs may be multisets or strings, defined in the well-known way. When the system *halts*, in case of computing with multisets we consider the number of objects from Σ contained in specific cells declared as *output cells* at the moment when the system halts as the *result* of the underlying computation in Π.

We would like to emphasize that as results we only take the objects from the terminal alphabet Σ in each of the output cells, all other objects are not counted to the result of a computation.

In the case of accepting or computing, the input is added to specific cells declared as *input cells*.

4   Tissue P Systems with Prescribed Teams of Channel Rules

We now consider the new general model of *tissue P systems with prescribed teams of channel rules*, where in one derivation step specific multisets of channel rules – called *teams* – are applied in the given derivation mode.

Definition 5. *Given a tissue P system* $\Pi = (n, V, \Sigma, w, Inf, \mathcal{R}, \delta)$, *instead of the interaction rules in* $\mathcal{R}$ *we now use* channel rules *of the form* $(K, \langle k, b, m \rangle)$ *(enforcing channel rule) or* $(K, \langle k, b, m |)$ *(permitting channel rule) which open a channel between cell* k *and cell* m, $1 \leq k, m \leq n$, *for one object to pass from cell* k *to cell* m. *In case of an enforcing channel rule* $(K, \langle k, b, m \rangle)$, *one object* b *must move from cell* k *to cell* m, *whereas in case of a permitting channel rule* $(K, \langle k, b, m |)$ *this channel only has to be used if cell* k *contains at least one object* b. *We emphasize that we allow* $k = m$ *in these channel rules. If no applicability conditions are used, we speak of channel rules without applicability conditions.*

With $\mathcal{R}$ just being a set of channel rules without applicability conditions, cooperation is missing and therefore some other control mechanism is needed to gain more computational power up to computational completeness, for example, graph or matrix control. In this paper, we consider the concept of *teams*, with a team of channel rules consisting of a multiset of channel rules which have to be applied in parallel.

Definition 6. *A* tissue P system with prescribed teams of channel rules – *a* TPPTCS *for short – of* degree $n \geq 1$ *is a construct*

$$\Pi = (n, V, \Sigma, w, Inf, \mathcal{R}, \delta) \quad \text{where}$$

– *n is the number of cells in* Π,

- V *is the alphabet of* objects;
- $\Sigma \subseteq V$ *is the alphabet of* terminal objects;
- $w = (w_1, \ldots, w_n)$, *with* $w_i \in \langle V, \mathbb{N} \rangle$, $1 \le i \le n$, *being the finite multiset of objects initially assigned to cell* i;
- $Inf = (Inf_1, \ldots, Inf_n)$, *with* $Inf_i \subseteq V$, $1 \le i \le n$, *being the set of objects available infinitely often in cell* i;
- $\mathcal{R}$ *is a finite set of* teams of channel rules *over* V, *where each team consists of a multiset of channel rules of the form* $(K, \langle k, b, m \rangle)$ *(enforcing channel rule) or* $(K, \langle k, b, m |)$ *(permitting channel rule) with* K *being an applicability condition as for tissue P systems;*
- δ *is the* derivation mode.

The following definitions nearly verbatim are the same as for tissue P systems, with the rules in $\mathcal{R}$ now being teams of channel rules.

Definition 7. *A configuration* C *of* Π *is an* n*-tuple of multisets over* V $(u'_1, \ldots, u'_n)$ *with* $u'_i \in \mathbb{N}_\infty$, $1 \le i \le n$; *in the following,* C *will also be described by its finite part* C_f *only, i.e., by* $(u_1, \ldots, u_n)$ *satisfying* $u'_i = u_i \cup Inf_i^\infty$ *and* $u_i \cap Inf_i = \emptyset$, $1 \le i \le n$.

The set of all multisets of teams of channel rules applicable to C *in the derivation mode* δ *is denoted by* $Appl(\Pi, C, \delta)$. *A computation in* Π *using the derivation mode* δ *is a sequence of configurations* $(C_0, C_1, \ldots)$ *where* C_{i+1} *is obtained from* C_i *by applying the teams in* $\mathcal{R}$ *in the derivation mode* δ. *A* halting computation *ends with a configuration to which no multiset of teams is applicable any more in the derivation mode* δ.

The number s of channel rules in a team is called its *size*. If all prescribed teams have at most size s, then Π is called a *TPPTCS of size* s. Π is called a *TPPTCS of type* (n, s), if it is of degree n and size s.

The applicability conditions K in the most general case again can be any computable/recursive features of the underlying configuration. As a special case we will consider *random context conditions*, i.e., given by two sets (P_i, Q_i) for each cell i, $1 \le i \le n$, with $P_i, Q_i \subseteq V$, where P_i is the set of *permitting contexts* and Q_i is the set of *forbidden contexts* in cell i, $1 \le i \le n$. Given a configuration C with its finite part being $(u_1, \ldots, u_n)$, then all elements from P_i must be in u_i and none from Q_i is allowed to be in u_i.

Example 1. Let $G = (N, \Sigma, w_0, P)$ be a regular multiset grammar where N is the alphabet of nonterminal symbols, Σ is the terminal alphabet, P is a set of regular (multiset) productions of the forms $A \to bC$ or $A \to \lambda$, with $A, C \in N$ and $b \in \Sigma$, and $w_0 \in \langle V, \mathbb{N} \rangle$, $w_0 \ne \lambda$, is the *axiom*. Regular multiset grammars characterize $PsREG$.

A TPPTCS of type $(2, 3)$ generating the same multiset language is

$$\Pi = (2, N \cup \Sigma, \Sigma, w = (\lambda, w_0), Inf = (N \cup \Sigma, \emptyset), \mathcal{R}, \delta),$$

$\delta \in \{sequ, max\}$. Cell 1 is the environment, cell 2 does the whole work by communicating with the environment using the following teams of enforcing channel rules in $\mathcal{R}$:

– A production $A \rightarrow bC$ is simulated by the team

$$\{\langle 2, A, 1\rangle, \langle 1, b, 2\rangle, \langle 1, C, 2\rangle\}.$$

– A final production of the form $A \rightarrow \lambda$ is simulated by the team $\{\langle 2, A, 1\rangle\}$.

All objects from $N \cup \Sigma$ are available in the environment in an unbounded number, whereas cell 2 at the beginning only contains the axiom w_0. At the end of a halting computation, cell 2 contains the terminal multiset. In order to avoid halting in Π with a multiset in cell 2 still containing a nonterminal symbol $X \in N$, without loss of generality we assume G to be a *reduced* regular multiset grammar fulfilling the condition that from each nonterminal symbol $X \in N$ a terminal multiset can be derived. We finally observe that both derivation modes yield exactly the same computations.

Notation 1. *In the following, we often will represent multisets in a more compact way by corresponding strings; for example, the team*

$$\{\langle 2, A, 1\rangle, \langle 1, b, 2\rangle, \langle 1, C, 2\rangle\}$$

can be written as the string $\langle 2, A, 1\rangle\langle 1, b, 2\rangle\langle 1, C, 2\rangle$ *or even as the string* $\langle 2, A, 1\rangle\langle 1, bC, 2\rangle$, *i.e., we may combine several channel rules to one when several objects pass from a cell k to a cell m.*

Definition 8. *A* random context multiset grammar *is a multiset grammar* $G = (N, \Sigma, w_0, R)$, *where N is the alphabet of nonterminal symbols, Σ is the alphabet of terminal symbols, $V := N \cup \Sigma$, $w_0 \in \langle V, \mathbb{N}\rangle$, $w_0 \neq \lambda$, and R is a finite set of random context rules of the form $(P, Q; u \rightarrow v)$, with $P, Q \subseteq V$ being the sets of permitting and forbidden contexts, respectively, $P \cap Q = \emptyset$, $u, v \in \langle V, \mathbb{N}\rangle$, $u \cap N \neq \emptyset$, and $u \cap (P \cup Q) = \emptyset$. A rule $(P, Q; u \rightarrow v)$ is applicable to a multiset x if all symbols from P and no symbol from Q appears in x and $u \leq x$; its application then yields the multiset $(x - u) + v$. The multiset language generated by G is the set of all terminal multisets obtained by a finite derivation starting with the axiom w using the rules in R in a sequential way.*

Theorem 1. *Any random context multiset grammar G can be simulated in real time by a TPPTCS of degree 3 in the sequential derivation mode using both enforcing and permitting channel rules, but no context conditions.*

Proof. Let $G = (N, \Sigma, w_0, R)$ be a random context multiset grammar, $V := N \cup \Sigma$. Then we define the corresponding TPPTCS of degree 3

$$\Pi = (3, V, \Sigma, w = (\lambda, w_0, \lambda), Inf = (V, \emptyset, \emptyset), \mathcal{R}, sequ),$$

where cell 1 acts as the environment containing all symbols in an unbounded number, cell 2 does the real-time simulation of the rules in R, i.e., after n derivation steps it contains exactly the same multiset as it has been derived in n steps by the corresponding derivation in G. The third cell acts as a trap, which causes infinite computations in case any object arrives there, using the teams $\langle 3, a, 3\rangle$,

$a \in V$. The rules in R are simulated by the corresponding teams in $\mathcal{R}$; for each rule $(P, Q; u \rightarrow v) \in R$ we take the following simulating team into $\mathcal{R}$:

$$\{\langle 2, a, 2 \rangle \mid a \in P\} \cup \{\langle 2, a, 3| \mid a \in Q\} \cup \{\langle 2, u, 1 \rangle\} \cup \{\langle 1, v, 2 \rangle\}$$

The enforcing channel rules $\{\langle 2, a, 2 \rangle \mid a \in P\}$ guarantee that the permitting contexts from P are available in cell 2, whereas the permitting channel rules $\{\langle 2, a, 3| \mid a \in Q\}$ guarantee that no object from Q is present in a successful simulation step, as otherwise with an object from Q arriving in cell 3 the computation will never stop. The assumption $u \cap N \neq \emptyset$ guarantees that as soon as G has derived a terminal multiset, also in Π no team of channel rules is applicable any more. Finally, to avoid halting in Π with a configuration not yet consisting of only terminal symbols, for all $X \in N$ we add the singleton team $\langle 2, X, 2 \rangle$, which will cause an infinite computation in Π if no simulating team is applicable any more. □

As is folklore, only forbidden contexts are needed for getting PsRE with random context multiset grammars, which immediately implies the corresponding result for TPPTCS of degree 3 working in the sequential derivation mode. As elaborated in the succeeding section, from a descriptional complexity point of view, some better results can be obtained when TPPTCSs are directly simulating register machines.

5   TPPTCSs Directly Simulating Register Machines

In this section we show how register machines can directly be simulated by TPPTCSs in different ways. First we establish the result for TPPTCSs working in the sequential or the maximally parallel derivation mode, by using applicability conditions represented by sets of (permitting and) forbidden contexts and only enforcing channel rules.

Notation 2. *Instead of writing the complete vector of context conditions* $(1 : (P_1, Q_1), \ldots, n : (P_1, Q_1))$ *for a channel rule with this context condition, in the following we will only specify the components which are relevant.*

Theorem 2. *The computations of a register machine can be simulated in real time by a TPPTCS of type* $(2, 3)$ *using forbidden contexts as applicability conditions for enforcing channel rules when working in the sequential or the maximally parallel derivation mode.*

Proof. Consider the register machine $M = (m, B, l_0, l_h, R)$. We now construct the TPPTCS $\Pi = (2, V, \Sigma, w = (\lambda, l_0 w_0), Inf = (V, \emptyset), \mathcal{R}, \delta)$, $\delta \in \{sequ, max\}$, of type $(2, 3)$ working in the sequential or the maximally parallel derivation mode using forbidden contexts for the channel rules as applicability conditions.

Throughout the computation of Π, cell 2 contains one symbol $p \in B$ representing the instruction from the register machine to be simulated next, and the number of symbols a_r represents the contents of register r, $1 \leq r \leq m$. Hence, we start with the empty multiset as the finite part w_1 of the initial configuration and with the axiom $w_2 = l_0 w_0$ in cell 2, where w_0 represents the initial contents of the registers. If the final label l_h appears, we know that the computation in M has been successful and finally can erase l_h, so that a multiset over Σ remains as the result of the computation; observe that as usual we assume that at the end of a successful computation in M all registers not being output registers are empty.

Moreover, the set of symbols V only consists of the labels in B and the symbols a_r representing the registers:

$$V = B \cup \{a_r \mid 1 \le r \le m\}.$$

The set of terminal symbols Σ consists of only those symbols from the set $\{a_r \mid 1 \le r \le m\}$ which represent output registers.

The teams of enforcing channel rules with applicability conditions for simulating the instructions of the register machine are defined as follows.

– $p : (ADD(r), q, s), p \in B_{ADD}$, is simulated by the two teams

$$\langle 2, p, 1\rangle\langle 1, a_r, 2\rangle\langle 1, q, 2\rangle \text{ and } \langle 2, p, 1\rangle\langle 1, a_r, 2\rangle\langle 1, s, 2\rangle.$$

As these teams of channel rules can anyway only be applied if p is present, no context conditions are needed.

– $p : (SUB(r), q, s), p \in B_{SUB(r)}$, is simulated by the following teams of enforcing channel rules:

$$\langle 2, p, 1\rangle\langle 2, a_r, 1\rangle\langle 1, q, 2\rangle \text{ and } \langle 2, p, 1\rangle((2 : \emptyset, \{a_r\}) : \langle 1, s, 2\rangle).$$

$\langle 2, p, 1\rangle\langle 2, a_r, 1\rangle\langle 1, q, 2\rangle$ covers the decrement case; it is only applicable if both p and at least one a_r are present in cell 2.

The team $\langle 2, p, 1\rangle((2 : \emptyset, \{a_r\}) : \langle 1, s, 2\rangle)$ covers the zero test case, i.e., the forbidden context condition $(2 : \emptyset, \{a_r\})$ with $Q_2 = \{a_r\}$ checks for the absence of a_r in cell 2.

– $l_h : HALT$ is simulated by the team $\langle 2, l_h, 1\rangle$.

Only in the case of applying the team

$$\langle 2, p, 1\rangle((2 : P_2 = \emptyset, Q_2 = \{a_{Reg(p)}\}) : \langle 1, s, 2\rangle)$$

a forbidden context condition is used for one channel rule.

The application of a team is only possible if the current label symbol p appears in the underlying configuration, and in the case of a SUB-instruction also the absence of $a_{Reg(p)}$ is necessary in the zero-test case.

If the register machine M is deterministic, then throughout any computation in Π exactly one team of channel rules is applicable before finally a configuration only containing terminal symbols is reached, hence, also Π works in a deterministic way.   □

The use of forbidden contexts can be avoided when using both enforcing and permitting channel rules and an additional cell as trap as already done in the proof of Theorem 1.

Theorem 3. *The computations of a register machine can be simulated in real time by a TPPTCS of type $(3,3)$ when working in the sequential or the maximally parallel derivation mode using both enforcing and permitting channel rules without applicability conditions.*

Proof. As in the proof of the preceding theorem we start with the register machine $M = (m, B, l_0, l_h, R)$ and construct an equivalent TPPTCS

$$\Pi = (3, V, \Sigma, w = (\lambda, l_0 w_0, \lambda), Inf = (V, \emptyset, \emptyset), \mathcal{R}, \delta),$$

$\delta \in \{sequ, max\}$, of type $(3,3)$.

Throughout the computation of Π, cell 2 contains one symbol $p \in B$ representing the instruction from the register machine to be simulated next, and the number of symbols a_r represents the contents of register r, $1 \le r \le m$. Hence, we start with the empty multiset as the finite part w_1 of the initial configuration and with the axiom $w_2 = l_0 w_0$ in cell 2, where w_0 represents the initial contents of the registers. Moreover, the initial contents of cell 3 is the empty multiset. If the final label l_h appears, the computation in M halts yielding the multiset over Σ in cell 2 as the result of the computation, but only if during the whole computation no object has arrived in cell 3. Again, the set of symbols V only consists of the labels in B and the symbols a_r representing the registers:

$$V = B \cup \{a_r \mid 1 \le r \le m\},$$

and the set of terminal symbols Σ consists of only those symbols from the set $\{a_r \mid 1 \le r \le m\}$ which represent output registers.

The teams of channel rules for simulating the instructions of the register machine are defined as follows.

- $p : (ADD(r), q, s)$, $p \in B_{ADD}$, is simulated by the two teams of enforcing channel rules
$$\langle 2, p, 1 \rangle \langle 1, a_r q, 2 \rangle \quad \text{and} \quad \langle 2, p, 1 \rangle \langle 1, a_r s, 2 \rangle.$$

- $p : (SUB(r), q, s)$, $p \in B_{SUB(r)}$, is simulated by the teams of channel rules

$$\langle 2, p, 1 \rangle \langle 2, a_r, 1 \rangle \langle 1, q, 2 \rangle \text{ and } \langle 2, p, 1 \rangle \langle 1, s, 2 \rangle \langle 2, a_r, 3 |.$$

$\langle 2, p, 1 \rangle \langle 2, a_r, 1 \rangle \langle 1, q, 2 \rangle$ covers the decrement case; it is only applicable if both p and at least one a_r are present in cell 2. The zero test case now is simulated by the team $\langle 2, p, 1 \rangle \langle 1, s, 2 \rangle \langle 2, a_r, 3 |$ with the permitting channel rule $\langle 2, a_r, 3 |$ only to be used if an unwanted object a_r is present in cell 2. In some sense, this rule is used in a kind of appearance checking mode, i.e., it has to be used if a_r is present in cell 2, but otherwise can remain unused; in that way we check for the absence of a_r in cell 2.

– $l_h : HALT$ is simulated by the team $\langle 2, l_h, 1 \rangle$.

In addition, we add the teams $\langle 3, a_r, 3 \rangle$, $1 \leq r \leq m$, to $\mathcal{R}$, which cause infinite loops in case that during at least one simulation of a SUB-instruction the wrong choice was taken by using the rule for the zero-test case, although at least one register object was present.

The main drawback of this construction is that even if the register machine M is deterministic, Π does not work in a deterministic way.   □

When only using the derivation mode max, both the use of the forbidden contexts as well as of permitting rules can be avoided, yet now the simulation of a SUB-instruction is not real-time anymore, but takes three steps.

Theorem 4. *The computations of a register machine can be simulated by a TPPTCS of type $(2,3)$ without applicability conditions and with only using enforcing channel rules working in the maximally parallel derivation mode.*

Proof. Following the proof of Theorem 2, the SUB-instruction $p : (SUB(r), q, s)$, $p \in B_{SUB(r)}$ now is simulated by the following teams of enforcing channel rules in three steps:

1. $\langle 2, p, 1 \rangle \langle 1, p', 2 \rangle \langle 1, p'', 2 \rangle$ replaces p by $p'p''$;
2. $\langle 2, p', 1 \rangle \langle 1, \tilde{p}, 2 \rangle$ replaces p' by $\tilde{p}$ and
   $\langle 2, p'', 1 \rangle \langle 2, a_r, 1 \rangle \langle 1, \hat{p}, 2 \rangle$ removes one register symbol a_r if it exists and in parallel replaces p'' by $\hat{p}$;
3. depending on whether p'' has been replaced by $\hat{p}$,
   – $\langle 2, \tilde{p}, 1 \rangle \langle 2, \hat{p}, 1 \rangle \langle 1, q, 2 \rangle$ (decrement case) or
   – $\langle 2, \tilde{p}, 1 \rangle \langle 2, p'', 1 \rangle \langle 1, s, 2 \rangle$ (zero-test case) is applied.

For each SUB-instruction now we use the additional objects $p', p'', \tilde{p}, \hat{p}$, i.e.,

$$V = B \cup \{p', p'', \tilde{p}, \hat{p} \mid p \in SUB\} \cup \{a_r \mid 1 \leq r \leq m\}.$$

The rest of the construction remains the same as in the proof of Theorem 2. We emphasize that this proof only works for the derivation mode max, which is essential in the second step.   □

6   Computational Completeness

According to Subsect. 2.1, register machines are a model being computationally complete for multisets, i.e., any partial recursive relation on multisets can be computed by a register machine. Hence, from the theorems established in the previous section, we immediately infer the following results:

Theorem 5. *TPPTCSs are computationally complete for multisets if*

- *they are of type* $(2,3)$ *using forbidden contexts as applicability conditions for enforcing channel rules working in the sequential derivation mode or in the maximally parallel derivation mode;*
- *they are of type* $(3,3)$ *without applicability conditions working in the sequential derivation mode or in the maximally parallel derivation mode using both enforcing and permitting channel rules;*
- *they are of type* $(2,3)$ *only using enforcing channel rules when working in the maximally parallel derivation mode.*

6.1   Specific Variants of Channel Rules

Antiport and Symport Rules

Antiport and symport rules first were introduced in [34] for hierarchical P systems, i.e., with a communication structure being a tree.

An antiport rule can be written as team of channel rules $\langle k, u, m \rangle \langle m, v, k \rangle$. As a special case, a symport rule is of the form $\langle k, u, m \rangle$, $u \neq \lambda$.

An overview on results obtained for P systems using specific variants of antiport and/or symport rules was given in [6].

Remark 1. For example, the teams of channel rules used in the proof of Theorem 4 correspond to antiport rules, except for the channel rule $\langle 2, l_h, 1 \rangle$ eliminating the label of the *HALT*-instruction used at the end of a successful simulation, which technically speaking is a symport rule. Yet this channel rule could even be omitted, as we have defined the results of a halting computation to only be the terminal symbols without taking into account garbage symbols not in Σ. This also has to be kept in mind when we refer to results listed in the rest of this paper.

Communicating P Systems

In [39], communicating P systems were introduced, also with the communication structure being a tree. The rules were special communication rules of the form $\langle k, a, m \rangle$, $\langle k, a, m \rangle \langle k, b, n \rangle$, and $\langle 2, a, m \rangle \langle 2, b, n \rangle \langle 1, c, 2 \rangle$ with cell 1 representing the environment and cell 2 representing the skin membrane. Further results for this variant were elaborated in [29].

Generalized Communicating P Systems

Specific variants of tissue P systems with channel rules were introduced in [40] as generalized communicating P systems. The special communication rules there are of the form $\langle i, a, k \rangle \langle j, b, \ell \rangle$. Depending on the cells i, j, k, ℓ used in these rules specific variants of minimal interaction rules were introduced. In the following table, we use the notations as, for example, defined in [18]; we emphasize that some of the cells can be equal. In the following representation as teams of channel rules, different symbols from i, j, k, ℓ indicate different numbers for these cells:

Definition 9. *Let V be an alphabet and let $\langle i, a, k \rangle \langle j, b, \ell \rangle$ be a minimal interaction rule with $a, b \in V$ ($\hat{=}$ means "corresponds to", written as a team of enforcing channel rules).*

1. $i = j = k \neq \ell \,\hat{=}\, \langle i, a, i \rangle \langle i, b, \ell \rangle$: *conditional uniport out rule;*
2. $i = k = \ell \neq j \,\hat{=}\, \langle i, a, i \rangle \langle j, b, i \rangle$: *conditional uniport in rule;*
3. $i = j \neq k = \ell \,\hat{=}\, \langle i, a, k \rangle \langle i, b, k \rangle \,\hat{=}\, \langle i, ab, k \rangle$: *symport2 rule;*
4. $i = \ell \neq j = k \,\hat{=}\, \langle i, a, k \rangle \langle k, b, i \rangle$: *antiport1 rule;*
5. $i = k \neq j \neq \ell \,\hat{=}\, \langle i, a, i \rangle \langle j, b, \ell \rangle$: *presence-move rule;*
6. $i = j \neq k \neq \ell \,\hat{=}\, \langle i, a, k \rangle \langle i, b, \ell \rangle$: *split rule;*
7. $k = \ell \neq i \neq j \,\hat{=}\, \langle i, a, k \rangle \langle j, b, k \rangle$: *join rule;*
8. $i \neq j = k \neq \ell \,\hat{=}\, \langle i, a, k \rangle \langle k, b, \ell \rangle$: *chain rule;*
9. $i \neq j \neq k \neq \ell \,\hat{=}\, \langle i, a, k \rangle \langle j, b, \ell \rangle$: *parallel-shift rule.*

Remark 2. We observe that using permitting context conditions, then both the conditional uniport rules and the presence-move rule can be represented by just one enforing conditional channel rule without using teams (Table 1):

Table 1. Representation of teams by one conditional channel rule

type of rule	as team	as conditional rule
conditional uniport out rule	$\langle i, a, i \rangle \langle i, b, \ell \rangle$	$((i, \{a\}, \emptyset) : \langle i, b, \ell \rangle)$
conditional uniport in rule	$\langle i, a, i \rangle \langle j, b, i \rangle$	$((i, \{a\}, \emptyset) : \langle j, b, i \rangle)$
presence-move rule	$\langle i, a, i \rangle \langle j, b, \ell \rangle$	$((i, \{a\}, \emptyset) : \langle j, b, \ell \rangle)$

Table 2. Generalized communicating P systems

type of rule	number of cells	reference
conditional uniport out rule	3	[17]
conditional uniport in rule	3	[17]
symport2 rule	3	[6,8]
presence-move rule	4	[18]
split rule	4	[16]
join rule	4	[16]
chain rule	4	[16]
parallel-shift rule	5	[18]

New computational completeness results for specific variants of generalized communicating P systems using only one type of the rules defined above can be found in [16–18]. In these papers it was shown that NRE can be obtained by only using one of these types of rules and a small number of cells (including the environment). Table 2 summarizes some of these results.

7   Computing with Strings

Based on P systems using antiport rules, in 2002 the idea of extending these systems for accepting string languages in parallel was presented in [13] and [25]. The main feature of these so-called *P automata* is that the sequence of symbols taken in from the environment into the skin membrane defines the string to be analysed and probably accepted by a halting computation. Following the model with activated/prohibited membrane channels considered in [24], also in [26] it was shown that any recursively enumerable string language can be accepted by these variants of P automata. Further variants of P automata were investigated in [23]. Restricted variants of P automata only accepting language classes below RE were investigated in [14] and [15]. An overview on various results for P automata was presented in [20]. The concept of P automata (based on antiport rules) was even extended to the acceptance of ω-words in [28].

As for example shown in the proof of Theorem 4, register machines can be simulated by specific variants of teams of enforcing channel rules, which easily can be recognized as antiport rules. Register machines can be extended by rules of the form $(p : (a, come), q)$ for a symbol $a \in \Sigma_{in}$, where Σ_{in} is a special input alphabet, from which the input strings are constructed, which means that the sequence of such symbols a taken from the environment constitutes the input string. In fact, such a rule $(p : (a, come), q)$ corresponds to an antiport rule, written as a team of enforcing channel rules, $\langle 2, p, 1 \rangle \langle 1, a, 2 \rangle \langle 1, q, 2 \rangle$. We call such a TPPTCS a *TPPTC automaton*.

As an immediate consequence of Theorem 4, we therefore obtain the following result for strings:

Corollary 1. *Any recursively enumerable string language can be accepted by a TPPTC automaton of type $(2, 3)$ with enforcing channel rules without context conditions in the maximally parallel derivation mode.*

Remark 3. The variant of TPPTC automata used in Corollary 1 is the most natural to be used when to be compared with other models of P automata based on antiport rules. Yet also the constructions presented in the (proofs of) Theorems 2 and 3 could be used as well.

The model of TPPTC automata can be extended to a generating as well as to a computing model very easily: we can use rules of the form $(p : (a, come), q)$ for a symbol $a \in \Sigma_{out}$, where Σ_{out} is a special output alphabet, from which the output strings are constructed, which means that the sequence of such symbols $a \in \Sigma_{out}$ taken from the environment constitutes the output string. Obviously, this only can work correctly with assuming $\Sigma_{out} \cap \Sigma_{in}$. Thus, TPPTC automata can be seen as a computationally complete model for computing with strings.

8   Going Beyond Turing

Usually computational completeness means that a computing model has the same computational power as Turing machines (for strings) or register machines (for multisets). In [32], red-green Turing machines were introduced as a computing model which allows to "go beyond Turing", i.e., more than only the languages from RE can be accepted. The basic idea behind this model is that the set of states is divided into two disjoint sets, one "colored" by red, the other one by green, and infinite computations on finite strings are considered with an input string w being accepted if and only if there exists an infinite run on w such that red states are only entered finitely often. In that way, the family Σ_2 of the *Arithmetical Hierarchy* can be characterized, which properly includes RE.

In [9], this idea of red-green automata was transferred to red-green register machines and to red-green P automata, simulating red-green register machines with antiport rules in a similar way as described in the proof of Theorem 4. Red-green register machines were considered in the context of Watson-Crick T0L systems in [12]. The behavior observed with accepting infinite runs of red-green P automata was investigated in [21].

When introducing the idea of red-green automata for TPPTC automata, we have two choices which constituents should be colored, i.e., either the whole teams of channel rules or only channel rules themselves. Coloring the teams may look more powerful, but it turns out that even coloring only the channel rules is sufficient: In order to correctly simulate the behaviour of accepting infinite runs of red-green register machines, in the proofs of Theorems 2 and 4, only the enforcing channel rules $\langle 1, t, 2 \rangle$ for red states t have to be colored by red, all other channel rules by green. This guarantees that also in the infinite computations of the simulating red-green TPPTCS/TPPTC automaton red channel rules $\langle 1, t, 2 \rangle$ are used as often as the corresponding red states t are used in the corresponding infinite computation of the red-green register machine.

Remark 4. As with red-green TPPTCSs/TPPTC automata we consider infinite computations, the construction with the trap cell used in the proof of Theorem 3 cannot be used, as also wrong simulations would cause infinite computations.

As a consequence of Theorem 4 and the discussion in the preceding section, we therefore obtain the following result for "going beyond Turing":

Corollary 2. *Any string language from Σ_2 can be accepted by a red-green TPPTC automaton of type $(2, 3)$ with enforcing channel rules without context conditions in the maximally parallel derivation mode.*

Remark 5. A similar result holds for multiset languages accepted by red-green TPPTCSs. Moreover, as a consequence of Theorem 2, similar results hold for red-green TPPTCSs/TPPTC automata of type $(2, 3)$ with enforcing channel rules with forbidden context conditions both in the maximally parallel and the sequential derivation mode.

9 Conclusion

In this paper we have considered the concept of tissue P systems using prescribed teams of channel rules, with the applicability of a team possibly depending on random context conditions. Various direct simulations of register machines have been proved. Moreover, we have shown how many variants of purely communicating (tissue) P systems can be mimicked within this model, especially when antiport, symport, or minimal communication rules are used. Based on these results, various computational completeness results could be presented. We also have extended our model of tissue P systems with prescribed teams of channel rules for computations on strings. Finally, we have explained how these systems can even "go beyond Turing".

Among others, the following interesting topics remain for future research:

– Throughout this paper, we have restricted ourselves to the two basic derivation modes, i.e., the sequential one and the maximally parallel derivation mode. A thorough investigation of tissue P systems with prescribed teams of channel rules using other derivation modes remains for future research.
– In many papers, the extension of the models investigated there to computations with strings is missing. Especially, for the different variants of generalized communicating P systems with minimal communication rules, e.g., see [18], it may be worth to investigate how the main features of how to compute with strings as elaborated in Sect. 7 can be implemented without violating the specific constraints for the rules used there.
– In most papers introducing variants of (tissue) P systems, the idea of "going beyond Turing" is not taken into account. Hence, for many models introduced so far it might be interesting to see how the ideas discussed in Sect. 8 can be implemented in these models.

Acknowledgements. Artiom Alhazov acknowledges Project 011301 "Information systems based on artificial intelligence" by Moldova State University.

References

1. Alhazov, A., Freund, R., Ivanov, S.: When catalytic P systems with one catalyst can be computationally complete. J. Membr. Comput. **3**(3), 170–181 (2021). https://doi.org/10.1007/s41965-021-00079-x
2. Alhazov, A., Freund, R., Ivanov, S.: Simple P systems with prescribed teams of sets of rules. In: Ciencialová, L. (ed.) Proceedings of the 24th International Conference on Membrane Computing (CMC 2023), 28–31 August 2023, Opava, Czech Republic, pp. 7–26. Silesian University, Opava (2023)
3. Alhazov, A., Freund, R., Ivanov, S., Oswald, M.: Variants of simple purely catalytic P systems with two catalysts. In: Vaszil, Gy., Zandron, C., Zhang, G. (eds.) International Conference on Membrane Computing ICMC 2021, Proceedings, pp. 39–53 (2021)
4. Alhazov, A., Freund, R., Ivanov, S., Verlan, S.: Variants of simple P systems with one catalyst being computationally complete. In: Vaszil, Gy., Zandron, C., Zhang, G. (eds.) International Conference on Membrane Computing ICMC 2021, Proceedings, pp. 21–38 (2021)

5. Alhazov, A., Freund, R., Ivanov, S., Verlan, S.: Prescribed teams of rules working on several objects. In: Durand-Lose, J., Vaszil, Gy. (eds.) Machines, Computations, and Universality – 9th International Conference, MCU 2022, Debrecen, Hungary, 31 August–2 September 2022, Proceedings. Lecture Notes in Computer Science, vol. 13419, pp. 27–41. Springer (2022). https://doi.org/10.1007/978-3-031-13502-6_6
6. Alhazov, A., Freund, R., Rogozhin, Y.: Computational power of symport/antiport: history, advances, and open problems. In: Freund, R., Păun, G., Rozenberg, G., Salomaa, A. (eds.) WMC 2005. LNCS, vol. 3850, pp. 1–30. Springer, Heidelberg (2006). https://doi.org/10.1007/11603047_1
7. Alhazov, A., Freund, R., Verlan, S.: P systems working in maximal variants of the set derivation mode. In: Leporati, A., Rozenberg, G., Salomaa, A., Zandron, C. (eds.) CMC 2016. LNCS, vol. 10105, pp. 83–102. Springer, Cham (2017). https://doi.org/10.1007/978-3-319-54072-6_6
8. Alhazov, A., Rogozhin, Yu., Verlan, S.: Minimal cooperation in symport/antiport tissue P systems. Int. J. Found. Comput. Sci. **18**(1), 163–180 (2007). https://doi.org/10.1142/S0129054107004619
9. Aman, B., Csuhaj-Varjú, E., Freund, R.: Red–green P automata. In: Gheorghe, M., Rozenberg, G., Salomaa, A., Sosík, P., Zandron, C. (eds.) CMC 2014. LNCS, vol. 8961, pp. 139–157. Springer, Cham (2014). https://doi.org/10.1007/978-3-319-14370-5_9
10. Csuhaj-Varjú, E.: Communicating P systems: bio-inspired computational models for complex systems. In: Holena, M., et al. (eds.) Proceedings of the 20th Conference Information Technologies – Applications and Theory (ITAT 2020), Hotel Tyrapol, Oravská Lesná, Slovakia, 18–22 September 2020. CEUR Workshop Proceedings, vol. 2718, pp. 3–8. CEUR-WS.org (2020). https://ceur-ws.org/Vol-2718/invited2.pdf
11. Csuhaj-Varjú, E., Dassow, J., Kelemen, J.: Grammar Systems: A Grammatical Approach to Distribution and Cooperation. Topics in Computer Mathematics, Gordon and Breach (1994)
12. Csuhaj-Varjú, E., Freund, R., Vaszil, Gy.: Watson-Crick T0L systems and red-green register machines. Fundamenta Informaticae **155**(1–2), 111–129 (2017). https://doi.org/10.3233/FI-2017-1578
13. Csuhaj-Varjú, E., Vaszil, G.: P automata or purely communicating accepting P systems. In: Păun, G., Rozenberg, G., Salomaa, A., Zandron, C. (eds.) WMC 2002. LNCS, vol. 2597, pp. 219–233. Springer, Heidelberg (2003). https://doi.org/10.1007/3-540-36490-0_14
14. Csuhaj-Varjú, E., Vaszil, Gy.: P automata with restricted power. Int. J. Found. Comput. Sci. **25**(4), 391–408 (2014). https://doi.org/10.1142/S0129054114400024
15. Csuhaj-Varjú, E., Vaszil, Gy.: On languages of P automata. Fundamenta Informaticae **171**(1–4), 133–149 (2020). https://doi.org/10.3233/FI-2020-1876
16. Csuhaj-Varjú, E., Verlan, S.: Computationally complete generalized communicating P systems with three cells. In: Gheorghe, M., Rozenberg, G., Salomaa, A., Zandron, C. (eds.) CMC 2017. LNCS, vol. 10725, pp. 118–128. Springer, Cham (2018). https://doi.org/10.1007/978-3-319-73359-3_8
17. Csuhaj-Varjú, E., Verlan, S.: Conditional uniport P systems with two cells. In: Ciencialova, L. (ed.) Proceedings of the Twenty-fourth International Conference on Membrane Computing (CMC 2023), 28–31 August 2023, Opava, Czech Republic, pp. 97–126. Silesian Unversity at Opava (2024)

18. Csuhaj-Varjú, E., Verlan, S.: Computational completeness of minimal communication with small number of cells. J. Membr. Comput. (2025). https://doi.org/10.1007/s41965-025-00192-1

19. Dassow, J., Păun, Gh.: Regulated Rewriting in Formal Language Theory. Springer (1989)

20. Freund, R.: P automata: new ideas and results. In: Bordihn, H., Freund, R., Nagy, B., Vaszil, Gy. (eds.) Eighth Workshop on Non-Classical Models of Automata and Applications, NCMA 2016, Debrecen, Hungary, 29–30 August 2016. Proceedings. books@ocg.at, vol. 321, pp. 13–40. Österreichische Computer Gesellschaft (2016)

21. Freund, R., Ivanov, S., Staiger, L.: Going beyond Turing with P automata: regular observer ω-languages and partial adult halting. Int. J. Unconventional Comput. **12**(1), 51–69 (2016). http://www.oldcitypublishing.com/journals/ijuc-home/ijuc-issue-contents/ijuc-volume-12-number-1-2016/ijuc-12-1-p-51-69/

22. Freund, R., Leporati, A., Mauri, G., Porreca, A.E., Verlan, S., Zandron, C.: Flattening in (tissue) P systems. In: Alhazov, A., Cojocaru, S., Gheorghe, M., Rogozhin, Y., Rozenberg, G., Salomaa, A. (eds.) CMC 2013. LNCS, vol. 8340, pp. 173–188. Springer, Heidelberg (2014). https://doi.org/10.1007/978-3-642-54239-8_13

23. Freund, R., Martín-Vide, C., Obtułowicz, A., Păun, G.: On three classes of automata-like P systems. In: Ésik, Z., Fülöp, Z. (eds.) DLT 2003. LNCS, vol. 2710, pp. 292–303. Springer, Heidelberg (2003). https://doi.org/10.1007/3-540-45007-6_23

24. Freund, R., Oswald, M.: P systems with activated/prohibited membrane channels. In: PĂun, G., Rozenberg, G., Salomaa, A., Zandron, C. (eds.) WMC 2002. LNCS, vol. 2597, pp. 261–269. Springer, Heidelberg (2003). https://doi.org/10.1007/3-540-36490-0_17

25. Freund, R., Oswald, M.: A short note on analysing P systems with antiport rules. Bull. EATCS **78**, 231–236 (2002)

26. Freund, R., Oswald, M.: P automata with membrane channels. Artif. Life Robot. **8**(2), 186–189 (2004). https://doi.org/10.1007/S10015-004-0312-X

27. Freund, R., Oswald, M., Păun, Gh.: Catalytic and purely catalytic P systems and P automata: control mechanisms for obtaining computational completeness. Fund. Inform. **136**(1–2), 59–84 (2015). https://doi.org/10.3233/FI-2015-1144

28. Freund, R., Oswald, M., Staiger, L.: ω-P automata with communication rules. In: Martín-Vide, C., Mauri, G., Păun, G., Rozenberg, G., Salomaa, A. (eds.) WMC 2003. LNCS, vol. 2933, pp. 203–217. Springer, Heidelberg (2004). https://doi.org/10.1007/978-3-540-24619-0_15

29. Freund, R., PĂun, A.: Membrane systems with symport/antiport rules: universality results. In: PĂun, G., Rozenberg, G., Salomaa, A., Zandron, C. (eds.) WMC 2002. LNCS, vol. 2597, pp. 270–287. Springer, Heidelberg (2003). https://doi.org/10.1007/3-540-36490-0_18

30. Freund, R., Păun, Gh., Pérez-Jiménez, M.J.: Tissue P systems with channel states. Theoret. Comput. Sci. **330**(1), 101–116 (2005). https://doi.org/10.1016/J.TCS.2004.09.013

31. Freund, R., Verlan, S.: A formal framework for static (tissue) P systems. In: Eleftherakis, G., Kefalas, P., Păun, G., Rozenberg, G., Salomaa, A. (eds.) WMC 2007. LNCS, vol. 4860, pp. 271–284. Springer, Heidelberg (2007). https://doi.org/10.1007/978-3-540-77312-2_17

32. van Leeuwen, J., Wiedermann, J.: Computation as an unbounded process. Theoret. Comput. Sci. **429**, 202–212 (2012). https://doi.org/10.1016/J.TCS.2011.12.040

33. Minsky, M.L.: Computation. Finite and Infinite Machines. Prentice Hall, Engle-wood Cliffs (1967)
34. Pâun, A., Pâun, G.: The power of communication: P systems with sym-port/antiport. N. Gener. Comput. **20**(3), 295–305 (2002). https://doi.org/10.1007/BF03037362
35. Păun, Gh.: Computing with membranes. J. Comput. Syst. Sci. **61**(1), 108–143 (2000). https://doi.org/10.1006/jcss.1999.1693
36. Păun, Gh.: Membrane Computing: An Introduction. Springer (2002). https://doi.org/10.1007/978-3-642-56196-2
37. Păun, Gh., Rozenberg, G., Salomaa, A. (eds.): The Oxford Handbook of Membrane Computing. Oxford University Press (2010)
38. Rozenberg, G., Salomaa, A. (eds.): Handbook of Formal Languages. Springer (1997). https://doi.org/10.1007/978-3-642-59136-5
39. Sosík, P., Matýsek, J.: Membrane computing: when communication is enough. In: Calude, C.S., Dinneen, M.J., Peper, F. (eds.) UMC 2002. LNCS, vol. 2509, pp. 264–275. Springer, Heidelberg (2002). https://doi.org/10.1007/3-540-45833-6_22
40. Verlan, S., Bernardini, F., Gheorghe, M., Margenstern, M.: Generalized communicating P systems. Theor. Comput. Sci. **404**(1), 170–184 (2008). https://doi.org/10.1016/j.tcs.2008.04.008. https://www.sciencedirect.com/science/article/pii/S0304397508002582
41. The P Systems Website. http://ppage.psystems.eu/

Multiset Reaction Systems

Paolo Bottoni[1], Victor Mitrana[2,3]($\boxtimes$), and Ion Petre[4]

[1] Department of Computer Science, Sapienza University of Rome, Viale Regina Elena 295, 00166 Rome, Italy
bottoni@di.uniroma1.it
[2] Department of Information Systems, Polytechnic University of Madrid, Calle Alan Turing s/n, 28031 Madrid, Spain
victor.mitrana@upm.es
[3] National Institute of Research and Development for Biological Sciences, 296 Independent Bd. District 6, 060031 Bucharest, Romania
[4] Department of Mathematics and Statistics, University of Turku, Turku, Finland
ion.petre@utu.fi

Abstract. A multiset reaction system is an extension of the classical reaction system model with three key differences. First, all components of a reaction are now multisets and not sets. Second, it modifies the permanency principle: in this model, resources which are not consumed by application of reactions do not vanish from the system, even if they are not supported by any enabled reaction. Third, each resource is available in a finite, specific quantity, which may constrain the number of reactions that can access it concurrently. As a result, the model is inherently quantitative and nondeterministic, and it operates on multisets of resources rather than on simple sets. We investigate several modes of simultaneous and parallel enabling of reaction within this framework and demonstrate that all of them can be effectively simulated using sequential enabling. Additionally, we prove that the computational power of multiset reaction systems with sequential evolution is equivalent to that of multiset Turing machines.

Keywords: Reaction · Reaction system · Multiset · Multiset reaction system · Activation mode · Register machine

1 Introduction

Reaction systems were introduced in [16] as a computational model inspired by the functioning of the living cell. The model is based on the interaction between

This study was supported by the Ministry of Research, Innovation, and Digitalization through the Core Program of the National Research, Development, and Innovation Plan 2022-2027, project no. PN 23-02-0101-Contract No. 7N/2023. It was also supported by the Ministry of Research, Innovation, and Digitalization through the Romanian National Recovery and Resilience Plan (PNRR), Pillar III, Component C9/Investment no. 8 (I8) - contract CF 68 and contract CF 53.

M. D. Jiménez López and G. Vaszil (Eds.): Erzsébet Csuhaj-Varjú Festschrift,
LNCS 15840, pp. 179–193, 2025.
https://doi.org/10.1007/978-3-031-97274-4_11

reactions that are enabled or disabled depending on the current state, on what other reactions were produced, and on what the environment introduces. In this framework a reaction is enabled on the basis of two fundamental principles: *activation* and *inhibition*. A reaction is *enabled* in a certain state if all of its *activators* (called *reactants*) are available in the state, but none of its *inhibitors* are. As a result, the reaction contributes a set of *products* to the successor state, which in effect may activate or inhibit other reactions.

The reaction systems model (in its basic formulation) is a qualitative framework in which a resource, if available in the current state, is available in unlimited amounts. This eliminates the competition on resources between reactions, makes the model qualitative in nature, and makes it rooted in set theory. This is known as *threshold principle*: When a resource is available, it is available in unlimited amounts. Another fundamental aspect of the model is the *non-permanency principle*: If a resource is not explicitly sustained/produced by reactions, it will not be available in the next state. As a result, the next state of a reaction system consists of only the species explicitly produced by the reactions enabled in the previous state. Additionally, reaction systems are open systems, in which the environment contributes a so-called context set to the current state at each step of the computation. The computation is a state-transition system in which each state is obtained through the combined contributions of the reactions enabled in the previous state and of the environment. In this paper, we are mainly concerned with dynamics induced only by reactions, i.e., with those which in the classical model are called *context-independent* processes.

A reaction is formally defined in [16] by a triplet of nonempty sets: its set of reactants, its set of inhibitors, and its set of products. A reaction is enabled in a state T if all of its reactant set is included in T and no inhibitor is in T. The result of enabling a reaction is its set of products.

The paper is organized as follows. After Sect. 3 defines the main concepts and notation: multiset reaction; multiset reaction system; and various types of evolution, Sect. 4 investigates the relationships between all these evolutions and shows that they can be simulated, at different costs, by sequential evolutions. The computational power of our model is then compared in Sect. 5 to that of multiset Turing machines employing the results regarding the relationships between the evolutions. Finally, Sect. 6 draws conclusions and points to future work.

2   Related Work

Several aspects of this initial model are discussed in [13]. First, all the substances of the substrate completely vanish after identifying the set of reactants such that the result does not contain any former component of the substrate unless it is produced by the reaction. Second, there is no counting for a reaction; hence, the model is a qualitative model rather than a quantitative one. In other words, each reactant appears in a sufficient quantity so that the reaction system performs all the reactions enabled on the current state. Finally, each inhibitor is universal; hence, it is nonselective, which means that it reacts with the enzyme-substrate complex without any affinity for the active sites of the enzyme. In [13] and subsequent work [30,31], various functions defined by reaction systems were investigated. It turned out that functions having complex behavior can be obtained with rather simple reaction systems. Actually, in biochemical systems we find universal inhibitors for some reactants, but not for all as most of the inhibitors are selective. Three types of selective enzyme inhibitors have been considered in [22]. Many quantitative properties of biological systems have been introduced to modeling with reaction systems in [1–3]: mass conservation, invariants, steady states, multistability, limit cycles, stationary processes, elementary fluxes, periodicity, bifurcation. They were qualitatively expressed through set-based formulations, and several algorithmic and decision problems were investigated. We continue here the work initiated in [22] on the *Quantitative Reaction System* (qRS) model. We consider a simplification of this model; namely, we discard the property of inhibitors to be selective, but we keep all the other features: the permanency principle and the multiset abstraction of the substrate.

There is a rich literature on computing with multisets. We briefly discuss a few key contributions to place our work in a wider context. In [18] a formalism based on multiset rewriting, called *constraint multiset grammar*, offers a high-level framework for the definition of visual languages. It has been further investigated in [21] from the point of view of parsing complexity. These grammars may be viewed as a bridge between the usual string grammars, dealing with string rewriting, and constraint logic programs, dealing with set rewriting. Other devices based on multiset rewriting have been reported in [6,32] where *abstract multiset rewriting systems* were used to model some characteristics of population development in artificial cell systems. Furthermore, a Chomsky-like hierarchy of grammars rewriting multisets was proposed in [19] and an accepting counterpart was proposed in [11]. In all these approaches, the multisets are processed in a sequential, non-distributed way. Other authors considered parallel or distributed ways of processing multisets to define computational models inspired by biochemistry [4,5,7] or microbiology [25–27]. Different properties of commutative languages (macrosets in our terminology) have been considered in a series of papers; see, e.g., [10,20] and their references. Moreover, other highly parallel and distributive models that manipulate multisets have been proposed: networks of multiset processors [9] and membrane systems [28], some of them considering also promoters/inhibitors [8] or catalysts [17]. Petri nets, in their numerous variants, can be typically interpreted as defining some transformation law over multisets, for a classic survey on the topic, see [23]. It has been proven that adding a new type of relation between places and transitions –namely *inhibitor arcs* which prevent a transition from firing if a token is present in any place connected to it through such an arc– brings the expressive power of Petri Nets to equal that of Turing machines over multisets, see [29].

Although the vast majority of these models are generative, some of them are accepting devices [9,11,12], such as this one. It is worth mentioning that the computational model considered in this paper presents features resembling the reaction automata model introduced in [24] (see also the survey [33]). A reaction automaton may also be seen as a reaction system, where a symbol from the input word is added to every current state, such that the input string is accepted when it was entirely consumed and a final state has been reached.

3   Preliminaries

We first recall some formal notions regarding reaction systems, as introduced in [15,16]. Given a finite set S with at least two elements, called the *background set*, we say that a *reaction* over S is a triplet $a = (R, I, P)$, where R, I, P are subsets of S, while R and I are disjoint. The elements of S are informally called *objects*, the elements of R are called *reactants*, the elements of I are called *inhibitors*, while the elements of P are called *products*. The reaction $a = (R, I, P)$ is *enabled* (or activated) in *state* $X \subseteq S$, denoted $\mathsf{en}_a(X)$, if $R \subseteq X$, while $I \cap X = \emptyset$. The mapping $\mathsf{res}_a(X)$ that computes the *result* of the reaction a activated in X is defined as follows: $\mathsf{res}_a(X) = P_a$, if $\mathsf{en}_a(X)$, and $\mathsf{res}_a(X) = \emptyset$, otherwise.

A *reaction system* on a finite background set S is a pair $\mathcal{A} = (S, A)$, where A is a finite set of reactions over S. The *computation* of a reaction system may be an interactive (there is an input from the environment) or a context-independent process. Here it is a context-independent process, that is a computation path, $X_0, X_1, \ldots$, in a state-transition system over S, where $X_n = \mathsf{res}_A(X_{n-1}) = \bigcup_{a \in A, \mathsf{en}_a(X_{n-1})} \mathsf{res}_a(X_{n-1})$ for all $n \geq 1$.

Obviously, any reaction system model defines a finite, state-transition system [14].

For a finite set X, $card(X)$ indicates its cardinality. A multiset is an extension of the concept of a set, in which each element is accompanied by its number of copies. Formally, given a finite set U, we define a *multiset* X over U via a *membership function* $\sigma_X : U \longrightarrow \mathbf{N}$, where $\sigma_X(x)$ gives the number of copies of element $x \in U$ in X. For a multiset X over U, we write $supp(X) = \{x \in U \mid \sigma_X(x) > 0\}$ for the support set of X. Note that a set X can be seen as a multiset with each of its elements having multiplicity 1.

The *empty multiset* is denoted by ε, that is, $\sigma_\varepsilon(a) = 0$ for all $a \in U$. The set of all multisets on U is denoted by U° while the set of all nonempty multisets is denoted by $U^\#$. A subset of U° is called *macroset*. The *weight* of a multiset X over U is $\|X\| = \sum_{a \in U} \sigma_X(a)$. Clearly, a multiset X of weight n over a set U can be formally defined by an unordered list of size n. For instance, $\{\{a_{i_1}, \ldots, a_{i_n}\}\}$ is a vector representing a multiset of weight n over the set $\{a_1, \ldots a_k\}$, for some $k \geq 1$. More precisely, $\sigma_X(a_r) = card(\{j \mid i_j = r\})$, for all $1 \leq r \leq k$.

We recall the standard operations on multisets. For two multisets X, Y over a set U, we define:

- the *inclusion* relation $X \sqsubseteq Y$, where $\sigma_X(x) \leq \sigma_Y(x)$ for all $x \in U$;
- the *addition* multiset $X + Y$, where $\sigma_{X+Y}(x) = \sigma_X(x) + \sigma_Y(x)$ for all $x \in U$;

- the *difference* multiset $X - Y$, where $\sigma_{X-Y}(x) = \sigma_X(x) - \sigma_Y(x)$ for each $x \in U$, provided that $Y \sqsubseteq X$;
- the *scalar multiplication* of the multiset X by the positive integer k, where $\sigma_{k \cdot X}(x) = k \cdot \sigma_X(x)$, for all $x \in U$.

We now propose our multiset reaction systems model. The key difference from (standard) reaction systems is that the components of each reaction, as well the states of the model, are multisets rather than sets. This has several consequences: reactions have now access to counted (hence, limited) resources and will compete among themselves on them, and the resources may not be enough for all enabled resources to be executed. Additionally, we also adopt the principle that resources are removed from the system only as a result of being consumed/used by an enabled reaction that got to be executed; otherwise, they are left to persist in the successor state. Consequently, a *multiset reaction* over a set S is actually a triple of multisets instead of sets. We now define the way of enabling a multiset reaction.

Definition 1. *Let S be a background set and $a = (R, I, P)$ a multiset reaction over S. Given a multiset $T \in S^{\#}$, we say that T enables a, denoted $\mathrm{en}_a(T)$, if $\sigma_T(x) \geq \sigma_R(x)$, for all $x \in R$, and $\sigma_T(y) = 0$, for all $y \in I$. The result of enabling a is $\mathrm{res}_a(T) = P + (T - R)$.*

Definition 2. *Let S be a background set of a mRS $\mathcal{A} = (S, A)$. For a multiset of reactions Δ, we define its resource and inhibitor multisets, R_Δ, I_Δ, as follows:*

$$R_\Delta = \sum_{a \in A} \sigma_\Delta(a) \cdot R_a, \quad I_\Delta = \bigcup_{\sigma_\Delta(a) \geq 1} I_a.$$

For a state $T \in S^{\#}$, we say that T enables simultaneously the reactions of Δ, denoted $\mathrm{en}_\Delta(T)$, if $R_\Delta \sqsubseteq T$ and $\sigma_T(x) = 0$ for all $x \in I_\Delta$. In this case, the result of applying a multiset of activated reactions Δ to the state T is given by

$$\mathrm{res}_\Delta(T) = \sum_{a \in A} \sigma_\Delta(a) \cdot P_a + (T - R_\Delta).$$

We define the macroset $SE_k(A, T)$ of multisets of weight k enabled in T as

$$SE_k(A, T) = \{\Delta \mid \Delta \in A^{\#}, \|\Delta\| = k, \mathrm{en}_\Delta(T)\}.$$

Then $SE(A,T) = \bigcup_{k \geq 1} SE_k(A, T)$ is the set of all multisets of reactions enabled in T.

We define various types of *events* generated by $T \in S^{\#}$. In particular, an event is:

(i) A *k-event*, for some $k \geq 1$, if there exists $\Delta \in A^{\#}$ of weight k such that $\mathrm{en}_\Delta(T)$ is true. The result of this *k*-event is $\mathrm{res}_\Delta(T)$. A 1 event is also called a *sequential event*, while Δ is called a *k-enabled multiset*.

(ii) A *-event* if there exists $k \geq 1$ such that T generates a k-event. In this case, Δ is called an *arbitrarily enabled multiset*

(iii) A $\leq_k$-*event* if there exists $1 \leq m \leq k$ such that T generates a m-event. Now, Δ is called an *at most k enabled multiset*.

(iv) A $\geq_k$-*event* if there exists $m \geq k \geq 1$ such that T generates an m-event. We say that Δ is an *at least k enabled multiset*.

(v) A *maximal event* if there exists $\Delta \in A^{\#}$ such that $\mathrm{en}_\Delta(T)$ is true, and there is no $\alpha \in A$ such that $\mathrm{en}_{\Delta+\{\{\alpha\}\}}(T)$ is true. A multiset Δ as above is called a *maximally enabled* multiset.

Example 1. For a better understanding of these events, we give an example. Let $\mathcal{A} = (S, A)$ be a mRS, where

$$S = \{a, b, c\}, \qquad\qquad A = \{\alpha_1, \alpha_2, \alpha_3\},$$
$$\alpha_1 = (\{a, b\}, \{c\}, \{a, c\}), \quad \alpha_2 = (\{a, c\}, \{b\}, \{b\}), \quad \alpha_3 = (\{a\}, \{c\}, \{a\})$$

Let T be the multiset $T = \{\{a, a, a, b, b\}\}$. We have the followings:

– An arbitrarily enabled multiset by T could be $\{\{\alpha_1\}\}$, $\{\{\alpha_3\}\}$, $\{\{\alpha_1, \alpha_1\}\}$, $\{\{\alpha_1, \alpha_3\}\}$, $\{\{\alpha_3, \alpha_3\}\}$, $\{\{\alpha_1, \alpha_1, \alpha_3\}\}$, $\{\{\alpha_1, \alpha_3, \alpha_3\}\}$ $\{\{\alpha_3, \alpha_3, \alpha_3\}\}$.

– A 2-enabled multiset could be $\{\{\alpha_1, \alpha_1\}\}$, $\{\{\alpha_1, \alpha_3\}\}$, $\{\{\alpha_3, \alpha_3\}\}$.

– An at most 1 enabled multiset could be $\{\{\alpha_1\}\}$, $\{\{\alpha_3\}\}$.

– An at least 2 enabled multiset could be $\{\{\alpha_1, \alpha_1\}\}$, $\{\{\alpha_1, \alpha_3\}\}$, $\{\{\alpha_3, \alpha_3\}\}$, $\{\{\alpha_1, \alpha_1, \alpha_3\}\}$, $\{\{\alpha_1, \alpha_3, \alpha_3\}\}$ $\{\{\alpha_3, \alpha_3, \alpha_3\}\}$.

– A maximally enabled multiset could be $\{\{\alpha_3, \alpha_3, \alpha_3\}\}$, $\{\{\alpha_1, \alpha_3, \alpha_3\}\}$, $\{\{\alpha_1, \alpha_1, \alpha_3\}\}$. Note that $\{\{\alpha_1, \alpha_1\}\}$ is not a maximally enabled multiset. □

Let $f \in \{*, maximal\} \cup \{\leq_k, k, \geq_k |\ k \geq 1\}$. Given a multiset reaction system $\mathcal{A} = (S, A)$, an f-*evolution* in $\mathcal{A}$, generated by $T \in S^{\#}$ is the sequence $D_0, D_1, \ldots$ of multisets over S, defined as follows:

(i) $D_0 = T$,

(ii) for $i \geq 0$, the multiset $D_{i+1} = \mathrm{res}_{\Delta_i}(D_i)$ is generated from D_i as the result of an f-event.

We now define the computation of macrosets according to f-evolutions. To this aim, we introduce to the background set S a special "universal inhibitor", denoted by †, and assume it to be present in the inhibitor set of each reaction. Then we call a reaction system with this property a *computing mRS (cmRS)*. Given a cmRS $\mathcal{A}$, we say that $T \in S^{\#}$ is computed by f-evolutions in $\mathcal{A}$ if there exists an f-evolution $C_0 = T, C_1, C_2, \ldots, C_m$, for some $m \geq 1$, such that $† \in C_m$, so that no further event is possible. The macroset of all multisets computed by f-evolutions in $\mathcal{A}$ is called the *macroset computed by* $\mathcal{A}$, and is denoted by $M_f(\mathcal{A})$.

4 Relationships Among the Evolutions in Multiset Reaction Systems

We first show that $*$-evolutions can be simulated by sequential evolutions.

Theorem 1. *Let $\mathcal{A}$ be a cmRS. There exists a cmRS $\mathcal{A}'$ such that a multiset is computed by $*$-evolutions in $\mathcal{A}$ if and only if it is computed by sequential evolutions in $\mathcal{A}'$. Hence, $M_*(\mathcal{A}) = M_1(\mathcal{A}')$ holds.*

Proof. Let $\mathcal{A} = (S, A)$ be a cmRS with $A = \{\alpha_1, \alpha_2, \ldots, \alpha_k\}$, for some $k \geq 1$, and $\alpha_i = (R_i, I_i, P_i)$, $1 \leq i \leq k$. We construct the cmRS $\mathcal{A}' = (S', A')$, where

$$S' = S \cup \{s' \mid s \in S\} \cup \{Z, Z'\}, Z, Z' \notin S,$$
$$A' = \{\alpha_j' \mid 1 \leq j \leq k\} \cup \{\alpha_j'' \mid 1 \leq j \leq k\} \cup \{\beta, \gamma\} \cup \{\beta_s' \mid s \in S\}.$$

We now define the reactions of A'. For each $1 \leq j \leq k$, we define

$$\alpha_j' = (R_j, I_j \cup \{Z, Z'\}, P_j' \cup \{Z\}),$$
$$\alpha_j'' = (R_j \cup \{Z\}, I_j, P_j' \cup \{Z\}),$$

where $P_j' = \{s' \mid s \in P_j\}$, for all $1 \leq j \leq k$. We further define $\beta = (\{Z\}, \{\dagger\}, \{Z'\})$, and $\gamma = (\{Z'\}, \{s' \mid s \in S\}, \emptyset)$.

Finally, for each $s \in S$, we set $\beta_s' = (\{s', Z'\}, \{\dagger\}, \{s, Z'\})$. Note that we allow empty sets of products, but this is just for sake of simplicity because all the results we are going to present hold also for reaction systems formed by reactions with all their components being nonempty sets.

If a $*$-evolution in $\mathcal{A}$ starts by enabling the multiset of reactions $\Delta = \{\{\alpha_{j_1}, \ldots, \alpha_{j_r}\}\}$, for some $r \geq 1$, the corresponding sequential evolution in $\mathcal{A}'$ enables successively the reaction $\alpha_{j_1}', \alpha_{j_1}'', \ldots, \alpha_{j_r}''$. Note that all the elements produced during these successive reactions are prime copies of the ones produced in the $*$-event. In this way, we prevent substances produced in one of these reactions from being used in the subsequent ones, such that the $*$-event is properly simulated. Therefore, the role of the new symbol Z is to regulate a proper simulation of a $*$-event in $\mathcal{A}$.

Now, by means of the second new symbol Z', all the prime symbols, if any, are restored. Note that this sequential evolution starts by enabling the reaction β, for changing the symbol Z into Z', and continues by enabling only reactions β_p', $p \in S$, until all prime symbols are restored. Finally, γ removes the symbol Z' and a new $*$-event in $\mathcal{A}$ can be simulated. Obviously, no $*$-event in A is possible if and only if no further sequential event is possible in $\mathcal{A}'$. In conclusion, each multiset computed by $*$-evolutions in $\mathcal{A}$ can be computed by sequential evolutions in $\mathcal{A}'$. By the construction of $\mathcal{A}'$, the converse statement is also true.

Conversely, each sequential evolution in $\mathcal{A}'$ starts by activating a reaction α_j', for some $1 \leq j \leq k$, and continues with a sequence of activations of reactions in the set $\{\alpha_1'', \alpha_2'', \ldots, \alpha_k''\}$. Now, the only possible continuation is to enable β and then enabling successively reactions in the set $\{\beta_p' \mid p \in S\}$ until all prime symbols are restored. As explained above, this whole evolution is simulated in $\mathcal{A}$ in just one $*$-event. □

We now investigate the relationships between k-evolutions and sequential ones. We prove that it is possible to simulate all the k-events in a k-evolution by sequential events.

Theorem 2. *Let $\mathcal{A}$ be a cmRS and $k \geq 1$. Then, there exists a cmRS $\mathcal{A}'$ such that a multiset is computed by k-evolutions in $\mathcal{A}$ if and only if it is computed by sequential evolutions in $\mathcal{A}'$. Therefore, $M_k(\mathcal{A}) = M_1(\mathcal{A}')$.*

Proof. Let $\mathcal{A} = (S, A)$ be a cmRS, with $A = \{\alpha_1, \ldots, \alpha_n\}$, for some $n \geq 1$, and $\alpha_i = (R_i, I_i, P_i)$, $1 \leq i \leq n$. We construct the cmRS $\mathcal{A}' = (S', A')$, where:

(i) $S' = S \cup \{s' \mid s \in S\} \cup \{Z_t \mid 1 \leq t \leq k\}$,
(ii) $A' = \{\alpha_j^p \mid 1 \leq j \leq n, 1 \leq p \leq k\} \cup \{\beta_s \mid s \in S\} \cup \{\gamma\}$.

We now define the multiset reactions of A'. For each $1 \leq j \leq n$, we define

$$\alpha_j^1 = (R_j, I_j \cup \{Z_t \mid 1 \leq t \leq k\}, P_j' \cup \{Z_1\}),$$
$$\alpha_j^p = (R_j \cup \{Z_{p-1}\}, I_j \cup \{Z_t \mid t \neq p - 1\}, P_j' \cup \{Z_p\}),$$
$$2 \leq p \leq k,$$

where $P_j' = \{s' \mid s \in P_j\}$. Moreover, $\beta_s = (\{s', Z_k\}, \{\dagger\}, \{s, Z_k\})$, $\gamma = (\{Z_k\}, \{s' \mid s \in S\}, \emptyset)$.

Now, let $T \in S^\#$ and $C_0, C_1, \ldots$ be a k-evolution generated by T in $\mathcal{A}$. We show that there is a sequential evolution $D_0, D_1, \ldots$ generated by T in $\mathcal{A}'$ such that for each $j \geq 0$, there is $i_j \geq 0$ with $C_j = D_{i_j}$. Our argument is based on the induction of j. Clearly $C_0 = D_0$, hence $i_0 = 0$.

Assume now that $C_{j+1} = res_{\Delta_j}(C_j)$, for some $\Delta_j \in SE_k(A, C_j)$, with $\Delta_j = \{\!\{\alpha_{t_1}, \ldots, \alpha_{t_k}\}\!\}$. By the induction hypothesis, there is i_j such that $C_j = D_{i_j}$. Obviously, each $\alpha_{t_q} \in \Delta_j$ also belongs to $SE_1(A, C_j)$. From the definition of A', it follows that $\alpha_{t_q} \in SE_1(A', D_{i_j})$ holds. Without loss of generality, we may take $q = 1$. We now show a sequence of sequential activation of reactions in A' that eventually leads to C_{j+1}. This sequence has two distinct parts.

The first part starts with the activation of $\alpha_{t_1}^1$ and continues with $\alpha_{t_2}^2, \alpha_{t_3}^3$, and so on, ending with the activation of $\alpha_{t_k}^k$. Let $D \subseteq S^\#$ be the multiset obtained at the end of this sequential evolution. As the products added in any event are marked by prime symbols, they cannot interfere with the conditions for activating the next reaction. Moreover, the symbol Z ensures that all the reactions in the multiset Δ_j have been activated in the order $t_1, \ldots, t_k$. Note that, as mentioned above, this order does not actually matter. A closer look at D reveals that, except for the object Z_k, if one restores the prime copies of the objects in D, the multisets D and C_{j+1} coincide.

The role of the second part is to restore the prime copies of the objects in D. A possible way to do this is to repeatedly activate the reaction β_s, for some $s \in S$, until all prime copies of s in D have been restored. The process continues with another object in S, until all the prime copies have been restored. Note that during this process, only these reactions may be activated due to the presence of

Z_k. When all the prime copies are restores, the reaction γ is activated, producing exactly C_{j+1}.

The converse inclusion follows by a similar argument used in the proof of Theorem 1. □

The techniques employed in the proofs of Theorems 1 and 2 may be extended to prove the next two results.

Theorem 3. *With $\mathcal{A}$ a cmRS, let $k \geq 1$. Then, there exists a cmRS $\mathcal{A}'$ such that a multiset is computed by $\leq_k$-evolutions in $\mathcal{A}$ if and only if it is computed by sequential evolutions in $\mathcal{A}'$. Therefore, $M_{\leq_k}(\mathcal{A}) = M_1(\mathcal{A}')$.*

Proof. We consider the construction in the proof of Theorem 2. Informally, in order to simulate a $\leq_k$-event, we just give $\mathcal{A}$ the possibility to start the restoring process in a state containing any symbol Z_p with $p \leq k$ and not only Z_k as in the proof of Theorem 2. This can be done by adding the reactions

$$\overline{\alpha}_j^p = (R_j \cup \{Z_{p-1}\}, I_j \cup \{Z_t \mid t \neq p - 1\}, P_j' \cup \{Z_k\}),$$

for all $1 \leq j \leq n$ and $2 \leq p \leq k - 1$, provided that $k \geq 3$. If $k = 2$, then the following reactions are to be added:

$$\overline{\alpha}_j^1 = (R_j, I_j \cup \{Z_t \mid 1 \leq t \leq k\}, P_j' \cup \{Z_2\}),$$

for all $1 \leq j \leq n$. □

Theorem 4. *With $\mathcal{A}$ a cmRS, let $k \geq 1$. Then, there exists a cmRS $\mathcal{A}'$ such that a multiset is computed by $\geq_k$-evolutions in $\mathcal{A}$ if and only if it is computed by sequential evolutions in $\mathcal{A}'$. Therefore, $M_{\geq_k}(\mathcal{A}) = M_1(\mathcal{A}')$.*

Proof. We consider again the construction in the proof of Theorem 2. In order to simulate a $\geq_k$-event, we just add a set of new reactions in $\mathcal{A}'$, which allows $\mathcal{A}'$ to simulate more than k events in a $\geq_k$-evolution of $\mathcal{A}$. The informal idea is to permit $\mathcal{A}'$ to continue with sequential evolutions as soon as the symbol Z_k is in the environment, such that Z_k plays the same role as Z in the proof of Theorem 1. Nondeterministically, Z_k is changed to Z' which regulates the process of restoring the prime symbols. Consequently, we make the following changes in the proof of Theorem 2:

- Add the new reactions defined by $\overline{\alpha}_j^k = (R_j \cup \{Z_k\}, I_j \cup \{Z_t \mid t \neq k\}, P_j' \cup \{Z_k\}), 1 \leq j \leq k$.
- Add the new reaction $\beta = (\{Z_k\}, \{\dagger\}, \{Z'\})$.
- Change the reactions β_s by $\beta_s = (\{s', Z'\}, \{\dagger\}, \{s, Z'\})$, $s \in S$.
- Change γ by $\gamma = (\{Z'\}, \{s' \mid s \in S\}, \emptyset)$.

If a $\geq_k$-evolution in $\mathcal{A}$ starts by enabling the multiset of reactions $\Delta = \{\{\alpha_{j_1}, \ldots, \alpha_{j_r}\}\}$, for some $r \geq k$, the corresponding sequential evolution in $\mathcal{A}'$ is identical to the one described in the proof of Theorem 2. up to the point where $\alpha_{j_k}^k$ was enabled. If $r = k$, then Z_k is replaced by Z', and $\mathcal{A}'$ passes to the second phase, that of restoring the prime symbols. If $r > k$, then the reactions $\overline{\alpha}_j^k$, $1 \leq j \leq n$, are enabled $r - k$ times, and then $\mathcal{A}'$ passes to the second phase, that of restoring the prime symbols. □

Theorem 5. *Let $\mathcal{A}$ be a cmRS. Then, there exists a cmRS $\mathcal{A}'$ such that a multiset is computed by maximal evolutions in $\mathcal{A}$ if and only if it is computed by sequential evolutions in $\mathcal{A}'$. Therefore, $M_{maximal}(\mathcal{A}) = M_1(\mathcal{A}')$.*

Proof. Let $\mathcal{A} = (S, A)$ be a cmRS, with $A = \{\alpha_1, \ldots, \alpha_n\}$, for some $n \geq 1$, and $\alpha_i = (R_i, I_i, P_i)$, $1 \leq i \leq n$. We construct cmRS $\mathcal{A}' = (S', A')$, where:

$$S' = S \cup \{s' \mid s \in S\} \cup \{Y_t \mid 1 \leq t \leq n+1\} \cup \{X, Z\},$$

while A' contains all reactions defined below.

Group 1. For all $1 \leq i \leq n$, the following reactions belong to A':

$$\alpha_i^1 = (R_i, I_i \cup \{X, Z\} \cup \{Y_j \mid 1 \leq j \leq n+1\}, P_i' \cup \{Z\}),$$
$$\alpha_i^2 = (R_i, I_i \cup \{X, Z\} \cup \{Y_j \mid 1 \leq j \leq n+1\}, P_i' \cup \{Y_1\}),$$
$$\alpha_i^3 = (R_i \cup \{Z\}, I_i \cup \{X\}, P_i' \cup \{Z\}),$$
$$\alpha_i^4 = (R_i \cup \{Z\}, I_i \cup \{X\}, P_i' \cup \{Y_1\}).$$

As before, $P_i' = \{s' \mid s \in P_i\}$ for all $1 \leq i \leq n$.

Group 2. For each $1 \leq i \leq n$, the following reactions belong to A':

$$\delta_a^i = (\{Y_i, a\}, \{\dagger\}, \{a, Y_{i+1}\}), a \in I_i,$$
$$\eta_a^i = (\{Y_i\}, \{a, \dagger\}, \{Y_{i+1}\}), a \in R_i.$$

Finally, $\theta = (\{Y_{n+1}\}, \{\dagger\}, \{X\}) \in A'$.

Group 3. A' contains the reactions $\beta_s = (\{s', X\}, \emptyset, \{s, X\})$, for all $s \in S$, as well as the reaction $\gamma = (\{X\}, \{s' \mid s \in S\}, \emptyset)$.

Now, with $T \in S^{\#}$, let $\Delta = \{\alpha_{i_1}, \ldots, \alpha_{i_r}\}$ be the reactions enabled by T in a maximal event, and let T' be the result of this event. We shall show how T' can be obtained in $\mathcal{A}'$ as the result of a series of consecutive sequential events. Initially, the simulation starts either by reaction $\alpha_{i_1}^2$, provided that $r = 1$, or by reaction $\alpha_{i_1}^1$, provided that $r > 1$. We continue with the case $r > 1$, the argument for $r = 1$ being identical to the last step of this reasoning. The computation in $\mathcal{A}'$ continues with reactions in the first group, namely $\alpha_{i_2}^3, \alpha_{i_3}^3, \ldots$, and the last reaction is $\alpha_{i_r}^4$. In this step, if we restore the prime symbols in the current state, we get exactly $T' + \{\{Y_1\}\}$.

The role of reactions in the second group is to check whether Δ was indeed a correct multiset of reactions that T can enable by maximal evolution. This is done as follows: for each $1 \leq i \leq n$, the reactions in the second group check whether $\Delta + \{\{\alpha_i\}\}$ could have been enabled by T. This process is divided into two subprocesses. On the one hand, δ_a^i checks whether the current state contains an inhibitor of reaction α_i, namely a. If this is the case, which means that $\Delta + \{\{\alpha_i\}\}\}$ cannot be enabled by T, the symbol Y_i is replaced by Y_{i+1}, and the same check process continue for the reaction α_{i+1}. On the other hand, η_a^i checks whether $a \in R_i$ is not present in the current state, thus indicating that $\Delta + \{\{\alpha_i\}\}$ cannot be enabled by T. Again, if a is not present in the current state, Y_i is substituted by Y_{i+1}.

When the current state contains Y_{i+1}, which means that Δ was indeed a correct multiset of reactions that T can enable by maximal evolution, Y_{i+1} is replaced by X. From now on, by the reactions in the third group, all the prime symbols are restored, and finally X disappears.   □

5   Computational Power of Multiset Reaction Systems

As we have seen in the previous section, each type of evolution can be simulated by sequential evolution. Note that cmRS is a particular variant of the quantitative reaction system [22], where the set of pairs (reactant, selective inhibitor) is empty. In [22], it was proven that the computational power of sequential evolutions in quantitative reaction systems equals the computational power of multiset Turing machine. Consequently, each macroset computed by a cmRS, with any type of evolution, is accepted by a multiset Turing machine. We shall investigate now whether the converse relation holds as well. To this aim, we here recall the definition of a multiset Turing machine (MTM for short).

Informally speaking, a MTM may be seen as having a bag able to store a multiset of symbols of infinite weight and a *pu-pb* head which can *pick up* one symbol from the bag and *put back* one symbol to the content of the bag. Furthermore, this machine is able to detect the absence of a symbol from the bag, being closely related to the multiset Turing machine with detection (MTMD) defined in [11]. We give the definition of a MTM which is a bit different than the definition of a MTMD in [11]. Formally, a MTM is a construct

$$\mathcal{M} = (Q, U, f, q_0, \nabla, F),$$

where Q and $F \subseteq Q$ is the finite set of states, and final states, respectively, U is the *bag alphabet*, ∇ is a special symbol of U which occurs infinitely many times in the bag, q_0 is the initial state, and f is the transition mapping from $Q \times U$ into the set of all subsets of $Q \times U$. A configuration is a pair (q, τ), where q is the current state and τ is a multiset representing the content of the bag. We write

$$(q, \tau) \models (s, \rho)$$

if one of the following conditions is satisfied:

(i) there are $a, b \in U \setminus \{\nabla\}$ such that $(s, b) \in f(q, a)$, $\tau(a) \geq 1$,

$$\rho(a) = \tau(a) - 1, \ \rho(b) = \tau(b) + 1, \ \rho(c) = \tau(c), \ \forall c \in U \setminus \{a, b\};$$

(ii) there is $a \in U \setminus \{\nabla\}$ such that $(s, \nabla) \in f(q, a)$, $\tau(a) \geq 1$,

$$\rho(a) = \tau(a) - 1, \ \rho(c) = \tau(c), \ \forall c \in U \setminus \{a\};$$

(iii) there is $b \in U \setminus \{\nabla\}$ such that $(s, b) \in f(q, \nabla)$,
$$\rho(b) = \tau(b) + 1, \ \rho(c) = \tau(c), \ \forall c \in U \setminus \{b\};$$
(iv) there is $a \in U \setminus \{\nabla\}$, $b \in U$ such that $(s, b) \in f(q, a)$,
$$\rho(a) = \tau(a) = 0, \ \rho(b) = \tau(b) + 1, \ \rho(c) = \tau(c), \ \text{for } c \in U \setminus \{a, b\}.$$

The reflexive and transitive closure of this operation is denoted by $\models^*$. We say that the multiset τ is accepted by $\mathcal{M}$ if $(q_0, \tau) \models^* (s, \beta)$ and $s \in F$. In words, the multiset τ is accepted if there is a computation in $\mathcal{M}$, starting in the initial state q_0 with τ the contents of the bag, which reaches a final state.

Theorem 6. *Given: a cmRS $\mathcal{A} = (S, A)$; $T \in S^{\#}$; and $f \in \{*, maximal\} \cup \{\leq_k , k, \geq_k | \ k \geq 1\}$, there exists an MTM $\mathcal{M}$ such that T is computed by f-evolutions in $\mathcal{A}$ if and only if T is accepted by $\mathcal{M}$.*

Proof. The proof is based on the following three statements. First, the f-evolution can be simulated by sequential evolutions, by the previous results. Second, each multiset reaction system is a particular variant of quantitative reaction systems (cqRS). Third, each multiset computed by sequential evolutions in a quantitative reaction system is accepted by an MTM [22]. □

Although cmRS is a particular variant of cqRS, the converse relationship holds as well.

Theorem 7. *Given an MTM $\mathcal{M}$ and a multiset T, there exists a cmRS $\mathcal{A}$ such that T is accepted by $\mathcal{M}$ if and only if T is computed by sequential evolutions in $\mathcal{A}$.*

Proof. Let $\mathcal{M} = (Q, U, f, q_0, \nabla, F)$ be a MTM and T be a multiset over U accepted by $\mathcal{M}$. We construct a cmRS $\mathcal{A} = (U \cup Q \cup \{\dagger\}, A)$, where the set of quantitative reactions A contains the following reactions:

- α_0 whose effect is to add q_0 to the initial substrate.
- For each transition $(s, b) \in f(q, a)$, $a, b \in U \setminus \{\nabla\}$, we add the reaction $\alpha_{(q,a,s,b)} = (\{q, a\}, \{\dagger\}, \{s, b\})$. As one can easily notice, the effect of this reaction is to remove a from the substrate, provided it exists, as well as q, and add s and b.
- For each transition $(s, \nabla) \in f(q, a)$, $a \in U \setminus \{\nabla\}$, we add the reaction $\beta_{(q,a,s)} = (\{q, a\}, \{\dagger\}, \{s\})$.
- For each transition $(s, b) \in f(q, \nabla)$, $b \in U \setminus \{\nabla\}$, we add the reaction $\gamma_{(q,s,b)} = (\{q\}, \emptyset, \{s, b\})$.
- For each transition $(s, b) \in f(q, a)$, $a \in U \setminus \{\nabla\}$, $b \in U$, we add the reaction $\delta_{(q,a,s,b)} = (\{q\}, \{a, \dagger\}, \{s, b\})$. As can be easily noticed, this reaction checks that a does not appear in the substrate and, if this is the case, removes q and adds s and b.
- For each final state $q_f \in Q$, We add the reaction $w_{q_f} = (\{q_f\}, \{\dagger\}, \{\dagger\})$.

This construction, together with the explanations accompanying the reactions, yield the conclusion that $T \in U$ is accepted by $\mathcal{M}$ iff T is computed by $\mathcal{A}$. □

6   Conclusion

We introduced reaction systems that compute over multisets. The computation in our framework begins with an initial multiset of resources, where multiple reactions may be enabled simultaneously. These reactions consume resources and produce new ones, forming the next state in the computation. The process halts when a special inhibitor appears in the state, at which point the input multiset is accepted.

Surprisingly, we found that all the evolution types we defined—both quantitative ($\leq_k, \geq_k, k$) and qualitative ($*, maximal$)—can be simulated sequentially, with only one reaction enabled at a time. We then proved cmRS with sequential evolution have the same computational power as multiset Turing machines.

In our approach, reactions follow the classic reaction system framework and are defined by sets of reactants, inhibitors, and products. When a reaction is enabled in a multiset state, it consumes one copy of each reactant and introduces one copy of each product into the next state. A natural extension of this framework allows reactions to be defined using multisets of reactants, inhibitors, and products. In this variant, a reaction is enabled if the current multiset contains the required reactants in the necessary multiplicities while lacking inhibitors in quantities sufficient to block it. It is worth mentioning that all the results proposed in this paper are valid for this variant of reaction system. Actually, the extension of the results presented here for the *maximal* evolution require some more intriguing work because it is necessary to introduce the possibility to count the number of occurrences of a reactant in the environment, but this can be done by means of some specific reactants.

An additional extension considers variations in reaction execution times, influencing how parallel reactions are enabled. This can be incorporated into the definition of k-events: a multiset of reactions with weight k is enabled if no sub-multiset of weight up to $k-1$ inhibits the remaining reactions. In other words, a multiset of reactions can proceed simultaneously as long as they do not interfere with one another.

References

1. Azimi, S., Gratie, C., Ivanov, S., Petre, I.: Dependency graphs and mass-conservation in reaction systems. Theor. Comput. Sci. **598**, 23–39 (2015)
2. Azimi, S., Gratie, C., Ivanov, S., Manzoni, L., Petre, I., Porreca, A.E.: Complexity of model checking for reaction systems. Theor. Comput. Sci. **623**, 103–113 (2016)
3. Azimi, S., Panchal, C., Mizera, A., Petre, I.: Multi-stability, limit cycles, and period-doubling bifurcation with reaction systems. Int. J. Found. Comput. Sci. **28**, 1007–1020 (2017)
4. Banâtre, J.P., Coutant, A., Le Metayer, D.: A parallel machine for multiset transformation and its programming style. Futur. Gener. Comput. Syst. **4**, 133–144 (1988)
5. Banâtre, J.P., Le Metayer, D.: Gamma and chemical reaction model: ten years after. In: Andreoli, J.M., Hankin, C. (eds.) Coordination Programming: Mechanisms, Models and Semantics, pp. 3–41. Imperial College Press (1996)

6. Bedau, M.A., McCaskill, J.S., Packard, N.H., Rasmussen, S.: Chemical evolution among artificial proto-cells. In: Artificial Life VII: Proceedings of the Seventh International Conference on Artificial Life, pp. 54–63. MIT Press (2000)
7. Berry, G., Boudol, G.: The chemical abstract machine. Theor. Comput. Sci. **96**, 217–248 (1992)
8. Bottoni, P., Martín-Vide, C., Păun, G., Rozenberg, G.: Membrane systems with promoters/inhibitors. Acta Informatica **38**, 695–720 (2002)
9. Bottoni, P., Labella, A., Mitrana, V.: Networks of polarized multiset processors. J. Comput. Syst. Sci. **85**, 93–103 (2017)
10. Crespi-Reghizzi, S., Mandrioli, D.: Commutative grammars. Calcolo **13**, 173–189 (1976)
11. Csuhaj-Varjú, E., Martín-Vide, C., Mitrana, V.: Multiset automata. In: Calude, C., Pŭn, G., Rozenberg, G., Salomaa, A. (eds.) Multiset Processing, Mathematical, Computer Science, and Molecular Computing Points of View, WMP 2000. Lecture Notes in Computer Science, vol. 2235, pp. 69–84. Springer, Heidelberg (2001)
12. Csuhaj-Varjú, E., Oswald, M., Vaszil, G.: P automata. In: Păun, G., Rozenberg, G., Salomaa, A. (eds.) Handbook of Membrane Computing, pp. 144–167. Oxford University Press (2010)
13. Ehrenfeucht, A., Main, M.G., Rozenberg, G.: Functions defined by reaction systems. Int. J. Found. Comput. Sci. **22**(1), 167–178 (2011)
14. Ehrenfeucht, A., Petre, I., Rozenberg, G.: Reaction systems: a model of computation inspired by the functioning of the living cell. In: Konstantinidis, S., Moreira, N., Reis, R., Shallit, J. (eds.) The Role of Theory in Computer Science, pp. 1–32. World Scientific (2017)
15. Ehrenfeucht, A., Rozenberg, G.: Basic notions of reaction systems. In: Calude, C.S., Calude, E., Dinneen, M.J. (eds.) DLT 2004. LNCS, vol. 3340, pp. 27–29. Springer, Heidelberg (2004). https://doi.org/10.1007/978-3-540-30550-7_3
16. Ehrenfeucht, A., Rozenberg, G.: Reaction systems. Fundam. Informaticae **75**(1–4), 263–280 (2007)
17. Freund, R., Ibarra, O.H., Păun, A., Sosík, P., Yen, H.-C.: Catalytic P systems. In: Păun, G., Rozenberg, G., Salomaa, A. (eds.) The Oxford Handbook of Membrane Computing. Oxford University Press, Oxford (2009)
18. Helm, R., Marriott, K., Odersky, M.: Building visual language parsers. In: Robertson, S.P., Olson, G.M. (eds.) Proceedings of ACM Conference on Human Factors in Computing, CHI 1991, pp. 105–112. Association for Computing Machinery, New York (1991)
19. Kudlek, K., Martin-Vide, C., Păun, G.: Toward FMT (formal macroset theory). In: Calude, C.S., Dinneen, M.J., Păun, G. (eds.) Pre-Proceedings of the Workshop on Multiset Processing (WMP 2000), CDMTCS–140, pp. 149–158 (2000)
20. Latteux, M.: Cónes rationnels commutativement clos. RAIRO. Informatique théorique **11**, 29–51 (1977)
21. Marriott, K.: Constraint multiset grammars. In: Ambler, A.L., Kimura, T. (eds.) Proceedings of IEEE Symposium on Visual Languages, pp. 118–125. IEEE Computer Society Press (1994)
22. Mitrana, V., Păun, M., Petre, I., Prelipcean, A.M.: Quantitative reaction systems (submitted)
23. Murata, T.: Petri nets: properties, analysis and applications. Proc. IEEE **77**, 541–580 (1989)
24. Okubo, F., Kobayashi, S., Yokomori, T.: Reaction automata. Theor. Comput. Sci. **429**, 247–257 (2012)

25. Păun, G., Rozenberg, G., Salomaa, A.: DNA Computing. New Computing Paradigms. Springer, Berlin (1998)
26. Păun, G.: Computing with membranes. An introduction. Bull. EATCS **67**, 139–152 (1999)
27. Păun, G.: Computing with membranes (P systems): Twenty six research topics, CDMTCS Report No. 119, Auckland University (2000)
28. Păun, G.: Membrane Computing. An Introduction. Springer (2002)
29. Peterson, J.L.: Petri Net Theory and the Modeling of Systems. Prentice Hall (1981)
30. Salomaa, A.: Functional constructions between reaction systems and propositional logic. Int. J. Found. Comput. Sci. **24**(1), 147–160 (2013)
31. Salomaa, A.: Functions and sequences generated by reaction systems. Theor. Comput. Sci. **466**, 87–96 (2012)
32. Suzuki, Y., Tanaka, H.: Symbolic chemical system based on abstract rewriting system and its behavior pattern. Artif. Life Robot. **1**, 211–219 (1997)
33. Yokomori, T., Okubo, F.: Theory of reaction automata: a survey. J. Membr. Comput. **3**(1), 63–85 (2021). https://doi.org/10.1007/s41965-021-00070-6

P Colonies Generating Strings

Rodica Ceterchi[1], Marian Gheorghe[2]([✉]), Lakshmanan Kuppusamy[3],
and K. G. Subramanian[4]

[1] Faculty of Mathematics and Computer Science, University of Bucharest, 14
Academiei Street, 010014 Bucharest, Romania
[2] School of Computer Science and Electronics, University of Bradford, West
Yorkshire, Bradford BD7 1DP, UK
m.gheorghe@bradford.ac.uk
[3] School of Computer Science and Engineering, VIT, Vellore 632 014, India
[4] School of Mathematics, Computer Science and Engineering, Liverpool Hope
University, Hope Park, Liverpool L16 9JD, UK

Abstract. In this paper P colonies are considered as a string generating mechanism, and thus producing languages. It is shown that this model with two agents and each having three objects computes, in both maximally parallel manner as well as in sequential mode, the family of recursively enumerable languages. This device is used to generate 2D structures, first as chain code languages and next an actual 2D shape is generated.

1 Introduction

P colonies are simple membrane computing devices inspired by the behaviour of multi-agent systems, where individual agents execute various tasks and communicate through a shared environment. They have been introduced in [11], being motivated by problems occurring in multi-agent communities. Colonies of simple formal grammars introduced in [10] have played an influential role in conceiving the concept of a P colony. The main P colony research problems and results are thoroughly described in the survey paper [5]. Most of the results are of a similar type with those investigated in membrane computing [15], a very active research area initiated in [14].

There are different variants of P colonies and they share some common characteristics: each agent has a finite multiset of objects of a constant size; the agents change their states, given by the finite multisets, by executing programs. Every agent has a finite number of programs, where each program consists of simple instructions that are rules changing objects or exchanging them with others through the environment. Handling multisets of objects is a common feature of many membrane computing systems [15]. As these membrane systems compute sets of numbers, the P colonies do similar computations. A P colony model

---

K. G. Subramanian—Honorary Visiting Professor.

© The Author(s), under exclusive license to Springer Nature Switzerland AG 2025
M. D. Jiménez López and G. Vaszil (Eds.): Erzsébet Csuhaj-Varjú Festschrift,
LNCS 15840, pp. 194–209, 2025.
https://doi.org/10.1007/978-3-031-97274-4_12

extended to an automaton-like device [4], is an accepting mechanism which handles multisets, but also reads input from an input tape, accepting languages.

In this paper we consider a P colony device that uses multisets of objects and strings in order to produce new strings as output of the system. Consequently, such a P colony computes a language. The model is formally introduced in Sect. 2 and some examples from context-free and non context-free languages are provided to explain how the introduced P colony model computes them. The main result in Sect. 3 shows that the family of languages computed by P colonies with strings having two agents is the family of recursively enumerable languages. Applications to generate 2D structures as chain code languages are given in Sect. 4. A P colony generating the 2D language of L-shaped arrays with equal arms is presented in Sect. 5.

2   Preliminaries and Definitions

We assume that the readers are familiar with formal languages and P systems. Below we recall some basic concepts and notations for the former and refer to [14, 15] for the latter and present here basic definitions used in the paper.

Let V be a finite set of characters (or symbols), called *alphabet* and let V^* denote the free monoid of all strings over the alphabet V under the concatenation operation. A *string* (or *word*) $x = a_1 a_2 \ldots a_n \in V^*$, with $a_i \in V, 1 \leq i \leq n$, is a finite sequence of symbols and the number of characters of x, i.e., n, defines the length of x and is denoted $|x|$. Let λ denote the empty string, with length 0. Let $V^+ = V^* - \{\lambda\}$.

A multiset over V is a mapping $f : V \to \mathbb{N}$, represented as a string $a_1^{f(a_1)} \cdots a_p^{f(a_p)}$, where the order is not important, and the elements which are not in the support of f (i.e., elements $a_j, 1 \leq j \leq p$, having $f(a_j) = 0$) are omitted. Similar to strings, for a multiset x, $|x|$ denotes the size, i.e., $f(a_1) + \cdots + f(a_p)$. When in the same context both strings and multisets are used then if the multiset $x = a_1 \cdots a_p, p \geq 1, a_i \in V, 1 \leq i \leq p$, has to be used as a string, with a_i appearing in that order, then this will be denoted $[x]$, whenever $p > 1$.

The family of *recursively enumerable languages* is denoted by RE. For more details of basic concepts in formal language theory we refer to [16].

A *matrix grammar with appearance checking* in a specific normal form is defined below.

Definition 1. *A matrix grammar with appearance checking in binary normal form is a tuple* $G = (N, T, S, M, F)$, *where* $N = N_1 \cup N_2 \cup \{S, \#\}$, *with the three sets mutually disjoint, is the finite set of non-terminal symbols, T is the finite set of terminal symbols, $N \cap T = \emptyset$, M is a finite set of sequences, called matrices, of one of the following forms:*

1. $(S \longrightarrow XA)$, *with* $X \in N_1, A \in N_2$;
2. $(X \longrightarrow Y, A \longrightarrow x)$, *with* $X, Y \in N_1, A \in N_2$ $x \in (N_2 \cup T)^*, |x| \leq 2$;
3. $(X \longrightarrow Y, A \longrightarrow \#)$, *with* $X, Y \subset N_1, A \subset N_2$;

4. $(X \longrightarrow \lambda, A \longrightarrow x)$, with $X \in N_1$, $A \in N_2$, $x \in T$.

There is only one matrix of type 1. The set F contains all the rules $A \longrightarrow \#$ that appear in matrices of type 3.

One can observe that each of the matrices in group 4 can be rewritten as follows. If $u = a_1 \cdots a_p$, then there are two case. When $p = 0$ or $p = 1$ the second rule is $A \longrightarrow u$, $u \in T \cup \{\lambda\}$, and the matrix in group 4 is $(X \longrightarrow \lambda, A \longrightarrow u)$. When $p > 1$, then the matrix can be replaced by $(X \longrightarrow X_1, A \longrightarrow a_1 A_1)$, $(X_1 \longrightarrow X_2, A_1 \longrightarrow a_2 A_2), \cdots, (X_{p-1} \longrightarrow \lambda, A_{p-1} \longrightarrow a_p)$, where X_i, $1 \leq i \leq p - 1$, are new symbols added to N_1 and A_i, $1 \leq i \leq p - 1$, are new symbols added to N_2. Then the matrix $(X_{p-1} \longrightarrow \lambda, A_{p-1} \longrightarrow a_p)$ will go to group 4 and the others will be included in group 2. As a conclusion, one can choose the grammar such that each rule in group 4 is $(X \longrightarrow \lambda, A \longrightarrow u)$, $u \in T \cup \{\lambda\}$.

We define a *derivation*, denoted $\Longrightarrow^m$, as a relationship between w, z and m, with $w, z \in (N \cup T)^*$ and m the label of a matrix from M, in the following way: if $w = X\alpha A\beta$, $z = Y\alpha x\beta$ and m is $(X \longrightarrow Y, A \longrightarrow x)$, then X and A in w are replaced by Y and x, respectively, generating z, where $\alpha, \beta \in (N_2 \cup T)^*$, $X \in N_1$, $A \in N_2$ and $Y \in N_1$, $x \in (N_2 \cup T)^*$, $|x| \leq 2$, or $Y = \lambda$, $x \in T^*$. If the matrix of label m is of type 2 or 4, then the two rules of m must be applied. If m is of type 3, $(X \longrightarrow Y, A \longrightarrow \#)$, then this is applied in *appearance checking* mode, which means that the second rule is applied when A appears in the string to be derived, otherwise the rule is skipped. When such a rule is applied, a trap symbol, $\#$, is introduced and this is never removed. The first derivation starts with S, where the only applicable matrix is that of type 1. When the label of the matrix m is not necessary in a derivation then this is dropped from the notation.

The language generated by a matrix grammar with appearance checking, G, is defined by $L(G) = \{w | S \Longrightarrow^* w, w \in T^*\}$, where $\Longrightarrow^*$ is the reflexive and transitive closure of $\Longrightarrow$.

It is known that the family of languages generated by matrix grammars with appearance checking is the same as RE [7].

We introduce now a *P colony with strings* shortly *PCol-s*. This concept is similar to a standard P colony [5] and P colony automaton [4], for string processing aspects.

Definition 2. *A P colony with strings (PCol-s) of capacity k and with n agents (or cells) is a tuple*

$$\Pi = (O, e, \mathcal{S}_0, w_{E,0}, B_1, \ldots B_n, F),$$

where O is a finite set of symbols, denoting the PCol-s alphabet, its elements are called objects; $e \in O$ is the environmental object available in a countably infinite number of copies; $\mathcal{S}_0$ is a finite set of initial strings – each of them over $O \setminus \{e\}$, $\mathcal{S}_0 = \{s_{1,0}, \cdots, s_{p,0}\}$, $p \geq 1$; $w_{E,0}$ is the initial multiset of objects from the environment different from e; B_i, $1 \leq i \leq n$, is the i-th agent, where $B_i = (w_{i,0}, P_i)$, with $w_{i,0}$ representing the initial contents of the agent, such that $|w_{i,0}| = k$, i.e., the initial number of objects, which is equal to the agent capacity,

and P_i is a finite set of programs - *every program consisting of at most k rules.*
$F \subseteq O$ *is the set of* final objects.

The programs contain the following types of rules: (i) *string rules*, of the
form $[x] \longleftrightarrow^S y$, with $[x]$ a string over O and y a multiset; such a rule is applied
to strings; and (ii) non-string rules, of the form $x \longrightarrow y$ or $x \longleftrightarrow y$, with x, y
multisets over O. A string rule $[x] \longleftrightarrow^S y$, when applied, will exchange the
string $[x]$ obtained from objects of the agent, with y, a multiset obtained from a
substring extracted from one of the strings. The objects from y will be added to
the current content of the agent and $[x]$ will replace the substring that produced
y. A non-string rule $x \longrightarrow y$ will replace x by y in the agent and $x \longleftrightarrow y$ will
exchange x from the agent with y from the environment.

We give a simple example to illustrate how string rule works. Assume that
there is a string $w = \alpha ab\beta$, where $\alpha, \beta \in O^*$, $a, b \in O$, and a rule $[bcd] \longleftrightarrow^S ab$,
with b, c, d objects of the agent. The rule is applicable and the string ab is
extracted from w and is moved to the agent as objects a, b; the string $[bcd]$
replaces ab in w, producing $w' = \alpha bcd\beta$. When such a rule is applied the balance
between what is taken out from the agent and what is brought in is broken
and this has to be re-established by other rules. In such circumstances rules
exchanging or rewriting with left and right side of unequal lengths, even λ are
allowed.

For a rule, r, either string or non-string type, $x \longrightarrow y$ or $x \longleftrightarrow^\sigma y$, $x, y \in O^*$,
$\sigma = S$ or $\sigma = \lambda$, one denotes $left(r) = x$ and $right(r) = y$.

One can have rules of type (iii) r_1/r_2, called *checking rules*, where r_1, r_2 are
of type (i) or (ii). When r_1/r_2 is applied it works as follows: if r_1 is applicable,
this must be applied, otherwise r_2 is applied.

A *string program* is a program containing one string rule, otherwise it is a
non-string program or simply *program*. In a non-string program, for any rule
r, we have $|left(r)| - |right(r)| - 1$. Consequently, any program has always
exactly k rules. If a string program contains the rules $r_1, \cdots, r_h$, $h \leq k$, then
$|left(r_1)| + \cdots + |left(r_h)| = |right(r_1)| + \cdots + |right(r_h)| = k$.

A PCol-s, Π, consists of an alphabet comprising all the symbols handled by
Π, agents, an environment, and a set of final symbols. Every agent B_i, $1 \leq i \leq n$,
has a multiset of objects, w_i, where $|w_i| = k$ (the PCol-s capacity), and a set of
programs. Each program, depending on its rules, can transform objects from the
agent, by rewriting them, and exchange objects with the environment or with
the strings. The environment consists of a finite number of non-environmental
objects (multiset of objects from O different from e) and a countably infinite
number of copies of e.

A *configuration* of Π is an $(n+p+1)$-tuple, $c = (s_1, \cdots, s_p; w_E; w_1, \cdots, w_n)$,
where s_i, $1 \leq i \leq p$, is a string, w_E is the contents of the environment and w_i,
$1 \leq i \leq n$, is the contents of the agent B_i.

A PCol-s Π computes in a stepwise manner starting from the *initial config-*
uration, given by $(s_{1,0}, \cdots, s_{p,0}; w_{E,0}; w_{1,0}, \cdots, w_{n,0})$.

For any two configurations $c = (s_1, \cdots, s_p; w_E; w_1, \cdots, w_n)$ and $c' = (s'_1, \cdots,$
$s'_p; w'_E; w'_1, \cdots, w'_n)$, a *transition* from c to c' may be defined in two ways: (i)

maximally parallel mode, when each agent which can use any of its programs in configuration c must use one, non-deterministically chosen; (ii) *sequential mode*, when only one single agent chooses non-deterministically one of its programs. The result produced in this step starting from c is c'.

A *computation* is a sequence of transitions starting from the initial configurations. A *halting computation* is a computation that arrives in a configuration where no program can be applied any more. The result of a halting computation is a set of strings $\{s_{1,f}, \cdots, s_{p,f}\}$, with $s_{i,f} \in F^*$, $1 \leq i \leq p$.

With a PCol-s Π one can associate the strings computed by Π. Their set, the language computed by Π, is denoted by $L(\Pi)$.

The number of agents in a PCol-s Π is called the *degree* of Π; the maximal number of programs of an agent of Π is called the *height* of Π; the number of objects inside any of the agents is called the *capacity* of Π; and the number of strings of Π is called its *size*. The family of languages computed by PCol-s with capacity at most $c \geq 0$, degree at most $n \geq 0$, height at most $h \geq 0$, size at most $s \geq 0$, using checking programs and working in α mode, is denoted by $\mathcal{L}PCOL_\alpha K(c, n, h, s)$, where $\alpha = par$ means the maximally parallel mode and $\alpha = seq$ means the sequential mode. If one of n or h is unbounded, then we replace it by $*$.

Example 1. Let us consider the following context-free language,

$$L_1 = \{a^n c^n | n \geq 1\}.$$

The following PCol-s computes L_1.

Let $\Pi_1 = (O, e, S_0, w_{E,0}, B_1, F)$ of capacity 2, with 1 agent, height 5 and size 1, where $O = \{A, C, a, c\}$, $S_0 = \{C\}$, $w_{E,0} = \lambda$, $B_1 = (w_{1,0}, P_1)$, $F = \{a, c\}$; $w_{1,0} = Aa$ and P_1 consists of the following programs:

$$p_1 : \langle [aA] \longleftrightarrow^S C; \lambda \longleftrightarrow e \rangle,$$
$$p_2 : \langle C \longrightarrow C; e \longrightarrow c \rangle,$$
$$p_3 : \langle [Cc] \longleftrightarrow^S A; \lambda \longleftrightarrow e \rangle,$$
$$p_4 : \langle A \longrightarrow A; e \longrightarrow a \rangle,$$
$$p_5 : \langle c \longleftrightarrow^S A; C \longrightarrow C \rangle.$$

The initial configuration is $c_0 = (C; \lambda; Aa)$. The transitions develop from c_0:
$c_0 = (C; \lambda; Aa) \Longrightarrow^{p_1} c_1 = (aA; \lambda; Ce) \Longrightarrow^{p_2} c_2 = (aA; \lambda; Cc) \Longrightarrow^{p_3}$
$c_3 = (aCc; \lambda; Ae) \Longrightarrow^{p_4} c_4 = (aCc; \lambda; Aa)$.

In c_4 we have again, as in c_0, C in the string and the same objects (i.e., Aa) in the agent B_1. Hence, this sequence of transitions can be repeated $n \geq 0$ times and we get the configuration $(a^n Cc^n; \lambda; Aa)$. If we apply p_1 and p_2, then $(a^{n+1}Ac^n; \lambda; Cc)$ is obtained and continuing with p_5 one gets $(a^{n+1}c^{n+1}; \lambda; AC)$, $n \geq 0$. The computation stops, as no program can be used in this configuration, and the result produced, $a^{n+1}c^{n+1}$, $n \geq 0$, is a string over F.

The above computation satisfies the requirements of both of the maximally parallel and the sequential.

A problem for the reader. Find a PCol-s of capacity 2, with 2 agents and of size 2 computing $L = L' \cup L''$, where $L' = \{a^n c^n | n \geq 1\}$ and $L'' = \{b^n d^n | n \geq 1\}$ such that the strings $a^n c^n$ and $b^n d^n$, $n \geq 1$, are computed in parallel.

The next example shows how to produce a non-context-free language using PCol-s pointing to similarities with the previous example, but also outlining differences as well.

Example 2. Let us consider the following crossed dependency non-context-free language, $L_2 = \{a^n b^m c^n d^m | n, m \geq 1\}$. In this case, each of the pairs of strings a^n, c^n and b^m, d^m, will be produced by an agent working similarly to Π_1 in Example 1. However, the difference is given by the use of the two agents and the fact that in the case of the current example the pairs are not adjacent, but scattered, requesting a slightly different way of switching from a component to the other one in each pair.

Let $\Pi_2 = (O, e, S_0, w_{E,0}, B_1, B_2, F)$ of capacity 2, with degree 2 (2 agents), height 6 and size 1, where $O = \{e, A, B, C, D, a, b, c, d\}$, $S_0 = \{ABCD\}$, $w_{E,0} = \lambda$, $B_1 = (w_{1,0}, P_1)$, $B_2 = (w_{2,0}, P_2)$, $F = \{a, b, c, d\}$; $w_{1,0} = Aa$ and $w_{2,0} = Bb$. P_1 and P_2 consisting the following programs:

$$p_{1,1} : \langle [Aa] \longleftrightarrow^S A; \lambda \longleftrightarrow e \rangle, \quad p_{2,1} : \langle [Bb] \longleftrightarrow^S B; \lambda \longleftrightarrow e \rangle,$$
$$p_{1,2} : \langle A \longrightarrow C; e \longrightarrow c \rangle, \quad\quad p_{2,2} : \langle B \longrightarrow D; e \longrightarrow d \rangle,$$
$$p_{1,3} : \langle [Cc] \longleftrightarrow^S C; \lambda \longleftrightarrow e \rangle, \quad p_{2,3} : \langle [Dd] \longleftrightarrow^S D; \lambda \longleftrightarrow e \rangle,$$
$$p_{1,4} : \langle C \longrightarrow A; e \longrightarrow a \rangle, \quad\quad p_{2,4} : \langle D \longrightarrow B; e \longrightarrow b \rangle,$$
$$p_{1,5} : \langle a \longleftrightarrow^S A; A \longrightarrow c \rangle, \quad p_{2,5} : \langle b \longleftrightarrow^S B; B \longrightarrow d \rangle,$$
$$p_{1,6} : \langle c \longleftrightarrow^S C; A \longrightarrow A \rangle; \quad p_{2,6} : \langle d \longleftrightarrow^S D; B \longrightarrow B \rangle;$$

The initial configuration is $c_0 = (ABCD; \lambda; Aa, Bb)$.

Assuming that PCol-s Π works in maximally parallel mode, the following transition develops from c_0:

$c_0 = (ABCD; \lambda; Aa, Bb) \Longrightarrow^{p_{1,1}, p_{2,1}} c_1 = (AaBbCD; \lambda; Ae, Be) \Longrightarrow^{p_{1,2}, p_{2,2}}$
$c_2 = (AaBbCD; \lambda; Cc, Dd) \Longrightarrow^{p_{1,3}, p_{2,3}} c_3 = (AaBbCcDd; \lambda; Ce, De) \Longrightarrow^{p_{1,4}, p_{2,4}}$
$c_4 = (AaBbCcDd; \lambda; Aa, Bb)$.

One can see that for each of the components of the two pairs, there is a placeholder (one of A, B, C, D) starting with the initial configuration. After four steps the pairs a, b and c, d are inserted next to their placeholders and the agents return to their initial contents, expressed as multisets.

This sequence of transitions may continue $n \geq 0$ times when one of the agents stops and the other one may continue with a sequence of programs where only the first four programs of that agent are used, maybe repeatedly. Let us consider that arriving at $(Aa^n Bb^n Cc^n Dd^n; \lambda; Aa, Bb)$, $n \geq 0$, the first agent will stop and the second one will continue up to step $m \geq n$. After step n the first agent will use in steps $n+1$ and $n+2$ the programs $p_{1,5}, p_{1,6}$, respectively, and the second agent has to use the programs $p_{2,1}, p_{2,2}$ leading to $(a^{n+1} Bb^{n+1} c^{n+1} Dd^n; \lambda; CA, Dd)$. From that configuration only the second agent will continue working until step m where the final configuration is reached, $(a^{n+1} b^{m+1} c^{n+1} d^{m+1}; \lambda; CA, DB)$, $n, m \geq 0$.

One can observe that the two agents do not have any dependencies and when the PCol-s works in sequential mode one gets the same result, as for any sequence of $k \geq 1$ transitions as above when in each step two programs are applied, one can get through interleaving a sequence of $2k$ transitions with a program being applied. Hence, the PCol-s generates the same language both in maximally parallel manner as well as in sequential mode.

3   The Computational Power of PCol-S

The following result shows that P colonies with strings characterize the class of recursively enumerable languages, RE. The proof below uses the fact that the family RE is obtained through matrix grammars with appearance checking.

Theorem 1. $\mathcal{L}PCOL_\alpha K(3, 2, *, 1) = RE$, $\alpha \in \{par, seq\}$.

Proof. Let $L \subseteq T^*$ be an arbitrary recursively enumerable language and $G = (N, T, S, M, F)$ a matrix grammar in binary normal form, as in Definition 1, where the matrices in M have one of the following forms:

1. $(S \longrightarrow XA)$, with $X \in N_1$, $A \in N_2$;
2. $(X \longrightarrow Y, A \longrightarrow x)$, with $X, Y \in N_1$, $A \in N_2$ $x \in (N_2 \cup T)^*$, $|x| \leq 2$;
3. $(X \longrightarrow Y, A \longrightarrow \#)$, with $X, Y \in N_1$, $A \in N_2$;
4. $(X \longrightarrow \lambda, A \longrightarrow u)$, with $X \in N_1$, $A \in N_2$, $u \in T \cup \{\lambda\}$.

We label the matrices above with $l_1, \cdots, l_k, \cdots, l_m$, where l_1 is the label of the first matrix, $(S \longrightarrow XA)$, l_2 to l_k are the labels of the rules in groups 2 and 3 and l_{k+1} to l_m are the labels of the rules in group 4. The set of these labels is H. Let us construct the PCol-s $\Pi = (O, e, S_0, w_{E,0}, B_1, B_2, F)$ of capacity 3, with 2 agents and size 1, where $O = N \cup T \cup \{e, t_1, t_2, \$\} \cup H \cup H'$, with t_1, t_2 two semaphore symbols, $H' = \{l'_h | l_h \in H\}$; e is as in Definition 2; $S_0 = \{s_{1,0}\}$, with $s_{1,0} = A$; $w_{E,0} = l_2 \cdots l_m t_1$; B_1 and B_2 contain programs corresponding to the matrix rules, as presented below, and $w_{1,0} = Xee$, $w_{2,0} = eee$, where X and A are the symbols on the right hand side of the rule from the matrix in group 1, $(S \longrightarrow XA)$; and $F = T$. Note that there is only one matrix of type 1.

The rules on the first position of any matrix with label l_h, $2 \leq h \leq m$, are written as $X_h \longrightarrow Y_h$, with $X_h, Y_h \in N_1$, when $1 \leq h \leq k$ and $X_h \longrightarrow \lambda$, with $X_h \in N_1$, when $k + 1 \leq h \leq m$. The rules on the second position have the form $A_h \longrightarrow y_h$, where (i) $y_h = x_{h,1} x_{h,2}$ or (ii) $y_h = x_{h,1}$ or (iii) $y_h = \lambda$ for rules in group 2 ($x_{h,1}, x_{h,2} \in N_2 \cup T$). Group 3 contains rules with their right hand side of type (ii) and $x_{h,1} = \#$; the rules in group 4 have the right hand side of type (ii) or (iii).

The programs of B_1 correspond to the rules on the first position in each of the matrices labelled l_2 to l_m.

For $X_h \longrightarrow Y_h$, with $X_h, Y_h \in N_1$, $2 \le h \le k$, and $X_h \longrightarrow \lambda$, with $X_h \in N_1$, $k+1 \le h \le m$, as above, we have:

$$p_{1,1,h} : \langle X \longrightarrow X; e \longleftrightarrow l_h; e \longleftrightarrow t_1 \rangle, \text{ for any } X \in N_1, \; X_h \longrightarrow Y_h,$$
$$2 \le h \le m, \text{ and } X = X_h,$$
$$p_{1,2,h} : \langle X \longrightarrow l'_h; l_h \longleftrightarrow e; t_1 \longrightarrow t_2 \rangle, \; 2 \le h \le m,$$
$$p_{1,3,h} : \langle l'_h \longleftrightarrow e; e \longrightarrow Y_h; t_2 \longleftrightarrow e \rangle, \; 2 \le h \le k,$$
$$p_{1,4,h} : \langle l'_h \longleftrightarrow e; e \longrightarrow \$; t_2 \longleftrightarrow e \rangle, \; k+1 \le h \le m.$$

One can observe that B_1 agent contains only non-string programs.

The programs of B_2 correspond to the rules on the second position in each of the matrices in groups 2 to 4, i.e., $A_h \longrightarrow y_h$ – see the presentation before starting the description of the rules of B_1.

For each rule $A_h \longrightarrow y_h$, $2 \le h \le m$, as above, we have:

$$p_{2,1} : \langle e \longrightarrow e; e \longleftrightarrow t_2; e \longleftrightarrow l'_h \rangle.$$

For a rule $A_h \longrightarrow x_{h,1} x_{h,2}$, $2 \le h \le m$, from group 2, the following programs are defined:

$$p_{2,2,h} : \langle e \longrightarrow x_{h,1}; t_2 \longrightarrow x_{h,2}; l'_h \longrightarrow l'_h \rangle,$$
$$p_{2,3,h} : \langle [x_{h,1} x_{h,2}] \longleftrightarrow^S A_h; l'_h \longrightarrow l'_h e \rangle.$$

For a rule $A_h \longrightarrow x_{h,1}$, $2 \le h \le m$, from groups 2 or 4, we have:

$$p_{2,4,h} : \langle e \longrightarrow x_{h,1}; t_2 \longrightarrow e; l'_h \longrightarrow l'_h \rangle,$$
$$p_{2,5,h} : \langle x_{h,1} \longleftrightarrow^S A_h; e \longrightarrow e; l'_h \longrightarrow l'_h \rangle.$$

For a rule $A_h \longrightarrow \lambda$, $2 \le h \le m$, from group 2, we have:

$$p_{2,6,h} : \langle \lambda \longleftrightarrow^S A_h; et_2 \longrightarrow e; l'_h \longrightarrow l'_h \rangle.$$

For a rule with appearance checking $A_h \longrightarrow \#$, $2 \le h \le m$, from group 3, we have:

$$p_{2,7,h} : \langle e \longrightarrow \#; t_2 \longrightarrow e; l'_h \longrightarrow l'_h \rangle,$$
$$p_{2,8,h} : \langle \# \longleftrightarrow^S A_h \; / \; \# \longrightarrow e; e \longrightarrow t_1; l'_h \longrightarrow l'_h \rangle,$$
$$p_{2,9,h} : \langle A_h \longrightarrow A_h; t_1 \longrightarrow t_1; l'_h \longrightarrow l'_h \rangle.$$

The rule $p_{2,8,h}$ is a checking rule. It requires that $\# \longleftrightarrow^S A_h$ is always executed when A_h is in the current string; otherwise, $\# \longrightarrow e$ is executed.

For any rule $A_h \longrightarrow y_h$, $2 \le h \le m$, as above, we have:

$$p_{2,10,h} : \langle A_h \longrightarrow e; e \longrightarrow t_1; l'_h \longrightarrow l'_h \rangle,$$
$$p_{2,11,h} : \langle e \longrightarrow e; t_1 \longleftrightarrow e; l'_h \longrightarrow e \rangle, \; 2 \le h \le k,$$
$$p_{2,12,h} : \langle e \longrightarrow e; t_1 \longrightarrow e; l'_h \longrightarrow e \rangle, \; k+1 \le h \le m.$$

The set of programs of B_2 includes string programs ($p_{2,3,h}$, $p_{2,5,h}$, $p_{2,6,h}$, $p_{2,8,h}$; $2 \le h \le m$). The rest are non-string programs.

The initial configuration is $(s_{1,0}; w_{E,0}; w_{1,0}, w_{2,0}) = (A; l_2 \cdots l_m t_1; Xee, eee)$. After applying the first matrix in G one gets XA. In Π, A is the initial string, $s_{1,0}$, and X is an object of $w_{1,0}$.

If in G the current sentential form is $XxDy$, $X \in N_1$, $x, y \in (T \cup N_2)^*$, $D \in N_2$ and the matrix with label l_h is $(X_h \longrightarrow Y_h, A_h \longrightarrow y_h)$, $2 \leq h \leq m$, where $X_h = X$ and $A_h = D$ is applied to $XxDy$, it yields $Y_h xy_h y$.

The computation in Π, corresponding to the above derivation step in G, starts in B_1 from the configuration $c_0 = (u; w_e; w_1, w_2)$, where $u = xDy$, w_e contains all the labels l_h, $2 \leq h \leq m$, and t_1, $w_1 = Xee$ and $w_2 = eee$, having the following transitions simulating the rule on the first position of the matrix with label l_h, $X_h \longrightarrow Y_h$, where $X_h = X$:

$c_0 = (xDy; l_2 \cdots l_m t_1; Xee, eee) \Longrightarrow^{p_{1,1,h}}$
$c_1 = (xDy; l_2 \cdots l_{h-1} l_{h+1} \cdots l_m; X l_h t_1, eee) \Longrightarrow^{p_{1,2,h}}$
$c_2 = (xDy; l_2 \cdots l_{h-1} l_h l_{h+1} \cdots l_m; l'_h et_2, eee)$.

Then $p_{1,3,h}$, $2 \leq h \leq k$, is applied and one gets:

$c_3 = (xDy; l_2 \cdots l_{h-1} l_h l'_h l_{h+1} \cdots l_k \cdots l_m t_2; eY_h e, eee)$.

If $p_{1,4,h}$, $k < h \leq m$, is applied, then one gets:

$c'_3 = (xDy; l_2 \cdots l_{k+1} \cdots l_{h-1} l_h l'_h l_{h+1} \cdots l_m t_2; e\$e, eee)$.

One can observe that the programs applied interact only with the components 2 and 3 of the configurations, corresponding to the environment multiset and the multiset representing the contents of B_1, respectively.

The first program, $p_{1,1,h}$, can be executed as the environment contains the semaphore object t_1 which is brought into the agent; also, the label of a matrix, l_h, with the rule on the first position having the left hand side X_h, such that $X = X_h$, is brought into B_1. The rule $p_{1,2,h}$ applied to $X l_h t_1$ yields $l'_h et_2$ and the object l_h is returned back to the environment. When either of the rules $p_{1,3,h}$ or $p_{1,4,h}$ is executed the objects t_2, l'_h are sent to the environment. The semaphore object t_2 indicates that B_2 can start a computation and l'_h points to the rule on the second position of the matrix of label l_h to be executed. In the case of using $p_{1,3,h}$ the object Y_h, the right hand side of the rule $X_h \longrightarrow Y_h$, is used in B_1 for the next iteration. If $p_{1,4,h}$ is executed, then the object $\$$ indicates that there is no continuation in B_1.

Now, the computation continues, from the last configuration c_3, by executing programs in B_2, and B_1 programs wait until t_1 is released back to the environment. The programs executed in B_2 simulate the rule on the second position in the matrix with label l_h, $2 \leq h \leq m$, i.e., $A_h \longrightarrow y_h$ and $D = A_h$.

First, we consider starting with configuration c_3, when $2 \leq h \leq k$. The rule $p_{2,1,h}$ can be applied, and we get:

$c_3 = (xA_h y; l_2 \cdots l_h l'_h \cdots l_k \cdots l_m t_2; eY_h e, eee) \Longrightarrow^{p_{2,1,h}}$
$c_4 = (xA_h y; l_2 \cdots l_h \cdots l_m; eY_h e, et_2 l'_h)$.

Now, there are different options depending on the type of rule $A_h \longrightarrow y_h$:

(i) when $y_h = x_{h,1} x_{h,2}$, then the rules $p_{2,2,h}$ and $p_{2,3,h}$ are applied and the following transitions are obtained:

$c_4 = (xA_h y; l_2 \cdots l_h \cdots l_m; eY_h e, et_2 l'_h) \Longrightarrow^{p_{2,2,h}}$
$c_5 = (xA_h y; l_2 \cdots l_h \cdots l_m; eY_h e, x_{h,1} x_{h,2} l'_h) \Longrightarrow^{p_{2,3,h}}$
$c_6 = (xy_h y; l_2 \cdots l_h \cdots l_m; eY_h e, A_h el'_h)$, where $y_h = x_{h,1} x_{h,2}$;

(ii) when $y_h = x_{h,1}$, then the rules $p_{2,4,h}$ and $p_{2,5,h}$ are applied and one gets:

$c_4 = (xA_h y; l_2 \cdots l_h \cdots l_m; eY_h e, et_2 l'_h) \Longrightarrow^{p_{2,4,y}}$

$c_5 = (xA_h y; l_2 \cdots l_h \cdots l_m; eY_h e, x_{h,1} el'_h) \Longrightarrow^{p_{2,5,y}}$

$c_6 = (xy_h y; l_2 \cdots l_h \cdots l_m; eY_h e, A_h el'_h)$, where $y_h = x_{h,1}$;

(iii) when $y_h = \lambda$, then the rule $p_{2,6,h}$ applied:

$c_4 = (xA_h y; l_2 \cdots l_h \cdots l_m; eY_h e, et_2 l'_h) \Longrightarrow^{p_{2,6,y}}$

$c_5 = (xy_h y; l_2 \cdots l_h \cdots l_m; eY_h e, A_h el'_h)$, where $y_h = \lambda$;

(iv.1) when a rule with appearance checking $A_h \longrightarrow \#$ is used then the rules $p_{2,7,h}$ $p_{2,8,h}$ and $p_{2,9,h}$ are applied:

$c_4 = (xDy; l_2 \cdots l_h \cdots l_m; eY_h e, et_2 l'_h) \Longrightarrow^{p_{2,7,h}}$

$c_5 = (xDy; l_2 \cdots l_h \cdots l_m; eY_h e, \# el'_h) \Longrightarrow^{p_{2,8,h}}$

$c_6 = (x\#ey; l_2 \cdots l_h \cdots l_m; eY_h e, A_h t_1 l'_h) \Longrightarrow^{p_{2,9,h}}$

$c_6 = (x\#ey; l_2 \cdots l_h \cdots l_m; eY_h e, A_h t_1 l'_h) \Longrightarrow^{p_{2,9,h}} \cdots.$

In this case, when $p_{2,8,h}$ is executed A_h is in the current string, i.e. $D = A_h$, and this leads to an infinite computation (as $p_{2,9,h}$ can be applied repeatedly many a times), the configuration c_6 being obtained.

(iv.2) when A_h is not present, i.e., there is no A_h in xDy, then only the first two rules are applied, i.e., $p_{2,7,h}$ and $p_{2,8,h}$:

$c_4 = (xDy; l_2 \cdots l_h \cdots l_m; eY_h e, et_2 l'_h) \Longrightarrow^{p_{2,7,h}}$

$c_5 = (xDy; l_2 \cdots l_h \cdots l_m; eY_h e, \# el'_h) \Longrightarrow^{p_{2,8,h}}$

$c_6 = (xDy; l_2 \cdots l_h \cdots l_m; eY_h e, et_1 l'_h).$

The configurations c_6, in cases (i) and (ii) and c_5, in case (iii) have the same multiset on the fourth position and one denotes them with $c_{5,6}$. In this configuration one can apply $p_{2,10,h}$:

$c_{5,6} = (xy_h y; l_2 \cdots l_h \cdots l_m; eY_h e, A_h el'_h) \Longrightarrow^{p_{2,10,h}}$

$c_7 = (xy_h y; l_2 \cdots l_h \cdots l_m; eY_h e, et_1 l'_h) \Longrightarrow^{p_{2,11,h}}$

$c_8 = (xy_h y; l_2 \cdots l_h \cdots l_m t_1; eY_h e, eee).$

In (iv.2), the last configuration is c_6 and its fourth component is the same with the fourth component of c_7 above. Then in (iv.2) one can continue with the rule $p_{2,11,h}$. In the final configuration, c_8, we obtain the result of the simulation of the rule on the second position of l_h. In the environment is released t_1 and a new iteration can start by resuming the computation from B_1.

One can observe that the programs applied interact only with the components 1, 2 and 3 of the configurations, corresponding to the string, environment multiset and the multiset from B_2, respectively.

Now, we consider the case when the computation in B_2 starts with configuration $c'_3 = (xDy; l_2 \cdots l_{k+1} \cdots l_{h-1} l_h l'_h l_{h+1} \cdots l_m t_2; e\$e, eee)$, when we simulate the execution of the rule on the second position of a matrix with label l_h from group 4, $(X_h \longrightarrow \lambda, A_h \longrightarrow u_h)$, $X_h \in N_1$, $A_h \in N_2$, $u_h \in T \cup \{\lambda\}$, where $D = A_h$, $k + 1 \leq h \leq m$.

In this configuration the computation stops in B_1 and starts in B_2. The program $p_{2,1,h}$ is executed, getting $(xA_h y; l_2 \cdots l_m; e\$e, et_2 l'_h)$; if $u \in T$, then $p_{2,4,h}$ and $p_{2,5,h}$ are executed and the configuration $(xuy; l_2 \cdots l_m; e\$e, Ael'_h)$ is obtained. When $u = \lambda$, one gets the same configuration by using the program $p_{2,6,h}$. Finally, by using $p_{2,10,h}$ and $p_{2,12,h}$, the final configuration is obtained, $(xuy; l_2 \cdots l_m; e\$e, eee)$. The string obtained in the last step of the derivation in G is the string of the final configuration in Π.

The above computation satisfies both maximally parallel and sequential modes.

4   Chain Code Picture Language Generated with PCol-S

A special class of 2D shapes, composed of only vertical and horizontal lines, can be described by strings, if properly codified. Such a codification was introduced by Maurer in [12], and uses the alphabet $V = \{u, d, r, l\}$, called the *chain code* alphabet. Its four letters stand for a unit line in the corresponding direction in a 2D space, respectively *up, down, right, left*. Alternatively, it can codify the movements of a writing head on the 2D grid (lattice), from a current position to one of its four neighbours. Families of such pictures, seen as languages, have made the object of numerous studies, like [6] and [8], devoted to finding alternative generative devices for chain code picture languages. P systems with parallel rewriting [2], alphabetic flat splicing P systems [13] and three classes of modified alphabetic splicing P systems [1] were proposed for their generation. Here we propose to generate such a language, the *double stairs*, with PCol-s models. The *double stairs* language $L = \{(ur)^n (rd)^n \mid n \geq 1\}$ is a context-free language. Two PCol-s devices computing L are given below. The first PCol-s uses only one agent (Fig. 1).

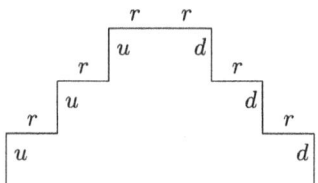

Fig. 1. A chain code picture of two "stairs" of equal height, represented by the chain code word $(ur)^3 (rd)^3$

Example 3. Let $\Pi_1 = (O, e, S_0, w_{E,0}, B_1, F)$ of capacity 2, with 1 agent and size 1, where $O = \{e, A, B, X, u, r, d\}$, $S_0 = \{B\}$, $w_{E,0} = \lambda$, $B_1 = (w_{1,0}, P_1)$, $F = \{u, r, d\}$; $w_{1,0} = uA$ and P_1 consists of the following programs:

$$p_1 : \langle [uA] \longleftrightarrow^S B; \lambda \longleftrightarrow e \rangle,$$
$$p_2 : \langle B \longrightarrow B; e \longrightarrow d \rangle,$$
$$p_3 : \langle [Bd] \longleftrightarrow^S A; \lambda \longleftrightarrow e \rangle,$$
$$p_4 : \langle e \longrightarrow r; A \longrightarrow X \rangle,$$
$$p_5 : \langle [rX] \longleftrightarrow^S B; \lambda \longleftrightarrow e \rangle,$$
$$p_6 : \langle B \longrightarrow B; e \longrightarrow r \rangle,$$
$$p_7 : \langle [Br] \longleftrightarrow^S X; \lambda \longleftrightarrow e \rangle,$$
$$p_8 : \langle e \longrightarrow u; X \longrightarrow A \rangle,$$
$$p_9 : \langle \lambda \longleftrightarrow^S B; uA \longrightarrow r \rangle.$$

The initial configuration is $c_0 = (B; \lambda; uA)$. A computation which is a sequence of transitions is the following:

$c_0 = (B; \lambda; uA) \Longrightarrow^{p_1} c_1 = (uA; \lambda; Be) \Longrightarrow^{p_2} c_2 = (uA; \lambda; Bd) \Longrightarrow^{p_3}$
$c_3 = (uBd; \lambda; Ae) \Longrightarrow^{p_4} c_4 = (uBd; \lambda; rX) \Longrightarrow^{p_5} c_5 = (urXd; \lambda; Be) \Longrightarrow^{p_6}$
$c_6 = (urXd; \lambda; Br) \Longrightarrow^{p_7} c_7 = (urBrd; \lambda; Xe) \Longrightarrow^{p_8} c_8 = (urBrd; \lambda; uA)$.

We have in c_8, as in configuration c_0, B in the string and the same objects in the agent B_1, u, A. Hence, this sequence of transitions can be repeated $n \geq 1$ times and we get the configuration $c_8 = ((ur)^n B(rd)^n; \lambda; Aa)$. If p_9 is applied, then it will remove B from the string and in B_1 we get Br resulting in the configuration $((ur)^n (rd)^n; \lambda; Br)$. The computation stops, as no program can be used in this configuration, and the result produced, $(ur)^n (rd)^n$, is a string over the set of final objects, F.

The above computation satisfies both maximally parallel and sequential modes.

The second PCol-s uses two agents computing each string $(ur)^n (rd)^n$ as follows: one agent is computes $(ur)^n$, the other one $(rd)^n$ and they work in parallel.

Example 4. Let $\Pi_1 = (O, e, S_0, w_{E,0}, B_1, B_2, F)$ of capacity 2, with 2 agents and size 1, where $O = \{e, A, B, C, D, u, r, d\}$, $S_0 = \{BD\}$, $w_{E,0} = \lambda$, $B_1 = (w_{1,0}, P_1)$, $B_2 = (w_{2,0}, P_2)$, $F = \{u, r, d\}$; $w_{1,0} = uA$, $w_{2,0} = Cd$ and P_1 consists of the programs $p_{1,i}, 1 \leq i \leq 5$:

$$p_{1,1} : \langle \lambda \longleftrightarrow e; [uA] \longleftrightarrow^S B \rangle,$$
$$p_{1,2} : \langle e \longrightarrow r; B \longrightarrow B \rangle,$$
$$p_{1,3} : \langle \lambda \longleftrightarrow e; [rB] \longleftrightarrow^S A \rangle,$$
$$p_{1,4} : \langle e \longrightarrow u; A \longrightarrow A \rangle,$$
$$p_{1,5} : \langle \lambda \longleftrightarrow^S BD; uA \longleftrightarrow \lambda \rangle,$$

P_2 consists of the programs $p_{2,i}, 1 \leq i \leq 4$:

$$p_{2,1} : \langle [Cd] \longleftrightarrow^S D; \lambda \longleftrightarrow e \rangle,$$
$$p_{2,2} : \langle D \longrightarrow D; e \longrightarrow r \rangle,$$
$$p_{2,3} : \langle [Dr] \longleftrightarrow^S C; \lambda \longleftrightarrow e \rangle,$$
$$p_{2,4} : \langle C \longrightarrow C; e \longrightarrow d \rangle.$$

The system Π_2 works similarly to Π_1 using maximally parallel mode with the agents B_1 and B_2 applying on the first and second halves of the string, the programs $p_{1,i}$, $1 \leq i \leq 4$, and $p_{2,i}$, $1 \leq i \leq 4$, respectively, in parallel. Finally, the program $p_{1,5}$ will stop the computation. It can be seen that the language generated by Π_2 is the same as the language generated by Π_1.

The solutions provided here based on PCol-s models use a number of agents which is less than or equal to the number of membranes of the models from [1,2,13]. The number of programs and the number of steps is higher for PCol-s than in the other cases, but this is explained by the constraints imposed on the limited capacity of the agents. One can improve the values of these two parameters, even when only one agent is used, by increasing the capacity.

5   Generating 2D Shapes with PCol-2d

Several types of array systems have been considered in the framework of formal language theory and membrane computing for generating two-dimensional (2D) array languages consisting of picture arrays, rectangular or non-rectangular [3, 9,17]. We now illustrate with an example how the PCol-s can be used with an array replacing its string component to generate a 2D array language. Some notions related to arrays are recalled here [3].

Given an alphabet V, a *horizontal* word w (or simply a word) is of the form $w = a_1 a_2 \cdots a_n, (n \geq 1)$ with $a_i \in V$ for $i = 1, \cdots, n$. A *vertical* word $t(w)$ is the transpose of the word w, as above, and is given as follows:

$$t(w) = \begin{matrix} a_1 \\ a_2 \\ \vdots \\ a_n \end{matrix} .$$

A 2D array consists of finitely many symbols from a given alphabet V, placed in the points of the 2D plane. The points not containing symbols of V are assumed to be empty indicated by the blank symbol #. An array is given by specifying the pixels of non-blank points, along with their associated symbols from V. We will exhibit pictorially a 2D finite array indicating their non-blank pixels and only the relative positions of non-blank pixels in the array are taken into account. For example, an L-shaped array with equal arms over a symbol a is formally described by a set of points in the plane as follows: $\{((0,0), a), ((1,0), a), ((2,0), a), ((3,0), a), (4,0), a), (((0,1), a), ((0,2), a), ((0,3), a), ((0,4), a)\}$. Figure 2 shows a pictorial form of this array.

$$\begin{matrix} a \\ a \\ a \\ a \\ a\ a\ a\ a\ a \end{matrix}$$

Fig. 2. L-shaped array with equal arms over a symbol a

Consider the following 2D array language

$$L = \{A \mid A \text{ is an L-shaped array with equal arms over an alphabet } V = \{a\}\}.$$

We consider a modified PCol-s, called a 2D string PCol (PCol-2d), with two kinds of string rules: a horizontal string rule of the form $[x] \longleftrightarrow^{S_h} y$ and a vertical string rule of the form $[t(x)] \longleftrightarrow^{S_v} t(y)$. As in the case of a string rule, a horizontal string rule replaces a substring y in a horizontal word in an array by $[x]$. Likewise a vertical string rule replaces a substring $t(y)$ in a vertical word in an array by $[t(x)]$. The following modified PCol-2d computes L.

Let $\Pi_2 = (O, e, S_0, w_{E,0}, B_1, F)$ of capacity 2, with 1 agent and array size 1, where $O = \{e, A, B, C, D, a\}$, $S_0 = \{ \begin{smallmatrix} A \\ a \ B \end{smallmatrix} \}$, $w_{E,0} = \lambda$, $B = (w_0, P)$, $F = \{a\}$; $w_0 = t(aC)$.

P consists of the programs $p_i, 1 \le i \le 10$:

$$p_1 : \langle \lambda \longleftrightarrow e; [t(Ca)] \longleftrightarrow^{S_v} A \rangle,$$
$$p_2 : \langle e \longrightarrow a; A \longrightarrow D \rangle,$$
$$p_3 : \langle [aD] \longleftrightarrow^{S_h} B; \lambda \longleftrightarrow e \rangle,$$
$$p_4 : \langle e \longrightarrow a; B \longrightarrow A \rangle,$$
$$p_5 : \langle [t(Aa)] \longleftrightarrow^{S_v} C; \lambda \longleftrightarrow e \rangle,$$
$$p_6 : \langle e \longrightarrow a; C \longrightarrow B \rangle,$$
$$p_7 : \langle [aB] \longleftrightarrow^{S_h} D; \lambda \longleftrightarrow e \rangle,$$
$$p_8 : \langle e \longrightarrow a; D \longrightarrow C \rangle,$$
$$p_9 : \langle \lambda \longleftrightarrow^{S_v} A; Ca \longrightarrow B \rangle,$$
$$p_{10} : \langle \lambda \longleftrightarrow^{S_h} B; AB \longrightarrow A \rangle.$$

The initial configuration is $c_0 = \left(\begin{smallmatrix} A \\ a \ B \end{smallmatrix} ; \lambda; Ca \right)$. A computation which is a sequence of transitions is the following:

$$c_0 = \left(\begin{smallmatrix} A \\ a \ B \end{smallmatrix} ; \lambda; Ca \right) \Longrightarrow^{p_1} c_1 = \left(\begin{smallmatrix} C \\ a \\ a \ B \end{smallmatrix} ; \lambda; eA \right) \Longrightarrow^{p_2}$$

$$c_2 = \left(\begin{smallmatrix} C \\ a \\ a \ B \end{smallmatrix} ; \lambda; aD \right) \Longrightarrow^{p_3} c_3 = \left(\begin{smallmatrix} C \\ a \\ a \ a \ D \end{smallmatrix} ; \lambda; eB \right) \Longrightarrow^{p_4}$$

$$c_4 = \left(\begin{smallmatrix} C \\ u \\ a \ a \ D \end{smallmatrix} , \lambda; uA \right) \Longrightarrow^{p_5} c_5 = \left(\begin{smallmatrix} A \\ a \\ a \\ a \ a \ D \end{smallmatrix} ; \lambda; eC \right) \Longrightarrow^{p_6}$$

$$c_6 = \left(\begin{smallmatrix} A \\ a \\ a \\ a \ a \ D \end{smallmatrix} ; \lambda; aB \right) \Longrightarrow^{p_7} c_7 = \left(\begin{smallmatrix} A \\ a \\ a \\ a \ a \ a \ B \end{smallmatrix} ; \lambda; eD \right) \Longrightarrow^{p_8}$$

$$c_8 = \left(\begin{smallmatrix} A \\ a \\ a \\ a \ a \ a \ B \end{smallmatrix} ; \lambda; aC \right).$$

As in the configuration c_0, we have in c_8, A and B in the array and the same objects in the agent B_1. Hence, this sequence of transitions can be repeated $n \ge 1$ times. If p_9 is applied, then it will remove A from the array and in B_1 we get AB. This can be followed by applying p_{10} which will remove B from the array and in B_1 we get BA. The computation stops, as no program can be used in this configuration, and the result produced is an L shaped array over $F = \{a\}$.

6 Conclusions and Further Work

In this paper we have introduced a new P colony model, denoted PCol-s, able to generate strings. Examples are provided to understand the working of the model. A proof has been given that the model is able to compute the family of recursively enumerable languages. We have illustrated its functioning by generating a chain code language and a 2D shape.

The proof that PCol-s are able to generate RE could be revisited using Kuroda and/or Geffert normal forms for type-0 grammars, in order to see if the resources used (capacity, number of agents, types of programs) in the model can be minimized or simplified.

Developing the present work towards generating chain code languages for more complex 2D structures, as well as studying various 2D languages with this formalism represent other potential research avenues to be investigated in the future.

Acknowledgement. The authors would like to thank the anonymous reviewers for their very useful and constructive comments that helped improving the paper. MG's and LK's work has been partially supported by the Royal Society grant IES\R3\213176, 2022-2024.

References

1. Ceterchi, R., Gheorghe, M., Kuppusamy, L., Subramanian, K.G.: Three classes of alphabetic flat splicing P systems. J. Membr. Comput. (accepted)
2. Ceterchi, R., Subramanian, K.G., Venkat, I.: P systems with parallel rewriting for chain code picture languages. In: Beckmann, A., Mitrana, V., Soskova, M. (eds.) CiE 2015. LNCS, vol. 9136, pp. 145–155. Springer, Cham (2015). https://doi.org/10.1007/978-3-319-20028-6_15
3. Ceterchi, R., Mutyam, M., Păun, G., Subramanian, K.G.: Array-rewriting P systems. Natural Comput. **2**, 229–249 (2003). https://doi.org/10.1023/A:1025497107681
4. Cienciala, L., Ciencialová, L., Csuhaj-Varjú, E., Vaszil, Gy.: PCol automata: recognizing strings with P colonies. In: 8th Brainstorming Week on Membrane Computing, pp. 65–76 (2010)
5. Ciencialová, L., Csuhaj-Varjú, E., Cienciala, L., Sosík, P.: P colonies - survey. J. Membr. Comput. **1**, 178–197 (2019)
6. Dassow, J., Habel, A., Taubenberger, S.: Chain-code pictures and collages generated by hyperedge replacement. In: Cuny, J., et al. (ed.) Graph Grammars 1994. LNCS, vol. 1073, pp. 412–427. Springer (1994)
7. Dassow, J., Păun, Gh.: Regulated Rewriting in Formal Language Theory. Springer, Berlin (1989)
8. Drewes, F.: Some remarks on the generative power of collage grammars and chain-code grammars. In: Ehrig, H., Engels, G., Kreowski, H.J., Rozenberg, G. (eds.) Theory and Application of Graph Transformations, pp. 1–14. Springer, Heidelberg (2000)

9. Giammarresi, D., Restivo, A.: Two-dimensional languages. In: Rozenberg, G., Salomaa, A. (eds.) Handbook of Formal Languages (Vol. 3): Beyond Words, pp. 215–267. Springer, Heidelberg (1997)
10. Kelemen, J., Kelemenová, A.: A grammar-theoretic treatment of multiagent systems. Cybern. Syst. **23**, 621–633 (1992)
11. Kelemen, J., Kelemenová, A., Păun, Gh.: Preview of P colonies: a biochemically inspired computing model. In: Workshop and Tutorial Proceedings. Ninth International Conference on the Simulation and Synthesis of Living Systems (Alife IX), Boston, Massachusetts, pp. 82–86 (2004)
12. Maurer, H.A., Rozenberg, G., Welzl, E.: Using string languages to describe picture languages. Inf. Control **54**, 155–185 (1982)
13. Pan, L., Song, B., Nagar, A., Subramanian, K.G.: Language generating alphabetic flat splicing P systems. Theoret. Comput. Sci. **724**, 28–34 (2018)
14. Păun, Gh.: Computing with membranes. J. Comput. Syst. Sci. **61**(1), 108–143 (2000). https://doi.org/10.1006/jcss.1999.1693
15. Păun, Gh., Rozenberg, G., Salomaa, A. (eds.): The Oxford Handbook of Membrane Computing. Oxford University Press (2010)
16. Rozenberg, G., Salomaa, A.: Handbook of Formal Languages (Vol. 1): Word, Language, Grammar. Springer, New York (1997)
17. Subramanian, K.G.: P systems and picture languages. In: Durand-Lose, J., Margenstern, M. (eds.) Machines, Computations, and Universality, pp. 99–109. Springer, Heidelberg (2007)

String Assembling Systems: Origins and Directions

Martin Kutrib$^{(\boxtimes)}$ and Matthias Wendlandt

Institut für Informatik, Universität Giessen, Arndtstr. 2, 35392 Giessen, Germany
{kutrib,matthias.wendlandt}@informatik.uni-giessen.de

Abstract. String assembling systems are biologically inspired mechanisms that generate strings from copies out of a finite set of assembly units. The underlying mechanism is based on piecewise assembly of a double-stranded sequence of symbols, where the upper and lower strand have to match. Since their introduction in 2011, several variants have been studied from various viewpoints. Although string assembling systems are a simple concept, their generative behavior can be already very complex and leads to undecidable problems on these devices such as, for example, emptiness, finiteness, universality, equivalence, etc. Here we tour a fragment of the literature on generative capacities, decidability problems, and other properties of string assembling systems. The capacities of different variants are compared to study the impact of the resources given to the variants. The results discussed obviously lack completeness, as one falls short of exhausting all the details considered in the literature.

Keywords: String Assembling · Double-Stranded Sequences · Stateless · Two-Head Finite Automata · Decidability · Closure Properties

1 Introduction

In 1965 Gordon E. Moore predicted that the number of components per integrated circuit will double every 18 months [17]. Up to now, this forecast – which is also known as *Moore's Law* – has become a reality. Nevertheless, there are many real world problems requiring such a huge computational complexity that they cannot be solved for an appropriate size of the instance in this day and age, and also will not be solvable under the assumption of Moore's Law in a thousand years unless new computing techniques are developed. This motivated the advent of investigations of devices and operations that are inspired by the study of biological processes, and the growing interest in nature-based problems modeled in formal systems. Examples of string generating mechanisms include Lindenmayer systems [24], splicing systems and sticker systems [22]. The latter two types of devices model operations on DNA molecules and are therefore based upon double-stranded strings as the raw material of the string generation process, where corresponding symbols are uniquely related. String assembling

M. D. Jiménez López and G. Vaszil (Eds.): Erzsébet Csuhaj-Varjú Festschrift,
LNCS 15840, pp. 210–237, 2025.
https://doi.org/10.1007/978-3-031-97274-4_13

systems, introduced in [11], are another string generating mechanism based on double strands. The generation process of string assembling systems is basically driven by the mechanisms of the Post Correspondence Problem [23]. So, its old control mechanism of the generation process has been rekindled. In particular, the basic assembly units are pairs of strings that have to be connected to the upper and lower string generated so far synchronously. In comparison to sticker systems, the strings are not connected to each other. This property enables the possibility to increase the length difference between the two strands arbitrarily and, moreover, to compare positions that are arbitrarily far away from each other in a given word. Thus, it is possible to generate non-context-free languages. Apart from the double strand, essentially, derivations in string assembling systems are controlled by the requirement that the first symbol of a string to be assembled has to match the last symbol of the strand generated so far. One can imagine that both symbols are glued together one at the top of the other and, thus, just one appears in the final string. Moreover, as for the notion of strictly locally testable languages [16, 29], we distinguish between assembly units that may appear at the beginning, during, and at the end of the assembling process. The lengths of the strings in the assembly units are finite but are not limited a priori.

In the following, we present and discuss some of the main results on string assembling systems. The capacities of different variants are compared to study the impact of the resources given to the variants. The results discussed obviously lack completeness. Moreover, we do not prove these results but we merely draw attention to the big picture and some of the main ideas involved.

2   Preliminaries and Definitions

We write Σ^* for the set of all words over the finite alphabet Σ. The empty word is denoted by λ, and $\Sigma^+ = \Sigma^* \setminus \{\lambda\}$. The reversal of a word w is denoted by w^R and for the length of w we write $|w|$. For the number of occurrences of a symbol a in w we use the notation $|w|_a$. Generally, for a singleton set $\{a\}$ we simply write a. We use $\subseteq$ for inclusions and $\subset$ for strict inclusions. In order to avoid technical overloading in writing, two languages L and L' are considered to be equal, if they differ at most by the empty word, that is, $L - \{\lambda\} = L' - \{\lambda\}$.

We start with a general definition and derive the restricted variants from this. A *bidirectional string assembling system* generates the double-stranded strings by assembling substrings to the upper and lower strand at both ends, so that both strands match. Moreover, a substring can only be assembled to the right when its first symbol matches the last symbol of the strand, and to the left when its last symbol matches the first symbol of the strand. In these cases the matching symbols are glued together one at the top of the other. The substrings to be assembled are given by so-called units. In *nonterminal controlled string assembling systems*, auxiliary symbols may appear at the ends of the strings of a unit which are replaced by associated ordinary symbols whenever an assembly unit is attached to them. The generation has to begin with a unit from the set of initial units. Then it may continue with units from different sets, and when a unit from the set of ending units is applied, the assembling process in the corresponding direction stops. During the assembling process, the overlapping part of the upper and lower strand must always be identical. When the process stops, nonterminals possibly appearing at the ends are replaced with their associated ordinary symbols. Then, the upper and the lower strand must completely coincide.

We denote *(incomplete) matching double strands* by sixtuples. More precisely, let Σ denote the set of symbols, Γ denote the disjoint set of auxiliary symbols, and $\sigma : \Sigma \cup \Gamma \to \Sigma$ be a letter-to-letter homomorphism that is the identity on Σ. Then $(v_1, v_2, u_1, u_2, w_1, w_2)$ is an (incomplete) matching double strand, where $v_1 u_1 w_1, v_2 u_2 w_2 \in (\Gamma \cup \{\lambda\})\Sigma^*(\Gamma \cup \{\lambda\})$ are the upper and the lower strand, $\sigma(u_1) = \sigma(u_2)$ is non-empty, at least one of v_1 and v_2 is empty and at least one of w_1 and w_2 is empty. It is understood that u_1, u_2 is the part where upper and the lower strand match, v_1 (v_2) denotes the part of the upper (lower) strand sticking out to the left, and w_1 (w_2) denotes the part of the upper (lower) strand sticking out to the right (see Fig. 1).

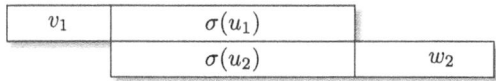

Fig. 1. Example of an incomplete matching double strand ($v_2 = w_1 = \lambda$).

The set of all (incomplete) matching double strands over alphabet Σ with nonterminals from Γ and homomorphism σ is denoted by $\Sigma_{\Gamma,\sigma}^{\rightleftarrows}$.

A *bidirectional nonterminal controlled string assembling system* (2NSAS) is a system $S = \langle \Sigma, \Gamma, \sigma, A, T_l, T_r, E_l, E_r \rangle$, where Σ is the finite, nonempty set of *symbols* or *letters*, Γ is the finite set of *auxiliary symbols* or *nonterminals*, $\Gamma \cap \Sigma = \emptyset$, $\sigma : \Sigma \cup \Gamma \to \Sigma$ is a letter-to-letter homomorphism such that $\sigma(x) = x$, for all $x \in \Sigma$, $A \subset \Sigma_{\Gamma,\sigma}^{\rightleftarrows}$ is the finite set of *axioms*, $T_l, T_r \subset (\Gamma \cup \{\lambda\})\Sigma^*(\Gamma \cup \{\lambda\}) \times (\Gamma \cup \{\lambda\})\Sigma^*(\Gamma \cup \{\lambda\})$ are the finite sets of *left and right assembly units*, where each unit is a pair of two non-empty strings, $E_l \subset \Sigma^*(\Gamma \cup \{\lambda\}) \times \Sigma^*(\Gamma \cup \{\lambda\})$ is the finite set of *left ending assembly units* of the forms $(u_1 v, u_2)$ or $(u_1, u_2 v)$, where $\sigma(u_1) = \sigma(u_2)$ are non-empty, and $E_r \subset (\Gamma \cup \{\lambda\})\Sigma^* \times (\Gamma \cup \{\lambda\})\Sigma^*$ is the finite set of *right ending assembly units* of the forms $(v u_1, u_2)$ or $(u_1, v u_2)$, where $\sigma(u_1) = \sigma(u_2)$ are non-empty.

The next definition formally says how the units are assembled (see Fig. 2). In order to keep the presentation simpler, we use the transformation $\sigma_{rl} \colon (\Sigma \cup \Gamma)^* \to (\Gamma \cup \{\lambda\})\Sigma^*(\Gamma \cup \{\lambda\})$ where a word $a_1 a_2 \cdots a_{n-1} a_n$ is mapped to $a_1 \sigma(a_2 \cdots a_{n-1}) a_n$, that is, possible nonterminals at both ends are unchanged while other nonterminals are replaced by their associated ordinary symbols. Similarly, σ_l (σ_r) are transformations that do not change the possible nonterminal at the left (right) end, but all the other ones.

The *derivation relation* $\Rightarrow$ is defined on $\Sigma^{\rightleftharpoons}_{\Gamma,\sigma}$ by

1. $(v_1, v_2, u_1, u_2, w_1, w_2) \Rightarrow (v_1, v_2, u'_1, u'_2, w'_1, w'_2)$ if

   (a) $u_1 w_1 = t\alpha$, $u_2 w_2 = s\beta$, and $(\alpha x, \beta y) \in T_r \cup E_r$, for $\alpha, \beta \in \Sigma \cup \Gamma$, $s, t \in \Sigma^*$, and

   (b) $\sigma(u_1 w_1 x) = \sigma(u_2 w_2 y)$, $u'_1 = \sigma_{rl}(u_1 w_1 x)$, $u'_2 = \sigma_{rl}(u_2 w_2 y)$, $w'_1 = w'_2 = \lambda$, or $\sigma(u_1 w_1 x) = \sigma(u_2 w_2 yz)$, $z \neq \lambda$, $u'_1 = \sigma_l(u_1 w_2 y)$, $w'_1 = \sigma_r(z)$, $u'_2 = \sigma_{rl}(u_2 w_2 y)$, $w'_2 = \lambda$, or $\sigma(u_2 w_2 y) = \sigma(u_1 w_1 xz)$, $z \neq \lambda$, $u'_1 = \sigma_{rl}(u_1 w_1 x)$, $w'_1 = \lambda$, $u'_2 = \sigma_l(u_2 w_1 x)$, $w'_2 = \sigma_r(z)$.

2. $(v_1, v_2, u_1, u_2, w_1, w_2) \Rightarrow (v'_1, v'_2, u'_1, u'_2, w_1, w_2)$ if

   (a) $v_1 u_1 = \alpha t$, $v_2 u_2 = \beta s$, and $(x\alpha, y\beta) \in T_l \cup E_l$, for $\alpha, \beta \in \Sigma \cup \Gamma$, $s, t \in \Sigma^*$, and

   (b) $\sigma(x v_1 u_1) = \sigma(y v_2 u_2)$, $u'_1 = \sigma_{rl}(x v_1 u_1)$, $u'_2 = \sigma_{rl}(y v_2 u_2)$, $v'_1 = v'_2 = \lambda$, or $\sigma(x v_1 u_1) = \sigma(z y v_2 u_2)$, $z \neq \lambda$, $u'_1 = \sigma_r(y v_2 u_1)$, $v'_1 = \sigma_l(z)$, $u'_2 = \sigma_{rl}(y v_2 u_2)$, $v'_2 = \lambda$, or $\sigma(y v_2 u_2) = \sigma(z x v_1 u_1)$, $z \neq \lambda$, $u'_1 = \sigma_{rl}(x v_1 u_1)$, $v'_1 = \lambda$, $u'_2 = \sigma_r(x v_1 u_2)$, $v'_2 = \sigma_l(z)$.

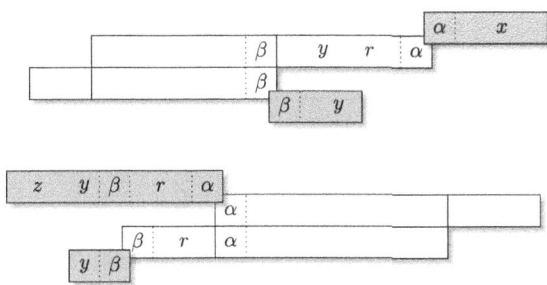

Fig. 2. Examples of assembling a unit $(\alpha x, \beta y)$ at the right (top) and a unit $(zy\beta r\alpha, y\beta)$ at the left (bottom). Possible nonterminals at the ends are depicted as their images under σ.

A derivation is said to be *successful* if it initially starts with an axiom from A, continues with assembling units from T_l and T_r, and ends with having assembled an ending unit from E_l to the left and an ending unit from E_r to the right. The process necessarily stops when both ending units have been added. The sets T_l, T_r, E_l, and E_r are not necessarily disjoint. During the process nonterminals can only appear at the ends of the strands. The generated language consists of the strings appearing both as lower and as upper strand of the double strands derived in successful derivations, where possible nonterminals at the ends are replaced by their associated ordinary symbols.

The *language $L(S)$ generated* by S is defined to be the set

$$L(S) = \{\, w \in \Sigma^+ \mid (v_1, v_2, u_1, u_2, w_1, w_2) \Rightarrow^* (\lambda, \lambda, u'_1, u'_2, \lambda, \lambda)$$
$$\text{with } w = \sigma(u'_1) = \sigma(u'_2) \text{ is a } successful \text{ derivation}\,\}$$

where $\Rightarrow^*$ refers to the reflexive, transitive closure of the derivation relation $\Rightarrow$.

A 2NSAS $\langle \Sigma, \Gamma, \sigma, A, T_l, T_r, E_l, E_r \rangle$ is a *bidirectional string assembling system* (2SAS) if Γ is the empty set and, thus, σ is the identity mapping and can be omitted. In this case, in (incomplete) matching double strands $\sigma(u_1) = \sigma(u_2)$ simply means $u_1 = u_2$. To simplify writing we use the notation (v_1, v_2, u, w_1, w_2) and write $\Sigma^{\rightleftharpoons}$.

A 2NSAS (2SAS) is said to be *unidirectional* (1NSAS, 1SAS) if $T_l = \emptyset$, $E_l = \{ (\alpha, \beta) \mid \alpha, \beta \in \Sigma \cup \Gamma, \sigma(\alpha) = \sigma(\beta) \}$, and all axioms are of the form $(\lambda, \lambda, u_1, u_2, w_1, w_2)$. That is, except for ending units that actually add no symbols, units are only assembled at the right. Now we may write (uw_1, uw_2) for (incomplete) matching double strands in the case of 1SAS. Moreover, we can simplify the notation of systems to $\langle \Sigma, \Gamma, \sigma, A, T, E \rangle$ or $\langle \Sigma, A, T, E \rangle$ when we are dealing with unidirectional generations.

3   Capacities and Properties of 1SAS

We start the tour with the structurally simplest systems, that is, with unidirectional string assembling systems, and then move on to more complex models. The results of this section originate in [11]. Let us first clarify their operation mode with three meaningful examples.

Example 1. The following 1SAS $\langle \{a, b, c\}, A, T, E \rangle$ generates the non-context-free language $\{ a^n b^n c^n \mid n \geq 1 \}$.

$$A = \{(a, a)\}, \quad T = T_a \cup T_b \cup T_c, \quad E = \{(c, c)\}, \text{ where}$$
$$T_a = \{(aa, a), (ab, a)\}, \quad T_b = \{(bb, aa), (bc, ab)\},$$
$$T_c = \{(cc, bb), (c, bc), (c, cc)\}.$$

The units in T_a are used to generate the prefixes $a^n b$. Initially, only the unit (aa, a) is applicable repeatedly. Then only (ab, a) can be used to generate the upper string $a^n b$ and the lower string a. After that the unit (bb, aa) from T_b has to be used exactly as many times as the unit (aa, a) has been applied before. Then an application of unit (bc, ab) is the sole possibility. This generates the upper string $a^n b^n c$ and the lower string $a^n b$. For the last part the units from T_c are used. Similarly as before, repeated applications of (cc, bb) yield to the upper string $a^n b^n c^n$ and the lower string $a^n b^n$. So, it remains to complement the c's in the lower string. This is done by the units (c, bc), which can be applied only once, and (c, cc) which can be applied arbitrarily often. However, the derivation is successful only if the number of c's in the upper and lower string match when the unit from E is applied.

The construction can be extended to an arbitrary number of symbols. Let $k \geq 1$ be a constant and $\Sigma = \{a_1, a_2, \dots, a_k\}$ be an alphabet. Then the language $\{ a_1^n a_2^n \cdots a_k^n \mid n \geq 1 \}$ is generated by an 1SAS.   ∎

The next example uses the same mechanism as the previous one, but extends the substrings generated. The mechanism is to copy parts of the string generated so far by using markers and the matching of the upper and lower strings.

Example 2. Let Σ be an alphabet not containing the symbols $\{\$_1, \$_2, \$_3\}$. The following 1SAS $\langle \Sigma \cup \{\$_1, \$_2, \$_3\}, A, T, E \rangle$ generates the non-context-free language $\{\, \$_1 w \$_2 w \$_3 \mid w \in \Sigma^+ \,\}$.

$$A = \{(\$_1, \$_1)\}, \quad T = T_1 \cup T_2 \cup T_3, \quad E = \{(\$_3, \$_3)\}, \text{ where for } x, y \in \Sigma,$$
$$T_1 = \{(\$_1 x, \$_1), (xy, \$_1), (x \$_2, \$_1)\}, \quad T_2 = \{(\$_2 x, \$_1 x), (xy, xy), (x \$_3, x \$_2)\},$$
$$T_3 = \{(\$_3, \$_2 x), (\$_3, xy), (\$_3, x \$_3)\}.$$

Similar as in Example 1, the units from T_1 are used to generate the upper string $\$_1 w \$_2$ and the lower string $\$_1$. Then units from T_2 are assembled to form the upper string $\$_1 w \$_2 w \$_3$ and the lower string $\$_1 w \$_2$. Finally, one obtains $\$_1 w \$_2 w \$_3$ as upper and lower string by the units in T_3.

The construction can be extended to an arbitrary number of copies of w. Let $k \geq 1$ be a constant and Σ be an alphabet not containing the symbols $\{\$_1, \$_2, \ldots, \$_k\}$. Then the language $\{\, \$_1 w \$_2 w \cdots \$_{k-1} w \$_k \mid w \in \Sigma^+ \,\}$ is generated by an 1SAS. ∎

Now we turn to a basic example where the underlying technique is to utilize the lengths difference between the upper and lower string.

Example 3. Let $k \geq 2$ be a constant. The following 1SAS $\langle \{a, b\}, A, T, E \rangle$ generates the language $\{\, bw \mid w \in \{a, b\}^*, |w|_a \bmod k = 0 \,\}$.

$$A = \{(b, b)\}, \quad E = \{\, (x, x) \mid x \in \{a, b\} \,\},$$
$$T = \{(xa, x), (xb, yz), (a, u), (b, u) \mid x, y, z \in \{a, b\}, u \in \{a, b\}^k \,\}.$$

The idea of the construction is to start with a b and then to add arbitrary symbols to the upper string. Whenever an a is added, the difference between the lengths of the upper and lower string is increased by one, while it remains as it is when a b is added. The only possibility to complement the lower string is to add substrings of length k. Therefore, in any situation, the difference between the lengths modulo k is equal to the number of a's in the upper string modulo k. So, if both strings are identical, they do belong to the language as stated. ∎

3.1 Generative Capacity

In order to explore the generative capacity of 1SAS we start with an upper bound. In particular, it is shown in [11] that any 1SAS can be simulated by some nondeterministic one-way two-head finite automaton. The family of languages accepted by such devices is known to be a proper subfamily of languages accepted by nondeterministic *two-way* two-head finite automata (see [6], for example). From the complexity point of view, the two-way case is well explored. There is a strong relation to the computational complexity class $\mathsf{NL} = \mathsf{NSPACE}(\log n)$. In [5] it has been shown that NL is characterized by the class of nondeterministic two-way multi-head finite automata. So, together with the next theorem, we obtain that the family of languages generated by 1SAS is properly included in NL.

Theorem 4. *Let S be an 1SAS. There exists a nondeterministic one-way two-head finite automaton that accepts $L(S)$.*

The previous theorem and its preceding discussion together with the proper inclusion of NL in $\mathsf{NSPACE}(n)$ (see, for example, [20]), which in turn is equal to the family of context-sensitive languages, reveals the following corollary.

Corollary 5. *The family of languages generated by 1SAS is properly included in NL and, thus, in the family of context-sensitive languages.*

It is well known that nondeterministic one-way two-head finite automata cannot accept the deterministic and linear context-free language $\{\, wcw^R \mid w \in \{a,b\}^* \,\}$. Therefore, combining Theorem 4 and Example 1 yields the following relation to context-free languages.

Lemma 6. *The family of languages generated by 1SAS is incomparable with the family of (deterministic) (linear) context-free languages.*

Knowing this, it is natural to compare the family of languages generated by 1SAS with regular languages, too. To this end, let us consider the regular language $L = \{a\} \cup \{\, a^{2n} \mid n \geq 2 \,\}$ and assume that it is generated by some 1SAS $\langle \{a\}, A, T, E \rangle$. Since $a \in L$, the unit (a, a) must belong to A as well as to E.

Now we define the three sets $T_e = \{\, (a^i, a^i) \in T \mid i \geq 2 \,\}$, $T_u = \{\, (a^i, a^j) \in T \mid i > j \geq 1 \,\}$, and $T_l = \{\, (a^i, a^j) \in T \mid 1 \leq i < j \,\}$.

If T_e is not empty, all its units are of the form (a^{4+2k}, a^{4+2k}), $k \geq 0$. Otherwise, starting with unit $(a, a) \in A$, assembling a unit from T_e not of this form, and ending with unit $(a, a) \in E$ results in a string of length greater than one but not of length a^{4+2k}. But this string does not belong to L. Now, starting with unit $(a, a) \in A$, assembling a fixed unit (a^{4+2k_0}, a^{4+2k_0}) from T_e twice, and ending with unit $(a, a) \in E$ results in the string $a^{4+2k_0+4+2k_0-1}$ of odd length. But the only string in L of odd length is a. So, we conclude that T_e must be empty.

If T_u or T_l is empty in addition, either the lower or the upper string gets longer and longer compared with the other string. In this case only a finite language is generated, which is a contradiction. Therefore, T_u and T_l both are not empty. Fix a unit (a^{i_1}, a^{j_1}) from T_u and a unit (a^{i_2}, a^{j_2}) from T_l. Now, assembling $j_2 - i_2$ units (a^{i_1}, a^{j_1}) and $i_1 - j_1$ units (a^{i_2}, a^{j_2}) extends the upper as well as the lower string by $i_1 j_2 - i_2 j_1 - i_1 - j_2 + i_2 + j_1$ symbols. So, the effect is as assembling a unit $(a^{i_1 j_2 - i_2 j_1 - i_1 - j_2 + i_2 + j_1 + 1}, a^{i_1 j_2 - i_2 j_1 - i_1 - j_2 + i_2 + j_1 + 1})$ from T_e. We conclude that T_u and T_l both have to be empty which is impossible. Therefore, the regular language L is not generated by any 1SAS.

Theorem 7. *The family of languages generated by 1SAS is incomparable with the family of (unary) regular languages.*

Though not all regular languages belong to the family of languages generated by 1SAS, all regular languages can be represented by an 1SAS and a weak homomorphism.

Theorem 8. *Let L be a regular language. There is an 1SAS S and a λ-free letter-to-letter homomorphism h such that $L = h(L(S))$.*

Following the discussion preceding Theorem 4, the simulation of 1SAS by nondeterministic one-way two-head finite automata gives only a rough upper bound for the generative capacity of 1SAS. Interestingly, the stateless version of the two-head finite automaton marks to some extent a lower bound for the generative capacity (cf. [7,27] for results and details of the model). More precisely, up to at most five additional symbols in the words generated, any stateless nondeterministic one-way two-head finite automaton can be simulated by some 1SAS.

Theorem 9. *Let M be a stateless nondeterministic one-way two-head finite automaton with input alphabet Σ, and %, \$, #, ?, ! $\notin \Sigma$. There exists a string assembling system S such that any word generated by S contains each of the symbols %, \$, #, ?, ! at most once, and $h(L(S)) = L(M)$, for the homomorphism $h(\%) = h(\$) = h(\#) = h(?) = h(!) = \lambda$ and $h(a) = a$, for $a \in \Sigma$.*

The underlying idea of the construction of S is to guess and assemble the next symbol to the corresponding strand whenever a head moves to the right. The guesses are subsequently verified by simulating transitions of M. Special care has to be taken for the situation where M accepts. Though it is an open problem whether the additional symbols used in the simulation of the previous proof are necessary, there is a language generated by 1SAS which is not accepted by any stateless nondeterministic one-way two-head finite automaton.

Lemma 10. *The language $\{a^{2n} \mid n \geq 1\}$ is generated by an 1SAS but not accepted by any stateless nondeterministic one-way two-head finite automaton.*

3.2   Decidability Problems

It seems to be an obvious choice to prove the undecidability of several problems for 1SAS by reduction of Post's Correspondence Problem (PCP) (see, for example, [25]). It is known that the PCP is still undecidable, if the length of the words is limited to two [4]. So, it seems that the reduction requires the construction of an 1SAS whose units are at least of length three. Moreover, if the reduction is such that an 1SAS is constructed from a given PCP that generates exactly the strings which are solutions of the PCP, then undecidability of emptiness follows, but what about semidecidability. So, instead of reducing from PCP, reductions from one-sided Turing machine computations are used in [14]. Since it is not even semidecidable whether such Turing machines accept one input at all, emptiness is not semidecidable for 1SAS. In particular, the construction requires only units at most of length two. From the undecidability of emptiness further undecidability results follow.

Theorem 11. *Emptiness, finiteness, infiniteness, equivalence, inclusion, regularity and context-freeness are not semidecidable for 1SAS whose units are two-length-restricted.*

In Subsect. 6.1 below, length restricted 1SAS are considered in more detail. Obviously, 1-length-restricted string assembling systems are not productive and generate finite languages only. In this case the mentioned problems are decidable. So, there is a sharp border between decidability and undecidability.

4   Bidirectional String Assembling Systems

Here we turn to several types of *two-sided or bidirectional* string assembling systems. The results of this section originate in [12]. The control of the generation process is weakened for centralized variants, where units are still assembled at both ends, but all units are centralized into one set, that is, it is not distinguished whether a unit may be assembled at the left or right. A stronger control of the generation process is obtained by synchronizing the assembling of units at both ends. Here we consider systems where units are assembled simultaneously at the right and at the left. The last variant in question are synchronized bidirectional string assembling systems, where the units simultaneously assembled must be related.

Example 12. The 2SAS $S = \langle \{a, b\}, A, T_l, T_r, E_l, E_r \rangle$ generates the deterministic context-free language $\{ a^n b^n \mid n \geq 1 \} \cup a^+$, where

$$A = \{(\lambda, \lambda, a, \lambda, \lambda), (\lambda, \lambda, b, \lambda, \lambda)\},$$
$$T_l = \{(bb, b), (ab, b), (aa, bb), (a, ab), (a, aa)\}, \quad T_r = \{(aa, aa)\},$$
$$E_l = \{(a, a)\}, \quad E_r = \{(b, b), (a, a)\}.$$

The units in T_l are used to generate the words from $\{ a^n b^n \mid n \geq 1 \}$ to the left of the axiom $(\lambda, \lambda, b, \lambda, \lambda)$. The units in T_r are used to generate the words of the form a^+ to the right of the axiom $(\lambda, \lambda, a, \lambda, \lambda)$. Starting with this axiom it is only possible to add units (aa, aa) to the right, and end up at both ends with the units $(a, a) \in E_l$ and $(a, a) \in E_r$. If the unit (a, aa) would be used at the left side, the lower strand gets longer, but cannot be completed in the upper strand. If the axiom containing a b is used, first the suffix ab^n is generated by repeatedly assembling unit (bb, b) followed by one unit (ab, b). After that the unit (aa, bb) has to be assembled exactly as many times as the unit (bb, b) before. Now the only possibility is to add (a, ab) and complete the lower strand with (a, aa). Because the units of T_r cannot be used at the left side, (aa, aa) cannot be added. ∎

Example 13. The 2SAS $S = \langle \{a, b\}, A, T_l, T_r, E_l, E_r \rangle$ generates the deterministic context-free language $\{ a^n b^n a^m \mid n, m \geq 1 \}$, where

$$A = \{(\lambda, \lambda, ba, \lambda, \lambda)\},$$
$$T_l = \{(bb, b), (ab, b), (aa, bb), (a, ab), (a, aa)\}, \quad T_r = \{(aa, aa)\},$$
$$E_l = \{(a, a)\}, \quad E_r = \{(a, a)\}.$$

Here, basically, the same mechanism as in the previous example is used. The main difference is that a derivation starts with an axiom consisting of a b at the left side and an a at the right, which leads to the generation of the concatenation of the languages $\{a^n b^n \mid n \geq 1\}$ and a^+.   ■

Now we turn to weaken the control of the generation process. So-called *centralized* bidirectional string assembling systems (C-2SAS) cannot distinguish between the units that may be assembled at the left and right. To this end, formally it suffices to require $T_l = T_r$ and $E_l = E_r$.

Example 14. The C-2SAS $S = \langle \{a, b\}, A, T_l, T_r, E_l, E_r \rangle$ generates the context-free language $\{a^n b^n a^m b^m \mid n, m \geq 1\}$, where

$$A = \{(\lambda, \lambda, ba, \lambda, \lambda)\}, \quad T_l = T_r = \{(bb, b), (ab, b), (aa, bb), (a, ab), (a, aa)\},$$
$$E_l = E_r = \{(a, a), (b, b)\}.$$

As in Example 12, the words from $\{a^n b^n \mid n \geq 1\}$ are generated to the left of the axiom $(\lambda, \lambda, ba, \lambda, \lambda)$. In addition, the same units are used to generate a second word from the same set to the right. When a word from $\{a^k b^k a^l b^l \mid k, l \geq 1\}$ has been assembled, the derivation cannot be extended successfully. Though the unit (bb, b) can repeatedly be added at the right, the lower strand cannot be completed afterwards. Similarly, the unit (a, aa) can be added at the left, but the upper strand cannot be completed afterwards.   ■

4.1   Generative Capacity

In [11] it has been shown that the language $\{a^n b^n a^m \mid n, m \geq 1\}$ is not generated by any 1SAS. Therefore, by Example 13 we obtain the following inclusion.

Theorem 15. *The family of languages generated by 1SAS is properly included in the family of languages generated by 2SAS.*

While the previous result is evident, we next turn to the question whether or not 2SAS generate merely the concatenation of two 1SAS languages. The next theorem shows that 2SAS are in fact at least as powerful as two 'concatenated' 1SAS. However, it turned out not only that 2SAS are strictly more powerful, but also that they can generate languages which have no representation as any finite concatenation of 1SAS languages.

Theorem 16. *Let S_1, S_2 be two 1SAS. There exists a 2SAS that generates the concatenation $L(S_1)L(S_2)$.*

The family of languages generated by 1SAS is not closed under concatenation. Moreover, there is an infinite, strict, and tight concatenation hierarchy of 1SAS [12]. The hierarchy is witnessed by four languages

$$L_0 = \{a^n b^n \mid n \geq 1\} \cup d^+, \qquad L_1 = \{c^n d^n \mid n \geq 1\} \cup a^+,$$
$$L_2 = \{b^n a^n \mid n \geq 1\} \cup c^+, \qquad L_3 = \{d^n c^n \mid n \geq 1\} \cup b^+$$

and, for $i \geq 1$, their cyclic concatenations $L^{(1)} = L_0$ and $L^{(i+1)} = L^{(i)} L_{i \bmod 4}$.

Theorem 17. *Let $k \geq 1$ be a constant. Then $L^{(k)}$ can be represented as concatenation of k 1SAS languages, but there is no representation as concatenation of less than k 1SAS languages.*

The concept of bidirectionality of string assembling systems is different from concatenations of 1SAS languages. In fact, there are languages on top of the infinite concatenation hierarchy that are generated by simple 2SAS. By Example 12, the language $L = \{ a^n b^n \mid n \geq 1 \} \cup a^+$ is generated by a 2SAS. Now assume in contrast to the assertion that it has a representation as concatenation of some $k \geq 1$ languages generated by the 1SAS $S_1, S_2, \ldots, S_k$. Since L includes infinitely many words of the form a^+, at least one of the systems, say S_i, generates infinitely many of them. None of the systems S_j, with $1 \leq j < i$, generates a word containing the letter b, since otherwise by concatenation a word is obtained where a b is followed by an a. Moreover, none of the systems S_j, with $i < j \leq k$, generates a word containing the letter b. Otherwise two concatenations which differ only by two different words of the form a^+ from $L(S_i)$ and which include the word from $L(S_j)$ containing the letter b, must yield a word not belonging to L.

We conclude that system S_i generates all factors containing the letter b. Since, in addition, $L(S_i)$ contains infinitely many words of the form a^+, Lemma 21 is applicable, which shows that there are words generated that do not belong to L, a contradiction. So, the next theorem follows.

Theorem 18. *There is a language generated by a 2SAS which cannot be represented as concatenation of any finite number of 1SAS languages.*

4.2   Synchronized 2SAS

This subsection is devoted to variants of 2SAS allowing a stronger control of the generation process. Basically, the idea is to synchronize the assembling of units at the right and left. First we consider S-2SAS (SC-2SAS), which are 2SAS (C-2SAS) where units are always assembled simultaneously at the right and at the left. In this way, the number of units assembled is the same for the right and left part of the strand.

Example 19. The SC-2SAS $S = \langle \{a, b\}, A, T_l, T_r, E_l, E_r \rangle$ generates the context-free language $\{ a^n b a^n \mid n \geq 1 \}$, where $A = \{(\lambda, \lambda, aba, \lambda, \lambda)\}$, $T_l = T_r = \{(aa, aa)\}$, and $E_l = E_r = \{(a, a)\}$.

The only possibility to start with is the axiom $(\lambda, \lambda, aba, \lambda, \lambda)$. Then $n - 1$ times the unit (aa, aa) is used, which is synchronously assembled at the left and at the right. Finally, the ending unit (a, a) completes the derivation.   ∎

Though for non-synchronized 2SAS the numbers of units assembled at the right and left may differ, they are special cases of synchronized systems. This can be seen as follows. Let $S = \langle \Sigma, A, T_l, T_r, E_l, E_r \rangle$ be a 2SAS. Then we construct an equivalent S-2SAS $S' = \langle \Sigma, A, T_l', T_r', E_l, E_r \rangle$ generating $L(S)$ by adding units that actually do not add anything to the strands. That is, we set $T_l' = T_l \cup$

$\{(a, a) \mid a \in \Sigma\}$ and $T_r' = T_r \cup \{(a, a) \mid a \in \Sigma\}$. Clearly, S' generates the language $L(S)$. Since centralized variants meet the condition $T_l = T_r$ and the construction extends T_l as well as T_r by the same set of units, the construction works fine also for C-2SAS and SC-2SAS.

Moreover, synchronized string assembling systems have been separated from non-synchronized ones by using the witness language $\{a^n b a^n \mid n \geq 1\}$ of Example 19.

Theorem 20. *(i) The family of languages generated by 2SAS is properly included in the family of languages generated by S-2SAS. (ii) The family of languages generated by C-2SAS is properly included in the family of languages generated by SC-2SAS.*

The next result is, to some extend, a pumping lemma for certain languages. It is an extension of a pumping lemma for 1SAS and has been shown in [11] for 1SAS.

Lemma 21. *Let $L \subseteq \Sigma^*$ be a language generated by an SC-2SAS. If $|a^+ \cap L| = \infty$, for some symbol $a \in \Sigma$, then there exist constants $p, q \geq 1$ such that $a^p v \in L$, $v \in \Sigma^*$, implies $a^{p+lq} v \in L$, for all $l \geq 1$.*

The lemma can be applied to separate centralized from non-centralized string assembling systems. Let L be the language $\{a^n b^n \mid n \geq 1\} \cup a^+$, and assume L is generated by an SC-2SAS. Then Lemma 21 can be applied with constants $p, q \geq 1$. Since $a^p b^p \in L$, we derive $a^{p+q} b^p \in L$, a contradiction. So, L does not belong to the family of languages generated by SC-2SAS and, thus, does not belong to the family of languages generated by C-2SAS, either. On the other hand, by Example 12 language L is generated by a 2SAS and, thus by an S-2SAS.

Theorem 22. *(i) The family of languages generated by C-2SAS is properly included in the family of languages generated by 2SAS. (ii) The family of languages generated by SC-2SAS is properly included in the family of languages generated by S-2SAS.*

Next, we compare the generative capacity of synchronized 2SAS with the computational capacity of nondeterministic one-way multi-head finite automata in order to derive languages that are not generated by any S-2SAS. In particular, it is well known that the mirror language $\{ww^R \mid w \in \{a, b\}^+\}$ is not accepted by any nondeterministic one-way multi-head finite automaton. The following relation has been shown in [10].

Theorem 23. *Let S be an S-2SAS. There exists a nondeterministic one-way 5-head finite automaton that accepts $L(S)$.*

4.3   Synchronized 2SAS with Related Units

The last variant in question are synchronized bidirectional string assembling systems, where the units which are simultaneously assembled must be related.

Formally, we introduce a relation $R \subseteq (T_l \times T_r) \cup (E_l \times E_r)$, where it is understood that when a unit p is assembled at the left simultaneously with a unit q at the right, then $(p, q) \in R$. We denote such systems by R-2SAS and their centralized versions by RC-2SAS.

Example 24. The following RC-2SAS $S = \langle \{a, b\}, A, T_l, T_r, E_l, E_r, R \rangle$ generates the context-free language $\{ ww^R \mid w \in \{a, b\}^+ \}$.

$$A = \{(\lambda, \lambda, aa, \lambda, \lambda), (\lambda, \lambda, bb, \lambda, \lambda)\}$$
$$T_l = T_r = \{(bb, bb), (aa, aa), (ab, ab), (ba, ba)\}$$
$$E_l = E_r = \{(a, a), (b, b)\}$$
$$R = \{((bb, bb), (bb, bb)), ((aa, aa), (aa, aa)), ((ab, ab), (ba, ba)),$$
$$((ba, ba), (ab, ab)), ((a, a), (a, a)), ((b, b), (b, b))\}$$

The derivation of ww^R starts in the center of the word with one of the axioms $(\lambda, \lambda, aa, \lambda, \lambda)$ or $(\lambda, \lambda, bb, \lambda, \lambda)$. The relation R associates a unit $(u, u) \in T_l$ with its reversed version $(u^R, u^R) \in T_r$. So, each time a unit of T_l is assembled at the left, the reversed counterpart is assembled at the right. Moreover, the units allow to add an a or a b regardless of the current symbol at the end of the strings. The derivation is simply completed by assembling an ending unit (a, a) or (b, b) at both ends. ∎

While for all variants of bidirectional string assembling systems considered so far the centralized versions are strictly weaker than the non-centralized ones, this difference disappears when the units of synchronized systems are related.

Theorem 25. *A language is generated by an R-2SAS if and only if it is generated by an RC-2SAS.*

Let $S = \langle \Sigma, A, T_l, T_r, E_l, E_r, R \rangle$ be an R-2SAS. To turn it into an equivalent RC-2SAS $S' = \langle \Sigma, A', T_l', T_r', E_l', E_r', R' \rangle$ we set $A' = A$, $T_l' = T_r' = T_l \cup T_r$ and $E_l' = E_r' = E_l \cup E_r$. In order to make sure that the units from T_r (T_l) are only assembled at the right (left) and similarly for E_r and E_l, the relation R' is used. To this end, it is simply defined to be R. In this way, clearly, in a derivation of S' only pairs of units are assembled that also can be assembled in S. Since the set of axioms is unchanged we obtain $L(S) = L(S')$.

It is worth mentioning that any S-2SAS is an R-2SAS, where the relation between units is $R = (T_l \times T_r) \cup (E_l \times E_r)$. Theorem 23 shows that every language generated by an S-2SAS is accepted by a nondeterministic one-way 5-head finite automaton. It is well known that the latter cannot accept the mirror language $\{ ww^R \mid w \in \{a, b\}^+ \}$. By Example 24 we obtain the following proper inclusions.

Theorem 26. *The families of languages generated by S-2SAS and SC-2SAS are properly included in the family of languages generated by R-2SAS (or RC-2SAS).*

At the top of the hierarchy are the synchronized 2SAS with related units. An upper bound on their generative capacity is given by the power of nondeterministic two-way 4-head finite automata. So, together with the next theorem, we obtain that the family of languages generated by R-2SAS is properly included in NL.

Theorem 27. *Let S be an R-2SAS. There exists a nondeterministic two-way 4-head finite automaton that accepts $L(S)$.*

Finally, we compare all language families generated by some variant of a 2SAS with (sub-) families of the Chomsky hierarchy. Theorem 27 revealed that all the former families are properly included in NL and, thus, in the family of context-sensitive languages. From Example 1 we know that even 1SAS can generate non-context-free languages. The next lemma and Theorem 7 allow to conclude the incomparability of all 2SAS families with the regular and, thus, with the (deterministic) (linear) context-free languages.

Lemma 28. *A unary language is generated by an R-2SAS if and only if it is generated by a 1SAS.*

Figure 3 summarizes the inclusions derived.

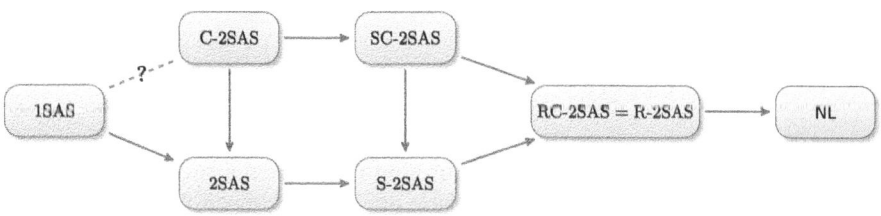

Fig. 3. Inclusion structure of language families generated by string assembling systems. The arrows indicate strict inclusions. The relation between 1SAS and C-2SAS is an open problem.

5   Nonterminal Controlled String Assembling Systems

As mentioned, a string assembling system is called *nonterminal controlled* if, in addition, there is a finite set Γ of auxiliary symbols (nonterminals) that may appear only at the ends of the strands. Such auxiliary symbols are also used in Lindenmayer systems and splicing systems in order to gain more control on the process of string generation. In Lindenmayer systems, for example, several different auxiliary symbols may represent one and the same living cell in different phases during the development of an organism. They are placeholders for associated ordinary symbols that may have distinguishable inner states. The results of this section originate in [1].

Example 29. The language $L = \{a^n b^n a^m \mid n, m \geq 1\}$ is generated by the 1NSAS $\langle \{a, b\}, \{X\}, \sigma, A, T, E \rangle$, where

$$A = \{(\lambda, \lambda, abX, aba, \lambda, \lambda), (\lambda, \lambda, a, a, a, \lambda)\},$$

$$T = \{(aa, a), (ab, a), (bb, aa), (bX, ab), (X, bb), (X, ba), (XX, aa)\},$$

$$E = \{(X, a)\}, \text{ and } \sigma(X) = a.$$

There are two different cases for generating words of L. The first case concerns words of the form aba^m, for $m \geq 1$. After starting with the axiom $(\lambda, \lambda, abX, aba, \lambda, \lambda)$ it is only possible to assemble the unit (XX, aa) arbitrarily often, what extends the strands by an arbitrary sequence of a's, and finally the ending unit.

In the second case, the assembling process starts with the axiom $(\lambda, \lambda, a, a, a, \lambda)$. Here the upper strand can be extended by a's with the unit (aa, a). Subsequently, the mode is switched with (ab, a). Then units (bb, aa) have to be assembled, so that there are as many b's added to the upper strand as are a's in the lower strand so far. Exactly when the a sequence in the lower strand is completely made up, the unit (bX, ab) can be assembled. Then the b's in the lower strand are completed with (X, bb). Finally, the only further possibility is to use the unit (X, ba) which enables assembling of units (XX, aa) for adding arbitrarily many a's at the end. ∎

5.1 Generative Capacity

In order to explore the generative capacity of string assembling systems they have been compared with multi-head finite automata. Theorem 4 says that any 1SAS can be simulated by some nondeterministic one-way two-head finite automaton. On the other hand, up to at most five additional symbols in the words generated, the 1SAS in turn can simulate any stateless nondeterministic one-way two-head finite automaton (Theorem 9). Moreover, any S-2SAS can be simulated by some nondeterministic one-way five-head finite automaton (Theorem 23).

For 2NSAS we have a somehow stronger result. The family of languages generated by 2NSAS is *characterized* by means of nondeterministic one-way two-head finite automata. Moreover, unidirectional and bidirectional systems are equally powerful.

Basically, the idea of the construction of an equivalent nondeterministic one-way two-head finite automaton M from a given 2NSAS is to guess dependent on the currently scanned input symbols which assembly unit comes next. Then the guess is verified by reading the upper strand with the first and the lower strand with the second head. As the last symbol of this unit is also the first symbol of the next unit, the heads stay on it for the new guess. At the beginning, one of the left ending units is guessed and verified, then possibly further left assembly units. After each verification, M guesses whether the assembling process to the left is completed and guesses one of the axioms. Subsequently, possibly further right assembly units are guessed and verified, where after each verification, M

determines whether the assembling process is completed, in which case a final right ending unit is guessed.

Theorem 30. *Let S be a 2NSAS. There exists a nondeterministic one-way two-head finite automaton that accepts $L(S)$.*

The next step to prove the characterization is the simulation of nondeterministic one-way two-head finite automata M by nonterminal controlled *unidirectional* string assembling systems S.

The underlying idea of the construction of S is to relate each head with a strand, and guess and assemble the next symbol to the corresponding strand whenever the head moves to the right. The new state of M is encoded by a nonterminal symbol that appears either at the end of the upper or lower strand. The guesses are subsequently verified by simulating transitions of M. However, special care has to be taken for the situations where the strand ending with the nonterminal encoding the current state is not extended, or where M accepts.

Theorem 31. *Let M be a nondeterministic one-way two-head finite automaton. There exists an 1NSAS that generates $L(M)$.*

The characterization shows that the availability of nonterminals increases the generative capacity of string assembling systems significantly. By Theorem 7 there are regular languages not generated by any classical 1SAS. The proper inclusion of the family of languages generated by 1SAS in the family of languages generated by 2SAS has no analog for nonterminal controlled string assembling systems, where unidirectionality is as powerful as bidirectionality. Moreover, even the strongest type of classical string assembling systems, namely 2SAS, does not capture the regular languages, not even the unary ones. As witness for this fact the language $\{a\} \cup \{a^{2n} \mid n \geq 2\}$ has been used in [10]. We summarize these observations in the following result.

Theorem 32. *The family of regular languages as well as the family of languages generated by 2SAS are properly included in the family of languages generated by 1NSAS (or 2NSAS).*

The family of languages generated by 1NSAS (or 2NSAS) is properly included in the complexity class NL and, thus, in the family of context-sensitive languages.

This upper bound also allows comparisons with further (sub-)families of the Chomsky hierarchy. As mentioned, it is well known that the mirror language $\{wcw^R \mid w \in \{a, b\}^+\}$ is not accepted by any nondeterministic one-way multi-head finite automaton. However, it is a deterministic, linear, context-free language. So, by Lemma 6, the following incomparabilities follow.

Theorem 33. *The family of languages generated by 1NSAS (or 2NSAS) is incomparable with the families of (deterministic) (linear) context-free languages.*

6   The Impact of The Model-Inherent Control Mechanisms

It is natural to ask for the role played by the model-inherent control mechanisms. These could be relaxed or complemented by further mechanisms. In this section, we report about results on the generative capacities and the mutual relationships of mechanisms for the simplest model studied so far, that is, for 1SAS. The results originate in [15].

6.1   Length-Restricted String Assembling Systems

The length difference of the strings in units can be seen as a very basic kind of memory. This length difference is bounded by the lengths of the units. So, it is natural to consider 1SAS where the lengths of the strings in units are restricted.

Let $k \geq 1$ be an integer. An 1SAS $S = \langle \Sigma, A, T, E \rangle$ is said to be k-length-restricted (k-1SAS), if $|u| \leq k$ and $|v| \leq k$ for each unit $(u, v) \in A \cup T \cup E$.

Example 34. Let $k \geq 1$ be an integer. The language $L_k = a(a^{(k-1)^2})^*$ is generated by the k-1SAS $S = \langle \{a\}, A, T, E \rangle$ with the following units.

1. $(a, a) \in A$ 2. $(a^k, a) \in T$ 3. $(a^2, a^k) \in T$ 4. $(a, a) \in E$

Assembling the sole axiom and the sole ending unit results in the word a. So, the assembling of units from T must result in equally long upper and lower strands. The length difference between upper and lower string is $k - 1$ in unit (2) and $k - 2$ in unit (3). Since for $k \geq 3$ the numbers $k - 1$ and $k - 2$ are relatively prime, each $k - 1$ units (3) and $k - 2$ units (2) have to be assembled in order to obtain equally long upper and lower strands. Assembling $k - 1$ units (3) extends the upper strand by $k - 1$ and the lower strand by $(k - 1)(k - 1)$ symbols. Assembling $k - 2$ units (2) extends the upper strand by $(k - 2)(k - 1)$ and the lower strand by 0 symbols. So, the current strands can be extended by strings of length $(k - 1) + (k - 2)(k - 1)$ or equivalently $(k - 1)(k - 1)$. Adding the initial symbol a shows that S generates L_k, for $k \geq 3$. For $k = 1$, unit (2) does not extend the current strands and, thus, unit (3) cannot contribute to a successful derivation. Therefore, the initial word a is the only one that can be derived. Since $L_1 = \{a\}$, the 1SAS S generates the language L_k for $k = 1$ as well. Finally, if $k = 2$ then unit (3) extends the current strands by 1, which shows that $a^+ = L_2$ is generated. ∎

The main technique to prove an infinite hierarchy dependent on the length restriction (see Fig. 4) is to consider gaps between consecutive word lengths in unary languages. A quadratic lower bound follows by Example 34. An upper bound of $(k - 1)^2$ is shown in [15].

Theorem 35. *Let $k \geq 1$ be an integer. The family of languages generated by k-1SAS is strictly included in the family of languages generated by $(k+1)$-1SAS.*

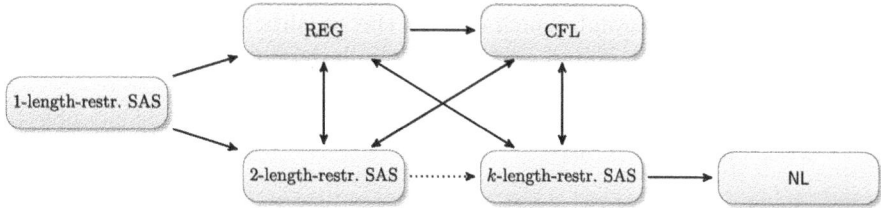

Fig. 4. Hierarchy on the length of the units. A single arrow means strict inclusion, a double arrow means incomparability, and the dotted arrow is for an infinite hierarchy depending on the maximal length of the units. Since 1-length-restricted 1SAS can only generate finite languages, they generate a subset of the regular languages.

6.2   Free String Assembling Systems

The next restricted variant are so-called *free* string assembling systems, where the control mechanism derived from the fact that the assembled strings have to overlap the last symbol of the current strand is relaxed. For this reason we allow the units to be subsets of $\Sigma^* \times \Sigma^*$.

Example 36. Let $h \colon \{a_1, b_1\} \to \{a_2, b_2\}$ be a homomorphism with $h(a_1) = a_2$ and $h(b_1) = b_2$. The language $\{ \$_0 w_1 \$_1 h(w_1) \$_2 \mid w_1 \in \{a_1, b_1\}^+ \}$ is not context free but generated by the free 1SAS $S = \langle \{a_1, a_2, b_1, b_2, \$_0, \$_1, \$_2\}, A, T, E \rangle$, where all following units are defined for all $x_1, y_1, z_1 \in \{a_1, b_1\}$.

1. $(\$_0 x_1, \lambda) \in A$
2. $(x_1 y_1, \lambda) \in T$
3. $(\$_1, \$_0) \in T$
4. $(x_1 \$_1, \$_0) \in T$
5. $(h(x_1)h(y_1), x_1 y_1) \in T$

6. $(h(x_1)\$_2, x_1 \$_1 h(z_1)) \in T$
7. $(h(x_1)h(y_1)\$_2, x_1 y_1 \$_1 h(z_1)) \in T$
8. $(\lambda, h(x_1)h(y_1)) \in T$
9. $(\lambda, \$_2) \in E$
10. $(\lambda, h(x_1)\$_2) \in E$

There are three basic ideas of the construction of S. First, the axiom (1) has an empty lower string. This ensures that subsequently only units (2) can be assembled until the derivation of the upper strand $\$_0 w_1 \$_1$ is completed by one of the units (3) or (4). Second, since the concluding $\$_2$ in the lower strand is only defined in the ending units (9) and (10), it is impossible to generate anything after $\$_2$. Third, the units assembling the upper w_1 extend the current strand at even positions and have length two, while units assembling w_1 in the lower strand extend the current strand at odd positions. Thus, they overlap, which ensures that the format of the generated words is correct, and that there are no symbols of $\{a_1, b_1\}$ and $\{a_2, b_2\}$ mixed up. These ideas are similarly applied to the construction of the units generating the subword $h(w_1)$. Here the units in the upper strand start at an odd position of $h(w_1)$ and at an even position in $h(w_1)$ in the lower strand.

Unit (5) copies the word w_1 with different indices after the $\$_1$ in the upper strand. The units (6) and (7) complete the derivation of the upper strand. Both place $\$_1$ in the lower strand, which ensures the equality of w_1 and $h(w_1)$. The generation of the lower strand and the whole derivation is completed by the units (8) and (9) or (10).

Since the order of the applications of the units is fixed, it is not possible to derive words of another form. ∎

In general, the loss of the control mechanism based on overlapping weakens the generative capacity of 1SAS. For example, neither the language

$$L = \{\, a^n b^n \$ a^m \mid m, n \geq 1 \,\}$$

nor its iterated version $L_+ = \{a\}L_0^*$ with $L_0 = \{\, a^{n-1} b^n \$ a^m \mid m, n \geq 1 \,\}$ can be generated by any free 1SAS. However, language L_+ is generated by some 1SAS.

Though there is a language that separates 1SAS from free 1SAS, the differences in the generative capacities disappear for unary languages. However, the general relation of 1SAS and free 1SAS is an open question.

6.3   One-Set String Assembling Systems

The next restricted variant are so-called *one-set* string assembling systems, where the control mechanism that the units are arranged in the three sets of axioms, assembling units, and ending units is relaxed. So, a string assembling system is said to be *one set*, if the sets A, T, and E are equal. In particular, a derivation can end at any point of the derivation where both strands have the same length.

Example 37. The language $L = \{\, a^m b^n \mid m + n \geq 2 \,\}$ is generated by the one-set 1SAS $S = \langle \{a, b\}, A, T, E \rangle$ with $A = T = E$ and the following units.

1. $(aa, aa) \in T$ 2. $(ab, ab) \in T$ 3. $(bb, bb) \in T$ ∎

The lost possibility to stop a generation explicitly is a strict weakening of the systems. It implies the following. Let S be a one-set 1SAS, $w_1, w_2 \in \Sigma^*$, and $x \in \Sigma$. If $w_1 x$ and $x w_2$ are generated by S then $w_1 x w_2$ is generated by S as well. So, we have the next inclusion.

Theorem 38. *The family of languages generated by one-set 1SAS is strictly included in the family of languages generated by 1SAS.*

A well-known useful fact related to number theory and Frobenius numbers (see, for example, [26] for a survey) can be used to settle the unary case.

Proposition 39. *Every unary language generated by a one-set 1SAS is either empty, the singleton $\{a\}$, or $L_z = \{\, a^n \mid n = z \cdot m + 1, \text{ for } a^m \in L_0 \,\}$, for a constant $z \geq 1$ and a cofinite language L_0.*

Proposition 39 reveals that, for example, the finite singleton language $\{aa\}$ cannot be generated by any one-set 1SAS. On the other hand, they are able to generate infinite languages.

Moreover, the two possibilities to relax one of the two control mechanisms studied and to keep the other yield incomparable generative capacities.

Theorem 40. *The families of languages generated by free 1SAS and by one-set 1SAS are incomparable.*

6.4   Pure String Assembling Systems

The last restriction considered in this section is a combination of both restrictions studied above. So-called *pure* string assembling systems are one-set *and* free. Since the remaining control mechanisms are equal to those of the Post Correspondence Problem (PCP), this family of languages can be seen as the family of languages generated by PCP instances.

Example 41. Let $S = \langle \{a, b, \bar{a}, \bar{b}\}, A, T, E \rangle$ be the pure 1SAS, where $A = T = E$ and the following units are defined for the homomorphism $h(a) = \bar{a}$ and $h(b) = \bar{b}$ and all $x \in \{a, b\}$.

1. $(x, \lambda) \in T$ 2. $(h(x), x) \in T$ 3. $(\lambda, h(x)) \in T$.

Since the context-free languages are closed under intersection with regular sets, and the intersection of the languages $L(S) \cap \{a, b\}^+ \{h(a), h(b)\}^+$ results in the non-context-free language $\{ wh(w) \mid w \in \{a, b\}^+ \}$, the language $L(S)$ is not context free.

In order to generate words from $L(S) \cap \{a, b\}^+ \{h(a), h(b)\}^+$ the derivation has to start with units (1). After assembling repeatedly units (1), the only possibility to obtain a matching lower string is to continue with a unit (2). Since the word generated has to belong to the regular set $\{a, b\}^+ \{h(a), h(b)\}^+$, units (2) have to be assembled until strands of the form $(wh(w), w)$ are derived. Again, the only possibility to obtain a matching lower string is to continue with units (3) until a word of the desired form is derived.   ∎

It follows immediately from the definition that every language L generated by a pure 1SAS is Kleene plus closed, that is, $L = L^+$.

For unary languages, the difference between one-set 1SAS and pure 1SAS is subtle. Following the argumentation in [13] a unary language L is said to be *stretched* from language L_0 by $z \geq 1$ if $L = \{ a^n \mid n = z \cdot m, \text{ for } a^m \in L_0 \}$. So, the difference between the properties of being stretched and being generated by one-set 1SAS is the addition of one to the word lengths of stretched languages.

Proposition 42. *Every unary language generated by a pure 1SAS is either empty or a stretched cofinite language.*

As corollary we obtain the incomparability of the families of languages generated by (unary) one-set 1SAS and (unary) pure 1SAS.

On the other hand, the family of languages generated by pure 1SAS is strictly included in the family of languages generated by free 1SAS.

The relations between the variants of string assembling systems studied so far are summarized in Fig. 5. We conclude the section by the relations with the language families of the Chomsky Hierarchy. While string assembling systems where the units are arranged in three sets, that is 1SAS and free 1SAS, can generate all finite languages by using corresponding axioms and a trivial ending unit, the absence of this control mechanism yields incomparability with the family of finite languages. Therefore, the families of languages generated by free 1SAS, one-set 1SAS, and pure 1SAS are incomparable with the families of regular and (deterministic) (linear) context-free languages, and are strictly included in NL.

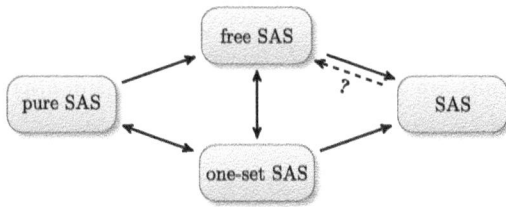

Fig. 5. Inclusion structure of language families. A single arrow means strict inclusion, a double arrow means incomparability, and the dashed line together with the solid line indicates the open problem whether there is a strict inclusion or incomparability.

6.5   String Assembling Systems with Multiple Strands

The most powerful mechanism of string assembling systems is the ability to have two strands that can grow independently from each other. This seems to be the reason for the strong connection to one-way two-head finite automata. It has been shown that one-way k-head finite automata are less powerful than one-way $(k + 1)$-head finite automata in [28]. Thus a proper head hierarchy can be concluded. Here we report on results for multi-stranded string assembling systems, where the number k of strands is a constant (SAS-k).

In line with previous results on 2-stranded 1SAS we can derive an upper bound for the generative capacity. The upper bound is given by the recognition power of nondeterministic one-way k-head finite automata.

It is known from [9] that nondeterministic one-way k-head finite automata cannot accept the linear context-free language $\{ wcw^R \mid w \in \{a, b\}^* \}$. Moreover, as mentioned above, the non-context-free language $\{ \$_1 w \$_2 w \$_3 \mid w \in \{a, b\}^+ \}$ is generated by some common 1SAS. So, again we obtain that, for $k \geq 2$, the family of languages generated by SAS-k is incomparable with the family of (deterministic) (linear) context-free languages.

By a slight modification of the languages used in [28] to show an infinite and tight head hierarchy for one-way multi-head finite automata, also an infinite and tight strand hierarchy for 1SAS can be shown.

It has been shown that k-stranded 1SAS are able to generate non-context-free languages. On the other hand, the unary regular language $\{a\} \cup \{a^{2n} \mid n \geq 2\}$ cannot be generated by any k-stranded 1SAS. Thus, the family of languages generated by k-stranded 1SAS is incomparable with the context-free languages as well as the regular languages.

Corollary 43. *Let $k \geq 1$ be an integer. (i) The family of languages generated by SAS-k is incomparable with the families of languages accepted by one-way k'-head finite automata if $k' < k$. (ii) The family of languages generated by SAS-k is strictly included in the families of languages accepted by one-way k'-head finite automata if $k' \geq k$. (iii) The family of languages generated by SAS-k is incomparable with the (unary) regular languages if $k \geq 2$.*

The results of this section concerning the generative power are summarized in Fig. 6.

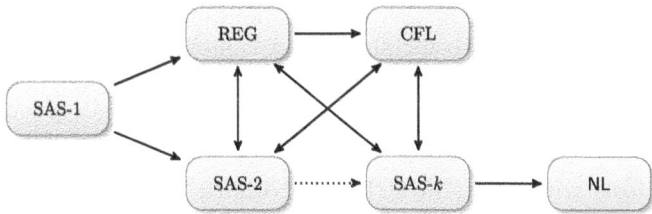

Fig. 6. Hierarchy of languages families dependent on the number of strands. A single arrow means strict inclusion, a double arrow means incomparability, and the dotted arrow is for an infinite hierarchy depending on the number of strands.

7   Closure Properties

Finally we summarize closure properties of the family of languages generated by string assembling systems in Table 1. Closure under certain operations indicates a certain robustness of the language families, while non-closure properties may serve, for example, as a valuable basis for extensions. As it turns out the language families considered here (except for R-2SAS) are not closed under five of the six AFL operations, where the remaining one, the iteration, is an open problem. Furthermore we obtain non-closure under complementation. The only positive closure property is for reversal.

Table 1. Summary of closure properties of families of languages generated by string assembling systems. The properties of k-length-restricted 1SAS are for all $k \geq 2$ except for the operation inverse homomorphism for which $k \geq 3$ is assumed.

Language Family	$\overline{}$	$\cup$	$\cap$	$\cap_{\mathrm{reg}}$	$\cdot$	$+$	$h_{\mathrm{len.pres.}}$	h^{-1}	R
1SAS	✗	✗	✗	✗	✗	?	✗	✗	✓
C-2SAS	✗	✗	✗	✗	✗	?	✗		✗
2SAS	✗	✗	✗	✗	✗	?	✗		✓
S-2SAS	✗	✗	✗	✗	✗	?	✗		✓
SC-2SAS	✗	✗	✗	✗	✗	?	✗		✓
R-2SAS	✗	✗	?	✗	✗	?	?		✓
free 1SAS	✗	✗	✗	✗	✗	?	✗	✗	✓
one-set 1SAS	✗	✗	✗	✗	✗	?	✗	✗	✓
k-length restricted 1SAS	✗	✗	✗	✗	✗	?	✗	✗	✓
1-stranded 1SAS	✗	✗	✗	✗	✗	?	✗	✗	✓
k-stranded 1SAS	✗	✗	✗	✗	✗	?	✗	✗	✓

8 Further Highlights

Here we turn briefly to some further investigations of string assembling systems. Exemplarily, we mention two highlights that compare the systems with other models that process double-stranded strings, namely Watson-Crick automata and sticker systems.

8.1 Relations with Watson-Crick Automata

Basically, Watson-Crick automata are similar to two-head finite automata. They work on a double-stranded input where the two strands are complementary. Each strand is read by one of the input heads which may move independently of each other. The close relationship with ordinary two-head finite automata reveals immediately that Watson-Crick automata can accept all regular and even non-context-free languages. They have been introduced in [2].

Since, on the one hand, nondeterministic one-way two-head finite automata can be simulated by Watson-Crick automata, and, on the other hand, cannot generate all regular languages, by Theorems 4 and 7 we know that the family of languages generated by 1SAS is properly included in the family of languages accepted by Watson-Crick automata.

In [18] the following improvement of Theorem 9 by means of Watson-Crick automata has been shown. The family of languages accepted by stateless Watson-Crick automata strictly includes the family of languages accepted by stateless two-head automata. One of the results in [18] is that for any stateless nondeterministic Watson-Crick automaton there is an 1SAS that generates the same language with *one* additional initial symbol. So, Theorem 9 is improved twofold. First the number of additional symbols is reduced from five to two. Second, the lower bound is increased by considering Watson-Crick automata.

Moreover, there is a language generated by some 1SAS which is not accepted by any Watson-Crick automaton [18].

The investigations of the relationships between string assembling systems and Watson-Crick automata are continued in [19]. A first remarkable result is that the computational capacity of stateless Watson-Crick automata is *equivalent* to the generative capacity of pure 1SAS. The induced language families coincide.

A step towards a solution of the open problem, whether the generative capacity of 1SAS is strictly stronger than the generative capacity of free 1SAS or whether the capacities are incomparable, is the result in [19] that says that any language generated by some free 1SAS is also generated by by some 1SAS provided that an initial symbol is added.

There are much more results in [19] with deep proofs. In general, relationships with Watson-Crick automata having one, two, or three states are obtained, in particular also for unary languages.

8.2 Relations with Sticker Systems

Sticker systems were introduced in [8] in their basic one-way variant. Basically, they consist of dominoes that can be seen as double-stranded molecules. The dominoes are sticked together in a derivation process until a complete double strand is derived. Different variants especially of two-way systems have been investigated in [3, 21, 22]. A main feature of sticker systems is that the upper and the lower fragment of the dominoes are glued together. So, when a domino is added to a double strand the length difference of the upper and the lower strand derived is the same as the length difference between the upper and the lower fragment of the dominoes. This implies that many variants of sticker systems are at most as powerful as linear context-free grammars [22].

By Example 2, the copy language $\{\,\$_1 w \$_2 w \$_3 \mid w \in \Sigma^+\,\}$ is generated by an 1SAS, while it is not generated by any sticker system. So, one could say that 1SAS can copy while sticker systems cannot. Conversely, some variant of the mirror language $\{\, w \mid w \in \{a, b\}^* \text{ and } w = w^R \,\}$ is generated by many variants of sticker systems (that can generate all linear context-free languages), but cannot be generated by any 1SAS. So, sticker systems can handle mirrored inputs while 1SAS cannot. Moreover, sticker systems can generate all regular languages, whereas it turned out that there is a regular language not generated even by 2SAS.

Several important types of restricted sticker systems have been considered. The maximal overhang of a double strand is called its delay. A derivation is said to be of delay m, if the maximal overhang that appears in it is at most m. A sticker system is one-sided if in each step a domino is added at one side of the strand only. It is regular if dominoes are added at the right end only, and it is simple if in each domino one of the fragments is empty.

Following the notation in [22], we denote by ASL the family of languages generated by general sticker systems, by OSL, RSL, and SSL the families of languages generated by one-sided, regular, and simple sticker systems, respectively, and use the notation SOSL and SRSL for the languages families generated by simple one-sided and simple regular systems. For all these families, it is distinguished between unrestricted derivations and derivations with bounded delay. So, (n) or (b) is added to the notation to indicate non-restricted and bounded-delay derivations.

Some results in [14] reveal incomparability of several families. The main comparisons are summarized as follows.

- The family of languages $SRSL(b) = SRSL(n)$ is a proper subfamily of the family of languages generated by 1SAS.
- The family of languages $OSL(b) = OSL(n) = RSL(b) = RSL(n)$ and the family of languages generated by 1SAS are incomparable.
- The families of languages $SSL(b)$ and $SSL(n)$ are incomparable with the family of languages generated by 1SAS.

These results show that even if the concepts of sticker systems and string assembling systems are similar, their computational power differs essentially. But the next representation theorem [14] shows that there are also deep connections between both models.

Theorem 44. *For any 1SAS S over an alphabet Σ, a sticker system $\hat{S}$ can effectively be constructed over an alphabet $\hat{\Sigma}$ such that there is an injective mapping $f \colon \Sigma^* \to \hat{\Sigma}^*$ and $L(\hat{S}) = \{f(w) \# w \mid w \in L(S)\}$.*

9 Conclusions and Further Research

The generative power of string assembling systems and their relation to other well-known language families has been examined. The results show that 1SAS form a language family that is incomparable with several classical families, such as regular, context-free, and deterministic context-free languages. This emphasizes the unique nature of their generative mechanism. At the upper bound, 1SAS are strictly contained in the class of languages accepted by nondeterministic one-way two-head finite automata, and thus also in the context-sensitive languages. Interestingly, every regular language can be described by an 1SAS via a letter-to-letter homomorphism, and any language accepted by a stateless nondeterministic one-way two-head finite automaton can be represented by an 1SAS through a homomorphism. We also discussed how 1SAS relate to other bio-inspired computational models. Although string assembling systems, sticker systems and Watson-Crick automata share some conceptual similarities, their generative capabilities differ fundamentally.

Several intriguing questions remain open. For instance, can we determine a more precise lower bound for the class of languages generated by 1SAS? Additionally, is the introduction of auxiliary symbols essential in the simulation of stateless Watson-Crick automata by 1SAS as proposed in [18]? Addressing these questions could further refine our understanding of the computational power of string assembling systems and their place within the landscape of formal languages.

We have analyzed several closure properties of string assembling systems and their variants. Notably, all variants are closed under reversal, demonstrating a certain robustness with respect to this operation. In contrast, none of the variants is closed under intersection. This non-closure is likely rooted in the close relationship between 1SAS and multi-head finite automata, specifically in the head hierarchy that relies on an intersection-sensitive language construction.

A significant open issue is the closure under iteration. For no variant of string assembling systems we could establish whether or not the language family is closed under this operation. This leads to the open question: is one of the considered language families closed under iteration? If not, it forms an anti-AFL. At first glance, an approach could be to combine the ending units and the axioms of a given system to new assembling units. The problem is that it cannot be ensured that the strands slip apart.

The undecidability of several classical decision problems for string assembling systems can be established via reductions from the Post Correspondence Problem (PCP), due to the strong conceptual connection between both models. Specifically, the undecidability of emptiness serves as a foundation from which the undecidabilities of finiteness, infiniteness, equivalence, inclusion, regularity, and context-freeness can be derived. The structural similarity between k-length-restricted 1SAS and $(k-1)$-length-restricted PCP instances is the basis for a more fine-grained analysis. Since the emptiness problem for PCP is undecidable for word lengths greater than or equal to two, this result directly transfers to string assembling systems with assembling units of length at least three. Moreover, even for 2-length-restricted string assembling systems, a simulation of the derivations of valid computations of a one-sided Turing machine can be constructed. This construction leads to the non-semidecidability of the same set of problems mentioned above, thereby strengthening the result. Despite these results, the question of the decidability of universality remains open. Establishing (un)decidability for this problem could offer deeper insights into the expressive boundaries of string assembling systems.

Moreover, there are still unresolved issues regarding specific variants of string assembling systems. These problems are more specialized but help for a deeper understanding of the overall picture:

– How is the relation between the generative capacity of 1SAS and C-2SAS?
– Also the general relation between the generative capacity of 1SAS and free 1SAS is an open question.
– Still open is the relation of the families of languages generated by SAS-k with the families of languages accepted by one-way k-head finite automata. Is the inclusion proper?

References

1. Bordihn, H., Kutrib, M., Wendlandt, M.: Nonterminal controlled string assembling systems. J. Autom. Lang. Comb. **19**, 33–44 (2014). https://doi.org/10.25596/jalc-2014-033
2. Freund, R., Păun, G., Rozenberg, G., Salomaa, A.: Watson-Crick finite automata. In: DIMACS Workshop on DNA Based Computers, pp. 305–317. University of Pennsylvania, Philadelphia (1997)
3. Freund, R., Păun, G., Rozenberg, G., Salomaa, A.: Bidirectional sticker systems. In: Pacific Symposium on Biocomputing (PSB 1998), pp. 535–546. World Scientific, Singapore (1998)
4. Halava, V., Hirvensalo, M., de Wolf, R.: Marked PCP is decidable. Theor. Comput. Sci. **255**(1–2), 193–204 (2001)
5. Hartmanis, J.: On non-determinancy in simple computing devices. Acta Inf. **1**, 336–344 (1972)
6. Holzer, M., Kutrib, M., Malcher, A.: Complexity of multi-head finite automata: origins and directions. Theor. Comput. Sci. **412**, 83–96 (2011)
7. Ibarra, O.H., Karhumäki, J., Okhotin, A.: On stateless multihead automata: hierarchies and the emptiness problem. Theor. Comput. Sci. **411**, 581–593 (2010)
8. Kari, L., Păun, G., Rozenberg, G., Salomaa, A., Yu, S.: DNA computing, sticker systems, and universality. Acta Inf. **35**, 401–420 (1998)
9. Kutrib, M., Malcher, A., Wendlandt, M.: Set automata. Int. J. Found. Comput. Sci. **27**, 187–214 (2016). https://doi.org/10.1142/S0129054116400062
10. Kutrib, M., Wendlandt, M.: Bidirectional string assembling systems. In: Non-Classical Models of Automata and Applications (NCMA 2012). books@ocg.at, vol. 290, pp. 107–121. Austrian Computer Society, Vienna (2012)
11. Kutrib, M., Wendlandt, M.: String assembling systems. RAIRO Inf. Théor. **46**, 593–613 (2012)
12. Kutrib, M., Wendlandt, M.: Bidirectional string assembling systems. RAIRO Inf. Théor. **48**, 39–59 (2014). https://doi.org/10.1051/ita/2013048
13. Kutrib, M., Wendlandt, M.: Expressive capacity of subregular expressions. RAIRO Inf. Théor. **52**, 201–218 (2018). https://doi.org/10.1051/ita/2018014
14. Kutrib, M., Wendlandt, M.: String assembling systems: comparison to sticker systems and decidability. In: Kostitsyna, I., Orponen, P. (eds.) UCNC 2021. LNCS, vol. 12984, pp. 101–115. Springer, Cham (2021). https://doi.org/10.1007/978-3-030-87993-8_7
15. Kutrib, M., Wendlandt, M.: Variants of string assembling systems. Nat. Comput. **23**, 131–156 (2024). https://doi.org/10.1007/S11047-022-09918-X
16. McNaughton, R.: Algebraic decision procedures for local testability. Math. Syst. Theory **8**, 60–76 (1974)
17. Moore, G.E.: Cramming more components onto integrated circuits. Electronics **38**, 114–117 (1965)
18. Murvai, A., Vaszil, G.: String assembling systems and watson-crick finite automata. In: Brejová, B., et al. (eds.) Information Technologies – Applications and Theory (ITAT 2021). CEUR Workshop Proceedings, vol. 2962, pp. 210–216. CEUR-WS.org (2021)
19. Murvai, A., Vaszil, G.: On the power of small watson-crick automata and variants of string assembling systems. In: Formenti, E., Durand-Lose, J. (eds.) Machines, Computations, and Universality (MCU 2024). LNCS, vol. 15270, pp. 89–102. Springer, Heidelberg (2024). https://doi.org/10.1007/978-3-031-81202-6_6

20. Papadimitriou, C.H.: Computational Complexity. Addison-Wesley, Boston (1994)
21. Păun, G., Rozenberg, G.: Sticker systems. Theor. Comput. Sci. **204**, 183–203 (1998)
22. Păun, G., Rozenberg, G., Salomaa, A.: DNA Computing: New Computing Paradigms. Texts in Theoretical Computer Science. Springer, Heidelberg (1998)
23. Post, E.L.: A variant of a recursively unsolvable problem. Bull. AMS **52**, 264–268 (1946)
24. Rozenberg, G., Salomaa, A.: The Mathematical Theory of L Systems. Academic Press, New York (1980)
25. Salomaa, A.: Formal Languages. Academic Press, New York (1973)
26. Shallit, J.: The frobenius problem and its generalizations. In: Ito, M., Toyama, M. (eds.) DLT 2008. LNCS, vol. 5257, pp. 72–83. Springer, Heidelberg (2008). https://doi.org/10.1007/978-3-540-85780-8_5
27. Yang, L., Dang, Z., Ibarra, O.H.: On stateless automata and P systems. In: Workshop on Automata for Cellular and Molecular Computing, pp. 144–157. MTA SZTAKI (2007)
28. Yao, A.C., Rivest, R.L.: $k+1$ heads are better than k. J. ACM **25**, 337–340 (1978)
29. Zalcstein, Y.: Locally testable languages. J. Comput. Syst. Sci. **6**, 151–167 (1972)

On P Colonies and Virus Machines

Mario J. Pérez-Jiménez[1,2(✉)] ⓘ, José A. Andreu-Guzmán[1,2] ⓘ,
Carmen Graciani[1,2] ⓘ, David Orellana-Martín[1,2] ⓘ,
Antonio Ramírez-de-Arellano[1,2] ⓘ, Agustín Riscos-Núñez[1,2] ⓘ,
Álvaro Romero-Jiménez[1,2] ⓘ, and Luis Valencia-Cabrera[1,2] ⓘ

[1] Research Group on Natural Computing, Department of Computer Science,
Universidad de Sevilla, Avda. Reina Mercedes, s/n, 41012 Sevilla, Spain
{jandreu,cgdiaz,dorellana,aramirezdearellano,ariscosn,romero.alvaro,
lvalencia}@us.es
[2] SCORE Lab, I3US, Universidad de Sevilla, Avda. Reina Mercedes, s/n,
41012 Sevilla, Spain
marper@us.es

Abstract. In the framework of membrane computing, different approximations have been taken from the perspective of the behaviour of the different compartments and types of objects. An interesting class of membrane systems is P colonies, taking inspiration from multi-agent systems where the cells act as agents and can interact with the environment, apart from being able to change the nature of the objects they are in contact with. It has been demonstrated that they are universal devices, thus their computational power is equivalent to Turing machines. Since some software simulators have been developed for P colonies, in this work we introduce the efficient simulation of a novel model of computation, virus machines, by means of P colonies. We describe the process of generation of a P colony and the analysis of computational resources.

Keywords: P colonies · Virus machines · Simulation

1 Introduction

In the framework of membrane computing, different classes of P systems are currently under research. Cell-like membrane systems [24], tissue-like membrane systems [23], or neural-like membrane systems [19]. These models are called, in general, membrane systems or P systems, they are computational devices inspired by the structure and behaviour of living cells. From the beginning, different scientists have been developing research in different lines, such as computability theory [25], computational complexity theory [27], software simulation [28], systems biology [18], ecological simulation [17], fault diagnosis [22], and machine learning [20], among others. A bibliometric analysis of the area is made in [26].

An interesting intersection between membrane systems and multi-agent systems are P colonies. This model, introduced in [21], takes the inspiration from

© The Author(s), under exclusive license to Springer Nature Switzerland AG 2025
M. D. Jiménez López and G. Vaszil (Eds.): Erzsébet Csuhaj-Varjú Festschrift,
LNCS 15840, pp. 238–251, 2025.
https://doi.org/10.1007/978-3-031-97274-4_14

membrane systems where rewriting rules make able the objects to evolve and to move from one region to another one, and from multi-agent systems, where different compartments can interact with the environment and the other agents. One of the most prominent researchers of this research line is Erzsébet Csuhaj-Varjú, from the Eötvös Loránd University. Her research has been focused on the study of P colonies and P automata. From theoretical properties [4,6,7,10,12,13,15] of these devices to their applications [2,8,9,11,14], she has delved into different types of P colonies and specific characteristics. An interesting research line is the relationship between different models of computation. In fact, in [3,16] P colonies are related to other models of computation, describing the process of simulation of such devices by means of P colonies. In this work, we describe the simulation of a novel model of computation, virus machines [29], by means of P colonies in an efficient way, only using two agents and a polynomial number of resources.

The rest of the work is structured as follows: In Sects. 2 and 3, P colonies and virus machines definitions are recalled. Section 4 is used for describing the process of simulation and analysis of this simulation of virus machines by P colonies. Section 5 is devoted to present the conclusions of the paper and some open research lines from this work.

2   P Colonies

First introduced in [21], P colonies are a bioinspired computing paradigm within the framework of membrane computing where the computational resources are managed by agents that are situated in an environment which they can interact with. The definition of P colonies from [5] is recalled.

Definition 1. *A P colony of degree n and capacity $k, k > 1$ is a tuple*

$$\Pi = (A, e, f, v_E, B_1, \ldots, B_n),$$

where:

1. *A is an alphabet whose elements are called objects;*
2. *$e \in A$ is the basic (or environmental) object of the colony;*
3. *$f \in A$ is the final object of the colony;*
4. *v_E is a finite multiset over $A \setminus \{e\}$, called the initial state of the environment;*
5. *$B_i, 1 \leq i \leq n$ are agents, where each agent $B_i = (o_i, P_i)$ is defined as follows:*
   - *o_i is a multiset over A consisting of k objects, called the initial state of the agent;*
   - *$P_i = \{p_{i,1}, \ldots, p_{i,k_i}\}$ is a finite set of programs, where each program P_i consists of k rules, which can be of the following forms:*
     - *$a \rightarrow b, a, b \in A$ (evolution rules);*
     - *$a \leftrightarrow b, a, b \in A$ (communication rules);*
     - *r_1/r_2 where r_1 and r_2 are both evolution rules or are both communication rules (checking rules);*

A P colony

$$\Pi = (A, e, f, v_E, B_1, \ldots, B_n)$$

of degree n and capacity k can be viewed as an ordered set of n agents, where each agent B_i initially contains k objects, represented by the multiset o_i. The environment plays an active role in the computation of this device, initially having the objects from the multiset v_E, and having an arbitrary number of objects e.

A *configuration* C_t at an instant t of a P colony is described by a tuple $(w_1, \ldots, w_n, w_E)$, where w_i and w_E are multisets over A. The meaning of C_t is the following: at an instant t, each agent B_i contains the multiset of objects $w_i, 1 \le i \le n$, and the environment contains the multiset w_E, apart from an arbitrary number of objects e. The initial configuration of a P colony $\Pi = (A, e, f, v_E, B_1, \ldots, B_n)$ is $C_0 = (o_1, \ldots, o_n, v_E)$. A configuration C_t yields configuration C_{t+1} in one *transition step* or *computation step* if we can pass from C_t to C_{t+1} (and we denote it by $C_t \Rightarrow_\Pi C_{t+1}$) in the way described next.

In this work, we only recall the maximal parallel mode, where each agent can use any of its programs in a single computation step. A program $p_{i,j}$ is applicable in an agent B_i if all of its rules are applicable.

An evolution rule $a \to b, a, b \in A$ is applicable if there exists an object $a \in w_i$ in an agent B_i. If this rule is applied, then the object a is removed from the agent and an object b is generated in such an agent.

A communication rule $a \leftrightarrow b, a, b \in A$ is applicable if there exists an object $a \in w_i$ in an agent B_i and an object $b \in w_E$ in the environment. If this rule is applied, then the object a from the agent and the object b from the environment are "interchanged", in the sense that the object a is moved to the environment and the object b is moved into the agent.

A checking rule r_1/r_2 is applicable if at least one of the rules r_1, r_2 is applicable. If such a rule is applied, then the following happens:

1. If r_1 is applicable, then it is applied;
2. If r_1 is not applicable, then r_2 is applied.

This can be seen as a *priority* of the rule r_1 over the rule r_2 to be applied.

If more than one program is applicable in a single agent, then the program to be applied is selected in a non-deterministic way. If two or more agents have an applicable communication rule that takes an object b from the environment, only one of them is able to be selected at the same time. A set of programs (at most one per agent) is selected from the set of sets of programs $\mathcal{P}$ in a non-deterministic way. Each set of programs is said to be maximal, in the sense that if a set $P \in \mathcal{P}$, then a set P' such that $P' \subseteq P$ cannot belong to $\mathcal{P}$. We denote as $C_t \Rightarrow_\Pi^{(n)} C_{t+n}$ as the natural extension of $C_t \Rightarrow_\Pi C_{t+1}$ where Π performs n computational steps, and $C_t \Rightarrow_\Pi^* C_n$ where Π performs one or more than one computational steps and C_n is a halting configuration.

P colonies have been demonstrated to be Turing-complete devices even when restricting some ingredients, such as the number of agents or the number of programs. For more information, we refer the reader to [5].

3   Virus Machines

Virus machines, first introduced in [29], can be seen as three well-differentiated graphs that describe the memory, the program and the flow of the program, respectively. Next, the definition of virus machines from [1] is recalled.

Definition 2. *A virus machine of degree* $(p,q), p,q \geq 1$ *is a tuple*

$$\Pi = (\Gamma, H, I, D_H, D_I, G_C, n_1, \ldots, n_p, i_1, h_{out}),$$

where:

1. $\Gamma = \{v\}$ *is a singleton alphabet, whose only element is an object representing a virus;*
2. $H = \{h_1, \ldots, h_p\}$ *and* $I = \{i_1, \ldots, i_q\}$ *are ordered sets such that* $v \notin H \cup I, H \cap I = \emptyset$ *and* $h_{out} \in H$ *or* $h_{out} = h_0$;
3. $D_H = (H \cup \{h_{out}\}, E_H, w_H)$ *is a weighted directed graph, where* $E_H \subseteq H \times (H \cup \{h_{out}\}), (h,h) \notin E_H$ *for each* $h \in H, out - degree(h_{out}) = 0$ *and* w_H *is a mapping from* E_H *on* $\mathbb{N} \setminus \{0\}$;
4. $D_I = (I, E_I, w_I)$ *is a weighted directed graph, where* $E_I \subseteq I \times I, w_I$ *is a mapping from* E_I *on* $\mathbb{N} \setminus \{0\}$ *and the out-degree of each node is less than or equal to 2;*
5. $G_C = (V_C, E_C)$ *is an undirected bipartite graph, with* $V_C = I \cup E_H$ *being* $\{I, E_H\}$ *the partition associated with it: every edge connects an element from* I *with, at most, one arc from* E_H;
6. $n_j \in \mathbb{N}(1 \leq j \leq p)$.

A *virus machine*

$$\Pi = (\Gamma, H, I, D_H, D_I, G_C, n_1, \ldots, n_p, i_1, h_{out})$$

of degree (p,q) can be viewed as an ordered set of p hosts labelled by elements from H, where each host h_j initially contains n_j viruses, and an ordered set of q *control instruction units* labelled by elements from I. h_{out} represents the output region, being a host if $h_{out} \in H$, and the *environment* of the machine if $h_{out} = h_0$. Arcs from the directed graph D_H represent *transmission channels* through which viruses can transmit from one host h_s (different from h_{out}) to another different host $h_{s'}$ or to the environment. The environment plays a passive role in virus machines, in the sense that it can only receive viruses from the device, but cannot take them back to it. Arcs from the directed graph D_I represent *instruction transfer paths*. Finally, the undirected bipartite graph G_C represents the *instruction-channel network* by which an edge $(i_j, (h_s, h_{s'}))$ indicates a control relationship between the instruction i_j and the channel $(h_s, h_{s'})$.

Usually, virus machines are described graphically as a heterogeneous network where the hosts are represented by rectangles, with the corresponding number of viruses represented as natural numbers, leaving them empty in the case of 0 viruses, and instructions are represented by circles. If the weight of an arc is not indicated, then it is equal to 1. In Fig. 1, a virus machine of degree $(3,4)$ is represented.

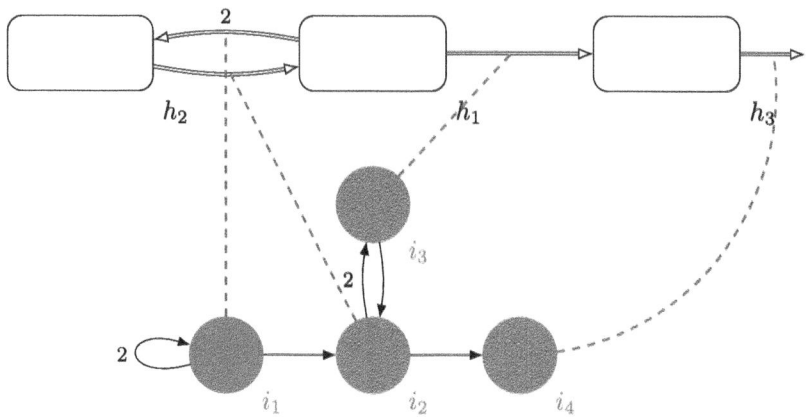

Fig. 1. Virus machine of degree $(3,4)$

A *configuration* C_t at an instant t of a virus machine is described by a tuple $(a_1, \ldots, a_p, u, a_0)$, where $a_0, a_1, \ldots, a_p \in \mathbb{N}$ and $u \in I \cup \{\#\}$, where $\# \notin H \cup \{h_0\} \cup I$ is a symbol that characterizes a halting configuration. The meaning of C_t is the following: at an instant t, each host h_j contains exactly a_j viruses, the environment contains exactly a_0 viruses and, if $u \in I$, then the instruction u will be activated at step $t + 1$, and if $u = \#$, then no instruction will be activated and the machine will halt. The initial configuration of a virus machine $\Pi = (\Gamma, H, I, D_H, D_I, G_C, n_1, \ldots, n_p, i_1, h_{out})$ is $C_0 = (n_1, \ldots, n_p, i_1, 0)$. A configuration C_t yields configuration C_{t+1} in one *transition step* or *computation step* if we can pass from C_t to C_{t+1} (and we denote it by $C_t \Rightarrow_\Pi C_{t+1}$) in the following form.

1. First, given that C_t is a non-halting configuration, we have that $u \in I$. Then, the control instruction unit u is activated.
2. If u is attached to a channel $(h_s, h_{s'})$, then the channel will be *opened* and:
   - If $a_s \geq 1$ then only one virus is consumed from host h_s and $w_{s,s'}$ copies of v are produced in the region $h_{s'}$, where $w_{s,s'}$ is the weight of the channel going from h_s to $h_{s'}$.
   - If $a_s = 0$ then no viruses are consumed from host h_s and no viruses are produced in the region $h_{s'}$.
3. If u is not attached to any channel then there is no transmission of viruses.
4. The next instruction to be executed is obtained as follows:

- If $out\text{-}degree(u) = 2$ then there are two different instructions u' and u'' such that $(u, u'), (u, u'') \in E_I$ (with weights $w_{u,u'}$ and $w_{u,u''}$, respectively).
  - If the instruction u is attached to a channel $(h_s, h_{s'})$:
    * If $a_s \geq 1$ then the next instruction corresponds to the *highest* weight path ($\max(\{w_{u,u'}, w_{u,u''}\})$).
    * If $a_s = 0$ then the next instruction corresponds to the *lowest* weight path ($\min(\{w_{u,u'}, w_{u,u''}\})$).
    * In either case, if $w_{u,u'} = w_{u,u''}$, the next instruction is selected in a non-deterministic way.
  - If instruction u is not attached to a channel, then the next instruction is selected in a non-deterministic way.
- If $out\text{-}degree(u) = 1$ then the system behaves deterministically and u' is the next instruction that verifies $(u, u') \in E_I$.
- If $out\text{-}degree(u) = 0$ then $u = \#$ and $\mathcal{C}_{t+1}$ is a halting configuration.

A *computation* $\mathcal{C} = (\mathcal{C}_0, \mathcal{C}_1, \ldots)$ of a virus machine Π is a (possibly infinite) sequence of configurations such that $\mathcal{C}_0$ is the initial configuration of Π and for each $t \in \mathbb{N}$, $\mathcal{C}_t \Rightarrow_\Pi \mathcal{C}_{t+1}$. A computation $\mathcal{C} = (\mathcal{C}_0, \mathcal{C}_1, \ldots, \mathcal{C}_k)$ is called a *halting computation* if there exists a k such that $\mathcal{C}_k$ is a *halting configuration*; that is, $u = \#$. We denote as $\mathcal{C}_t \Rightarrow_\Pi^{(n)} \mathcal{C}_{t+n}$ as the natural extension of $\mathcal{C}_t \Rightarrow_\Pi \mathcal{C}_t$ where Π performs n computational steps, and $\mathcal{C}_t \Rightarrow_\Pi^* \mathcal{C}_n$ where Π performs one or more than one computational steps and $\mathcal{C}_n$ is a halting configuration.

Virus machines have been demonstrated to be Turing-complete devices even when restricting some ingredients, such as the number of agents or the number of programs. For more information, we refer the reader to [5].

4   Simulation of Virus Machines by P Colonies

In this section, the simulation of virus machines by means of P colonies will be carried out. Different modules will be provided, describing essential aspects on their behavior and relationship with other modules.

4.1   Description of a P Colony Simulating a Virus Machine

First, let

$$M = (\Gamma, H, I, D_H, D_I, G_C, n_1, \ldots, n_p, i_1, h_{out})$$

be a virus machine of degree $(p, q), p, q \geq 1$. Then, the virus machine M will be simulated by a P colony

$$\Pi_M = (A, e, f, v_E, B_1, B_2)$$

of degree 2 and capacity 2 where:

1. $A = \{i_k, i'_k \mid 1 \le k \le q\} \cup \{v_j \mid 1 \le j \le p\} \cup \{v_{j,t}, v'_{j,t} \mid 1 \le j \le p, 0 \le t < w_{j,M}\} \cup \{i, \#, v, v', v'', v_{fin}, e, f\}$, where $w_{j,M}$ is the maximum weight of the incoming channels of host h_j;
2. $v_E = \{i_1, v_1^{n_1}, \dots, v_p^{n_p}\}$;
3. $B_1 = (o_1, P_1)$, where:
   - $o_1 = \{i, v\}$
   - P_1 is a set of programs.
4. $B_2 = (o_2, P_2)$, where:
   - $o_2 = \{i, v\}$
   - P_2 is a set of programs.

For each instruction i_k in the virus machine M such that it is not connected to any channel and has a single following instruction i_l, as depicted in Fig. 2, it will be simulated by the following programs:

In P_1:

$p_{k,1} \equiv \langle i \leftrightarrow i'_k \rangle$
$p_{k,2} \equiv \langle i'_k \rightarrow i_l \rangle$
$p_{k,3} \equiv \langle i_l \leftrightarrow i \rangle$

In P_2:

$p_{k,4} \equiv \langle i \leftrightarrow i_k \rangle$
$p_{k,5} \equiv \langle i_k \rightarrow i'_k \rangle$
$p_{k,6} \equiv \langle i'_k \leftrightarrow i \rangle$

The module works as follows: First, the instruction i_k is located in the environment. By the successive application of the programs p_4, p_5, p_6, the instruction is moved into the agent B_2, evolved into i'_k and moved back to the environment (thanks to the object i). From this point, the successive application of the programs p_1, p_2, p_3, the instruction will be transformed into the instruction i_l, that will be present at the environment.

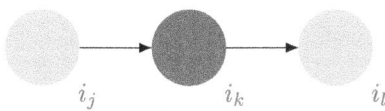

Fig. 2. Module for each non-connected simple instruction

If the instruction i_k is not connected to any other instruction (that is, if i_k leads to a halting configuration), then in the programs $p_{k,2}, p_{k,3}$ the object i_l is replaced by the object $\#$.

The simulation of an instruction i_k to two different instructions as depicted in Fig. 3 is performed in a similar way, by adding the programs $\langle i'_k \rightarrow i_m \rangle$ and $\langle i_m \leftrightarrow i \rangle$ to P_1. Since the selection of the program to be executed in each agent

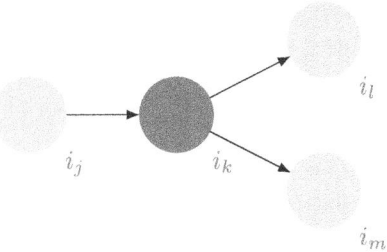

Fig. 3. Module for each non-connected instruction

is made in a non-deterministic way, the next instruction to be simulated will be selected as it would be selected in the original virus machine.

For each instruction i_k in the virus machine M such that it is connected to a channel from host h to host h' and has a single following instruction i_l, as depicted in Fig. 4, it will be simulated by the following programs:

In P_1:

$$p_{k,1} \equiv \langle v \rightarrow v'; i \leftrightarrow i'_k \rangle$$
$$p_{k,2} \equiv \langle v' \rightarrow v''; i'_k \leftrightarrow v_h/i'_k \leftrightarrow i \rangle$$
$$p_{k,3} \equiv \langle v'' \rightarrow v_{h',w-1}; v_h \rightarrow v_{h'} \rangle$$
$$p_{k,4,t} \equiv \langle v_{h',t} \rightarrow v'_{h',t}; v_{h'} \leftrightarrow e \rangle, 0 < t < w$$
$$p_{k,5,t} \equiv \langle v'_{h',t} \rightarrow v_{h',t-1}; e \rightarrow v_{h'} \rangle, 0 < t < w$$
$$p_{k,4,0} \equiv \langle v_{h',0} \rightarrow v'_{h',0}; v_{h'} \leftrightarrow i'_k \rangle$$
$$p_{k,5,0} \equiv \langle v'_{h',0} \rightarrow v_{fin}; i'_k \rightarrow i_l \rangle$$
$$p_{k,6} \equiv \langle v_{fin} \rightarrow v; i_l \leftrightarrow i \rangle$$
$$p_{k,7} \equiv \langle v'' \rightarrow v_n; i \leftrightarrow i'_k \rangle$$
$$p_{k,8} \equiv \langle v_n \rightarrow v_{n'}; i'_k \rightarrow i_l \rangle$$
$$p_{k,9} \equiv \langle v_{n'} \rightarrow v, i_l \leftrightarrow i \rangle$$

In P_2:

$$p_{k,10} \equiv \langle i \leftrightarrow i_k \rangle$$
$$p_{k,11} \equiv \langle i_k \rightarrow i'_k \rangle$$
$$p_{k,12} \equiv \langle i'_k \leftrightarrow i \rangle$$

The first four computational steps of this module work in the same way independently on the number of viruses of the host h.

The object i_k, situated in the environment, will be interchanged with the object i situated in the agent B_2. Then, it will be transformed into the object i'_k and will be interchanged again with the object i situated now in the environment, thus inducing the second part of the module, that is carried out by the agent B_1. Now the program $p_{k,1}$ is executed, evolving the object v into the object v' and introducing the object i'_k into the agent B_1.

From this point, the module works differently depending on the number of viruses at host h. Let n_h be the number of viruses in the host h at a given configuration.

If $n_h = 0$, then the program $p_{k,2}$ is applicable. Since there are no objects v_h at the environment, the rule $i'_k \leftrightarrow i$ is selected. Then, $p_{k,3}$ is not applicable (due to the fact that an object v_h is not present in the agent), but $p_{k,7}$ is applicable. Thus, by the application of such a program, the object v'' evolves into the object v_n and the object i'_k is introduced back into the agent B_1, where it evolves into an object i_l (the following instruction to be executed) while the object v_n evolves into $v_{n'}$, and finally i_l is sent to the environment while $v_{n'}$ evolves back into v, to restart the objects for the next instruction to be simulated.

If $n_h > 0$, then the program $p_{k,2}$ is applicable. Since at least one object v_h is present at the environment, the rule $i'_k \leftrightarrow v_h$ is selected. Then, $p_{k,7}$ is not applicable (due to the fact that an object i is not present in the agent), but $p_{k,3}$ is applicable. Thus, by the application of such a program, the object v'' evolves into the object $v_{h',w-1}$ (where w is the weight of the channel that goes from the host h to the host h'), and v_h is transformed into an object $v_{h'}$. The idea is the following: the second subscript of the object $v_{h',t}$ indicates how many objects $v_{h'}$ are still to be generated. Then, by the successive application of the programs $p_{k,4,t}$ and $p_{k,5,t}$, a new object $v_{h'}$ is generated and sent to the environment while the second subscript of the object $v_{h',t}$ is decreased by one until it reaches 0. When this happens, the program $p_{k,4,0}$ is executed, interchanging the last object $v_{h'}$ with the object i'_k that was at the environment and changing the object $v_{h',0}$ into an object $v'_{h',0}$, letting the program $p_{k,5,0}$ to run in the next step. By its application, objects v_{fin} and i_l are generated, the first one evolving to v and the second one being sent to the environment, both of them by means of the execution of the program $p_{k,9}$, preparing the objects for the simulation of the next instruction.

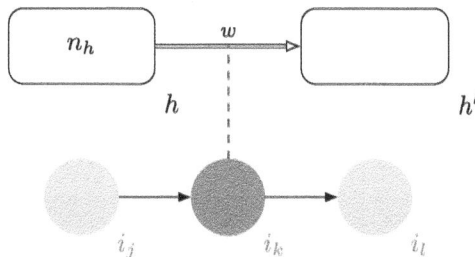

Fig. 4. Module for each simple connected instruction

If the instruction i_k is not connected to any other instruction (that is, if i_k leads to a halting configuration), then in the programs $p_{k,8}, p_{k,9}$ the object i_l is replaced by the object #.

If the instruction i_k is connected to two instructions i_l, i_m by edges of weight $2, 1$, respectively, as represented in Fig. 5, then the programs $p_{k,8}, p_{k,9}$ are replaced by the following ones:

$$p'_{k,8} \equiv \langle v_n \rightarrow v_{n'}; i'_k \rightarrow i_m \rangle$$
$$p'_{k,9} \equiv \langle v_{n'} \rightarrow v; i_m \leftrightarrow i \rangle$$

The module still works as the previous version. The only difference is that, if the host h does not have viruses (that is, $n_h = 0$), then the next instruction to be simulated is i_m. Since the program $p'_{k,8}$ can only be executed after $p_{k,7}$ (that is, when $n_h = 0$), the module works correctly.

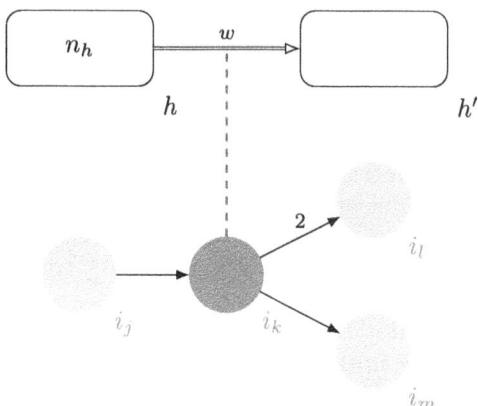

Fig. 5. Module for each connected instruction

If both next instructions i_l, i_m are connected by edges of the same weight, then the following programs are included in the original module (but no programs are removed):

$$p''_{k,5,0} = \langle v'_{h',0} \,\rangle\, v_{fin}; i'_k \,\rangle\, i_m \rangle$$
$$p''_{k,6} \equiv \langle v_{fin} \rightarrow v; i_m \leftrightarrow i \rangle$$
$$p''_{k,8} \equiv \langle v_n \rightarrow v_{n'}; i'_k \rightarrow i_m \rangle$$
$$p''_{k,9} \equiv \langle v_{n'} \rightarrow v; i_m \leftrightarrow i \rangle$$

The idea is the following: since the selection of the next instruction of the virus machine is made in a non-deterministic way, no matter what is the number of viruses in the host h, then the same non-deterministic behaviour must be observed in this simulation. In that sense, programs $p_{k,5,0}, p_{k,8}$ and $p''_{k,5,0}, p''_{k,8}$, respectively, will be selected non-deterministically, simulating this behaviour. Once the next instruction is "selected", then the corresponding instruction $p_{k,6}, p_{k,9}$ or $p''_{k,6}, p''_{k,9}$, respectively, will be executed according to the previous application.

4.2   Description of a Simulation of a Virus Machine by a P Colony

The computation of M is simulated in the following way:

1. First, the P colony Π_M is constructed taking into account the details described in this section; that is, the number of viruses situated in each host h_i is recreated as the same number of objects v_i in the environment of Π_M. For each instruction $i \in I$, the corresponding programs are created in both agents B_1 and B_2. Thus, the initial configuration of Π_M is $\mathcal{C}_0 = (\{i, v\}, \{i, v\}, \{i_1, v_1^{n_1}, \ldots, v_q^{n_q}\})$.

2. Then, the function $\mathcal{D}$ can be defined as the transformation of a configuration $\mathcal{C}_t$ of the virus machine M to the corresponding configuration $\mathcal{D}(\mathcal{C}_t)$ of Π_M simulating the former.

3. From $\mathcal{C}_0$, the successive configurations of Π_M are computed in such a way that a configuration $\mathcal{C}_{t+1}$ is obtained from $\mathcal{C}_t$ by the application of programs in a maximal parallel way; that is, $\mathcal{C}_t \Rightarrow_{\Pi_M} \mathcal{C}_{t+1}$.

4. Taking into account that $\mathcal{D}^{-1}$ is only defined when an object $i_k, 1 \le k \le p$ is present in the environment, then only configurations where such an object appears in the environment represent a configuration from M, such that if the configuration $\mathcal{C}_t$ of Π_M is $\mathcal{C}_t = (\{i, v\}, \{i, v\}, \{i_k, v_1^{a_1}, \ldots, v_q^{a_q}, v_0^{a_0}\})$, then the corresponding simulated configuration $\mathcal{D}^{-1}(\mathcal{C}_t)$ of M is $\mathcal{D}^{-1}(\mathcal{C}_t) = (a_1, \ldots, a_q, i_k, a_0)$.

5. The rest of the computational steps of Π_M (i.e. the steps where no object $i_k, 1 \le k \le p$ is present in the environment) correspond to the simulation of a single computational step of M.

6. When an object $\#$ appears in the Π_M, no programs will be applicable in the configuration, corresponding to the halting configuration of M. In fact, let $\mathcal{C}_t = (\{i, v\}, \{i, v\}, \{i_k, v_1^{a_1}, \ldots, v_q^{a_q}, v_0^{a_0}\})$. Then, the corresponding halting configuration of M is defined by $\mathcal{D}^{-1}(\mathcal{C}_t) = (a_1, \ldots, a_q, \#, a_0)$.

4.3 Computational Resources

If M is a virus machine as described above, then the number of resources used in Π_M is:

- Number of agents: $2 \in O(1)$.
- Number of objects in A: $O(2q + p + 2p \cdot w_M + 8) = O(q + p \cdot w_M)$, where q is the number of instructions of M, p is the number of hosts and w_M is the maximum weight of the graph of hosts D_H of M.
- Number of initial objects in the environment: $O(1 + n_1 + \ldots + n_p)$, where n_i is the initial number of viruses in the host h_i.
- Capacity of each agent: $2 \in O(1)$.
- Number of programs of each agent:
  1. $|P_1| \in O(q(7 + 2w_M)) = O(q \cdot w_M)$, where q is the number of instructions of M and w_M is the maximum weight of the graph of hosts D_H of M.
  2. $|P_2| \in O(3q) = O(q)$, where q is the number of instructions of M.
- Number of rules of each program: $1, 2 \in O(1)$.
- Computation time: The simulation of a single computational step is bounded by the function $2w_M + 10$, where w_M is the maximum weight of the graph of hosts D_H of M, thus a computation $\mathcal{C} =$

$$(\mathcal{C}_0, \mathcal{C}_1, \ldots, \mathcal{C}_n)$$

of M, being $\mathcal{C}_n$ a halting configuration, is simulated by a computation $\mathcal{D}^*(\mathcal{C}) = (\mathcal{D}(\mathcal{C}_0), \mathcal{C}_0^{(1)}, \ldots, \mathcal{C}_0^{(k_0-1)}, \mathcal{D}(\mathcal{C}_1), \mathcal{C}_1^{(1)}, \ldots, \mathcal{C}_1^{(k_1-1)}, \ldots, \mathcal{C}_{n-1}^{(1)}, \ldots, \mathcal{C}_{n-1}^{(k_{n-1}-1)}, \mathcal{D}(\mathcal{C}_n))$ of Π_M, where $k_j \leq w_M, 1 \leq j \leq n$ is the number of steps that takes to simulate the computational step $\mathcal{C}_j \Rightarrow_M \mathcal{C}_{j+1}$ by Π_M and $\mathcal{D}^*$ is the natural extension of $\mathcal{D}$ to computations as described. Then, $|\mathcal{D}(\mathcal{C})| \in O(n(w_M + 10)) = O(n \cdot w_M)$. The schema of the simulation of a single computational step is depicted in Fig. 6.

$$
\begin{array}{c|ccc}
M & \mathcal{C}_t & \Rightarrow_M & \mathcal{C}_{t+1} \\
\hline
\Pi_M & \mathcal{D}(\mathcal{C}_t) & \Rightarrow_{\Pi_M}^{(k_t)} & \mathcal{D}(\mathcal{C}_{t+1})
\end{array}
$$

Fig. 6. Description of the simulation of a single computational step

5   Conclusions and Future Work

In this work, a reduction from virus machines to P colonies is presented. A P colony with 2 agents and 2 objects in each agent is enough to simulate any basic (sequential) virus machine. Of course, since both P colonies and virus machines are universal devices, they are supposed to be able to simulate each other, but the objective is to minimize the number of resources used for this purpose. In fact, the number of programs of both agents B_1 and B_2 is bounded by a polynomial with respect to the number of instructions of the virus machine being simulated. Besides, for simulating a computation of n computation steps, the number of computational steps needed for simulating it is bounded by $O(n \cdot w_M)$, demonstrating a very efficient simulation by these devices. Simulators in the paradigm of P colonies are very advanced, and it would be interesting to take advantage of this fact to simulate the behaviour of virus machines by simulating them in software applications dedicated to P colonies. This will be carried out in future work.

Since virus machines are universal devices, it would be interesting to study the simulation of P colonies by means of a virus machine. This bi-simulation can lead to the study of interesting properties of both computing paradigms, and it can allow the use of proof techniques from one paradigm in the other one. Since the study of invariant formulas have been widely studied in virus machines, a research line of the use of this type of proof will be available by the simulation of P colonies with virus machines.

Acknowledgement. The authors are very grateful to Erzsébet Csuhaj-Varjú for her unconditional support, efforts for the community and continuous collaborations with the Sevilla Team, that had lead to strong scientific and personal bounds.

Disclosure of Interests. The authors have no competing interests to declare that are relevant to the content of this article.

References

1. Ramírez-de Arellano, A., Orellana-Martín, D., Pérez-Jiménez, M.J.: Generating, computing and recognizing with virus machines. Theor. Comput. Sci. **972**, 114077 (2023). https://doi.org/10.1016/j.tcs.2023.114077
2. Cienciala, L., Ciencialová, L., Csuhaj-Varjú, E.: P colonies processing strings. Fund. Informaticae **134**(1–2), 51–65 (2014). https://doi.org/10.3233/FI-2014-1090
3. Ciencialová, L., Cienciala, L., Csuhaj-Varjú, E.: P colonies and reaction systems. J. Membr. Comput. **2**(4), 269–280 (2020). https://doi.org/10.1007/S41965-020-00051-1
4. Ciencialová, L., Csuhaj-Varjú, E., Kelemenová, A., Vaszil, G.: Variants of P colonies with very simple cell structure. Int. J. Comput. Commun. Control **4**(3), 224–233 (2009). https://doi.org/10.15837/IJCCC.2009.3.2430
5. Ciencialová, L., Csuhaj-Varjú, E., Cienciala, L., Sosík, P.: P colonies. J. Membr. Comput. (2019)
6. Csuhaj-Varjú, E.: P automata: membrane systems as acceptors. In: Beckmann, A., Dimitracopoulos, C., Löwe, B. (eds.) CiE 2008. LNCS, vol. 5028, pp. 149–151. Springer, Heidelberg (2008). https://doi.org/10.1007/978-3-540-69407-6_16
7. Csuhaj-Varjú, E.: P automata: concepts, results, and new aspects. In: Păun, G., Pérez-Jiménez, M.J., Riscos-Núñez, A., Rozenberg, G., Salomaa, A. (eds.) WMC 2009. LNCS, vol. 5957, pp. 1–15. Springer, Heidelberg (2010). https://doi.org/10.1007/978-3-642-11467-0_1
8. Csuhaj-Varjú, E.: P and dP automata: unconventional versus classical automata. In: Yen, H.-C., Ibarra, O.H. (eds.) DLT 2012. LNCS, vol. 7410, pp. 7–22. Springer, Heidelberg (2012). https://doi.org/10.1007/978-3-642-31653-1_2
9. Csuhaj-Varjú, E.: P automata: automata-like constructs modeling complex natural systems. In: Bensch, S., Drewes, F., Freund, R., Otto, F. (eds.) Fifth Workshop on Non-Classical Models for Automata and Applications - NCMA 2013, Umeå, Sweden, 13 August–14 August 2013, Proceedings. books@ocg.at, vol. 294, pp. 13–30. Österreichische Computer Gesellschaft (2013)
10. Csuhaj-Varjú, E., Ibarra, O.H., Vaszil, G.: On the computational complexity of P automata. Nat. Comput. **5**(2), 109–126 (2006). https://doi.org/10.1007/S11047-005-4461-1
11. Csuhaj-Varjú, E., Kántor, K., Vaszil, G.: Deterministic parsing with P colony automata. In: Graciani, C., Riscos-Núñez, A., Păun, G., Rozenberg, G., Salomaa, A. (eds.) Enjoying Natural Computing. LNCS, vol. 11270, pp. 88–98. Springer, Cham (2018). https://doi.org/10.1007/978-3-030-00265-7_8
12. Csuhaj-Varjú, E., Margenstern, M., Vaszil, G.: P colonies with a bounded number of cells and programs. In: Hoogeboom, H.J., Păun, G., Rozenberg, G., Salomaa, A. (eds.) WMC 2006. LNCS, vol. 4361, pp. 352–366. Springer, Heidelberg (2006). https://doi.org/10.1007/11963516_22
13. Csuhaj-Varjú, E., Vaszil, G.: P automata. Scholarpedia **5**(4), 9344 (2010). https://doi.org/10.4249/SCHOLARPEDIA.9344
14. Csuhaj-Varjú, E., Vaszil, G.: Finite dP automata versus multi-head finite automata. In: Gheorghe, M., Păun, G., Rozenberg, G., Salomaa, A., Verlan, S. (eds.) CMC 2011. LNCS, vol. 7184, pp. 120–138. Springer, Heidelberg (2012). https://doi.org/10.1007/978-3-642-28024-5_10

15. Csuhaj-Varjú, E., Vaszil, G.: On the power of P automata. In: Mauri, G., Dennunzio, A., Manzoni, L., Porreca, A.E. (eds.) UCNC 2013. LNCS, vol. 7956, pp. 55–66. Springer, Heidelberg (2013). https://doi.org/10.1007/978-3-642-39074-6_7

16. Csuhaj-Varjú, E., Verlan, S.: Bi-simulation between P colonies and P systems with multi-stable catalysts. In: Gheorghe, M., Rozenberg, G., Salomaa, A., Zandron, C. (eds.) CMC 2017. LNCS, vol. 10725, pp. 105–117. Springer, Cham (2018). https://doi.org/10.1007/978-3-319-73359-3_7

17. Duan, Y., Rong, H., Qi, D., Valencia-Cabrera, L., Zhang, G., Pérez-Jiménez, M.J.: A review of membrane computing models for complex ecosystems and a case study on a complex giant panda system. Complexity **2020**(1), 1312824 (2020). https://doi.org/10.1155/2020/1312824

18. Frisco, P., Gheorghe, M., Pérez-Jiménez, M.J.: Applications of Membrane Computing in Systems and Synthetic Biology. Springer, Heidelberg (2014)

19. Ionescu, M., Păun, G., Yokomori, T.: Spiking neural P systems. Fund. Inf. **71**(2,3), 279–308 (2006)

20. Ipate, F., Niculescu, I., Lefticaru, R., Konur, S., Gheorghe, M.: A model learning based testing approach for kernel P systems. Theor. Comput. Sci. **965**, 113975 (2023). https://doi.org/10.1016/j.tcs.2023.113975

21. Kelemen, J., Kelemenová, A., Păun, Gh.: Preview of P colonies: a biochemically inspired computing model. In: Workshop and Tutorial Proceedings. Ninth International Conference on the Simulation and Synthesis of Living Systems (Alife IX), pp. 82–86 (2004)

22. Liu, Y., Chen, Y., Paul, P., Fan, S., Ma, X., Zhang, G.: A review of power system fault diagnosis with spiking neural P systems. Appl. Sci. **11**(10) (2021). https://doi.org/10.3390/app11104376

23. Martín-Vide, C., Păun, Gh., Pazos, J., Rodríguez-Patón, A.: Tissue P systems. Theor. Comput. Sci. **206**(2), 295–326 (2003). https://doi.org/10.1016/S0304-3975(02)00659-X

24. Păun, Gh.: Computing with membranes. J. Comput. Syst. Sci. **61**(1), 108–143 (2000). https://doi.org/10.1006/jcss.1999.1693

25. Păun, A., Păun, G.: Small universal spiking neural P systems. Biosystems **90**(1), 48–60 (2007). https://doi.org/10.1016/j.biosystems.2006.06.006

26. Rong, H., Duan, Y., Zhang, G.: A bibliometric analysis of membrane computing (1998–2019). J. Membr. Comput. **4**(2), 177–207 (2022)

27. Sosík, P.: P systems attacking hard problems beyond NP: a survey. J. Membr. Comput. **1**(3), 198–208 (2019). https://doi.org/10.1007/s41965-019-00017-y

28. Valencia-Cabrera, L., Orellana-Martín, D., Martínez-del Amor, M.Á., Pérez-Jiménez, M.J.: An interactive timeline of simulators in membrane computing: depicting two decades of evolution in the simulation of P systems. J. Membr. Comput. **1**, 209–222 (2019)

29. Valencia-Cabrera, L., Pérez-Jiménez, M.J., Chen, X., Wang, B., Zeng, X.: Basic virus machines. In: 16th International Conference on Membrane Computing (CMC16), pp. 323–342 (2015)

On Some Relationships Between P Colonies and Computing by Plasmids

José M. Sempere$^{(\boxtimes)}$

Valencian Research Institute for Artificial Intelligence (VRAIN) and Valencian Graduate School and Research Network of Artificial Intelligence (VALGRAI), Universitat Politècnica de València, Valencia, Spain
jsempere@dsic.upv.es

Abstract. Computing by plasmids is a recent proposal in the field of membrane computing where mobile elements that only contain rules can move around the regions of the structure of a P system. In this work, we explore some preliminary relations between this new computation model with other models that have had a long history in membrane computing such as P colonies.

Keywords: Membrane Computing · Computing by plasmids · P colonies

1 Introduction

Membrane computing was proposed at the end of the last century by Gh. Păun [16]. It is a computational model inspired by the living eukariotic cell where the information is encoded through objects (inspired by biomolecules and biomaterials) that can be modified using rules (inspired by biochemical reactions). Furthermore, the physical structure of the organelles within the living cell marks out differentiated workspaces separated by membranes in which objects can be sent and received, inspired by the actual transport of materials inside and outside the cell. In this way, a highly parallel, non-deterministic and distributed model was proposed, capable of proposing efficient solutions to complex problems of very diverse nature. The models to achieve membrane computing are named P systems.

From the beginning, membrane computing has been influenced by real biological phenomena from large to biomolecular scale. Thus, to cite some of these works, mutienvironment P systems were influenced and proposed to model real ecological systems [2], tissue P systems [13] was inspired by the inter-cellular communications by means of protein channels, spiking neural P systems [7] was a new model of artificial neural networks, and metabolic P systems [12] intend to model metabolic systems where matter is subject to transformations or reactions of different types. In addition, some ingredients of P systems that have been fruitfully used to achieve universality and computational efficiency come from

M. D. Jiménez López and G. Vaszil (Eds.): Erzsébet Csuhaj-Varjú Festschrift,
LNCS 15840, pp. 252–266, 2025.
https://doi.org/10.1007/978-3-031-97274-4_15

real biological aspects of the living matter, such as the use of active membranes that includes membrane division, membrane dissolution and electric charges [17], the use of catalysts [16], or the use of proteins on membranes [15], to mention some of them.

In the last years, some models of P systems have been influenced by the processes of biological infection and dissemination. Thus, virus machines [3,18] and objects inspired by genetic plasmids in neural computing models [1,11] have been proposed as new models of computation. In both cases, the objects (viruses and plasmids) acted in a passive role, that is, they were used as distinguished objects but without any direct influence on the rules governing the system.

In this work, we propose genetic plasmids, and we offer a new perspective that is closer to the active biological role played by this mobile genetic agent. In this work, plasmids become active sets of rules that, once introduced into a region, behave as a component that can dynamize the computations in the different regions of a P system. In addition, we relate our computational model with another model that has had a notable presence in the field of membrane computing: P colonies [5,9]. P colonies are composed by active agents that play a computational role in a shared environment. Every agent is defined by a set of objects together with a finite set of rules. In later work [4], a P colony model was proposed where agents have mobility rules in a two-dimensional space organized by a 2D grid.

This paper is structured as follows: first, basic concepts of genetic plasmids and membrane computing are introduced, which are necessary for understanding the rest of this work. Then, the computation by plasmids model is presented as a variant of P systems. The basic concepts of P colonies are introduced, and some relationships between P colonies and computation by plasmids in transition P systems are proposed. Finally, we end this work by providing some conclusions.

2   Basic Concepts

In the following, we introduce basic concepts of the biology of genetic plasmids taken from [10,14,22], and from membrane computing and P systems taken from [19].

2.1   The Biology of Plasmids

Plasmids are nonessential extrachromosomal genetic elements that replicate autonomously and control their own replication [14]. They are also known to be mobile genetic elements that can be horizontally transferred among different organisms [22]. Some bacterial plasmids take a circular shape based on a super-coiled DNA molecule, and they exist in a characteristic number of copies per cell. Plasmids are generally classified acording to the genetic information specified by their DNA. For example, most of the R plasmids consist of two components: the resistance transfer factor (RTF), and one or more r-determinants that are genes that confer resistance to antibiotics or mercury as shown in Fig. 1.

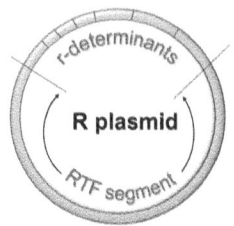

Fig. 1. A R plasmid containing resistance transfer factors (RTFs) and r-determinants

Plasmids can be considered as the bacterial fertility factor (F factor) in conjugation processes. Conjugation is a process by which genetic information from one bacterium is transferred to and recombined with that of other bacterium [10]. We can see in Fig. 2 a scheme for conjugation between two bacteria one donor and one receiver.

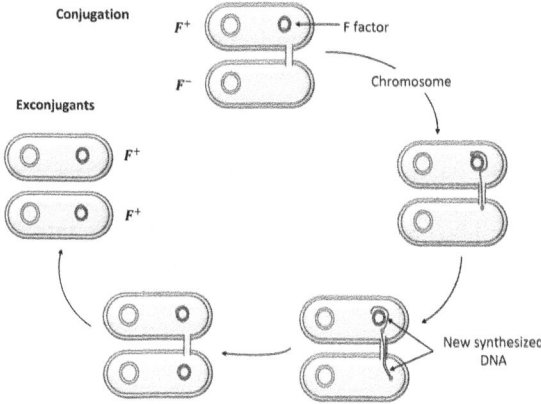

Fig. 2. A scheme of bacterial conjugation. The scheme shows how the recipient F^- cell converts to F^+

The most relevant aspects that we consider in this work are the following:

1. They are mobile genetic elements, meaning they encode genes that can be transferred and recombined.
2. They allow copying and self-replication.
3. Once transferred, they provide the host with an additional set of genetic instructions that can be at the same level as the recipient's native instructions.

2.2   P Systems

Now, we will introduce some basic concepts on P systems according to [19]. We assume that the reader is familiar with the basics of language theory and multisets.

Definition 1. *A cell-like* transition P system of degree m *is a construct*

$$\Pi = (V, \mu, w_1, \cdots, w_m, (R_1, \rho_1), \cdots, (R_m, \rho_m), i_0),$$

where:

- *V is the alphabet of objects;*
- *μ is a membrane structure consisting of m membranes labeled in a one-to-one manner with the natural numbers $\{1, .., m\}$. The outermost membrane is called the skin membrane;*
- *w_i, $1 \leq i \leq m$, is a string representing a multiset over V associated to the region i of μ;*
- *R_i, $1 \leq i \leq m$, are finite sets of evolution rules over V associated with the regions of μ; the evolution rules are of the forms $u \rightarrow v$ or $u \rightarrow v\delta$, where u is a multiset over V and v is a string from $(V \times \{here, out, in_k : 1 \leq k \leq m\})^*$ that denotes a multiset with target addressings.*
  In the rest of the work, we will omit the addressing here, so that the symbol a in the right-hand side of any rule will denote a_{here};
  The δ symbol is used to define dissolution rules where the membrane at region i disappears after the application of the rule. In such a case, all the rules of R_i dissapear. Observe that the dissolution rules cannot be applied in the skin membrane.
- *ρ_i, $1 \leq i \leq m$, is a partial order in the rules of R_i that denotes the priorities*
- *$i_0 \in \{1, ..., m\} \cup \{\infty\}$ specifies the output membrane of Π (in the case that it equals to ∞, the output is read outside the system).*

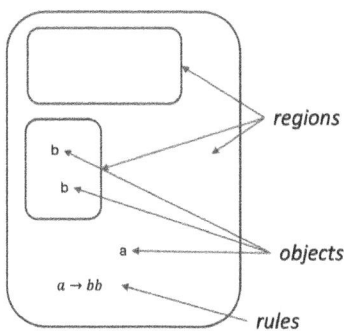

Fig. 3. A scheme of a P systems. The external membrane is named the skin membrane.

A scheme of a P system is shown in Fig. 3. A configuration of the system consists of the membrane structure and the multisets of objects at every region. The change of a configuration of the system is obtained by applying the rules at every region, for example in a maximally parallel manner [6]. That is, the maximum number of rules that can be applied (with or without repetition) are applied at each computation step. The system halts when no rule can be applied in any of the region. A computation of the system is a finite sequence of configurations that starts from the initial configuration. The result of a computation can be considered as the number of objects present in the output region when the system halts.

It is a well known result that transition P systems are universal and complete models of computation (given that they are equivalent to Turing machines and register machines). Furthermore, the P systems solve efficiently problems that are catalogued as difficult and intractable problems in the computational complexity theory [19] (they solve NP-complete problems in the P systems polynomial time).

3   Computing by Plasmids

In this section, we introduce plasmids as mobile agents that change the behavior of local regions at P systems. In the context of P systems, we consider that plasmids are membranes that only contain rules (there are no objects inside them). They can move throughout the space of regions of the P system by using predefined rules. Whenever a plasmid enters into a region, all its rules are inherited by such a region and its rules compete for the objects at the same level as the rest of the rules that were defined in that region. In addition, there are rules that can move the plasmids by using communication rules as in the classical transition P systems.

In the following, we provide a formal definition of P systems with plasmids.

Definition 2. *A* cell-like *transition P system of degree m with q plasmids is a construct*

$$\Pi = (V, H, \mu, w_1, \cdots, w_m, R_o, R_p, \rho, z_1, \cdots, z_m, z_E, p_1, \cdots, p_q, i_0),$$

where:

- *V is the alphabet of objects;*
- *H is the alphabet of membrane labels;*
- *μ is a membrane structure;*
- *w_i, $1 \leq i \leq m$, is a string representing a multiset over V associated to the region i of μ;*
- *R_o is a finite set of rules for objects and membranes, defined in the same way as the sets R_i in Definition 1. Observe that every rule can be referred to a different region by labeling its corresponding membrane;*
- *R_p is a finite set of rules for plasmid mobility, plasmid replication, and plasmid dissolution of the following types*

1. *in-symport movement*
   $p_i u[\ ]_k \rightarrow v[\ p_i\ ]_k$ *where p_i is a plasmid with $1 \leq i \leq q$, and $u, v \in V^*$*
2. *out-symport movement*
   $[p_i u]_k \rightarrow p_i[v]_k$ *where p_i is a plasmid with $1 \leq i \leq q$, and $u, v \in V^*$*
3. *antiport movement*
   $p_i u[p_j v]_k \rightarrow p_j w[p_i x]_k$ *where p_i, p_j are plasmids with $1 \leq i, j \leq q$, and $u, v, w, x \in V^*$*
4. *replication*
   $[p_i u]_k \rightarrow [p_i p_i v]_k$ *where p_i is a plasmid with $1 \leq i \leq q$, and $u, v \in V^*$*
5. *dissolution*
   $[p_i u]_k \rightarrow [v]_k$ *where p_i is a plasmid $1 \leq i \leq q$, and $u, v \in V^*$*

- *ρ is a partial order over the rules from R_o and R_p that denotes the priorities;*
- *$z_1, z_2, ..., z_m$ are the initial multiset of plasmids at every region in μ;*
- *z_E is the initial multiset of plasmids in the environment;*
- *$p_1, p_2, \cdots, p_q$ are plasmids, where every plasmid is defined by a pair (R_{p_i}, ρ_{p_i}) such that R_{p_i} is a finite set of evolution rules of the form $u \rightarrow v$ where $u \in V^+$, and $v \in (V \times \{here, out, in_k : 1 \leq k \leq m\})^*$, and ρ_{p_i} is a partial order over the rules in R_{p_i} that denotes the priorities*
- *$i_0 \in \{1, ..., m\} \cup \{\infty\}$ specifies the output membrane of Π (in the case that it equals to ∞, the output is read outside the system)*

We make some remarks to the previous definition:

1. when a dissolution rule is applied within a region, it causes all plasmids within that region to disappear (they are not moved to the upper region)
2. plasmid rules affect only to objects (they do not affect to other plasmids or membranes).
3. plasmid replication rules are applied in a minimal parallel manner: the rules are applied only to one plasmid regardless of how many copies of that plasmid there are in the region. Therefore, they only produces one copy of every plasmid at every computational step.

The system configuration takes into account not only the objects in each region but also the plasmids it contains. The change of a configuration is carried out similarly to that in a cell-like transition P system without plasmids. However, when applying rules to objects, the rules of the plasmids compete for objects at the same level as the rest of the rules. The system halts when no rule can be applied within the system, including plasmid mobility rules and the rules contained within each plasmid. The result of the computation can be considered the number of objects found in the output region when the system halts. Note that, in this sense, plasmids cannot be considered objects.

In the Fig. 4, we show a scheme of a P system with plasmids. Observe that red circles are plasmids and they are membranes that only contain only rules and do not contain objects.

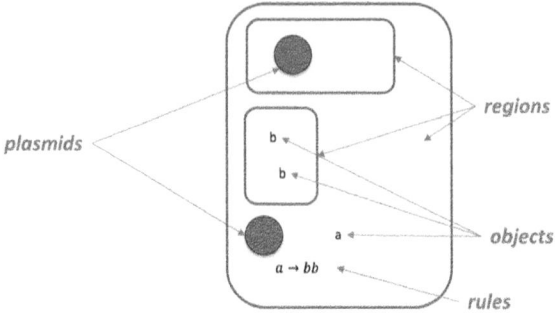

Fig. 4. An scheme of a P systems with plasmids

Example 1. Let us consider the following P systems with plasmids:

- $V = \{a, b, c, p, q\}$
- $H = \{1, 2, 3\}$
- $\mu = [\,[\,]_2\,[\,]_3\,]_1$
- $w_1 = pq$, $w_2 = a^n$ and $w_3 = b^m$
- $R_o = \{\,[a[\,]_3]_1 \to [\,[a]_3]_1\}$
- $R_p = \{p_1[\,p\,]_1 \to [p_1]_1,\ p_2[\,q\,]_1 \to [p_2]_1,\ p_1[\,]_2 \to [p_1]_2,\ p_2[\,]_3 \to [p_2]_3\}$
- $\rho = \emptyset$
- $z_1 = z_2 = z_3 = \emptyset$ and $z_E = p_1 p_2$
- $R_{p_1} = \{a \to a_{out}\}\ R_{p_2} = \{ab \to c_{out}\}\ \rho_{p_1} = \rho_{p_2} = \emptyset$
- $i_0 = 3$

The system we have defined calculates the function $f(n, m) = |n - m|$. It uses two plasmids p_1 and p_2. Plasmid p_1, when entering a region, sends out all the a symbols from it, while plasmid p_2, when entering a region, pairs symbols a and b and rewrites them as c. The symbols that have not been paired constitute the difference in absolute value of n and m. In Fig. 5, we show an example of a computation in the system. Observe that the parameter n is stored in region 2, while the parameter m is at region 3.

The family of P systems of degree m with q plasmids is denoted by Ppl_m^q. It has been shown in [20] that for every set A in NRE (that denotes the sets of numbers that can be algorithmically calculated) there exist positive integers $m, q > 0$ such that A can be calculated by a P system in Ppl_m^q. Hence, P systems with plasmids are complete models of computation.

4   P Colonies

In this section, we refer to [5] that is a survey on the subject. P colonies were first introduced in [9]. This computational model is based on communities of agents interacting in a shared environment that they can influence by their actions.

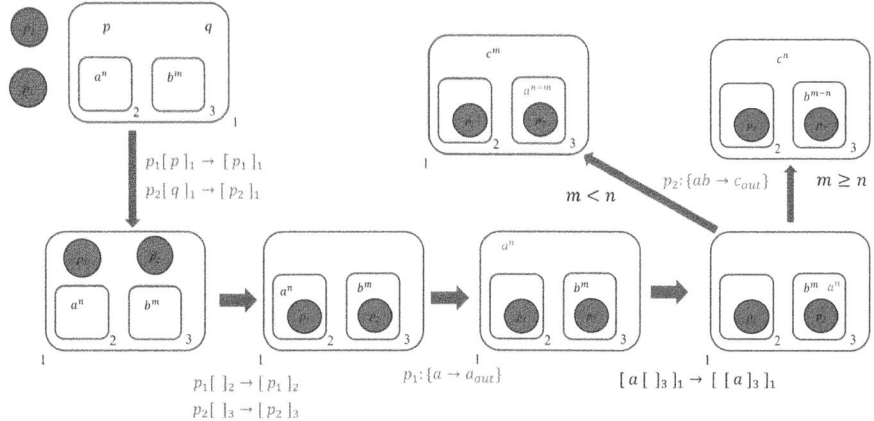

Fig. 5. An example of computing by plasmids to calculate $|n - m|$.

The sources of inspiration are multiple, as one can observe the influence of classic multi-agent systems in artificial intelligence [21], but also the work by tissue-like P systems [13], and classical works in formal language theory as in [8].

In this model, every agent consists of a finite multiset of objects (usually they are limited by the agent capacity), and a finite set of rules acting on the objects (*programs*). In addition, all the agents share an environment that contains a multiset of objects. Among all the objects there is a distinguished one (*the environment object*). During a computation, the agents can change the objects in the environment and they can change their own objects. The result of a computation in a P colony is the number of copies of a distinguished object (the *final object*).

Formally, we can define a P colony as follows:

Definition 3. *A P colony of capacity k, $k \geq 1$, is a construct*

$$\Pi = (A, e, f, v_E, B_1, \ldots, B_n),$$

where

- *A is an alphabet, its elements are called objects;*
- *$e \in A$ is the basic (or environmental) object of the colony;*
- *$f \in A$ is the final object of the colony;*
- *v_E is a finite multiset over $A - \{e\}$, called the initial state (or initial content) of the environment;*
- *B_i, $1 \leq i \leq n$, are agents, where each agent $B_i = (o_i, P_i)$ is defined as follows:*
  - *o_i is a multiset over A consisting of k objects, the initial state (or initial content) of the agent;*
  - *$P_i = \{p_{i,1}, \ldots, p_{i,k_i}\}$ is a finite set of programs, where each program consists of k rules, which are in one of the following forms each:*

* $a \rightarrow b$, $a, b \in A$, called an evolution rule;
* $c \leftrightarrow d$, $c, d \in A$, called a communication rule;
* r_1/r_2 , called a checking rule; r_1, r_2 are both evolution rules or both communication rules.

In a P colony, at each computation step, the state of the environment and that of the agents changes, for example, in the maximally parallel derivation mode, where each agent which can use any of its programs should use one (non-deterministically chosen) [5]. The result of a computation is given as the number of copies of the objects f present in the environment in the halting configuration.

A few years after the first proposal of P colonies, a variant of the model was formulated in which the colony's agents were provided with rules for mobility in the environment [4]. The environment was modeled as a two-dimensional space (2D) organized into cells arranged in a grid. In the proposed model, mobility rules were prioritized over rules of communication with the environment. The capacity of the agents (that is, the number of objects they can contain), as well as the instructions of their programs, are limited to 2.

A computation step in a 2D P colony consists of three parts: First, the set of applicable programs must be selected, then a program must be selected in such a way that there is no collision between communication rules and, finally, the selected programs are executed. The result of a computation is the number of final objects placed in the environment at the end.

In the following we provide the formal definition of a 2D P colony.

Definition 4. *A 2D P colony is a construct*

$$\Pi = (A, e, Env, B_1, \ldots, B_k, f), k \geq 1$$

where

- *A is an alphabet, its elements are called objects;*
- *$e \in A$ is the basic object of the 2D colony;*
- *Env is a pair $(m \times n, w_E)$, where $m, n \in \mathbb{N}$ is the size of the environment and w_E is the initial contents of environment, it is a matrix of size $m \times n$ of multisets of objects over $A - \{e\}$*
- *B_i, $1 \leq i \leq k$, are agents, where each agent $B_i = (o_i, P_i[o, p])$ is defined as follows:*
  - *o_i is a multiset over A, the initial state (or the initial content) of the agent, $|o_i| = 2$;*
  - *$P_i = \{p_{i,1}, \ldots, p_{i,l_i}\}$ is a finite set of programs, where each program contains exactly 2 rules, which are in one of the following forms each:*
    * *$a \rightarrow b$, $a, b \in A$, called an evolution rule;*
    * *$c \leftrightarrow d$, $c, d \in A$, called a communication rule;*
    * *$[a_{q,r}] \rightarrow s$, $0 \leq q, r \leq 2$, $s \in \{\Leftarrow, \Rightarrow, \Uparrow, \Downarrow\}$, called the motion rule,*

- $f \in A$ is the final object of the colony.

It has been proved that different combinations of the ingredientes of P colonies within different number of agents, different agent capacities, and different number of programs go to universality [19].

5 Some Relations Between P Colonies and Computing by Plasmids

In this section, we explore preliminary ideas about the relationship between computing by plasmids and P colonies. Our intention is to establish a direct transformation from one into the other. Hence, we will provide a general outline on how to obtain a P system with plasmids from a P colony.

5.1 A Proposal for the General Case

First, we analyze the general case where we consider a P colony

$$\Pi = (A, e, f, v_E, B_1, \ldots, B_n).$$

We can build a P system with plasmids

$$\Pi' = (V, H, \mu, w_{col}, R_o, R_p, \rho, z_{col}, z_E, p_1, \cdots, p_q, i_o),$$

starting from Π as follows

- $V = A \cup \{m_1, m_1', \cdots, m_n, m_n'\} \cup \bigcup_{1 \leq i \leq n} A_i$, where $A_i = \{a_i : a \in A - \{e\}\}$ and objects m_j, m_j' are used for the plasmids mobility;
- $H = \{col\}$, the P systems consists of only one membrane that we name col;
- $\mu = [\ ]_{col}$;
- $w_{col} = v_E \cup \{m_1, \cdots, m_n\} \cup \bigcup_{1 \leq i \leq n} w_i$, where $w_i = h_i(o_i)$ is obtained from the initial contents of every agent by applying the morphism $h_i(a) = a_i$ for all $a \in A$;
- $z_{col} = \emptyset$ and $z_E = \prod_{1 \leq i \leq n; 1 \leq j \leq l_i} p_{i,k}$, it means that all the plasmids are outside the system;
- For every program $p_{i,k}$ a plasmid $p_{i,k}$ is defined as follows:
  1. if the rule $a \to b$ belongs to program $p_{i,k}$ the the rule $a_i \to b_i$ belongs to $R_{p_{i,k}}$;
  2. if the rule $c \leftrightarrow d$ belongs to program $p_{i,k}$ then the rule $c_i d \to c d_i$ belongs to $R_{p_{i,k}}$;
  3. $\rho_{p_{i,k}} = \emptyset$
- $R_o = \emptyset$
- R_p is defined as follows: for every plasmid $p_{i,k}$ the following rules are defined:
  1. $p_{i,k}[\ m_i app(p_{i,k}]_{col} \to [\ p_{i,k} m_i' app(p_{i,k}]_{col}$, and

2. $[p_{i,k}m'_i]_{col} \rightarrow p_{i,k}[m_i]_{col}$

The function $app(p_{i,k})$ returns a multiset by taking the symbols in the left-hand side of the rules. It is used to select only those plasmids that can be applicable. For the checking rules r_1/r_2 different combinations are obtained;

- the definition of ρ goes as follows: if the checking rule r_1/r_2 belongs to agent B_i then $r_1 > r_2$ belongs to ρ;
- $i_o = col$

The proposed plasmid system works as explained in the following: The system works with a single membrane that models the environment of the P colony. To distinguish between objects in the environment and local objects of each agent, indexed copies of each object are introduced. Thus, for example, object a_i means that object a belongs to agent i. All plasmids in the P system are outside the system and they are in its environment. For each agent's program, a plasmid is created that interacts with that agent's indexed objects. Note that the exchange of objects between the agent and the environment through communication rules is established by rules for the evolution of indexed objects to non-indexed ones and vice versa. For the selection of each agent's program, note that only one plasmid can be selected since there is only one object m_i per agent in the system. The plasmid selection is carried out by evaluating its applicability. Once the plasmid has entered the system, it can apply its program (which is the same as that of the agent in the P colony). Note that while the plasmid executes its program, another plasmid cannot enter since the object m_i has changed to m'_i. Finally, the plasmid is sent out from the system into the environment and the simulation of a computational step is completed.

Note that with this strategy, the simulation of a P colony using a P system with plasmids can be performed effectively.

5.2   A Proposal for the 2D Case

Next, we will analyze the case of 2D P colonies. In this case, we will start from the colony defined as $\Pi = (A, e, Env, B_1, \ldots, B_s, f)$. with a grid of $m \times n$ size. The first modification with respect to the general case is that the membrane structure changes. We model the colony grid by introducing regions indexed by their spatial coordinates as showed in Fig. 6. In addition, an auxiliary region named tr is defined inside the skin region.

Next, we formally define the P system with plasmids proposed to simulate the 2D P colony. It is denoted by the following tuple

$$\Pi' = (V, H, \mu, w_{(1,1)}, \cdots, w_{(m,n)}, w_{tr}, w_{col}, R_o, R_p, \rho, z_{(1,1)}, \cdots, z_{(m,n)}, z_{tr},$$
$$z_{col}, z_E, p_1, \cdots, p_q, i_o), \text{where}$$

- $V = A \cup \{t\} \cup \bigcup_{\substack{1 \leq i \leq s; \\ 1 \leq j \leq m; \\ 1 \leq l \leq n}} \{m_{(i,j,l)}, m'_{(i,j,l)}, m''_{(i,j,l)}, m'''_{(i,j,l)}, m^{iv}_{(i,j,l)}\} \cup \bigcup_{1 \leq i \leq s} A_i \cup$

$A'_i \cup \hat{A}_i$, where $t \notin V$, $A_i = \{a_i : a \in A - \{e\}\}$, $A'_i = \{a'_{i,l,r} : a \in A - \{e\}, 1 \leq$

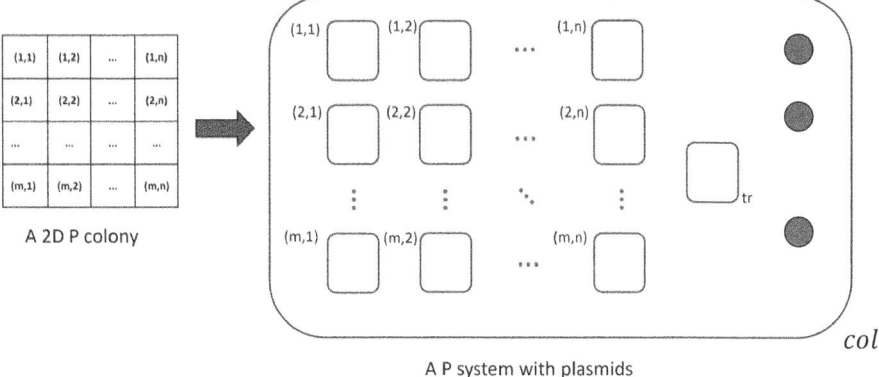

Fig. 6. A scheme to obtain a P system with plasmids from a 2D P colony.

$l \leq m, 1 \leq r \leq n\}$, $\hat{A}_i = \{\hat{a}_{i,p} : a \in A - \{e\}, 1 \leq p \leq l_i\}$ and objects $m_{(i,j,l)}, m'_{(i,j,l)}, m''_{(i,j,l)}$ are used for the plasmids mobility. Observe that s is the number of agents in the 2D P colony;

– $H = \{col, tr\} \cup \{(1,1), \cdots, (m,n)\}$, the P systems consists of one membrane that we name col and as many membranes within it as there are cells in the grid of the 2D P colony, and an auxiliary membrane tr;

– $\mu = [\,[\,]_{(1,1)} \cdots [\,]_{(m,n)}[\,]_{tr}]_{col}$;

– the objects in w_{col} are defined in the following way: if $B_i = (o_i, P_i, [l, r])$ then $m_{(i,l,r)} \in w_{col}$ for $1 \leq l \leq m, 1 \leq r \leq n$;

– $w_{(i,j)} = Env[(i,j), w_E]$, the contents of the regions are the same as in the 2D grid, and $w_{tr} = t$;

– $z_{col} = \prod_{\substack{1 \leq i \leq s; \\ 1 \leq j \leq l_i}} p_{i,j} \prod_{\substack{1 \leq i \leq s; \\ 1 \leq j \leq l_i}} \{p'_{i,j}, p''_{i,j}, p'''_{i,j}\}$, $z_{tr} = \emptyset$, $z_E = \emptyset$, and $z_{(i,j)} = \emptyset$ for $1 \leq i \leq m$ $1 \leq j \leq n$;

– For every program $p_{i,k}$, a plasmid $p_{i,k}$ is defined as follows:
  1. if the rule $a \rightarrow b$ belongs to program $p_{i,k}$ then the rule $\hat{a}_{i,k} \rightarrow \hat{b}_{i,k}$ belongs to $R_{p_{i,k}}$;
  2. if the rule $c \leftrightarrow d$ belongs to program $p_{i,k}$ then the rule $\hat{c}_{i,k} d'_{i,l,r} \rightarrow c'_{i,l,r} \hat{d}_{i,k}$ for $1 \leq l \leq m, 1 \leq r \leq n$, belongs to $R_{p_{i,k}}$;
  3. $\rho_{p_{i,k}} = \emptyset$;

– For every program $p_{i,k}$, a plasmid $p'_{i,k}$ is defined as follows:
  1. for every object $a \in A$, the following rules belong to $R_{p'_{i,k}}$
     $[[m_{(i,l,r)} a\,]_{(l,r)}]_{col} \rightarrow [[m_{i,l,r}\,]_{(l,r)} a'_{i,l,r}]_{col}$ (rule r_1), and
     $[[m_{(i,l,r)}\,]_{(l,r)}]_{col} \rightarrow [[\,]_{(l,r)} m''_{i,l,r}\,]_{col}$ (rule r_2)
  2. $r_1 > r_2$ is defined in $\rho_{p'_{i,k}}$

– For every program $p_{i,k}$, a plasmid $p''_{i,k}$ is defined as follows:
  1. for every object $a'_{i,l,r} \in A'_i$, the following rules belong to $R_{p''_{i,k}}$:
     $[[m'''_{(i,l,r)}\,]_{(l,r)} a'_{i,l,r}]_{col} \rightarrow [[m'''_{i,l,r} a\,]_{(l,r)}]_{col}$ (rule r_3), and
     $[[m'''_{(i,l,r)}\,]_{(l,r)}]_{col} \rightarrow [[\,]_{(l,r)} m'^v_{i,l,r}\,]_{col}$ (rule r_4)

2. $r_3 > r_4$ is defined in $\rho_{p''_{i,k}}$

- For every program $p_{i,k}$, a plasmid $p'''_{i,k}$ is defined as follows:

1. for every object $a_i \in A_i$, the following rules belong to $\rho_{p'''_{i,k}}$:

$[[m'''_{(i,k)}t \ ]_{tr}a_i]_{col} \rightarrow [[m'''_{i,k}t\hat{a}_{i,k} \ ]_{tr}]_{col}$ (rule r_5),

$[[m'''_{i,k}t\hat{a}_{i,k} \ ]_{tr}]_{col} \rightarrow [[m'''_{i,k}t]_{tr}\hat{a}_{i,k} \ ]_{col}$ (rule r_6), and

$[[m'''_{(i,k)}t \ ]_{tr}]_{col} \rightarrow [[t \ ]_{tr}m'^v_{(i,k)}) \ ]_{col}$ (rule r_7)

2. $r_5, r_6 > r_7$ is defined in $\rho_{p'''_{i,k}}$

- The set of plasmids in the system $p_1, \cdots, p_q$ enumerates the plasmids defined before
- R_o is defined to change the objects $m'^v_{(i,j,l)}$ to symbols $m_{(i,q,r)}$ according to the motion rules of the agents. In order to simplify the exposition, we will not specify the rules, but we must emphasize that each rule takes into account the object $m_{(i,j,l)}$ together with the contents of the regions surrounding the region (j, l). Collisions between agents will be avoided by proposing rules that prevent the simultaneous creation of objects $m_{(i,q,r)}$ and $m_{(i',q,r)}$. Note that since the number of possible cases is finite, one can precalculate all possible collisions and create the appropriate rules.
- R_p is defined as follows: for every plasmid $p_{i,k}$ the following rules are created:

1. $[\ p'_{i,k}m_{(i,j,l)}app(p_{i,k})[\ ]_{(j,l)}]_{col} \rightarrow [\ app(p_{i,k})[\ m'_{(i,j,l)}p'_{i,k}]_{(j,l)} [p'''_{i,k}m'''_{i,k}]_{tr}]_{col}$,

2. $[\ m''_{(i,j,l)}[p'_{i,k} \ ]_{(j,l)}]_{col} \rightarrow [\ m'''_{(i,j,l)}p'_{i,k}[\ ]_{(j,l)}]_{col}$,

3. $[\ m''_{(i,k)}[p''_{i,k} \ ]_{tr}]_{col} \rightarrow [\ p''_{i,k}[\ ]_{tr}]_{col}$, and

4. $[\ p''_{i,k}m'''_{(i,j,l)}[\ ]_{(j,l)}]_{col} \rightarrow [\ [\ m'''_{(i,j,l)}p''_{i,k}]_{(j,l)}]_{col}$

The function $app(p_{i,k})$ returns a multiset by taking the symbols in the left-hand side of the rules. It is used to select only those plasmids that can be applicable on the environment.

- $\rho = \emptyset$ (there are only priorities in the plasmid rules)
- $i_o = col$ (the result is obtained in the membrane related to the colony environment. If a different output is required then the output region should be changed).

The system works as explained in the following: for each cell in the grid, a region is created containing its objects. The outer region, called *col*, holds the objects for each agent, as well as the objects used to mobilize the plasmids. At the beginning of each computation cycle, the objects $m_{i,l,r}$ indicate in which cells each agent will be executed. A plasmid is sent through the objects $m'_{(i,l,r)}$, which enters the corresponding cell and sends all the objects in that cell to the region *col*. In addition, the objects of the agent are renamed in region *tr* to work only with a selected program $p_{i,k}$. The evolution and communication rules of every agent are then executed with their corresponding plasmids. Once executed, the objects are sent back to each grid cell, and new addressing objects are created according to the motion rules of every agent. The computation halts when no agent can be executed in any of the regions.

6 Conclusions

In this work we have presented the computing by plasmids model in the framework of membrane computing. Given the similarity between plasmids and the agents of P colonies, we have been able to establish a preliminary simulation of these systems by using computing by plasmids systems. This is the beginning of further works where we will be able to observe new relationships between the different variants of P colonies with respect to computing by plasmids.

Acknowledgement. Over the years, the work of Prof. Dr. Csuhaj-Varjú has always been a source of inspiration for my work. Furthermore, I am tremendously grateful for the friendship that Erzsi has shown me during all these years. Her honesty and scientific quality are combined with the personal qualities of kindness, respect, and friendship that I have been fortunate enough to enjoy. Therefore, my participation in this tribute volume is an act of recognition and gratitude to Erzsi.

Disclosure of Interests. The author has no competing interests to declare that are relevant to the content of this article. This work has received funding from the Generalitat Valenciana within the Prometeo program in the project *"A disruptive way to ameliorate the diagnosis and treatment of sensorineural diseases."* CIPROM/2023/026.

References

1. Cabarle, F., Zeng, X., Murphy, N., Song, T., Rodríguez-Patón, A., Liu, X.: Neural-like P systems with plasmids. Inf. Comput. **281**, 104766 (2021)
2. Cardona, M., et al.: A computational modeling for real ecosystems based on P systems. Nat. Comput. **10**, 39–53 (2011)
3. Chen, X., Pérez-Jiménez, M.J., Valencia-Cabrera, L., Wang, B., Zeng, X.: Computing with viruses. Theor. Comput. Sci. **623**, 146 159 (2016)
4. Cienciala, L., Ciencialová, L., Perdek, M.: 2D P colonies. In: Csuhaj-Varjú, E., Gheorghe, M., Rozenberg, G., Salomaa, A., Vaszil, G. (eds.) CMC 2012. LNCS, vol. 7762, pp. 161–172. Springer, Heidelberg (2013). https://doi.org/10.1007/978-3-642-36751-9_12
5. Ciencialová, L., Csuhaj-Varjú, E., Cienciala, L., Sosík, P.: P colonies. J. Membr. Comput. **1**, 178–197 (2019)
6. Freund, R.: How derivation modes and halting conditions may influence the computational power of P systems. J. Membr. Comput. **2**, 14–25 (2020)
7. Ionescu, M., Păun, G., Yokomori, T.: Spiking neural P systems. Fundamenta Informaticae **71**, 279–308 (2006)
8. Kelemen, J., Kelemenová, A.: A grammar-theoretic treatment of multiagent systems. Cybern. Syst. **23**(6), 621–633 (1992)
9. Kelemen, J., Kelemenová A., Păun, Gh.: Preview of P colonies: a biochemically inspired computing model. In: Ninth International Conference on the Simulation and Synthesis of Living Systems (Alife IX), Workshop and Tutorial Proceedings, pp. 82–86 (2004)
10. Klug, W.S., Cummings, M.R., Spencer, C.A., Palladino, M.A., Killian, D.J.: Essentials of Genetics, 10th edn. Pearson, London (2021)

11. Li, Y., Song, B., Zeng, X.: Neural-like P systems with plasmids and multiple channels. IEEE Trans. NanoBiosci. **22**(2), 420–429 (2023)
12. Manca, V., Bianco, L., Fontana, F.: Metabolic P systems. In Mauri, G., Păun, Gh., Pérez-Jiménez, M.J., Rozenberg, Gr., Salomaa, A. (eds.) 5th International Workshop WMC, LNCS, vol . 3365, pp. 63–84. Springer, Heidelberg (2005)
13. Martín-Vide, C., Păun, G., Pazos, J., Rodríguez-Patón, A.: Tissue P systems. Theor. Comput. Sci. **296**, 295–326 (2003)
14. Novick, R.P. : Plasmids. Encyclopedia of Life Sciences. John Wiley & Sons, Hoboken (2001)
15. Păun, A., Popa, B.: P systems with proteins on membranes. Fund. Inf. **72**, 467–483 (2006)
16. Păun, Gh.: Computing with membranes. J. Comput. Syst. Sci. **61**(1), 108–143 (2000)
17. Păun, Gh.: P systems with active membranes: attacking NP-complete problems. J. Autom. Lang. Comb. **6**, 75–90 (2001)
18. Romero-Jiménez, Á., Valencia-Cabrera, L., Riscos-Núñez, A., Pérez-Jiménez, M.J.: Computing partial recursive functions by virus machines. In: Rozenberg, G., Salomaa, A., Sempere, J.M., Zandron, C. (eds.) CMC 2015. LNCS, vol. 9504, pp. 353–368. Springer, Cham (2015). https://doi.org/10.1007/978-3-319-28475-0_24
19. Păun, G., Rozenberg, G., A. Salomaa, A. (eds.): The Oxford Handbook of Membrane Computing. Oxford University Press, Oxford (2010)
20. Sempere, J.M.: Computing by plasmids. In: 21st Brainstorming Week on Membrane Computing (BWMC) (2025)
21. Wooldridge, M.J.: An Introduction to Multiagent Systems. John Wiley & Sons, Chichester (2009)
22. Yano, H., Shintani, M., Tomita, M., Suzuki, H., Oshima, T.: Reconsidering plasmid maintenance factors for computational plasmid design. Comput. Struct. Biotechnol. J. **17**, 70–81 (2019)

An Overview on Applications of Spiking Neural Networks and Spiking Neural P Systems

Claudio Zandron$^{(\boxtimes)}$ (iD)

Dipartimento di Informatica, Sistemistica e Comunicazione,
Univeristá di Milano-Bicocca, Milan, Italy
`claudio.zandron@unimib.it`

Abstract. Spiking Neural Networks (SNNs) and Spiking Neural P Systems (SNPSs) are advanced computational models inspired by the biological processes of the human brain. SNNs use discrete spikes to transmit information between neurons, offering a more energy-efficient and biologically plausible approach compared to traditional neural networks. These networks are particularly well-suited for resource-constrained environments, processing temporal information with reduced energy consumption. On the other hand, SNPSs combine the principles of SNNs with membrane computing, enabling efficient distributed computing and complex problem-solving. Both models are capable of modeling biological neural processes and offer advantages in tasks such as image recognition, classification, and diagnostics. Their sparse, asynchronous activity and ability to adapt through spike-timing dependent plasticity make them a promising tool for a range of applications, from artificial intelligence to medical fields. Despite some challenges, particularly in training algorithms, these models present exciting opportunities for more efficient and biologically inspired computational systems.

Keywords: Spiking Neural Networks · Spiking Neural P Systems · Energy-efficient computing

1 Introduction

Spiking Neural Networks (SNNs) and Spiking Neural P Systems (SNPSs) are recent models of artificial neural networks, inspired by the functioning of the human brain. These models offer a more biologically plausible approach to neural processing compared to traditional Artificial Neural Networks (ANNs). In fact, in biological systems neurons communicate by emitting electrical signals known as spikes [27,50], which are transmitted through synapses. This mechanism allows neurons to influence the activity of neighbor neurons, where a spike generated by one neuron can be transmitted as an input to another one [27].

The design of artificial neural networks has gradually shifted toward more biologically realistic models [1,2,21,38]. While traditional neural networks have

M. D. Jiménez López and G. Vaszil (Eds.): Erzsébet Csuhaj-Varjú Festschrift,
LNCS 15840, pp. 267–278, 2025.
https://doi.org/10.1007/978-3-031-97274-4_16

proven effective in numerous applications, they often demand high computational power and are difficult to scale. Consequently, these networks may not be ideal in resource-limited environments. SNNs present an appealing alternative by significantly reducing energy consumption [19,20,49] and allowing for efficient processing with fewer neurons [55]. The efficiency of SNNs are a consequence of their sparse, asynchronous operation: neurons in an SNN can spike independently, without needing all components to be active at once, thus resulting in significative energy reduction. In SNNs, neurons are characterized by their internal state, which represents their action potential. As they receive spikes, this potential either increases or decreases, depending on the synaptic inputs. Synapses can modify their strength (through a process known as synaptic plasticity), which play a key role in learning and adaptation in the brain. This feature allows SNNs to effectively model biological communication mechanisms, making them valuable tools for investigating the brain's processes, such as information encoding and learning.

Unlike conventional artificial neural networks that rely on continuous activation values, SNNs transmit discrete spikes over time, capturing the temporal dynamics of neural activity. A neuron's action potential is determined by a threshold, which when exceeded, triggers the emission of a spike. This discrete operation of SNNs enables more efficient information encoding and processing, based on the timing and frequency of spikes. However, training SNNs presents challenges due to the discrete nature of spikes, requiring specialized learning algorithms. Despite these hurdles, SNNs have been successfully applied in numerous fields, as we will show in the following sections.

Another similar approach is Spiking Neural P Systems [26,30], introduced in 2006 as a variation of membrane systems [42]. These systems merge the principles of SNNs with the parallel [23,63] and distributed [6,14] aspects of membrane computing. Motivated by the neurophysiological features of biological neurons and the concepts of Spiking Neural Networks, SNPSs operate based on the emission and propagation of spikes within a membrane structure. Research on SNPSs has focused on their computational capabilities, including topics like communication on request [41,57], the impact of synaptic delays [53], and non-linear system behaviors [43]. Following similar lines common in the area of membrane computing [3,31–33,40,51], SNPSs have also been explored both for their computational properties as well as to find solutions for complex computational problems [17,22,29,37,54,56], in addition to investigating the intricacies of various algorithms in distributed environments.

The applicability of SNPSs extends to high-dimensional, multi-class classification tasks. As with SNNs, the use of SNPSs is advantageous because of their energy-efficient properties, especially in the context of increasingly complex deep neural networks. In SNPSs, neurons only become active when they accumulate enough spikes to trigger a rule, which allows many neurons to remain inactive, further reducing energy consumption. This sparse and asynchronous activity is a defining characteristic that enhances the efficiency of SNPSs.

SNNs and SNPSs represent two distinct models of third-generation neural networks that rely on spike-based communication. While similar under various aspects, they are mainly different in the following aspects. While the model of SNPSs is grounded in a formal language-theoretic framework, SNNs are primarily inspired by biological systems; moreover, while SNNs support various encoding schemes for handling continuous-valued inputs and outputs, SNPS models encode information through the number of spikes or discrete time delays.

Both of them offer high benefits in energy efficiency, adaptability, and computational capability. Their capacity to simulate biological processes with high fidelity makes them highly promising for a broad spectrum of applications, including medical diagnostics, complex classification problems, and much more.

In this paper, we aim to present an overview of studies from the literature, highlighting the use of these models in addressing various real-world challenges.

2   Spiking Neural Networks: Definition

A Spiking Neural Network [38] is formally defined as a computational model consisting of a finite set V of spiking neurons, a set $E \subseteq V \times V$ of synapses, a weight $W_{u,v} \geq 0$, and a response function $s_{u,v} : \mathbb{R}^+ \to \mathbb{R}$ for each synapse $(u, v) \in E$ (where $\mathbb{R}^+ := \{x \in \mathbb{R} : x \geq 0\}$), and a threshold function $\theta_v : \mathbb{R}^+ \to \mathbb{R}^+$ for each neuron $v \in V$.

If $F_u \subset \mathbb{R}^+$ represents the set of firing times of a neuron u, then the membrane potential at the trigger zone of neuron v at time t is calculated by:

$$P_v(t) := \sum_{(u,v)\in E} \sum_{s\in F_u:s<t} W_{u,v}\, \varphi_v(t - s) \tag{1}$$

where φ_v is a function defining the shape of the postsynaptic potential.

In a noise-free model, a neuron v fires at time t if and only if its potential $P_v(t)$ reaches the threshold $\theta_v(t - t')$, where t' is the time of the most recent firing of neuron v.

The network contains a specified subset $V_{\text{input}} \subset V$ of input neurons, whose firing times are provided externally rather than being determined by the model. The network also designates a subset $V_{\text{output}} \subset V$ of output neurons, whose firing times constitute the network output. For all other neurons $v \in V \setminus V_{\text{input}}$, firing times are determined by the previously described rules.

Biological evidence suggests that real neurons do not always fire deterministically, and they only fire reliably only under some specific conditions. To model this apsect, a stochastic version of the basic SNN model has also been proposed, where the difference $P_v(t) - \theta_v(t - t')$ determines the probability that neuron v fires at time t. A neuron v may not fire during a time interval I even when $P_v(t) - \theta_v(t - t') > 0$, or it may fire spontaneously at time t even when $P_v(t) - \theta_v(t - t') < 0$. While differences exist between these models (mainly regarding refractory period after firing) these distinctions do not significantly impact the computational properties of the network.

3   Spiking Neural P Systems: Definition

Informally, a Spiking Neural P system consists of a set of *neurons* arranged as nodes in a directed graph. Each neuron can contain any number of *spikes* (denoted by symbol a) and, under specific conditions based on its internal spike count, can fire, producing a spike that travels along the graph's arcs (representing *synapses*) to all connected post-synaptic neurons. The system evolves from an initial configuration according to defined rules and may produce output. These ideas were formalized in [8, 26] as follows.

A *Spiking Neural P system* (SNPS, for short) of degree $m \geq 1$ is defined as:

$$\Pi = (O, \sigma_1, \ldots, \sigma_m, syn, i_0)$$

where:

1. $O = \{a\}$ is the singleton alphabet (where a represents a *spike*);
2. $\sigma_1, \ldots, \sigma_m$ are *neurons*, each defined as $\sigma_i = (n_i, R_i)$ for $1 \leq i \leq m$, with:
   - $n_i \geq 0$ representing the *initial number* of spikes in neuron σ_i;
   - R_i being a finite set of *rules* of the following forms:
     - *Spiking rules*: $E/a^c \to a^k; d$, where E is a regular expression over $\{a\}$, $c, k \geq 1$, and $d \geq 0$;
     - *Forgetting rules*: $a^s \to \lambda$, where $s \geq 1$, with the restriction that $a^s \notin L(E)$ for any spiking rule $E/a^c \to a; d$ in R_i;
3. $syn \subseteq \{1, 2, \ldots, m\} \times \{1, 2, \ldots, m\}$ with $i \neq j$ for all $(i, j) \in syn$ represents the set of *synapses* between neurons;
4. $i_0 \in \{1, 2, \ldots, m\}$ indicates the *output* neuron.

If for every spiking rule $E/a^c \to a^k; d$ the language $L(E)$ is finite, the system is called a *finite* SNPS.

The system operates synchronously according to a global discrete clock. A spiking rule $E/a^c \to a^k; d$ in neuron σ_i is *enabled* when the neuron contains n spikes such that $a^n \in L(E)$ and $n \geq c$. When fired, the rule consumes c spikes from the neuron and prepares k spikes (a single spike, in the first definition of such system [26]) for delivery to all neurons connected via outgoing synapses, with a delay of d time units. During this delay period, the neuron enters a *refractory period*, remaining closed to incoming spikes and unable to fire new rules.

A forgetting rule $a^s \to \lambda$ can only be applied if the neuron contains exactly s spikes and no spiking rules are enabled, resulting in the removal of all s spikes.

A *configuration* of the system at time t is described by $C_t = \langle k_1/t_1, \ldots, k_m/t_m \rangle$, where each k_i represents the number of spikes in neuron σ_i and $t_i \geq 0$ indicates the remaining refractory period ($t_i = 0$ means the neuron is open).

The rule application follows two principles:

- *Sequentiality* at the neuron level: if multiple rules are enabled within a neuron, only one can be applied, chosen non-deterministically;

– *Maximal parallelism* at the system level: all neurons that can apply rules must do so simultaneously.

A *computation* is a sequence of transitions between configurations, starting from the initial state. A computation *halts* when it reaches a configuration where all neurons are open and no rules are enabled.

If the system is designed so that for any neuron, the regular expressions of any two spiking rules have disjoint languages ($L(E_1) \cap L(E_2) = \emptyset$), then at most one rule can be enabled at any time, making the system *deterministic*.

4   SNN Applications

As stated before, despite the challenges posed by the learning phase for SNNs, they have found applications in various domains. Some first applications of SNNs concerned their use to the recognition of numbers, considering the MNIST dataset.SNPSs In [5] the authors presented a model of spike-driven synaptic plasticity, with a network of integrate-and-fire neurons. A network consisting of two-thousand input neurons was used to accurately classify a high number of overlapping patterns, including three-hundred classes of preprocessed LaTeX characters (eachclass consisting of 30 patterns) and a subset of the NIST character dataset. In [47] the authors described an unsupervised algorithm that is able to learn sparse features. The model employs a linear encoder and decoder, with a sparse non-linearity applied beforehand, transforming a code vector into a nearly binary, sparse code vector. When trained on handwritten digits, like those in the common MNIST dataset, the model generates "stroke detectors," and when trained on natural image patches, it produces Gabor-like filters. Both inference and learning processes are highly efficient, requiring no preprocessing or costly sampling. By utilizing the proposed unsupervised method to initialize the first layer of a convolutional network, they achieved a slightly lower error rate than the best previously reported result on the MNIST dataset. In [24] the authors performed a case study for a hardware implementation of a spiking/non-spiking deep net on the MNIST dataset and clearly outline the design prospects involved in implementing neural computing platforms in the spiking mode of operation.

In [28], a supervised learning rule for multilayer SNNs that use a form of temporal coding was proposed. In the proposed coding scheme, each neuron fires exactly one spike per stimulus, with the firing order encoding the information. In the final readout layer, the first firing neuron identifies the stimulus class. This method achieved state-of-the-art performance with supervised multi-fully connected layer SNNs, achieving a test accuracy of 97.4% on the MNIST dataset and an accuracy of 99.2% on the Caltech Face/Motorbike dataset.

In [48] a Spiking Neural Network inspired by the so-called center-surround structure of retinal receptive fields was proposed, utilizing the Integrate-and-Fire (IF) neuron model. The performance of the proposed network was evaluated using both the Iris dataset and MNIST dataset. When using 60 input neurons, the network achieved an accuracy of 96.33% on the Iris dataset and converged in only 45 iterations, thus showing a good convergence rate. For the MNIST dataset, where the gray level of each pixel was used as input, the network required 600 input neurons, and it achieved an accuracy level of 90.5%.

Recent advancements in neuromorphic hardware [4,10,11,64] have further foster the research and development of SNNs in artificial intelligence. Considering this possibility, more recent results propose the use of variants and more complex spiking neural networks to approach different kind of problems. For example, in [16,18,65] the use of SNNs for complex classification tasks was considered. Other works have considered their use for robot control, like e.g. [35] or medical applications [7,39,62]. Additionally, research has explored non-linear neural spiking networks [36,58,69]. In all cases, SNNs proved their ability in reaching very good results, close to those of ANNs, but with a significant lower energy consumption.

5   SNPS Applications

As for SNNs, also SNPSs have found diverse applications across multiple domains, showing their ability to solve complex problems in fields such as power systems, microgrid management, language processing, graph theory, cybersecurity, federated learning, and medical imaging. These systems, inspired by biological neural networks, have been leveraged for optimization, fault diagnosis, pattern recognition, and decentralized learning tasks. Below, we discuss some of the key applications of SNPSs, highlighting their impact and effectiveness.

Numerous studies have focused on classification tasks, such as those in [52,66], where a layered SNPS with supervised learning was proposed. This system, structured as a multi-layer network, was specifically designed to address classification problems. Experimental results, evaluated using datasets from the UCI machine learning repository and the MNIST dataset, demonstrated the effectiveness of the proposed approach. Additionally, several other works tackling a variety of classification problems have emerged, including those in [9,15,68].

Related work, considering image classification, but more oriented on medical aspects were considered [13], where Magnetic Resonance Imaging analysis for brain tumors detection was implemented. In particular, a threshold segmentation approach based on SNPSs was proposed, that proved to be able to give results very lose (and sometimes better) with respect to various optimization algorithms usually employed for this task. Other SNPSs applied to various medical tasks have appeared in the literature. Among them, some recently appeared works have been presented in [25,46,59].

Microgrid management has also benefited from SNPS applications. In the context of distributed energy systems, the work [61] introduced a fuzzy spiking neural system for coordinated control of microgrids. The model helped optimize energy distribution across interconnected microgrids, improving efficiency and stability. Subsequent work [60] extended this framework by integrating autapses in the SNPS model, which allowed for more adaptive control of multi-microgrid systems. This enhancement resulted in better energy management, demonstrating the potential of SNPSs for real-time decision-making in dynamic power networks.

Another promising area of SNPS applications is language processing. SNPSs have been used to recognize and classify various languages and dialects. The authors of [67] applied gated SNPSs to the task of Chinese dialect tone recognition. Their approach demonstrated high accuracy, outperforming traditional machine learning methods in recognizing tonal variations across different dialects. Similarly, the work [12] utilized adaptive optimization SNPSs for English letter recognition. Their method, based on spiking neural systems, effectively classified handwritten letters, showcasing the ability of SNPSs to handle complex pattern recognition tasks in the domain of natural language processing.

Graph theory problems, particularly node classification in large networks, have also benefited from SNPSs. In [34] the use of hierarchical SNPSs with weighted connections for graph-based node classification was explored. By exploiting the temporal dynamics of spiking neurons, the model was able to efficiently process large-scale graph data and classify nodes with high accuracy. This application of SNPSs demonstrated their potential to address challenges in graph-based problems, such as network analysis and social media analytics, where data is inherently interconnected.

SNPSs have been also applied in the field of cybersecurity, to detect malicious activities such as malware or phishing attacks. In [45], Cyber-SNPSs were trained to classify cybersecurity-related data, proposing a model that demonstrated superior performance in detecting cyber threats, with fewer training epochs and higher accuracy than traditional machine learning approaches. This research underscores the potential of SNPSs for enhancing the security of digital infrastructures, where fast and accurate threat detection is crucial.

Recently, the use of SNPSs in the active framework of federated learning, a decentralized machine learning paradigm, has raised interest. In [44], authors explored the integration of Layered SNPSs in federated learning settings. Their study revealed that LSNPSs achieved faster convergence and higher accuracy compared to other federated learning algorithms, making them an attractive solution for privacy-preserving machine learning. By processing data locally on decentralized devices, SNPS-based federated learning models help protect sensitive information while ensuring efficient learning across distributed networks.

Overall, the diverse applications of Spiking Neural P Systems in fields such as power systems, microgrid management, language processing, graph theory, cybersecurity, federated learning, and medical imaging highlight their versatility and potential. As research in SNPSs continues to advance, we can expect these systems to become increasingly integrated into both theoretical and practical applications, driving innovation in multiple domains.

6   Conclusions

Spiking Neural Networks (SNNs) and Spiking Neural P Systems (SNPSs) represent significant advancements in neural computation models, providing a more biologically plausible approach to processing information compared to traditional ANNs. These models are inspired by the communication mechanisms of biological neurons, where spikes are used to transmit signals, leading to more efficient and energy-conscious designs. SNNs, with their sparse, asynchronous operation, are well-suited for resource-constrained environments and can process temporal information with high efficiency. Similarly, SNPSs, combining the principles of SNNs and membrane computing, offer robust computational capabilities for tasks such as multi-class classification and complex problem-solving.

Despite the clear advantages of these models in terms of energy efficiency and biological accuracy, challenges remain, particularly in the development of training algorithms for SNNs and SNPSs, and their integration into broader computational frameworks. Future research should focus on improving training methods, addressing the discrete nature of spikes, and advancing neuromorphic hardware to fully exploit their potential. Additionally, further exploration of SNPSs in real-world applications, such as medical diagnostics, cryptography, and fault detection, could reveal new use cases and unlock further efficiencies.

The ongoing development of both SNNs and SNPSs promises to not only enhance artificial intelligence but also provide new insights into the computational processes of the human brain. Future research could also explore hybrid models that combine the strengths of SNNs and SNPSs to overcome existing limitations and extend their applicability across various domains.

Acknowledgements. Work partially supported by the MUR under the grant "Dipartimenti di Eccellenza 2023-2027" of the Department of Informatics, Systems and Communication, University of Milano-Bicocca, Italy.

References

1. Adeli, H., Ghosh-Dastidar, S., Dadmehr, N.: Alzheimer's disease and models of computation: imaging, classification, and neural models. J. Alzheimers Dis. **7**, 187–199 (2005)
2. Adeli, H., Ghosh-Dastidar, S., Dadmehr, N.: Alzheimer's disease: models of computation and analysis of EEGs. Clin. EEG Neurosci. **36**(3), 131–140 (2005)
3. Alhazov, A., Leporati, A., Mauri, G., Porreca, A.E., Zandron, C.: Space complexity equivalence of p systems with active membranes and turing machines. Theor. Comput. Sci. **529**, 69–81 (2014). https://doi.org/10.1016/j.tcs.2013.11.015
4. Bekolay, T., et al.: Nengo: a python tool for building large-scale functional brain models. Front. Neuroinf. **7** (2014). https://doi.org/10.3389/fninf.2013.00048
5. Brader, J.M., Senn, W., Fusi, S.: Learning real-world stimuli in a neural network with spike-driven synaptic dynamics. Neural Comput. **19**(11), 2881–2912 (2007). https://doi.org/10.1162/neco.2007.19.11.2881
6. Buño, K., Adorna, H.: Distributed computation of ak P systems with active membranes for sat using clause completion. J. Membr. Comput. **2**(2), 108–120 (2020)
7. Cavaleri, M., Zandron, C.: Exploring the versatility of spiking neural networks: applications across diverse scenarios. Int. J. Neural Syst., 2550007 (2024). https://doi.org/10.1142/S0129065725500078. in press

8. Chen, H., Ionescu, M., Ishdorj, T.O., Păun, A., Păun, Gh., Pérez-Jiménez, M.J.: Spiking neural P systems with extended rules: universality and languages. Nat. Comput. **7**, 147–166 (2008)

9. Dalvand, M., Fathi, A., Kamran, A.: Spiking neural P system with weight model of majority voting technique for reliable interactive image segmentation. Neural Comput. Appl. **35**(12), 9035–9051 (2023). https://doi.org/10.1007/s00521-022-08162-9

10. Davies, M., et al.: Loihi: a neuromorphic manycore processor with on-chip learning. IEEE Micro **38**(1), 82–99 (2018). https://doi.org/10.1109/MM.2018.112130359

11. Davies, M., et al.: Advancing neuromorphic computing with Loihi: a survey of results and outlook. Proc. IEEE **109**(5), 911–934 (2021). https://doi.org/10.1109/JPROC.2021.3067593

12. Deng, Q., Huang, Z., Chen, X., Li, X., Du, Y.: English letter recognition based on adaptive optimization spiking neural P systems. J. Membr. Comput. **6**(2), 109–129 (2024). https://doi.org/10.1007/s41965-024-00140-5

13. Dong, J., Zhang, G., Hu, Y., Wu, Y., Rong, H.: An optimization numerical spiking neural membrane system with adaptive multi-mutation operators for brain tumor segmentation. Int. J. Neural Syst. **34**(08), 2450036 (2024). https://doi.org/10.1142/S0129065724500369. pMID: 38686911

14. Dong, J., Zhang, G., Xiao, D., Luo, B., Rong, H.: Migration strategy in distributed adaptive optimization spiking neural P systems. J. Membr. Comput. **4**(4), 314–328 (2022)

15. Ermini, I., Zandron, C.: Modular spiking neural membrane systems for image classification. Int. J. Neural Syst. **34**(06), 2450021 (2024)

16. Gambosi, B., et al.: A model with dopamine depletion in basal ganglia and cerebellum predicts changes in thalamocortical beta oscillations. Int. J. Neural Syst. **34**(09), 2450045 (2024). https://doi.org/10.1142/S012906572450045X

17. Gatti, M., Leporati, A., Zandron, C.: On spiking neural membrane systems with neuron and synapse creation. Int. J. Neural Syst. **32**(8) (2022). https://doi.org/10.1142/S0129065722500368

18. Gatti, M., Barbato, J.A., Zandron, C.: Spiking neural network classification of X-ray chest images. Knowl. Based Syst. **314**, 113194 (2025)

19. Ghosh-Dastidar, S., Adeli, H.: A new supervised learning algorithm for multiple spiking neural networks with application in epilepsy and seizure detection. Neural Netw. **22**(10), 1419–1431 (2009)

20. Ghosh-Dastidar, S., Adeli, H.: Third generation neural networks: spiking neural networks. In: Yu, W., Sanchez, E. (eds.) Advances in Computational Intelligence, pp. 167–178. Springer, Heidelberg (2009). https://doi.org/10.1007/978-3-642-03156-4_17

21. Ghosh-Dastidar, S., Adeli, S.: Neural network-wavelet microsimulation model for delay and queue length estimation at freeway work zones. J. Transp. Eng. **132**(4), 331–341 (2006)

22. Grillo, A., Zandron, C.: On the computational complexity of spiking neural membrane systems with colored spikes. Int. J. Neural Syst., 2550035 (2025). https://doi.org/10.1142/S0129065725500352

23. Gutiérrez-Naranjo, M.A., Pérez-Jiménez, M.J., Riscos-Núñez, A.: On the degree of parallelism in membrane systems. Theor. Comput. Sci. **372**(2–3), 183–195 (2007)

24. Han, B., Sengupta, A., Roy, K.: On the energy benefits of spiking deep neural networks: a case study. In: 2016 International Joint Conference on Neural Networks (IJCNN), pp. 971–976 (2016). https://doi.org/10.1109/IJCNN.2016.7727303

25. Hu, Y., Dong, J., Zhang, G., Wu, Y., Rong, H., Zhu, M.: Cancer gene selection with adaptive optimization spiking neural P systems and hybrid classifiers. J. Membr. Comput. **5**(4), 238–251 (2023). https://doi.org/10.1007/s41965-023-00133-w

26. Ionescu, M., Păun, G., Yokomori, T.: Spiking neural P systems. Fund. Inf. **71**(2-3), 279–308 (2006)

27. Kandel, E., Mack, S., Jessell, T., Schwartz, J., Siegelbaum, S., Hudspeth, A.: Principles of Neural Science, 5th edn. McGraw-Hill's Access Medicine, McGraw-Hill Education (2013)

28. Kheradpisheh, S.R., Masquelier, T.: Temporal backpropagation for spiking neural networks with one spike per neuron. Int. J. Neural Syst. **30**(06), 2050027 (2020). https://doi.org/10.1142/S0129065720500276. pMID: 32466691

29. Lazo, P., Cabarle, F., Adorna, H.N., Yap, J.: A return to stochasticity and probability in spiking neural P systems. J. Membr. Comput. **3**(2), 149–161 (2021). https://doi.org/10.1007/s41965-021-00072-4

30. Leporati, A., Mauri, G., Zandron, C.: Spiking neural P systems: main ideas and results. Nat. Comput. **21**, 629–649 (2022). https://doi.org/10.1007/s11047-022-09917-y

31. Leporati, A., Manzoni, L., Mauri, G., Porreca, A.E., Zandron, C.: Characterising the complexity of tissue P systems with fission rules. J. Comput. Syst. Sci. **90**, 115–128 (2017). https://doi.org/10.1016/j.jcss.2017.06.008

32. Leporati, A., Manzoni, L., Mauri, G., Porreca, A.E., Zandron, C.: A turing machine simulation by P systems without charges. J. Membr. Comput. **2**(2), 71–79 (2020). https://doi.org/10.1007/s41965-020-00031-5

33. Leporati, A., Zandron, C., Ferretti, C., Mauri, G.: On the computational power of spiking neural P systems. Int. J. Unconv. Comput. **5**(5), 459–473 (2009)

34. Li, D., Liu, X., Sun, M.: Hierarchical spiking neural p systems with weights on multiple channels for graph-based node classification. J. Membr. Comput. (2024). https://doi.org/10.1007/s41965-024-00177-6

35. Liu, X., Rong, H., Neri, F., Yu, Z., Zhang, G.: Entropy-weighted numerical gradient optimization spiking neural system for biped robot control. Int. J. Neural Syst. **34**(06), 2450030 (2024). https://doi.org/10.1142/S0129065724500308. pMID: 38616292

36. Long, L., et al.: A time series forecasting approach based on nonlinear spiking neural systems. Int. J. Neural Syst. **32**, 2250020 (2022)

37. Lv, Z., Yang, Q., Peng, H., Song, X., Wang, J.: Computational power of sequential spiking neural P systems with multiple channels. J. Membr. Comput. **3**(4), 270–283 (2021). https://doi.org/10.1007/s41965-021-00089-9

38. Maass, W.: Lower bounds for the computational power of networks of spiking neurons. Neural Comput. **8**(1), 1–40 (1996). https://doi.org/10.1162/neco.1996.8.1.1

39. Nichols, E., McDaid, L., Siddique, N.: Case study on a self-organizing spiking neural network for robot navigation. Int. J. Neural Syst. **20**(06), 501–508 (2010). https://doi.org/10.1142/S0129065710002577. pMID: 21117272

40. Pan, L., Song, B., Zandron, C.: On the computational efficiency of tissue P systems with evolutional symport/antiport rules. Knowl. Based Syst. **262**, 110266 (2023). https://doi.org/10.1016/j.knosys.2023.110266

41. Pan, L., Păun, Gh., Zhang, G., Neri, F.: Spiking neural P systems with communication on request. Int. J. Neural Syst. **27**(8), 1750042 (2017). https://doi.org/10.1142/S0129065717500423

42. Păun, Gh.: Computing with membranes. J. Comput. Syst. Sci. **61**(1), 108–143 (2000)

43. Peng, H., et al.: Nonlinear spiking neural P systems. Int. J. Neural Syst. **30**(10), 2050008 (2020). https://doi.org/10.1142/S0129065720500082

44. Pleşa, M.I., Gheorghe, M., Ipate, F., Zhang, G.: A federated learning protocol for spiking neural membrane systems. Int. J. Neural Syst. **34**(12), 2450062 (2024). https://doi.org/10.1142/S012906572450062X. pMID: 39212939

45. Pleşa, M.I., Gheorghe, M., Ipate, F., Zhang, G.: Applications of spiking neural P systems in cybersecurity. J. Membr. Comput. **6**(4), 310–317 (2024). https://doi.org/10.1007/s41965-024-00166-9

46. Qiu, C., Xue, J., Liu, X., Li, Q.: Deep dynamic spiking neural P systems with applications in organ segmentation. J. Membr. Comput. **4**(4), 329–340 (2022). https://doi.org/10.1007/s41965-022-00115-4

47. Ranzato, M., Poultney, C., Chopra, S., Cun, Y.: Efficient learning of sparse representations with an energy-based model. In: Schölkopf, B., Platt, J., Hoffman, T. (eds.) Advances in Neural Information Processing Systems, vol. 19, MIT Press (2006)

48. Rashvand, P., Ahmadzadeh, M.R., Shayegh, F.: Design and implementation of a spiking neural network with integrate-and-fire neuron model for pattern recognition. Int. J. Neural Syst. **31**(03), 2050073 (2021). https://doi.org/10.1142/S0129065720500732. pMID: 33353527

49. Schliebs, S., Kasabov, N., Defoin-Platel, M.: On the probabilistic optimization of spiking neural networks. Int. J. Neural Syst. **20**(06), 481–500 (2010)

50. Schuetze, S.: The discovery of the action potential. Trends Neurosci. **6**, 164–168 (1983)

51. Song, B., Li, K., Zeng, X., Pérez-Jiménez, M.J., Zandron, C.: Monodirectional evolutional symport tissue P systems with channel states and cell division. Sci. China Inf. Sci. **66**(3) (2023).https://doi.org/10.1007/s11432-021-3478-8

52. Song, T., et al.: Spiking neural P systems with learning functions. IEEE Trans. Nanobiosci. **18**(2), 176–190 (2019). https://doi.org/10.1109/TNB.2019.2896981

53. Song, X., Valencia-Cabrera, L., Peng, H., Wang, J., Pérez-Jiménez, M.J.: Spiking neural P systems with delay on synapses. Int. J. Neural Syst. **31**(01), 2050042 (2020). https://doi.org/10.1142/S0129065720500422

54. Sosík, P.: P systems attacking hard problems beyond NP: a survey. J. Membr. Comput. **1**(3), 198–208 (2019). https://doi.org/10.1007/s41965-019-00017-y

55. VanRullen, R., Guyonneau, R., Thorpe, S.: Spike times make sense. Trends Neurosci. **28**(1), 1–4 (2005)

56. Verlan, S., Freund, R., Alhazov, A., Ivanov, S., Pan, L.: A formal framework for spiking neural P systems. J. Membr. Comput. **2**(4), 355–368 (2020). https://doi.org/10.1007/s41965-020-00050-2

57. Wu, T., Neri, F., Pan, L.: On the tuning of the computation capability of spiking neural membrane systems with communication on request. Int. J. Neural Syst. **32**, 2250037 (2022)

58. Xian, R., Lugu, R., Peng, H., Yang, Q., Luo, X., Wang, J.: Edge detection method based on nonlinear spiking neural systems. Int. J. Neural Syst. **33**(01), 2250060 (2023). https://doi.org/10.1142/S0129065722500605. pMID: 36328966

59. Yin, X., et al.: Deep synergetic spiking neural P systems for the overall survival time prediction of glioblastoma patients. Expert Syst. Appl. **245**, 123032 (2024). https://doi.org/10.1016/j.eswa.2023.123032

60. Yu, W., Gu, Q., Wu, J., Zheng, L., Xie, B.: Application of spiking neural p systems with autapses in coordinated control of multi-microgrid. J. Membr. Comput. **7**(1), 14–24 (2025). https://doi.org/10.1007/s41965-024-00141-4

61. Yu, W., Xiao, X., Wu, J., Chen, F., Zheng, L., Zhang, H.: Application of fuzzy spiking neural DP systems in energy coordinated control of multi-microgrid. J. Membr. Comput. **5**(1), 69–80 (2023). https://doi.org/10.1007/s41965-023-00118-9

62. Zahra, O., Navarro-Alarcon, D., Tolu, S.: A neurorobotic embodiment for exploring the dynamical interactions of a spiking cerebellar model and a robot arm during vision-based manipulation tasks. Int. J. Neural Syst. **32**, 2150028 (2022)

63. Zandron, C.: On maximal parallel application of rules in rewriting P systems. J. Membr. Comput. **5**(3), 170–181 (2023). https://doi.org/10.1007/s41965-023-00127-8

64. Zhan, Q., Wang, B., Jiang, A., Xie, X., Zhang, M., Liu, G.: A two-stage spiking meta-learning method for few-shot classification. Knowl.-Based Syst. **284**, 111220 (2024). https://doi.org/10.1016/j.knosys.2023.111220

65. Zhang, G., et al.: A layered spiking neural system for classification problems. Int. J. Neural Syst. **32**(08), 2250023 (2022). https://doi.org/10.1142/S012906572250023X

66. Zhang, G., et al.: A layered spiking neural system for classification problems. Int. J. Neural Syst. **32**(08), 2250023 (2022). https://doi.org/10.1142/S012906572250023X. pMID: 35416762

67. Zhang, H., Liu, X., Shao, Y.: Chinese dialect tone's recognition using gated spiking neural P systems. J. Membr. Comput. **4**(4), 284–292 (2022). https://doi.org/10.1007/s41965-022-00113-6

68. Zhang, L., Xu, F., Neri, F.: An asynchronous spiking neural membrane system for edge detection. Int. J. Neural Syst. **34**(06), 2450023 (2024). https://doi.org/10.1142/S0129065724500230. pMID: 38490956

69. Zhang, Y., Yang, Q., Liu, Z., Peng, H., Wang, J.: A prediction model based on gated nonlinear spiking neural system. Int. J. Neural Syst. **33**(6), 2350029 (2023)

Author Index

M. D. Jiménez López and G. Vaszil (Eds.): Erzsébet Csuhaj-Varjú Festschrift,
LNCS 15840, p. 279, 2025.
https://doi.org/10.1007/978-3-031-97274-4

The manufacturer's authorised representative in the EU is Springer
Nature Customer Service Centre GmbH, Europaplatz 3, 69115 Heidelberg,
Germany. If you have any concerns regarding our products, please
contact ProductSafety@springernature.com

Printed and bound by CPI Group (UK) Ltd, Croydon, CR0 4YY
24/04/2026
02096367-0011